The Tender Detail

The Tender Detail

Ornament and Sentimentality in the Architecture of Louis H. Sullivan and Frank Lloyd Wright

Daniel E. Snyder

BLOOMSBURY VISUAL ARTS
LONDON • NEW YORK • OXFORD • NEW DELHI • SYDNEY

BLOOMSBURY VISUAL ARTS
Bloomsbury Publishing Plc
50 Bedford Square, London, WC1B 3DP, UK
1385 Broadway, New York, NY 10018, USA
29 Earlsfort Terrace, Dublin 2, Ireland

BLOOMSBURY, BLOOMSBURY VISUAL ARTS and the Diana logo
are trademarks of Bloomsbury Publishing Plc

First published in Great Britain 2020
Paperback edition first published in Great Britain, 2022

Copyright © Daniel E. Snyder, 2022

Daniel E. Snyder has asserted his right under the Copyright, Designs and
Patents Act, 1988, to be identified as Author of this work.

For legal purposes the Acknowledgments on p. xix constitute an
extension of this copyright page.

Cover design: Daniel E. Snyder Cover image: Sullivan, Louis Henri (1856-1924). *A System of Architectural Ornament*, Plate 17, A Geometrical Play-Ground. 1922. Graphite on Strathmore paper, 57.7 × 73.5 cm (22 3/4 × 29 in.). Signed and dated at bottom right of design, "Louis H. Sullivan del: 12/15/22". Image has been cropped. Commissioned by The Art Institute of Chicago.1988.15.12. The Art Institute of Chicago, Chicago, U.S.A. Photo credit: The Art Institute of Chicago/Art Resource, NY. Wright, Frank Lloyd (1867–1959). Midway Gardens, Chicago, IL., 1913–1914. Drawing of all railings for gardens. Image has been cropped. The Frank Lloyd Wright Foundation Archives (Museum of Modern Art | Avery Architectural & Fine Arts Library, Columbia University, New York).

All rights reserved. No part of this publication may be reproduced or
transmitted in any form or by any means, electronic or mechanical, including
photocopying, recording, or any information storage or retrieval system,
without prior permission in writing from the publishers.

Bloomsbury Publishing Plc does not have any control over, or responsibility for,
any third-party websites referred to or in this book. All internet addresses given
in this book were correct at the time of going to press. The author and publisher
regret any inconvenience caused if addresses have changed or sites have ceased
to exist, but can accept no responsibility for any such changes.

A catalogue record for this book is available from the British Library.

A catalogue record for this book is available from Library of Congress.

ISBN:	HB:	978-1-3500-9961-6
	PB:	978-1-3502-3671-4
	ePDF:	978-1-3500-9962-3
	eBook:	978-1-3500-9963-0

Typeset by Integra Software Services Pvt. Ltd.

To find out more about our authors and books visit www.bloomsbury.com
and sign up for our newsletters.

for Jamie

Frank Lloyd Wright drawings and text excerpts are Copyright © 2019 Frank Lloyd Wright Foundation, Scottsdale, AZ. All rights reserved. Used with permission.

The Frank Lloyd Wright Foundation Archives (The Museum of Modern Art | Avery Architectural & Fine Arts Library, Columbia University, New York)

CONTENTS

List of Illustrations x
Acknowledgments xix
Preface xx

1 Introduction: Frank Lloyd Wright—
   Sentimentalizing over the Dead 1

Part One: Louis H. Sullivan 27

2 The Plastic Decorations Are Distinctly
   Architectural in Conception 29

3 That Object He Became 41

4 Femininity 61

Part Two: Frank Lloyd Wright 79

5 No Damned Sentimentality Either 81

6 Integral Ornament at Last 103

7 'Like a Man' 127

Part Three: Louis H. Sullivan and Frank Lloyd Wright 151

8 That Supreme Erotic Adventure of the Mind 153

9 Ornament Purely as Such 171

10 Epilogue: When We Are Dead 197

Notes 204
Bibliography 256
Index 268

ILLUSTRATIONS

P.1 Independent Presbyterian Church, Savannah, GA. Cornice Detail. Photo by author. xxii

1.1 Cathedral of Notre-Dame, Reims, France, late nineteenth or early twentieth century. The façade of the cathedral of Notre Dame de Reims, where the kings of France used to be crowned. The cathedral dates from the late thirteenth century and is one of the finest Gothic cathedrals in France. It was seriously damaged by German artillery in the First World War and underwent major restoration work before reopening in 1937. Photo credit: HIP/Art Resource, NY. 7

1.2 Palladio, Andrea (1508–1580). Façade of the Church of Redentore. Il Redentore. Photo credit: Scala/Art Resource, NY. 8

1.3 Milwaukee County Courthouse, 1931. Courtesy of courthousehistory.com. 13

1.4 Independent Presbyterian Church, Savannah, Georgia. Built in 1817, burned in 1889 and rebuilt in 1891. Courtesy of the Georgia Historical Society. MS 1361-PH-03-21-0535. 21

1.5 Jerusalem Church, Rincon, 1769. Photograph by Van Jones Martin, from Mills Lane's *Architecture of the Old South: Georgia* (Savannah: The Beehive Press, 2017), 25. Courtesy of Beehive Press. 22

2.1 Carnegie Hall from Balcony. Courtesy of Carnegie Hall, Jeff Goldberg/Esto. 32

2.2 Auditorium Building, Chicago, IL, 1887–1889. Adler and Sullivan, architects. Photograph attributed to J. W. Taylor. Historic Architecture and Landscape Image Collection, Ryerson & Burnham Archives, The Art Institute of Chicago. Digital File # 49666. 33

2.3 Carrie Eliza Getty Tomb, Graceland Cemetery, Chicago, IL, 1890–1891. Louis H. Sullivan, architect. Richard Nickel, photographer. Richard Nickel Archive, Ryerson & Burnham Archives, The Art Institute of Chicago. Digital File # 201006_119A.9. 35

2.4 Historic American Buildings Survey, Creator, Ellis Wainwright, Adler & Sullivan, and Charles K Ramsey. *Wainwright Building, Seventh & Chestnut Streets, Saint Louis, Independent City, MO.*, *c.* 1933. Documentation Compiled After. Photograph by Lester Jones, 1940. (https://www.loc.gov/resource/hhh.mo0297.photos/?sp=2 [accessed September 18, 2018]). Library of Congress, Prints and Photographs Division, HABS. Reproduction number HABS MO, 96-SALU, 49–1. 36

2.5 Historic American Buildings Survey, Creator, Ellis Wainwright, Adler & Sullivan, and Charles K Ramsey. *Wainwright Building, Seventh & Chestnut Streets, Saint Louis, Independent City, MO.*, *c.* 1933. Documentation Compiled After. Photograph. (https://www.loc.gov/resource/hhh.mo0297.photos/?sp=8 [accessed September 18, 2018]). Library of Congress, Prints and Photographs Division, HABS. Reproduction number HABS MO, 96-SALU, 49–7. 37

2.6 Guaranty Building, exterior, 28 Church Street, Buffalo, *c.* 1900. Courtesy of the Buffalo History Museum. 38

2.7 Guaranty Building exterior cornice, 2018. © James Caulfield. 38

3.1 Sullivan, Louis Henri (1856–1924). *System of Architectural Ornament*, Plate 2, Manipulation of the Organic. 1922. Graphite on Strathmore paper, 57.7 × 73.5 cm (22 ¾ × 29 in.). Initialed and dated at bottom center of design, "LHS 1922." Commissioned by the Art Institute of Chicago. 1988.15.12. The Art Institute of Chicago, Chicago, USA. Photo credit: The Art Institute of Chicago/Art Resource, NY. 49

3.2 Sullivan, Louis Henri (1856–1924). *System of Architectural Ornament*, Plate 3, Manipulations of Forms in Geometry. 1922. Graphite on Strathmore paper, 57.7 × 73.5 cm (22 ¾ × 29 in.). Initialed and dated at bottom center/left of design, "LHS 1922." Commissioned by the Art Institute of

Chicago. 1988.15.12. The Art Institute of Chicago, Chicago, USA. Photo credit: The Art Institute of Chicago/Art Resource, NY. *50*

3.3 Sullivan, Louis Henri (1856–1924). *System of Architectural Ornament*, Plate 4, Fluent Geometry, 1922. Graphite on Strathmore paper, 57.7 × 73.5 cm (22 ¾ × 29 in.), initialed and dated at bottom right of design, "LHS 2.'22.'22." Commissioned by the Art Institute of Chicago. 1988.15.4. The Art Institute of Chicago, Chicago, USA. Photo credit: The Art Institute of Chicago/Art Resource, NY. *51*

3.4 Irving K. Pond, *The Meaning of Architecture: An Essay of Constructive Criticism*. Boston: Marshall Jones Company, 1918, 123. Photo by author. *55*

3.5 Sullivan, Louis Henri (1856–1924). *System of Architectural Ornament*, Plate 3, Manipulations of Forms in Geometry. 1922. Graphite on Strathmore paper, 57.7 × 73.5 cm (22 ¾ × 29 in.). Initialed and dated at bottom center/left of design, "LHS 1922." Commissioned by the Art Institute of Chicago. 1988.15.12. The Art Institute of Chicago, Chicago, USA. Photo credit: The Art Institute of Chicago/Art Resource, NY. *59*

4.1 Merchants National Bank, Grinnell, IA, 1913–1914. Louis H. Sullivan, architect. Henry Fuermann and Sons, photographer. Historic Architecture and Landscape Image Collection, Ryerson & Burnham Archives, The Art Institute of Chicago. Digital File # 25419. *72*

4.2 Peoples Savings and Loan Association, Sidney, OH, 1916–1918. Louis H. Sullivan, architect. Henry Fuermann and Sons, photographer. Historic Architecture and Landscape Image Collection, Ryerson & Burnham Archives, The Art Institute of Chicago. Digital File # 25419. *72*

4.3 Home Building Association Bank, Newark, OH, 1914–1915. Louis H. Sullivan, architect. Henry Fuermann and Sons, photographer. Historic Architecture and Landscape Image Collection, Ryerson & Burnham Archives, The Art Institute of Chicago. Digital File # 25456. *74*

4.4 Sullivan, Louis Henri (1856–1924). *System of Architectural Ornament*, Plate 14, Fantasy. 1922. Graphite on Strathmore paper, 57.7 × 73.5 cm (22 ¾ × 29 in.). Signed and dated at bottom right of design, "Louis H. Sullivan fecit Chicago: 7-18-1922." Commissioned by the Art Institute of Chicago. 1988.15.12. The Art Institute of Chicago, Chicago, USA. Photo credit: The Art Institute of Chicago/Art Resource, NY. 76

5.1 William H. Winslow House, Auvergne Place, River Forest, IL. The Frank Lloyd Wright Foundation Archives (The Museum of Modern Art | Avery Architectural & Fine Arts Library, Columbia University, New York). 89

5.2 Historic American Buildings Survey, Creator, and Frank Lloyd Wright. William H. Winslow House, Auvergne Place, River Forest, Cook County, IL., *c.* 1933. Documentation Compiled After. Photograph by Richard Nickel, 1965. (https://www.loc.gov/resource/hhh.il0316.photos/?sp=6 [accessed September 18, 2018]). Library of Congress, Prints and Photographs Division, HABS. Reproduction number HABS ILL, 16-RIVFO, 1–6. 90

5.3 Avery Coonley Residence, Riverside, IL, 1907. Frank Lloyd Wright, architect. Henry Fuermann, photographer. Historic Architecture and Landscape Image Collection, Ryerson & Burnham Archives, The Art Institute of Chicago. Digital File # 17828. 91

5.4 Wright, Frank Lloyd (1867–1959) ©ARS, NY. Unity Temple, Oak Park, IL. Exterior view from the northeast. The Frank Lloyd Wright Foundation. © 2019, The Frank Lloyd Wright Foundation, AZ/Art Resource, NY. All Rights Reserved. Licensed by Artist Rights Society. 92

5.5 Wright, Frank Lloyd (1867–1959). ©ARS, NY. The Larkin Company Administration Building, exterior. The Frank Lloyd Wright Foundation. © 2019, The Frank Lloyd Wright Foundation, AZ/Art Resource, NY. All Rights Reserved. Licensed by Artist Rights Society. 93

5.6 Thomas Hovenden. *Breaking Home Ties*. 1890 (Oil on canvas, 52 ⅛ inches × 6 feet ¼ inches (132.4 × 183.5 cm). Philadelphia Museum of

Art, Gift of Ellen Harrison McMichael in memory of C. Emory McMichael, 1942-60-1. 95

5.7 John Rogers. *Coming to the Parson,* patented 1870, painted plaster. Courtesy of Smithsonian American Art Museum, Gift of John Rogers and Son. 96

5.8 Denman W. Ross PhD. *A Theory of Pure Design: Harmony, Balance, Rhythm.* Boston: Houghton, Mifflin, and Company, 1907, 180. Photo by author. 98

6.1 Midway Gardens, Summer Garden, Chicago, IL, 1913–1914. Frank Lloyd Wright, architect. Henry Fuermann, photographer. Historic Architecture and Landscape Image Collection, Ryerson & Burnham Archives, The Art Institute of Chicago. Digital File # 17845. 103

6.2 Midway Gardens, Chicago, IL, 1913–1914. Frank Lloyd Wright, architect. Henry Fuermann, photographer. Historic Architecture and Landscape Image Collection, Ryerson & Burnham Archives, The Art Institute of Chicago. Digital File # 17860. 104

6.3 Midway Gardens, Chicago, IL, 1913–1914. Frank Lloyd Wright, architect. Henry Fuermann, photographer. Historic Architecture and Landscape Image Collection, Ryerson & Burnham Archives, The Art Institute of Chicago. Digital File # 17861. 104

6.4 Midway Gardens, Chicago, IL, Detail of Concrete Mural, *c*. 1914. The Frank Lloyd Wright Foundation Archives (The Museum of Modern Art | Avery Architectural & Fine Arts Library, Columbia University, New York). 105

6.5 Midway Gardens, Winter Garden, Chicago, IL, 1913–1914. Frank Lloyd Wright, architect. Henry Fuermann, photographer. Historic Architecture and Landscape Image Collection, Ryerson & Burnham Archives, The Art Institute of Chicago. Digital File # 17852. 106

6.6 Midway Gardens, Summer Garden, Chicago, IL, 1913–1914. Frank Lloyd Wright, architect. Henry Fuermann, photographer. Historic Architecture and Landscape Image Collection, Ryerson &

Burnham Archives, The Art Institute of Chicago. Digital File # 17855. 107

6.7 Wright, Frank Lloyd (1867–1959) © ARS, NY. Midway Gardens, Cottage Grove Avenue and 60th Street, Chicago, Illinois. Block from Façade, 1913–1914. Cast Concrete, 17 ¾ × 20 ¾ × 2 ¾ in. Gift of Mr. and Mrs. Hal Chalmers and Rexford Battenberg (1972.811). The Art Institute of Chicago, Chicago, USA. Photo credit: The Art Institute of Chicago/Art Resource, NY. © 2019 Frank Lloyd Wright Foundation. All Right Reserved. Licensed by Artist Rights Society. 108

6.8 Midway Gardens, Chicago, IL, 1913–1914. Frank Lloyd Wright, architect. Henry Fuermann, photographer. Historic Architecture and Landscape Image Collection, Ryerson & Burnham Archives, The Art Institute of Chicago. Digital File # 17862. 109

6.9 Unity Temple, Oak Park, IL, Perspective Sketch. The Frank Lloyd Wright Foundation Archives (The Museum of Modern Art | Avery Architectural & Fine Arts Library, Columbia University, New York). 113

6.10 Unity Temple, Oak Park, IL, Working Drawing #3, Plan Auditorium Level. The Frank Lloyd Wright Foundation Archives (The Museum of Modern Art | Avery Architectural & Fine Arts Library, Columbia University, New York). 114

6.11 "The Grammar of Ornament." *Via III: Ornament*. University of Pennsylvania Fine Arts Press, 1977, Fig. 128. Courtesy of Thomas Beeby, FAIA. 114

6.12 Drawing of interlocking figures (drawing by author). 116

6.13 Sullivan, Louis Henri (1856–1934). *System of Architectural Ornament*, Plate 17, A Geometrical Play-ground. 1922. Graphite on Strathmore Paper, 57.7 × 73.5 cm (22 ¾ × 29 in.). Signed and dated at bottom right of design, "Louis H. Sullivan del: 12/15/22." Commissioned by The Art Institute of Chicago. 1988.15.12. The Art Institute of Chicago, Chicago, USA. Photo credit: The Art Institute of Chicago/Art Resource, NY. 116

6.14 Sullivan, Louis Henri (1856–1934). *System of Architectural Ornament*, Plate 17, A Geometrical Play-ground. 1922. Graphite on Strathmore Paper, 57.7 × 73.5 cm (22 ¾ × 29 in.). Signed and dated at bottom right of design, "Louis H. Sullivan del: 12/15/22." Commissioned by The Art Institute of Chicago. 1988.15.12. The Art Institute of Chicago, Chicago, USA. Photo credit: The Art Institute of Chicago/Art Resource, NY. Drawing overlay by author. 117

6.15 Ernst Wasmuth. *Frank Lloyd Wright: Ausgeführte Bauten.* Berlin, 1911. Volume 2, Plate LXIV, "Lageplan und Grundriss vom Unity Tempel." Image has been cropped. Avery Architectural & Fine Arts Library, Columbia University. 117

6.16 Drawing representation of three dimensions (drawing by author). 118

6.17 Unity Temple, Oak Park, IL, Working Drawing #7, Long Section/Ceiling Plan. The Frank Lloyd Wright Foundation Archives (The Museum of Modern Art | Avery Architectural & Fine Arts Library, Columbia University, New York). 119

6.18 Unity Temple, Oak Park, IL, Section with Notes. The Frank Lloyd Wright Foundation Archives (The Museum of Modern Art | Avery Architectural & Fine Arts Library, Columbia University, New York). 119

6.19 Spatial trim diagram (drawing by author). 120

6.20 Unity Temple interior, from Pulpit, 2018. © James Caulfield. 120

6.21 Avery Coonley Playhouse, Riverside IL, floor plan. The Frank Lloyd Wright Foundation Archives (The Museum of Modern Art | Avery Architectural & Fine Arts Library, Columbia University, New York). 121

6.22 Niles Club floor plan. Mahoney, Marion and Griffin, Walter, *The Western Architect.* August 1913. Photo by author. 122

6.23 Ernst Wasmuth. *Frank Lloyd Wright: Ausgeführte Bauten.* Berlin, 1911. Volume 1, Plate XXXI, "Aussenansicht vom Stadtischen Wohnhause fur Frau Dana, Springfield, Illinois." Image has been cropped. Avery Architectural & Fine Arts Library, Columbia University. 123

6.24 Ernst Wasmuth. *Frank Lloyd Wright: Ausgeführte Bauten.* Berlin, 1911. Volume 1, Plate XXXIb, "Inneres des Festhaales for Frau Dana." Avery Architectural & Fine Arts Library, Columbia University. 124

6.25 Midway Gardens, Chicago, Illinois, USA, 1915. Postcard view of one of the interior rooms showing cloth-covered tables and a checked tile floor. Featuring a concert garden, restaurant, and dance hall, the Midway Gardens complex was designed by Frank Lloyd Wright and completed in 1914. It was demolished in 1929. Photo credit: HIP/Art Resource, NY. 126

7.1 *Advertisement for the Imperial Hotel, Tokyo: Main Building Designed by Lloyd Wright.* Japanese, Taishô—early Shôwa era. Leonard A. Lauder Collection of Japanese Postcards. 2002.10943. Photograph © 2020 Museum of Fine Arts, Boston. 128

7.2 Wright, Frank Lloyd (1867–1959) © ARS, NY. Imperial Hotel #2 [1509]. Exterior, north entrance, north wing. 1922–1923. Photograph by Henry Fuermann. The Frank Lloyd Wright Foundation. © 2019 Frank Lloyd Wright Foundation, AZ/Art Resource, NY. All Rights Reserved. Licensed by Artist Rights Society. 130

7.3 *Advertisement for the Imperial Hotel, Tokyo: Lobby Designed by Frank Lloyd Wright.* Japanese, Taishô—early Shôwa era. Leonard A. Lauder Collection of Japanese Postcards. 2002.10952. Photograph © 2020 Museum of Fine Arts, Boston. 130

7.4 Imperial Hotel, Tokyo, Japan. Scheme 2, Banquet Hall Plan. The Frank Lloyd Wright Foundation Archives (The Museum of Modern Art | Avery Architectural & Fine Arts Library, Columbia University, New York). 131

7.5 *Advertisement for the Imperial Hotel, Tokyo: Interior Designed by Frank Lloyd Wright.* Japanese, Taishô era. Leonard A. Lauder Collection of Japanese Postcards. 2002.4664. Photograph © 2020 Museum of Fine Arts, Boston. 132

7.6 Hollyhock House fireplace. *Wendingen: Frank Lloyd Wright.* C. A. Mees Santpoort Holland, 1925. Photo by author. 137

7.7 Mrs. George Madison Millard Residence, Pasadena, CA, 1923. Frank Lloyd Wright, architect. Historic Architecture and Landscape Image Collection, Ryerson & Burnham Archives, The Art Institute of Chicago. Digital File # M525580. 139

7.8 Historic American Buildings Survey, Creator, Frank Lloyd Wright, Samuel Freeman, and Rudolph M. Schindler. *Samuel Freeman House*, Glencoe Way, Los Angeles, Los Angeles County, CA, 1933. Documentation Compiled After. Photograph. https://www.loc.gov/resource/hhh.ca0228.sheet/?sp=2 [accessed September 18, 2018]. Library of Congress, Prints and Photographs Division, HABS. Reproduction number HABS CAL, 19-LOSAN, 62- (sheet 2 of 7). 140

7.9 Ennis House and Freeman House block detail (drawing by author). 141

7.10 Alexander Burran, Photo of Ennis House block detail (2018). Courtesy of Alexander Burran. 142

7.11 Cabanel, Alexandre (1823–1889). *Birth of Venus*. 1865. Musee d'Orsay. Photo credit: Scala/Art Resource, NY. 145

8.1 Auditorium Building, Chicago, IL, 1887–1889. Adler and Sullivan, architects. Sullivaniana Collection, Ryerson & Burnham Archives, The Art Institute of Chicago. Digital File #193101.080609–05. 153

8.2 A. Raguenet, *Matériaux & Documents d'Architecture Classés par Ordre Aphabétique*, 1872, 3. Photo by author. 162

8.3 Owen Jones, *The Grammar of Ornament*. New York: J. W. Bouton, 1880, plate LXXXI. Photo by author. 163

8.4 Chicago Stock Exchange Building, 1892–1894. Adler and Sullivan, architects. Barnum and Barnum/Commercial Photographic Company/J. W. Taylor, photographer. Richard Nickel Archive, Ryerson & Burnham Archives, The Art Institute of Chicago. Digital File # 201006_157A.233. 168

ACKNOWLEDGMENTS

I thank the many people who have helped with this book. I am indebted to my readers, Jane Bridges, Jane Fishman, Brian Martine, Tom Schantz, and Jerry Wright. Each time I thought I was done, they found more to critique. I thank the folks at Yale's Robert B. Haas Family Arts Library, especially Lindsay King, and at Columbia's Avery Architectural and Fine Arts Library, especially Pamela Casey. They cheerfully provided the necessary threads through the archive's maze. I thank all the people at Yale's Master of Environmental Design program. They offered me a rare opportunity to pursue this topic in an environment of extraordinary support. I thank its director, Eeva Liisa Pelkonen; my thesis committee, Eeva Liisa Pelkonen, Peggy Deamer, and Karsten Harries (chair); my classmates, Juana Salcedo and Saga Blane; and the faculty and invited jurors who read and critiqued my early chapters. Each helped turn an inchoate set of ideas into something resembling a thesis. Even more importantly, they encouraged me to turn it into a book.

I thank Kent Bloomer for his support and encouragement from the beginning of this project. He was one of the first persons at Yale to express an interest in it, even before I was a student. His classes, writings, scholarship, and individual tutelage provided an incomparable knowledge base into the understanding of ornament.

I owe a special debt of gratitude to Karsten Harries who showed me behind myself looking forward in the revelation of a more comprehensive worldview.

Finally, I am forever indebted to Jamie Maury, without whom none of this would have happened, nor would it have been worth it anyway. I promise I'll do the dishes.

Dan
Savannah, GA
October 7, 2019

PREFACE

His heart, twice its normal size, took sympathy from the warm open hand that rubbed his back. Sullivan would be dead in the morning. It was Sunday, April 13, 1924. For the past fourteen years he had been living in the Warner Hotel, down at 33rd and Cottage Grove, on the south side of Chicago. It was such a comedown from 1899 when he had moved into the lavish Windermere Hotel. Then internationally famous, Sullivan led an architectural practice so significant he would be dubbed "the dean of American architecture," "the father of the skyscraper," and "prophet of modern architecture."[1] Now, this father had no children, no family, and few friends. Divorced, broke, living alone in a bare room with cut-out magazine pictures on the walls and some reference books shelved in the bathroom, Sullivan subsisted on the compassion of a few former colleagues who paid his bills. For he owned nothing that really mattered: a small piece of jade, a scant wardrobe of clothing, and a daguerreotype of his mother, brother, and himself. His rare remaining drawings and the equipment used in their execution gathered dust in an office uptown. Unable to pay the rent, he accepted its use from a manufacturer of ornament—*gratis*.

Wright wanted to see the dying man more than once a week. But it was a four-hour trip from Taliesin, his home/office outside Spring Green, Wisconsin. It had been thirty-six years since they had first met. Wright was just twenty. He had been hired by Sullivan to work on ornament. In no time he was calling his boss "*Lieber Meister*," his beloved master, as the term of affection for a relationship of intense closeness that lasted just five years. By all accounts, Wright cheated on Sullivan.[2] Irreconcilable, the two hardly spoke for another twenty-eight years. In 1918, at Taliesin, Wright received an unexpected phone call. It was Sullivan.[3] The two men reconciled. They renewed an affection that would last until the end.

And now, alone in the Warner, they sat on the master's bed. Sullivan had his feet on the floor. His spirits were lifted by their chat. Wright held him, rubbed his back, felt his enlarged heart, laid him down, drew the blanket over him, and remained seated as the dying man fell asleep. For Wright, this relationship could not be overestimated. Grieving, he wrote, "To know him well was to love him well."[4]

Despite the expression of love, this story is about the repression of sentimentality. It begins in the United States during the second half of the nineteenth century and tells of its manifestations in architectural terms through the practice of ornament. The protagonists are Louis H. Sullivan (1856–1924) and Frank Lloyd Wright (1867–1959), two of the most important architects and designers of ornament in American history. Both Sullivan, the late romantic who marked its apogee for the era, and Wright, the proto-modernist who prefigured its demise, believed that the popular turn-of-the-century ornamentation was problematic. Sullivan proposed that architects not "use" it for a while.[5] Wright considered it "as pitiful as it [was] costly" and likewise proposed that architects "do away with most of it; to make us feel safer and more comfortable with plain things."[6] While both curtailed its "use" in varying degrees and for different periods of time, neither gave it up entirely; rather they preferred to solve the problem. In their respective responses, the two architects developed widely disparate solutions. They nonetheless shared something in common: for both men, their responses involved sentimentality. Sullivan attempted to solve the problem by eliciting it; Wright by consciously repressing it. This encapsulates the overriding thrust of the story. But it is much too simplistic. It might be better to consider their respective responses metaphorically as something like a tangled knot. One kinked line suggests that while Sullivan worked to solve the problem sentimentally, he never characterized his practice or himself as "sentimental." Another twisted line suggests that while Wright worked to solve it by actively repressing sentimentality, he nonetheless characterized himself as "the most sentimental person [he] ever knew."[7] Despite the entanglement, whether for good or for bad, their understanding of the problem of ornament was a problem of sentimentality, all of which invites questions.

As this story unfolds, there are three lines of questioning that I follow. The first is a simple one of definitions. What is "sentimentality?" What is "ornament?" Confronted with the impossibility of determining some static definition, I interrogate instead how the two architects might have understood and used these words within their given context. A clearer understanding is critical given that "sentimentality" underwent a semantic shift, and Wright developed a wholly new conception of ornament that he called "integral ornament."

The second line of questioning begins to ask why. Why did both architects appeal to the emotions of sentimentality at the same time that Wright insisted on their repression in his work? In his insistence, does this not presuppose some anterior power? Indeed, what were those effects of power, whether they were intrapersonal, interpersonal, or broadly cultural, that Wright chose to assert and deploy and that Sullivan chose seemingly to ignore? The aim is to excavate and reveal those repressive effects, especially in the practice of ornament. Not to posit their truths but rather to explore why it was that the two architects made their respective decisions and took such divergent paths.

The third line of questioning interrogates the specific relationship between sentimentality and ornament as put into practice by these two men. How might we interpret Sullivan's practice? Wright's? While impossible to definitively know, we can nonetheless begin to contextualize the contemporary discourse. For now, at the beginning of the twenty-first century, with a renewed interest in affect and the emotions, and ornament returning, we might ask: what about sentimentality?[8] If even one of these two titans of American architecture convincingly establishes a direct and mutually dependent relationship between the two, then it remains incumbent upon us to at least reevaluate it.

One might say, "So what?" It's the twenty-first century. We have a new conception of both. Sentimentality is repressed, and it is repressed in ornament too. That could be a good thing! From the realm of triglyphs and guttae (Figure P.1), the upright acroterion, or a border bubbling with guilloche, untangling these questions may seem of little more consequence than a long-outmoded understanding of ornament itself, slight doodads that once embroidered the otherwise tough fabric of our forebears' daily lives. But following each thread has proven more significant than even this tangled knot suggests. For it seems that both architects evinced a kind of drive to ornamentation. Both wondered if it might be as intrinsic to their persons as say "instinct" or "will." These questions therefore are not just about interrogating an exhausted architectural problem of ornament as exteriority, out there, on buildings. Rather they raise a broader set of aesthetic questions regarding how one may in fact be in the world. As both

FIGURE P.1 *Independent Presbyterian Church, Savannah, GA. Cornice Detail. Photo by author.*

men indicated, this inquiry is as basic as their often capitalized, and often in quotation marks, "Life" itself. When the two raised questions regarding the nature of "ornament" and "sentimentality," they were fully aware that they were asking much more than questions of semantics and etymology. Indeed, both men understood that they were asking questions of ontology. The very nature of being as negotiated through the contemporaneous architectural and philosophical debates was the etiological subject of ornament as such.

My aim is to place the original line of questioning back within this broader context. This is crucial. For while the two architects articulated different yet compelling worldviews, *both* engaged in acts of repression—*and repression has a silencing effect*. When Sullivan partook of a sentimental practice, yet never called it that, he silenced the word itself.[9] When Wright repressed what he understood to be the sentimentality within his work, he effectively silenced that quality of his architecture. Freud characterized repression as "strangulated affect," like the result of an ever more entangling knot around the throat that ultimately silences its effusion.[10] The full affective discourse, that is, inclusive of the architectural and philosophical discourses of sentimentality, and consequently ornament, has been repressed by acts of forceful muting. In Freud's terms, we have inherited a legacy of violent silencing. My process therefore is little more than a kind of untangling of that strangulating knot—to release the pent-up pneumatic gush of heartfelt respiration across the vocal folds—*to emote and speak*. With the contemporaneous return of ornament, the ultimate aim is to give voice, that is, to abreact the repressed affects of sentimentality.

I have limited the time frame of the narrative to the duration of Sullivan's life: September 3, 1856, to April 14, 1924. It was during this period that both men worked their hardest to solve the problem of ornament. All of their buildings from that period were candidates for consideration, but not after. Even though Wright lived another thirty-five years, his later buildings evince a noticeably waning interest in the problem. After 1924, he removed all of what was then understood to be "ornament" from his most iconic buildings. What remained on his other works offered little that was new to the discourse.

However, all of the writings of both men, including Wright's into the 1950s, were considered. The two texts that proved most informative have been their respective autobiographies. Both offer a particularly sentimental value. Sullivan's, *The Autobiography of an Idea*, was published just days before he died. The first edition of Wright's *An Autobiography* was published eight years later in 1932. Moreover, Wright published three editions, each with subtle edits, the differences of which have proven illustrative. Biographers and historians have severely, yet justifiably, criticized each as factually unreliable because of their glaring omissions, creeping exaggerations, and bald-faced lies. Nonetheless, they convey how the men placed themselves within some of the most important architectural and philosophical issues of their era.

Even more importantly, they convey how the two *felt* about those issues or at least how they wanted their readers to believe they felt. As *creative* acts, both autobiographies form some nexus between a self-generated idea of the "real" man and his theoretically constructed understanding as a way of being in the world. As such, they constitute some *poetic truth* resident within the reality of their lives that potentially reveals more about either man than the flawlessly accurate biography or the rigorously argued expository text.

That is not to say that the facts do not matter. More than enough has been assiduously written to determine the two books' numerous faults. In the text and footnotes that follow, I acknowledge the referenced autobiographical "facts" that have been proven false by subsequent critical readers. Still, many of the included stories simply cannot be corroborated. Though unlikely, they might have no more correspondence with actual events than the two men's dreams. Yet they mattered enough to their respective authors for inclusion. As such, they still reveal much about Sullivan and Wright. They do however require a different kind of reading. More like myth, legend, parable, and the good fairy tale, they offer their own ethical, poetic, and qualified truth.

Consequent with the release of strangulated affect, the following text is necessarily contingent. Initiated by the tender emotions of sentimentality, it should never be construed as some cool, rational exegesis exclusive of all but absolute factuality or objectifying reason. Even though I strive for a thoughtful well-reasoned case study, I concede to the subjectivity, emotionality, particularity, temporality, and inherent contradictions of three architects: Sullivan, Wright, and myself. I know that our shared profession is inadequate to warrant a discourse about architecture, much less the human condition. From this yielding foundation I do not pretend to offer a universal truth. Instead, I subjectively untangle a version of this knot. I emote and speak in the hopes that we might mutually share an affective yet thoughtful contact zone, a tender moment between us. From this fleeting moment you will go on to better things—and so shall I.

1

Introduction: Frank Lloyd Wright—Sentimentalizing over the Dead

Wright sat in silence. It was a Sunday night in Chicago's Oak Park. He was twenty years old.[1] He and his mother, two sisters, and their landlady had gathered for supper. His mother gave him inquiring looks; she knew something was wrong. What she didn't know was that he was angry at her. Earlier that day, he had learned that she had colluded with his best friend Cecil Corwin in an effort to forestall his growing affections for a young girl, his first love, Catherine (Kitty) Lee Tobin.[2] Corwin had broached the subject. The girl was too young. She was "a child." Wright was "a child." Neither had any experience dating. It was all happening too fast. As the arguments mounted it hit him.

"Look here, old man Cecil. Have you been talking to Mother about this thing?"

"No … She talked to me about it."

"What did she say?"

"You may ask her."

Wright was indignant. He seethed about it the whole way home. And now, after dinner, upstairs in his room his mother came up to find out what was wrong.

"What is it, my son?"

He didn't hesitate.

"Mother! Why go around to Cecil about Kitty and me?"

She didn't even look surprised. She smiled. "Why, indeed!"

Affronted, he burst out, "What's all the anxiety and fuss over a perfectly natural thing all about anyway? It's making Nature monstrous. Where is the sense in it?"

As she countered, his anger increased.

"I don't get it at all. I've never seen *you* like this. It doesn't seem like you, Mother. You have always said, 'If you have to choose between the good and the true, choose truth!' And—God—Mother! What in this matter *is* Truth?"

She ignored his point.

"Don't swear, my son."

The cooler she got, the more profane he got.

Rising to a fevered pitch he went off on the necessity of swearing. "'Damned' is a wonderful, necessary word!"

She got up and left.[3]

Wright couldn't let it go. He interpreted their interference as the imposition of some "foolish regulations," that he qualified as "'social'" (in quotes), that for some reason "'they'" (in more quotes) insisted on believing.[4] In contrast, his love expressed a "truth" which transcended the mere "good" of their "regulations."[5] After all, in his mind he and Kitty were happy—in love.

As he obsessed over their arguments he concluded that the difference between his sincere affections and their interference came from two different ways of understanding "Nature."[6] He wrote, "I began to see that in spite of all the talk about Nature that 'natural' was the last thing in this world they would let you be if they could prevent it. What did they mean when 'they' used the word 'nature'? Just some sentimental feeling about animals, grass and trees, the out-of-doors?"[7] He construed "'natural'" (still more quotes) to be something "internal" to things, like some essence. He compared it to "the nature of boys and girls" or the "nature of wood, glass and iron." In contrast, "sentimental" was some "measly, external way." He proudly held that when he read or used the word "nature," he "meant that interior way. Not in an external way." He railed: "Fools! They have no sentiment for nature. What they mean by 'nature' is just a sentimentalizing of the rudimentary animal. That's why they suffer all this confusion of ideas and make all these senseless rules—foolish regulations and unwise laws." Distinguishing between his love for Tobin as an "interior" "sentiment" understood as "truth" and their "regulations" as "external" conceptions understood as the "good," he designated the difference between their respective ways of understanding: his was "'natural;'" theirs was "sentimental."[8]

—

Despite his protestations, Wright nonetheless conceded to his mother's demands of the "good." He compromised his version of the "truth." Though he ultimately married Tobin, he lied about their ages. Confiding the marriage plans to his employer, Sullivan, he claimed that there was just two years' difference.[9] It was more like four.[10] But of truth and meaning, that is a relatively minor infraction. Indeed, what did he mean by "sentimental"? Is this an example of his using the word any way he wanted, or as his biographer Brendan Gill characterized it, as an "Alice-in-Wonderland liberality" with his key words?[11] If words are a medium to his understanding of "truth," and if Gill is correct, might this have been the greater infraction?

To be fair, by the end of the nineteenth century, "sentimental" was already polysemous. Having undergone a semantic shift over the previous 150 years, by 1900, it held multiple meanings, each with its own complex set of social implications. But Wright seems to compound the confusion. Even in this brief story we only get a hint of what he meant. If we are to take him seriously, and I believe we should, his semantics require a more careful interrogation.

I begin therefore with the dry assertions of the dictionary. Recognizing that they provide at best a skeletal framework, I have gathered a few other sources which begin to flesh out Wright's meanings. It is unlikely, in some cases impossible, that he had read any of them. But as it should become clear, he grappled with the ideas they expressed. As such, each source begins to place him in a broader theoretical context. Admittedly tendentious, I chose them simply to illustrate my point: despite Gill's criticism, Wright was careful enough with his words. Moreover, to take him seriously and contextualize his work, even within a biased selection of a few sources, is to open a world into "sentimentality."

The *Oxford English Dictionary* (*OED*) states that of persons, their dispositions, and actions, "sentimentality" is "characterized by sentiment." As it pertains to "sentiment," it means "arising from or determined by feeling rather than reason." Sentiment is variously defined as "a mental feeling, an emotion," or "what one feels with regard to something; mental attitude," or "a thought or reflection coloured by or proceeding from emotion." It generally applies "to those feelings which involve an intellectual element or are concerned with ideal objects."[12] Those feelings are not the coarse emotions of hatred, anger, or revenge. Suggesting Wright's characterization as "the good," they are defined as the "refined," "elevated," and "aesthetic" emotions. Importantly for architects, in the work of art they are understood as the expression of, or appeal to, the tender emotions, "especially those of love."

Note that both "sentiment" and "sentimentality" simultaneously link feeling and thought. Coming from the Latin *sentire in mente*, their root translates as "feeling in the mind" or "feeling in idea." Etymologically, neither word comes from a simple unalloyed effusion of the emotions. Even though the dictionary recognizes that in generalized usage, "sentiment" may mean just that, at their root both words denote some conflation of the two. More than addressing their problematic separation (as if feeling and thought could be discrete from each other), *sentire in mente* suggests a unique category that actively engages both. As an example, one might love an individual child. If that love comes from the idea of "children" and it no longer matters which child, it becomes sentimental. In this case, the feeling is entirely contingent on abstract thought: the apprehension of the idea of children.

Additionally, the dictionary includes definitions that acknowledge the semantic shift. "Sentiment" qualifies the appeal to the tender emotions in the arts by adding that it is "now chiefly in derisive use, conveying an imputation of either insincerity or mawkishness." "Sentimentality" includes the later definition of "addicted to indulgence in superficial emotion" and "apt to be swayed by sentiment." Clearly degrading attributes, both words can be summarized as having two antipodal sets of connotations: commendatory and pejorative. However, in the arts they are more often construed as the latter.

In the untangling of Wright's meaning, the dictionary unfortunately fails to straighten it out. Consider that he contrasted his "natural" understanding of nature from his mother's "sentimental" based on an implied categorical distinction between "sentiment" and "sentimentality." That distinction runs counter to the dictionary's declaration that the latter is "characterized" by the former. The only definitive way to construe the two words as that different would be to assume that Wright defined "sentiment" by its commendatory definitions and "sentimentality" by its pejorative definitions. Then the two words would be different enough to justify the distinction.[13] But if that were his interpretation it would mean that he was describing his mother as either "addicted to indulgence in superficial emotion" or too easily "swayed by sentiment." Wouldn't that be ironic? After all, it was he who had fallen in love while she apparently behaved rationally. Clearly a more thorough untangling is required.

—

Wright's distinction between "natural" and "sentimental" calls to mind Friedrich Schiller's distinction between "naïve" and "sentimental." "Natural" and "naïve" may be used synonymously. Schiller used them interchangeably.[14] Even though he wrote over a hundred years earlier, his essay *Naïve and Sentimental Poetry* (1795) shares uncanny similarities to Wright's story of first love. Moreover, his elaboration of the terms provides clarification to Wright's otherwise vague meanings. Following in the romantic tradition, he stated that the poet's subject, like Wright's, was nature. He characterized the difference between the "naïve" and "sentimental" poet (both invariably men) with this telling distinction. "The poet ... either *is* nature or he will *seek* her. The former is the naïve, the latter the sentimental poet."[15]

According to Schiller, the naïve poet enjoyed such an extraordinary immediacy with nature in a unity so complete as to constitute essence. The naïve poet *is* nature. Citing a direct correspondence between feeling and thought, he described a manifest unity such that the poet's thoughts, the substance of the poem itself, were "the completest possible *imitation of actuality*." Attempting to further convey the degree of immediacy Schiller added: "At that stage man still functions with all his powers simultaneously as a harmonious unity and hence the whole of his nature is expressed completely in actuality."[16] To read the work of the naïve poet is to be moved by the essence of nature herself, "by sensuous truth."[17]

In contrast, the sentimental poet is *distanced* from nature. As Schiller put it, "He will seek her." Coming out of the eighteenth-century enlightenment, when "nature" was rationally conceptualized, analyzed, objectified, *and romanticized*, Schiller blamed this distancing on "civilization."[18] He characterized it as a condition where humans became ever more alienated from nature. Once realized "as *experience* and as the (active and perceiving) *subject*," nature, for the civilized, became available only as "*idea* and *object*."[19] Having passed into this presumably higher state, the harmonious unity of the naïve poet is consequently split in two. No longer essentially within himself, that correspondence between his feeling and his thought, as it pertains to nature, is "outside of him, as an idea still to be realized."[20] The sentimental poet "can now express himself only as a *moral* unity, i.e., as striving after unity."[21] While the tender feelings for nature remain, they have been redirected toward the idea of it. The substance of the work becomes "the elevation of actuality to the ideal or, amounting to the same thing, the *representation of the ideal*."[22]

Still consistent with an idea of *sentire in mente*, the example of the child still applies. Adding nuance to the dictionary's linkage of feeling and thought, Schiller indicated that the sentimental poet "reflects upon the impression that objects make upon him, and only in that reflection is the emotion grounded which he himself experiences and which he excites in us. The object here ... is referred to an idea [like 'nature,' or 'children'] and his poetic power is based solely upon this referral."[23] The tender emotions are grounded through reflection: a process of thinking.

Schiller illustrated the specific consequences of that idealization. Identifying the particularity of nature as finite, and the representation of its ideal as infinite, he indicated that "the sentimental poet is thus always involved with two conflicting representations and perceptions—with actuality as a limit and with his idea as infinitude; and the mixed feelings that he excites will always testify to this dual source."[24] Unlike the naïve, where nature is immanent and *finite*, the sentimental arises from *both* the finitude of actuality *and* the infinitude of transcendent ideation. Recognizing that the idea as infinitude is never attainable in actuality, he characterized the two representations as "conflicting." Never finally resolved, sentimentality somehow reconciles the poet with that impossibility.

As illustrated, Schiller effectively outlined three critical areas of conflict that the sentimental poet reconciles. Unlike the naïve poet who enjoys unification *with and as* nature as some *essence*, where nature is a living *subject* immanently realized in all its *finitude*, the civilized sentimental poet who is distanced from nature defaults to its representation as *idea*, *object*, and transcendent *infinity*. For Schiller, sentimentality adequately reconciles the irresoluble conflict between three binary representations: subject and object, essence and ideal, finitude and infinity. While he described the unity of the naïve as a kind of "perfection," he asserted that sentimentality, though never perfect, enables the poet to participate in a more important advantage: the progress of civilization.[25]

Any reading of Schiller resonates with Wright's story. With the shared categorization into the two ways of understanding nature using synonymous terms and overlapping explanations, their similarities are as frequent and compelling as to suggest agreement. After all, couldn't Schiller's "naïve" poet, whose correspondence with nature is so thoroughly incorporated into himself as to constitute some essential, unified, perfection, be the same as Wright's "natural" architect whose correspondence with nature is so thoroughly incorporated as to be "internal?" Couldn't Schiller's naïve, "sensuous truth" be the same as Wright's "natural" "truth?" And couldn't Schiller's "sentimental" poet, who complies with the demands of "civilization" as to find nature so "outside" of himself that he must "seek her," not be one and the same as Wright's "sentimental" architect who complies with the demands of the "social" as to find nature "external" to himself? Isn't Schiller's sentimental "moral unity" comparable to Wright's "the good?" Finally, are not Wright's mother's "social" "rules and regulations" the manifestations of her "idealization" of "nature" and "civilization?" Certainly—in each case. But that is not the point. After all, in his brief story, Wright did not give us enough to determine any correspondence with Schiller. But if we value Schiller's argument as a thoughtful contribution to the discourse, then we must concede to the legitimacy of Wright's definition of "sentimental." In this case, Gill's characterization as "Alice-in-Wonderland liberality" in defining his key words is humorous, but inaccurate.

While this reading of Schiller provides elaboration to Wright's meaning, it also provides a more carefully articulated context to the broader themes of this work. Pivotal to today's debates around a nature/culture divide, Schiller pinpoints one of its most critical issues: the role that sentimentality plays in the understanding of "nature" from a cultured or "civilized" perspective.[26] For once humanity has passed into a state of "civilization" and has dissected "her" formerly sacred body into its rationally objectified parts, might nature ever again return as the "active and perceiving agent" in human lives, that is, *as subject*? In his story of first love, Wright answered this question with an almost willful performance of a pre-civilized yet somewhat qualified (in scare quotes) conception of "'natural.'" Refusing to embrace his own sentimentality, Wright willed himself to be naïve. In contrast, Schiller ceded to the benefits of civilization and performed a civilized "sentimentality." And it is precisely here that the two men go their separate ways. For even though they shared similar definitions for their key words, Schiller never construed "sentimental" as a pejorative term. Wright did.

We must therefore look somewhere else if we are to better understand Wright's terms. When writing about architecture, he often characterized buildings he disliked as "sentimental;" and he occasionally characterized buildings he admired as "natural." More frequently calling the latter "organic," he indicated that "organic building is natural building."[27] Believing that the best architecture in the world was "organic," he implied that in the West it occurred in ancient times; it disappeared during the Classical period of the ancient Greeks and Romans, only to reappear under Christianity and Gothic architecture. Sounding much like Schiller, whose naïve poetry was "the completest possible *imitation of actuality*," Wright concluded that during the Gothic period, architecture was "the chief register of humanity," and characterized it as "genuine construction, its effects noble because true to causes. The forms were sculpted from materials according to the nature of construction and the life of the time—decorated by indigenous carving and painting."[28] He construed the Gothic as the last great period of architecture that was spiritually realized and emotionally experienced as the *actuality* of its subject, or at least as close as one can get when mediated through architecture. And then, "in the fifteenth century everything changes."[29] In a theme that he repeated multiple times, Wright characterized the Renaissance as initiating a 500-year period of decline. Moreover, he characterized it as sentimental.[30]

FIGURE 1.1 *Cathedral of Notre-Dame, Reims, France, late nineteenth or early twentieth century. The façade of the cathedral of Notre Dame de Reims, where the kings of France used to be crowned. The cathedral dates from the late thirteenth century and is one of the finest Gothic cathedrals in France. It was seriously damaged by German artillery in the First World War and underwent major restoration work before reopening in 1937. Photo credit: HIP/Art Resource, NY.*

Positing the split between "natural" and "sentimental," Wright fundamentally assigned the characteristics of the former to Gothic architecture and those of the latter to Renaissance architecture, and to most of what followed thereafter. Despite the generalizations, and oversimplified categorizations of eras and styles, when viewed through Schiller's lens, we can at least begin to see his point. Compare for example a paradigmatic high Gothic cathedral such as Reims (1211–c: 1250) (Figure 1.1) with a paradigmatic late-Renaissance church such as Andrea Palladio's Il Redentore in Venice (1576–1592) (Figure 1.2). For Wright, all of the cathedral's character-defining features, such as the flying buttresses, pointed arches, bosses and crockets, ribbed vaults, and skeletal masonry structure, were virtually unprecedented. As a style, it made no obvious reference to any other architectural style. Rather it seems to have come directly from a building evolution that Wright qualified as the "universal writing of humanity."[31] With its soaring interior spaces, radiant in an ecstasy of narrative-rich stained glass, it was "true to causes," the indices of the aspirations of its builders. Its very structure was its expression. Like the love for *that* child, the cathedral expressed the unified and direct feelings of the Medieval community for their god—the *Civitas Dei* as subject.

FIGURE 1.2 *Palladio, Andrea (1508–1580). Façade of the Church of Redentore. Il Redentore. Photo credit: Scala/Art Resource, NY.*

In contrast, Il Redentore explicitly refers to much earlier styles of *architecture*. Its temple front with Corinthian pilasters, engaged composite columns, and denticulated pediments makes obvious references to the architecture of ancient Greece and Rome. Wright may have known that these were not casual references. He may have appreciated an architecture based on a Platonic cosmology, a timeless infinite ideal realized through the objectifying practices of geometry, proportional systems, mathematically constructed perspective, and optical corrections. He may have even understood that Il Redentore strove for the "elevation of actuality to the ideal or amounting to the same thing, the representation of the ideal," the very definition of Schiller's sentimentality. And like Schiller he would have called it "sentimental." But his invective was against something else.

While he always preferred the "natural" to the "sentimental," in his mind, the architecture of the Renaissance was made even worse because it imitated an even earlier architecture. He directed his criticism more broadly against the idea of imitation and, in particular, the imitation of earlier architectural styles based on the ideals that they were presumed to represent. It was not so much that he deviated from Schiller's definition of sentimentality. Rather, he focused on one of its effects. For is not every imitation of a *style*, when based on its ideation, some attempt at a re-presentation or reinterpretation of the presumed ideals of that style?[32] Is this not a yet once removed "elevation of actuality to the ideal," or "the representation of the ideal?" Is not every imitation of a previously recognized architectural style, when *based on its ideals*, in Schiller's term, "sentimental?"[33] Certainly—and *both* men would have characterized it so. But there remains a significant difference. For Wright, who sought an authentic architecture autochthonous to the United States, unified with nature in the way he believed the Gothic to have been, any architecture that imitated any other architecture from any other culture, regardless of the power of its ideas, would be reason enough for him to forsake it. He only preferred the "natural."[34]

—

The significant differences with Schiller and the fervor of Wright's denunciation suggest the effects of "sentimentality's" semantic shift. A good source to better understand that change of meaning would be Kierkegaard. Writing less than fifty years after Schiller, he had already witnessed the risks of sentimentality in mid-nineteenth-century European culture. In another tale of first love, his "The First Love" from *Either/Or* (1843), he provided a humorous social satire. Referring even less directly to architecture than Schiller's essay on poetry, Kierkegaard's essay nonetheless has particular relevance to an understanding of Wright. Moreover, it is one of the earlier and more trenchant critiques of the evolving understanding of sentimentality.

In the essay, the narrator, "A," reviewed Augustin Eugène Scribe's (1791–1861) play, *The First Love*.[35] The play is a farce of multiple mistaken identities and mismatched loves of the kind that appealed to the mid-nineteenth-century Parisian bourgeoisie. As a light-hearted morality tale, for Kierkegaard, it illustrated the contemporaneous notions of sentimentality. Its protagonists are Emmeline and Charles. Both educated "on romances," Emmeline is seriously entangled in a "web of sentimentality," and Charles, in his own way, is just as tangled.[36] She is described as a romantic who adamantly believes the fatuous notion that "the first love is the true love, and one loves only once."[37] Curiously however, after an eight-year absence she fails to recognize her "first" and "true love" Charles because he does not conform to what the narrator A calls the "picture" she has of him. That picture is comprised of a "multitude of accidents, especially by the ring upon his finger." When another man wears the ring, she thinks he is Charles.[38] Emmeline suffers from an illusion. The reader soon recognizes the problem. Her love for the "picture" that she holds so dear is not for the *actual* Charles. Nor is it for a *representation of the ideal* of him. Rather it is for the *idea of being in love with the first love*. Charles is not even in the picture! Emmeline's love is not for a *beloved*, but for a pitiably vacuous, twice-removed *idea* that does not warrant the desire. The narrator A—and we can assume Kierkegaard—calls this "sentimental."

For us, Kierkegaard has written a fatal definition for the term. He effectively leapfrogged Schiller's definition for a meaning that goes from the emotive expression in *actuality*, say love, (Schiller's "naïve"), over the *representation of the ideal* of love (Schiller's "sentimentality"), to an emotive expression generated from no more than the idea of the ideal of love (Kierkegaard's "sentimentality"). Based solely on the value of the tender emotions for their own sake as virtuous, ennobling, and good, this "sentimentality" no longer requires a beloved, nor even its ideal. It only requires that the proper emotions be effused. With his incisive critique he portrayed sentimentality as the exaggerated display of emotion for an unfounded object. Where Schiller took it from the finitude of actuality to the infinitude of the transcendent ideal, Kierkegaard returned it to the finitude of an emotion that *seems* utterly empty. But it isn't. Doubly distanced from the virtuous expression of the engaged tender emotions, Kierkegaard has taken Schiller's reflection upon the beloved to an autogenetic emotive expression focused entirely upon the self. What remained of Emmeline's "love" was directed not toward another, but toward herself in the delicious assurance of her own self-righteous goodness. And that is it! The finite love that Kierkegaard portrayed is essentially a self-love. It's narcissistic.

Kierkegaard's definition offers considerable insight into Wright's. When the young architect dismissed his mother's "regulations" as "sentimental," he characterized her in much the same way that Kierkegaard characterized Emmeline. Both men portrayed women who held notions about love that they implied were foolish. Conflating the two, we can imagine Wright defining his mother's notion as something like this: *only the experienced love is true love, and one finds true love only after having experience*. Contrasted to the luminous *truth* of his inexperienced love for Kitty, his mother's "social" notions of "the good" seemed just as fatuous as Emmeline's. For certainly his love could have been "true." Given the foolishness of his mother's belief, Wright recognized that his mother's love was not bestowed upon him. Nor upon such a silly notion of the good. Rather it was warranted solely by the belief that she was doing good. With her smug and smiling "Why indeed!" she inadvertently revealed her self-satisfaction in her own self-righteous maternal goodness. Like Emmeline, and as if quoting the *OED*, she was "addicted to indulgence in superficial emotion"—in love with herself. To be sure, the disinterested observer might argue that Wright's mother's beliefs were grounded in a reasoned assessment based on experience and a genuine concern. But to the angry and smitten young son, that didn't matter. He characterized his mother's notions as being based on a seriously misguided conception of Nature, love, and the "nature of boys and girls." Wright understood the definition much like Kierkegaard. He brandished it like a curse, and called her "sentimental."

Like Schiller's, Kierkegaard's definition conveys legitimacy to Wright's. Through his clever satire we begin to see the failure of "sentimentality" and the reasons for Wright's construal of it as pejorative. Moreover, what Kierkegaard portrayed as a social symptom of the era had direct correlation as an architectural symptom. Writing in 1844, just one year after the publication of *Either/Or*, Schopenhauer (1788–1860) made a similar critique. He called to account the nineteenth-century desire among the general populace of Western Europe to finally complete the many unfinished Medieval Gothic churches. Living in Frankfurt, he was certainly aware of the extravagant construction then undertaken on the Cologne Cathedral just down the Rhine River. Most of its funding came from *secular* associations and the Prussian state, with less than 7 percent coming from cathedral taxes and collections.[39] Like the cathedral of Reims, the original funding for the incomplete structure had come from the faithful Medieval believers. While Schopenhauer did not designate it as "sentimental," he described its effects. He contrasted the "enlightened" intentions of his era with the faith-based beliefs of the original builders. He chided, "Now when I see how this unbelieving age so diligently finishes the Gothic churches left uncompleted by the believing Middle ages, it seems to me as if it were desired to embalm a Christianity that has expired."[40] Schopenhauer characterized this trend in the language of the mortician, like the preparation for honoring the dead. More specifically, he located its cause in the contemporaneous "unbelieving age." He suggested that after enlightenment reason had overcome the Medieval Christian faith, there remained some unresolved feeling that was subsequently satisfied in a kind of architectural embalming of the Gothic church.

Using the same language of death, Wright characterized this feeling as "sentimentalizing over the dead."[41] Ironically, in another example where he denigrated those intervening years from the end of the Gothic period as "500 years of elaborate reiteration of restatement," he concluded in similar terms that by 1900 "all finally became moribund."[42] For Wright knew that the end-of-the-century architecture was even more problematic than Schiller's "representation of the ideal." He recognized, like Schopenhauer, that the faith, beliefs, *and ideals* that had generated it, the sources of its very transcendence, were dying or were already dead.[43] When he chose the Gothic as the apex, Wright believed he had identified an architecture that fulfilled the religious, social, and cultural aspirations of the people that generated it. For him, a living architecture arose from those living aspirations. When they were no longer viable, for whatever reasons, the architecture died.

Wright was certainly not the first architect to raise these concerns.[44] Understood as questions of meaning and intention, they generally manifested as questions of "style." They were a regular topic for discussion of the Western Association of Architects, even before Wright was old enough to join. At the convention of 1886, John Wellborn Root (1850–1891) identified "the one grave difficulty" that he and his colleagues faced: to answer the question, "What is the style of that house?" Root depicted the then popular styles as diseases, calling the Romanesque "Dropsical," the Queen Anne "Tubercular Style," and a style that was "supposed to have originated in New England" as "Cataleptic."[45] At the same convention Sullivan's partner, Dankmar Adler (1844–1900), used the same somatic analogies of birth, life, sickness, and death, and called "not for a Renaissance, but a naissance in architecture. For there is surely being born into our world a new style, the style of America."[46] It would not be long before Wright would pick up the same cant. But he, writing many years later, designated a cause of the problem. Once again, he called it "sentimental."

Surveying the contemporaneous profusion of styles, Wright denounced,

> Here was a mess. Were these meaningless monstrosities like the people whose houses they were—like the men and women who lived in them? Was all this waste what "they" *deserved*? [...] Why were they all satisfied with pretentious attitudes and stupid gestures? Were they all sentimental instead of sensible?[47]

From his first employer Joseph Lyman Silsbee's (1843–1918) "arty" work that "aimed to be uncommon—unusual—pictorial;" to the "expensive mummery" and "ambitious Eastlake mimicry" of Oak Park and Chicago; to the Spanish-Mexican-style "missionaries'" houses of southern California; and to the huge Milwaukee County Courthouse that would "set Milwaukee back fifty years from any cultural standpoint" (Figure 1.3); for Wright, all these and more were some variant of "sheer ordinary sentimentality."[48]

As imitative of earlier styles of architecture they already qualified. But Wright knew it was more than that. Consider just the courthouse.[49] Wright would have construed it to be a hybridized, imitative version of the ancient and presumably autochthonous Greek architecture to which it refers. It is in the style of "Neoclassical Revival."[50] The appellation as "revival" denotes an imitation and, as indicated, could be constitutive of Schiller's ideated

FIGURE 1.3 *Milwaukee County Courthouse, 1931. Courtesy of courthousehistory.com.*

"sentimentality." But "*Neo*-classical *Revival*" denotes an exponential distancing from some presumed "original:" an imitation of an imitation. It refers to the architecture of the ancient Greeks as imitated and modified by ancient Romans, as imitated and modified by Italian Renaissance Classicists, as imitated and modified by eighteenth-century "Classical Revivalists," and finally, as imitated and modified by Wright's *neo-revival* peers. For Wright, this lineage of imitation was further compounded by his belief that the "original" stone architecture of the Greeks was in fact another imitation of an earlier painted wood version.[51] After centuries of imitation reassembled in an "arty" fashion, only a fragmented and disconnected *image* system remained. For him, the courthouse was not founded on the beliefs that informed the original architecture, but on the image of the architecture itself. Gone were the references to the religious, social, and cultural aspirations of the ancient Greek builders. Gone were the transcendent ideals of Schiller's sentimentality as exemplified in Il Redentore. Downtown Milwaukee was neither the ancient Athenian Acropolis nor sixteenth-century Venice. No one believed that the new courthouse was some religious medium between humanity and the gods, much less the Greek gods.

Nonetheless, late-romantic architects persisted in the validation and celebration of the appeal to the tender emotions for their own sake as good. Like a thousand Emmelines, they sighed sentimentally over their imitative drawings. Unable to conjure a suitable replacement that warranted the effusion, they defaulted to *a love for the idea of being in love with ancient architecture*. As a kind of *meta*-scholarship for the past, it wasn't the content that mattered, but the idea of scholarship itself. Each persevered with a love based on a *picture* comprised of a few accidents. The beloved, that is, all of what generated the original architecture, what Wright considered to be the architecture itself, wasn't even in the picture. What remained of the emotion was redirected back toward its originators: the owners, developers, architects, and users, each another foolish Emmeline confident in the narcissistic assurance of her own self-righteous goodness. That empty "scholarship" was the only evidence necessary to validate the effusion, which after all was really for its own sake anyway. Wright aptly called it "a pretentious attitude and stupid gesture." Clearly intentional in his use of the trope, he wrote: "The picture had now triumphed over architecture."[52] While Kierkegaard's A found Scribe's play "comedic," Wright could not enjoy the irony. He called the architecture "a mess." And like Kierkegaard, he called it "sentimental."

Wright would make similar arguments for each of the other architectural styles to which he referred. He knew that they too were derivative, imitative, emotive pictures, devoid of substantive ideation. Yet the architects persisted as if providing endless examples of the *OED*'s definition: "addicted to indulgence in superficial emotion." Wright was correct. They were sentimental, *in the pejorative sense of the term*. By the end of the century, the semantic shift was complete. That architecture conceived as the finite, ornamented, and "arty" amalgamation, emptied of the infinitude of substantive transcendent ideation in the creation of an emotive picture for its own sake as good, was in fact "sentimental."

—

It is easy to understand Wright's disdain because clearly, if that is sentimentality, it does not make good architecture. Or as contemporary philosopher Karsten Harries explains, what Kierkegaard described makes "kitsch." In his commentary on "The First Love," Harries indicates that the term was unknown to Kierkegaard. But what is described in Emmeline is "something like an anatomy of the Kitsch personality."[53] Emmeline, in love with the idea of being in love with the first love, is a good example of that quality of kitsch that "does not so much arouse love or desire, but their simulacrum—their simulacrum precisely because love or desire are no longer related to what would warrant it."[54] In his *The Meaning of Modern Art* (1968), Harries describes the effects of kitsch in the work of art. "When we look at such a painting we don't really confront anything. In the end all that remains is an atmosphere, and it is precisely this atmosphere which Kitsch seeks to elicit."[55] Most scholars imply that in the work of kitsch, the emotive appeal, or Harries's "atmosphere," is self-evident, requires little effort on the part of the spectator, and is constituted as a system of "effects" so familiar as to be cliché.[56]

Wright's autobiography was published before most of the important texts on kitsch. When he wrote it, he might not have even known the term. But he would have agreed with the characterization. For the life traditions that once manifested in the highest realizations of Gothic architecture had been distanced and sequentially exhausted through their representation as an ideal, the imitation of that representation, and the imitation and re-imitation of the imitation. Yet the emotive desires remained, even heightened by the late-romantic architect who effused the tender emotions for their own sake as good. The expression of those desires through an architecture that no longer warranted them could arouse no more than their simulacrum, an atmosphere, the manipulation of feeling. Indeed, the Milwaukee County Courthouse is sentimental. And it is kitsch.

If this is the received end-of-the-century cultural definition, it is then surprising to find books in Sullivan's library that expressed precisely the same debased "sentimentality" as found in Scribe's *The First Love*. He owned, for example, the limited edition set of *The Works of Charles Paul de Kock* (1793–1871).[57] Primarily a novelist, de Kock also wrote for the popular theaters and at the exact same time of his fellow Parisian, Scribe. The two authors certainly knew of each other and, for a brief period of time, competed as playwrights for the same stages. They also shared more than a similar style of writing. Like Scribe, de Kock wrote humorous and light-hearted tales with convoluted twists of plot about and for the Parisian bourgeoisie. Generally, there was a moral as exemplified in *The First Love*. From today's perspective, these funny stories of piffle challenge all credulity. Like A's critique, these morality tales can only be seen through an ironic lens as comical. Yet Sullivan bought the entire twenty-five-*volume set* in the *twentieth* century.[58] Moreover, as he began his financial decline, he continued buying similar books as late as 1906. Apparently he derived some pleasure from them.

Undoubtedly, few contemporary academics would honor these books for inclusion within the esteemed Sullivan archive. Most would see them as an embarrassment. But there is at least one such scholar. In his book, *In Defense of Sentimentality* (2004), the late philosopher Robert Solomon argued for the toleration of kitsch in the sentimental work. He acknowledged the persistent correlation between the two.[59] Seeking to clarify the terms, he distinguished between them by limiting the definition of "sentimentality" to only its commendatory meaning. He defined it as "nothing more nor less than the 'appeal to tender feelings.'"[60] In so doing, he removed much of the problem. For few would say that in the work of art, "the appeal to the tender emotions" (or Solomon's "feelings") categorically results in kitsch. In contrast, the "indulgence in superficial emotion" usually does.[61]

While Solomon made a cogent six-point rebuttal to the correlation, he offered a much more interesting point.[62] For him, *sentimentality supersedes kitsch*. He suggested that if the tender emotions "provide us with an easy sigh or tear, that only shows how central they are to the very foundations of ethics and character. The work that evokes these emotions may not be great or even good art, but the emotions seem to me to be perfectly sound, and feeling them is a virtue and not a vice."[63] Whether or not Sullivan saw his occasional sigh as virtuous is beside the point. What concerns us here is that, for the experience of that sigh, both men were able to overlook the violation of kitsch. For Solomon, the appeal to the tender emotions was that important.[64] Perhaps for Sullivan too.

And here we get to the crux of the problem: what is the relative value of the appeal to the tender emotions in the work of art or architecture? Should we, like Solomon, be willing to tolerate kitsch in order to experience it? Is it that virtuous? That *good*? When Wright rejected that architecture now understood as kitsch, did he likewise intend to reject that appeal? In other words, did he reject *both* the pejorative and commendatory definitions of sentimentality? Moreover, at what point on a spectrum between the two might the whole work be rejected? For if the appeal to the tender emotions no longer holds any compelling value, then certainly sentimentality doesn't either.

—

Even so, "sentimentality" was not the primary focus of the day-to-day lives of Sullivan and Wright. For the two men working together in Chicago in 1890, it was the building requirements of architecture that demanded their utmost attention. In what could have been nothing short of exhilarating, the two men invented, designed, and constructed buildings in one of the most important and rapid periods of industrial and technological advancement in the history of architecture, *and* humankind. Consider that until his first night in Chicago, Wright, at age nineteen, had never even seen the illumination of an electric light bulb. With mixed feelings he described it as a "sputtering white arc-light," "dazzling and ugly," cutting through the drizzling, dreary, spring, night.[65] In no time he would conceal the naked bulb with indirect lighting. And Sullivan would take credit for being the first to incorporate it as a decorative element in his ornamentation.[66]

Moreover, Chicago itself, their home, was the site of some of the most rapid development of the period. When Wright first entered the city, it was in the midst of an explosive demographic and economic boom. In the decade from 1880 to 1890, it doubled in population to over a million people, surpassing Philadelphia to become the second largest city and manufacturing center in the United States.[67] By 1900, Chicago, not quite seventy years old, was the sixth largest city in the world, trailing only London, Paris, Berlin, Vienna, and New York.[68] While its downtown business area had been decimated by the Great Fire of 1871, most of its bustling economic infrastructure of manufacturing, transportation, and labor remained unscathed. Encircling this rare tabula rasa, that infrastructure sat, impatiently waiting for the architects and developers to resurrect its burnt, dead core. It is little wonder that historians cite Chicago as the source of the "first modern architectural movement."[69] For out of this rare opportunity surged some of the first skyscrapers, modern steel frame construction, the curtain wall system, the large plate glass of the Chicago Window, the Chicago School, and the Prairie style; and Sullivan and Wright were renowned participants in the design of each. Within this extraordinary arena of future-oriented progress, sentimentality seems simply incongruous.

But this burgeoning city raised serious questions regarding the appeal to the tender emotions. During the decade when Wright first moved to Chicago, growth was due largely to immigration. At a time when nationality and race were conflated, this was seen as a racial threat.[70] In 1890 more than three quarters of Chicago's one million citizens were immigrants.[71] Many were packed in tenements that enclosed some of the most densely populated areas in the world.[72] Even worse, in this city where so many were employed in slaughterhouses, 97 percent of the tenement units were without bathtubs.[73] Chicago was the city of the Pullman Strike, the Haymarket Affair, Jane Addams's Hull House, the race riots of 1919, and that disturbing paragon of America's self-image, the inglorious white city that was *The World's Columbian Exposition of 1893*.[74] Not surprisingly, it was also the city of Upton Sinclair's *The Jungle* (1906), a book whose aim was to "shake the popular heart and blow the top off the industrial tea-kettle." When Sinclair asserted that "fundamentally, it will be identical with [*Uncle Tom's Cabin*]—or try to be," he compared his novel to Stowe's exemplar of mid-nineteenth-century sentimentality.[75] From the extremes of progress, wealth, poverty, and immigration, Chicago provoked questions of what constitutes place, home, city, and nation. As the distillation of the best and worst of the still young and growing United States, the city provoked questions of what it meant to be civilized.

Social historian, Gail Bederman, thoroughly investigates the American turn-of-the-century conception of "civilization." She uncovers the broader social issues that inform an understanding of sentimentality.[76] She illustrates how the operative set of ideas used in the generation of that conception intersected with the discourses of class, race, and gender, and in particular what was then understood as "manliness." Believing that civilization was the most developed phase of a Darwinian evolution of progress, the American self-image was founded on notions of racial purification and masculine strength. As a form of Social Darwinism this implied that humanity evolved from savagery through barbarism to an advanced stage of civilization. As Bederman indicates, many believed that only white races had evolved to the civilized stage.[77] Manliness was understood to be instrumental to, and the manifestation of, that progress. Where the gender roles of the "savage" "were believed to be almost identical," the roles of the "men and women of the civilized races had evolved pronounced sexual differences. Civilized women were womanly—delicate, spiritual, dedicated to the home. And civilized men were the most manly ever evolved."[78] Consistent with the prevailing mores of Victorian respectability, manliness evinced a "strong character," a "powerful will," and the decorous requirements of "sexual self-restraint." By 1890 it had all the connotations of the moral rectitude of the "civilized" (meaning white, middle-class, American) male. Used to reinforce his privileged status, these disturbing conceptions of race and gender became the character-defining attributes of civilization itself.

Challenging that status were a number of perceived threats. According to Bederman, the separation of more and more men from their traditional sources of power and status like agriculture and the conquest of nature, the woman's movement and women's suffrage, the huge influx of immigrants seen as racially inferior and primitive, and the alienation experienced in the cities, all threatened the gender construct. It was further exacerbated by warnings from the medical establishment that the male body was vulnerable to two relatively newly identified assaults. "Neurasthenia" was seen as symptomatic of an industrializing economy that required an echelon of specialized businessmen engaged in intensive *mental* labor. And the recent categorization and labeling of "homosexuality" as a disorder of sexuality and gender, and its claim as a moral issue by the religious community, further intensified the risk. Each of these challenges to their power and manhood was construed as feminizing. Consequently, at the same time that the evolution of humankind was seen as leading to a more pronounced differentiation within the gender binary, "civilization" was also seen as emasculating to men and jeopardizing to that differentiation. Characterized as an "over-civilized" society, these threats precipitated a modification to the social construct of manliness. Many Americans, led by the likes of Teddy Roosevelt, Frederic Remington, Stanley Hall, and even Wright himself, called for a broad cultural response: "Americans," that is, white American men, were to be made strong and "masculine." By the turn of the century there began a shift in terms and conception from "manliness" to "masculinity."

In the 1890s "masculinity" was still a relatively new word. It had a significantly different meaning from "manliness." "Masculinity" had originally meant "any characteristic, good or bad, that all men had," or at least were thought to have had.[79] As an attribute of gender, it was a kind of clinical descriptor, devoid of moral, emotional, or value content. It could be applied across race and class. "By definition, *all* men were masculine."[80] However as "manliness" was thought to be ever more challenged, "masculinity" as a different quality of male power came to replace it. By 1917 masculinity began to connote a system of values, and it had evolved to describe "the essence of admirable manhood."[81] By the time of Wright's autobiography in 1932, it came to represent a "mix of 'masculine' ideals:" those "like aggressiveness, physical force, and male sexuality."[82] If "manliness" expressed moral ideals, self-restraint, and signs of constrained power, "masculinity" expressed the ideals of unchecked power. Compared to "civilized" "manliness," "masculinity" had connotations of the primitive, unrestrained and savage.[83]

Even before this masculine trend, many understood sentimentality as a feminine expression. Bederman takes this as a given. With a wave of the hand she declares, "'Sentimental' of course, was synonymous with 'unmanly.'"[84] Solomon wrote, "It is no secret that the charge of sentimentalism has long had sexist implications as a weakness that is both more common (even 'natural') and more forgivable in women than in men."[85] Neither indicates whether that came from its commendatory or pejorative definitions. Whether it was believed that women were more likely to appeal to the tender emotions, or more likely to indulge in superficial emotion, it hardly seems to matter. The characterization of "civilized women" could have been either.

Sullivan and Wright, each in his own way, were aware of and often spoke to these social issues. Their personal narratives are filled with references to some of the era-defining people and events. Wright was intimately related to two of the most renowned *and notorious* of them. His first cousin was Richard Lloyd Jones, owner and editor of the *Tulsa Tribune*, author of the racist and incendiary articles that fueled the Tulsa Race Riot of 1921.[86] Over the years, his family would distance themselves from his record. Ten years after the "riot," Wright designed his house, named of all things, "Westhope."[87] In stark contrast, Jones's father, Wright's uncle, was the Rev. Jenkin Lloyd Jones, the nationally renowned Unitarian minister who worked with Jane Addams, William Jennings Bryan, Susan B. Anthony, and Booker T. Washington.[88] An advocate for women's rights, racial equality, and pacifism, Jones drew crowds of followers to Spring Green, Wisconsin. There, in the family chapel and at the more intimate family gatherings, Wright heard and apprehended the preacher's beliefs. In Chicago, Wright enjoyed dinners at Jones's home where he met some of the leading social and religious leaders of the era. It was there that he met Addams. He later attended events at her nationally known settlement house, Hull House. Sullivan did too.

Both men admired Walt Whitman (1819–1892), one important yet iconoclastic voice in a particular construction of masculinity and race. Sullivan initially admired and Wright altogether rejected the writing of Herbert Spencer, one of the most important authors of Social Darwinism.[89] And both architects worked on Sullivan's Transportation Building for the *Columbian Exposition*, the one colorful intervention in the otherwise white "White City." Certainly they attended the fair, and surely they walked down the Midway Plaisance, that pleasure village to the west. As they left the White City and passed what Bederman describes as "the civilized" German and Irish villages, they might have been bemused by "the barbarous" Turkish, Arabic, and Chinese villages, until they finally arrived at "the savage" American Indians and Dahomey village.[90] And the architects might have recalled the *Chicago Tribune*'s glowing assessment, "What an opportunity was here afforded to the scientific mind to descend the spiral of evolution ... tracing humanity in its highest phases down almost to its animalistic origins."[91] Sullivan and Wright were not mere observers of these social events; they were participants. Both architects revealed their positions polemically in their architecture, in their writings, and by their identified influences and relationships. How they felt about and understood sentimentality informed those modes of participation.

But by the twentieth century, "sentimentality" was broadly and culturally repressed. While it still connoted two general types of definitions, they could no longer be diametrically characterized as commendatory and pejorative. Yes, the pejorative meanings persisted as such. The throbbing heart of the late romantic still effused the tender emotions for their own sake as good; the cool mind of the dispassionate philosopher still exposed the self-indulgence in the elevated emotions as narcissistic; and the critical eye of the astute purveyor of the fine arts still ridiculed kitsch. But now, the once commendatory meanings had become pejorative too. For even the slaughterhouse butcher who killed the fatted calf knew that sentimentality was bad. In an era of new masculinity those privileged white men who defined "America," to include the butcher, believed that even the appeal to the tender emotions understood as "feminine" was dangerous. Out of an imagined need to protect their "civilization," any appeal to those "refined," "elevated," "aesthetic," and "tender emotions, especially those of love," had to be likewise repressed. Consequently, even the positive attributes of "sentimentality" were negative. *Every* meaning of the word was construed as pejorative. Utterly vitiated, sentimentality seems unworthy of reconsideration.

Sullivan nonetheless upheld his own expression of it.

And Wright still called himself "the most sentimental person I ever knew."

In a case study of these two men, any use of the word must consequently remain qualified. In the following chapters when I use the term I, like Solomon, mean the "appeal to the tender feelings," those he defined as "pity, sympathy, fondness, adoration, and compassion." Yet, like the *OED*, and unlike Solomon, I also include "love."[92] It should go without saying that I attach no gender attributes to these feelings. Moreover, unlike Solomon, I recognize and concede to the general usage of the pejorative definitions as the "indulgence in superficial emotion" and "apt to be swayed by sentiment." I will occasionally even use the term accordingly. The context will be adequate to determine the intended meaning. Where needed, I explain my usage. My intention is not to modify or rewrite the definition. Rather, I seek only to untangle that knot.

—

Fortunately, "ornament," at least on the surface, is not as polysemous as "sentimentality." Figures 1.4 and 1.5 are photographs of two early American houses of worship. The Independent Presbyterian Church of Savannah, GA, built in 1817–1819 and restored after a fire in 1889, is resplendent in decoration. The Jerusalem Church, built in 1769, just up the river in Rincon, GA, is stripped bare. While most would agree that the quoins, mutules, triglyphs, and pilasters of the Presbyterian Church are "ornament," one might ask, "Is the steeple?"

"Ornament" comes from the Latin *ornamentum* for "equipment, trapping or ornament," which is rooted in the Latin *ornare*, which meant to "fit out, equip or adorn." It has often been a part of ceremonial services such

FIGURE 1.4 *Independent Presbyterian Church, Savannah, Georgia. Built in 1817, burned in 1889 and rebuilt in 1891. Courtesy of the Georgia Historical Society. MS 1361-PH-03-21-0535.*

as the "accessories or furnishings of the church and its worship." And it may be "a quality or circumstance that confers beauty, grace, or honour."[93] While ornament scholar Kent Bloomer indicates that there have been shifts of meaning "as vast as the development and vicissitudes of Western culture," he concedes that historically scholars say "more or less the same thing."[94] The basic meaning has not changed much since ancient times. The *OED* states that in architecture "ornament" is "something employed to adorn, beautify, or embellish, or that naturally does this; a decoration, embellishment."[95]

FIGURE 1.5 *Jerusalem Church, Rincon, 1769. Photograph by Van Jones Martin, from Mills Lane's* Architecture of the Old South: Georgia *(Savannah: The Beehive Press, 2017), 25. Courtesy of Beehive Press.*

Like a jewel on the body, by definition it postulates an ornament bearer, that body/thing that is adorned or accessorized. But unlike the diamond broach, it is not something you take off at night and put in a safe. Nor is it like the autonomous work of art that may be moved from wall to wall, or from pedestal to pedestal, or church to museum. In architecture, there is something quite fixed and mutually dependent in the relationship between ornament and its bearer.

Unlike the *OED*, Bloomer makes an emphatic and critical distinction between "ornament" and "decoration." He works to clarify what would have been understood and debated by fin-de-siècle architects.[96] He finds this necessary, especially today when the conception remains in transition. For him, ornament is neither a "fine art" nor "decoration," but "a category of art unto itself." He traces its etymology back to the Greek *Kosmos* (the opposite of *Chaos*) and links it to the Greek understanding of a harmonious, systemic, and timeless order of the universe. Not a casual instrument, ornament was the physical medium between humankind and their way of being in the world. Bloomer calls it a "natural and universal system of human communication that can present a valuable segment of human thought."[97] That thought, or the meaning conveyed, is integrally linked to the meaning of its bearer, the building itself.

Decoration on the other hand need not have any of these characteristics. Bloomer characterizes it as a "more changeful concept."[98] Generally understood as the tasteful arrangement of things, it suggests "the decorous, a condition marked by propriety, good taste, good conduct, and good appearance."[99] Tomorrow, the same decorative things could be rearranged quite differently. As architects, and the designers of what is affixed to buildings, it was the problem of ornament that Wright and Sullivan sought to solve. As this story progresses, I honor both architects' intentions and allow that all of their "decoration" rose to the level of "ornament." I consequently use the latter term unless the context clearly demands otherwise.

After tracking a history of the term, Bloomer summarily states that "ornament incorporates an amount of adherence into something that possesses and manifests an inherent utilitarian form."[100] His somewhat tortured sentence conveys the difficulty, and desire, to define it exactly. His words "adherence" as a fixed attachment, "incorporates" as uniting into one body, and "into" instead of "onto," all suggest an effort to define ornament as more integral to the "utilitarian form," that is, its bearer. And as we begin to determine a definition, already the contested territory is revealed. How integral is it? What is the nature of that integration? Indeed, must the bearer be "utilitarian?" These questions only begin to anticipate the current debates regarding the phenomenal, figural, and scalar relationships of ornament to its bearer; the language and grammar of ornament; and its meaning, politics, and the construction of subjectivity.

These too were the contested arenas that Sullivan and Wright began to address. Even though Wright was broadly writing about architecture when he decried the five-century decline of the "great art;" and Root and Adler were talking about "style;" by the very nature of most nineteenth-century building, they were implicitly talking about ornament. One needs only to consider that the most definitive character-defining features of the imitative architectural styles were chiefly their ornamentation. An architectural style, even a debased style, was identified by it. Wright reinforced this notion when he indicated that the evidence of that decline was through "the reiteration of restatements by classic column, entablature and pediment."[101] Or as he bemoaned, "The pilaster again!"[102] The contemporaneous and much deplored problem of style could be distilled as a problem of ornament.

To be sure, by the end of the nineteenth century, most Western architects understood ornament as problematic. Nonetheless, they persisted in the imitation of debased historic styles that no longer came from or spoke to the life traditions of the culture. They offered up their narcissistic vanities, effused for their own sake, just because they thought they were "good." It was unsustainable—and sentimental—in the pejorative sense of the word. It seemed as if architects had essentially two options. They could either follow Sullivan's and Wright's suggestion and stop using it entirely or work to develop some new style of ornamentation appropriate to their era that had sufficient meaning and relevance to whatever life traditions they might articulate. Ultimately, it was the former that modernism would favor.[103] Using arguments as varied as economics, morality, hygiene, gender politics, evolutionary doctrine, racial difference, and more, the leading modernist architects disparaged ornament and ultimately removed it from their buildings.[104]

—

While these manifold reasons were offered for the removal of ornament, there is an even broader issue at stake. Karsten Harries provides a framework to understand that issue and it uncannily dovetails with Wright's. Harries defines the problem of late-nineteenth-century architecture as coming from an art that was no longer in the service of the "ethos" of a given community. Harries notes that "ethos," as it pertains to the broader community, refers "to the spirit that presides over its activities. 'Ethos' here names the way human beings exist in the world: their way of dwelling."[105] Understanding "dwelling" in Heidegger's ontological sense, as "the basic character of human being," he qualifies it "not primarily as a being cast into boundless space but as a being at home in the world." Something more than the traditions of the culture, ethos connotes a kind of communal metaphysical "spirit."[106] Reminding us that the English word "ethical" derives from it, Harries suggests that architecture carries an "ethical function," by which he means "its task to help articulate a common ethos."[107] When Wright described the architecture of the Gothic period as "the chief register of humanity," we might suggest that for him it fulfilled its ethical function.[108] Comparable to "being at home in the world," one could argue that the "natural" architect helped in the articulation of that ethos.

Harries indicates that instead of the ethical function an alternative understanding of art and architecture has presided over much of modernity. He calls it the "aesthetic approach." Coming from that same eighteenth-century culture of enlightenment, Schiller's "civilization," the aesthetic approach understands "aesthetics" as one of the main branches of philosophy, an analogue to logic governed by reason.[109] Privileging rational thought over feelings, it was this same culture of reason that challenged the authority of an absent and unprovable god, the blind obeisance to a questionable crown, and the value of the seemingly irrational emotions. The aesthetic approach is the complement of a process of *rationalization and secularization*.

Harries illustrates its effects on architecture and, in particular, on ornament. He indicates that the "aesthetic approach" manifests as "the ideal of the artwork as an autonomous aesthetic object, serving neither church, nor state, nor love, serving only art."[110] It culminates as the contested art for art's sake. In architecture it manifests as an understanding of the work "as a functional building with an added aesthetic component."[111] Wright understood this as well. In the same way that he characterized Gothic architecture as fulfilling its ethical function, he likewise characterized the post-Gothic as evidence of the aesthetic approach.[112] He decried it as "decadence." "Sculpture becomes statuary, the image trade becomes painting, the canon becomes music." The arts "emancipate themselves, break the yoke of the architect, and take themselves off, each in its own direction."[113] While never specifically calling it the "aesthetic approach," he effectively described its manifestation: the transition to art for art's sake. In his commentary on the continued use of the ornamental Greek-revival cornice, he described it as "aesthetic effect, an aesthetic that had got itself into Greek and, therefore, into Roman life as Art for Art's sake, this arbitrary convention, became our accepted Academic pattern."[114]

Harries characterizes the manifestations of the aesthetic approach on ornament. He uses the same adjective as Wright: "decadent." He warns that the ornamentation that had become "the eclectic decoration of the nineteenth century is decadent in this sense: an aesthetic object added onto a building that could survive quite well without this addition."[115] Like Bloomer he distinguishes between "ornament" and "decoration," calling the former that which "articulates a communal ethos," and the latter that which "we experience primarily as an aesthetic addition to building. […] So understood, *decoration is the aesthetic analogue to ornament.*"[116] Through his distinction Harries suggests a return to the etymological root of ornament in *Kosmos*: it helps to articulate the way human beings exist in the world. It fulfills its ethical function. In contrast, decoration does not. The "ornamentation" of the aesthetic approach, now understood as decoration, has been divorced and/or liberated from its integration into both the communal ethos and the building itself. Like Bloomer's understanding as the tasteful arrangement of things, or Wright's shift to art for art's sake, it is just decoration.

Harries references Ruskin as a voice who spoke to the approach. Ruskin analytically distinguished between "building" and "architecture," where the latter is essentially the former but with some "added aesthetic component." He held that this component, while it "impresses" onto building "certain characters venerable and beautiful," is "otherwise unnecessary."[117] Ornament, as that which is "employed to adorn, beautify or embellish," clearly falls under that categorization of "added aesthetic component." It is "otherwise unnecessary." When architecture is so understood, and *when reason demands utility and justification*, ornament must rise to become a self-sufficient and self-justifying presence. *It must warrant its own necessity.* However, unlike painting or sculpture, it can never be entirely autonomous. It cannot exist as art for art's sake or ornament for ornament's sake. As

Harries reminds us, ornament by definition is in a specific relationship to its bearer. "To succeed as ornament, ornament must serve the ornament bearer. Where ornament aspires to the self-sufficient presence of a pure aesthetic object it dies."[118] By definition it is no longer ornament. "This death is demanded by the aesthetic approach, which would replace ornament with art for art's sake."[119] Again, we are left with decoration.

Harries offers a compelling argument. But we should remind ourselves that it is essentially based on the validity of a static definition. Ornament "must serve the ornament bearer." While that does not diminish its value, we might ask what would happen if the definition were to change. With questions that frame the chapters that follow, I ask whether "ornament" could, like "sentimentality," undergo a semantic shift. When Wright provided his conception of "integral ornament," did he in fact rewrite the definition? Is it possible that he developed some living "ornament" compatible with the aesthetic approach? Or had Sullivan? While these questions might seem to be an issue of definition, Schiller, Wright, and Harries illustrate that they are contingent upon a more significant ground than semantics. As Harries puts it, they are contingent upon "the way human beings exist in the world." All of which suggests that, to change the definition of ornament might require a different way of being.

PART ONE

Louis H. Sullivan

2

The Plastic Decorations Are Distinctly Architectural in Conception

The ravine called him "for friendship." It was a distant call that he answered in denial of school.[1] On that sunny morning he played hooky, collected baked goods from his grandparent's pantry, filled his "blouse" with rolls and doughnuts and cookies, a small tin cup, and "buttoned up;" "set forth" over hill crest and down through the countryside, jumping fence gates on his quest, seemingly alone.[2] At a bright spot in the bottom of a wooded ravine ran a "rivulet," a narrowing of a local creek where the constricted water passed rapidly over fieldstones under a canopy of "tall arching oaks."[3] And there, determined to test his engineering skills against the ineluctable forces of nature, a young Louis H. Sullivan built a dam.

It was the early summer of 1862; he was five years old. Sheltered from the grim realities of the Civil War, Sullivan had just spent a wonder-filled winter with his maternal grandparents on the outskirts of the small town of South Reading, Massachusetts.[4] Exploring their farm, he plotted to spend all of his time outdoors. He could not understand why he had to be pent-up within the walls of the West Ward Grammar school, all "imprisoned and sad."[5] He had already rebelled so ardently against the strictures of church, with its disturbing messages, rigors, and artifice, "all distorted, cruel and sugary," that his grandparents no longer required his attendance.[6] He was determined to have the same liberation from the much-reviled school.

For Sullivan, both institutions, the church and the school, were factitious contrivances that he believed alienated him from nature and hence from himself. As the evidence of civilization he reckoned that "it is education's crime that it has removed us from Nature."[7] He believed "that his world, his life, which he had frankly felt to be one, was being torn in two."[8] Like Schiller's sentimental poet, Sullivan intuited that the effects of civilization alienated the self that *is* nature.[9] And as a young boy he did not understand that in reflecting upon nature he would again approach it. He wrote:

> They never told him, never permitted him, to guess for himself how these things [what the student learns in books], were actually intense symbols, complex ratios, representing man's relation to Nature and his fellow man; they never told him that his mathematics, etc. etc., came into being in response to a *desire* in the human breast to come nearer to nature—that the full moon looked round to the human eye ages before the circle was dreamed of.[10]

He had made up his mind. Sullivan answered that distant call. He played hooky to build a dam. He immediately set to work.

Using the masonry walls that he had watched being laid as his model, he constructed his dam from those same fieldstones, mortared with mud, twigs, and grass. In no time it was holding water, forcing him to work faster, widen the barrier, increase its height until "at last child power and water power became unequal. Now was at hand the grand climax—the meaning of all this toil."[11]

In the retelling of his story of self-assertion, Sullivan called himself a "proud hydraulic engineer," "a strong boy." He compared himself to the "big men" who worked and accomplished great things.[12] He was designing *and* building, working with his hands in physical labor, testing the limits of his own creativity and strength. And for Sullivan it was the paradigmatic story of power: the power of human choice. By the time "a miniature lake had formed," at that precise moment of stasis when those engineered powers stabilized in seeming equipoise, yet brimmed pregnant with imminent rupture, as each additional drop of the gurgling creek inexorably filled the lake, at that moment of "grand climax," Sullivan "tore out the upper center of the wall, stepped back quickly and screamed with delight, as the torrent started, and, with one great roar, tore through in huge flood, leaving his dam a wreck. What joy!" Surrendering to this wild exhibition of power, "he laughed and screamed."[13]

—

At age thirty-one, Sullivan had long since given up the idea of becoming a hydraulic engineer. Having just hired Frank Lloyd Wright, he had a more vexing problem on his drafting table: what to do about ornament. Unwilling to give it up entirely, he knew that he had to find a way to fully incorporate it into the building project. He had already begun to articulate such a method. According to Wright, it was one of the most important things that the master had taught him. He characterized it as "of-the-thing-not-on-it."[14] Even though the expression is probably Wright's alone, it is more than just sententious. Wright described it as "the philosophy of which Louis H. Sullivan was now champion."[15] At its most simplistic, it meant that all the various components and elements of a building should be *of* the building, not *on* it. In Sullivan's terms, ornament should not appear "'stuck on,' so to speak."[16] The concept represented an architectural ideal that manifested as an integrity and unity of all the aggregate components of building. And it was based on his understanding of nature.

Like many Americans in the latter half of the nineteenth century, Sullivan construed nature as inherently good and a source of beauty. Synthesized with his readings of Charles Darwin and Herbert Spencer he developed a particular conception as the appropriate model for his understanding of ornament. As he expressed it, all things in nature have a shape that has evolved from and refined through an endless cycle of birth and death. Beauty is evinced in the way "life seeks and takes on its forms in an accord perfectly responsive to its needs. It seems ever as though the life and the form were absolutely one and inseparable, so adequate is the sense of fulfillment."[17] For him, ornament on a building would be as natural and presumably as integrated as the serrations of the elm leaf or the iridescent azure "eyes" of the peacock feathers.[18] From Wright's perspective, Sullivan's first and perhaps most successfully realized example was the interior of the Chicago Auditorium theater (1889).[19] The term that both men used to describe its ornamentation was "plastic."[20] Wright wrote that it "was the first *great* room for audience that really departed from the curious prevailing traditions. The magic word *plastic* was used by the Master in reference to his ornament, and the room itself began to show the effects of this ideal."[21] *Plastic* was not a new term, but it was problematic.[22] Writing forty-three years after the Auditorium was built, and with tongue firmly in cheek, Wright qualified it as "magic." Something of a nineteenth-century buzzword, it might always have been just a little too slippery. In *A Sentimental Education*, Flaubert satirized the glories of the craze in his portrayal of the facile painter Pellerin, who "finally recognized the stupidity of *Line*" and proclaimed: "everything's *plastic*."[23] And that was 1869. Sullivan and Wright's architectural colleague, Irving K. Pond (1857–1939), challenged their practice of it by obliquely calling them, without naming them, the "leaders of this self-styled cult." Characterizing it as an "oft-occurring offense against reality" he defined "plastic" architecture as one of "manipulation as against articulation, an architecture wanting the moral and aesthetic qualities of real structure."[24] As a definition Pond's is not particularly helpful. Unfortunately, neither Sullivan nor Wright *carefully* defined what they meant.[25] While Wright indicated that Sullivan "was fond" of using the term for a kind of integrated ornamentation as distinguished from something "stuck on," he nonetheless questioned whether even the master understood the term.[26] "That the word 'plastic' got itself understood at all in relation to architecture then is doubtful—even by Sullivan himself."[27]

As far as Wright was concerned, few architects were able to put it into practice. He indicated that among Sullivan's contemporaries, the only one who accomplished it was John Root in his Monadnock Building.[28] Comprised of brick bearing walls with flared base and cornice, it is characterized by the gentle bodily curves and the swelling of its modeling. Built immediately after the completion of the Auditorium, it rises like a cliff of carved, molded, and fired clay, that definitive "plastic" material. The Monadnock is easily recognizable as such. It is plastic. But it is basically without ornament.

In his essay "Plastic and Color Decoration of the Auditorium," Sullivan used the term in the title and first sentence and never repeated it. We nonetheless begin to get some sense of what he meant from the first two sentences. "The plastic and color decorations are distinctly architectural in conception. They are everywhere kept subordinate to the general effect of the larger structural masses and subdivisions, while lending to them the enchantment of soft tones and of varied light and shade."[29] His words recall his response of four years earlier to the question "what is the just subordination of details to mass?" In the symposium of the Illinois State Association of Architects of April 1887, he stated, "I prefer such subdivision of the masses into detail as is strictly called for by the utilitarian requirements of the buildings; and that they should comport with its size, location and purpose."[30] Even though he qualified this statement by privileging the "spiritual results" of the architecture over any "pedagogic scarecrow" of a "fixed rule," he nonetheless posited that details were to be kept subordinate to massing determined by "utilitarian requirements."[31]

FIGURE 2.1 *Carnegie Hall from Balcony. Courtesy of Carnegie Hall, Jeff Goldberg/Esto.*

This is a start. For Sullivan, plastic had something to do with modeling "the larger structural masses and subdivisions" while keeping the ornamentation "subordinate." Compare the interior ornamentation of William Burnet Tuthill's (1855–1929) Carnegie Hall (Figure 2.1), with Sullivan's Auditorium (Figure 2.2), its contemporary.[32] The differences are striking. Even though Carnegie Hall is a model of ornamental restraint, it is nonetheless typical of the stylization of the era. It has a stage defined by a Renaissance-Revival blind colonnade where the ornamentation articulates and organizes the five-bay enclosure. While the stage is basically a domed box with chamfered sides, what one sees and experiences is the colonnade—*and that is generated solely from the ornamentation*. Moreover, the colonnade and its components have adequate visual autonomy to read as *figures* on a background. One reads an entablature with engaged columns against a blank wall. For Tuthill, historical scholarship and meaning were conveyed in the choice of style as determined by the selected system of ornamentation and its arrangement. However, it should be noted that from today's perspective, it seems just as likely that the colonnade could have been Greek Revival, Baroque, or Roman arcading. What is clear is that in Carnegie Hall, *the character defining formal arrangement comes entirely from the ornamentation*.

FIGURE 2.2 *Auditorium Building, Chicago, IL, 1887–1889. Adler and Sullivan, architects. Photograph attributed to J. W. Taylor. Historic Architecture and Landscape Image Collection, Ryerson & Burnham Archives, The Art Institute of Chicago. Digital File # 49666.*

In contrast, the Auditorium, while strewn with Sullivan's typically exuberant decoration, is of indeterminate style. In his entire essay, Sullivan never even mentions "style." Here the overriding impression comes from the carefully delineated stage, proscenium, and ceiling of telescoping arches, all of which are the result of stage design and acoustic calculations. The ornamentation follows and repeats the formal directionality of the "utilitarian requirements." A large decorative lunette on either side of the proscenium (one is shown in Figure 2.2) repeats the arch motif and is integrated into the ornamental scheme. Murals infill some of the panels. The strongest figural ornament with adequate visual autonomy, that is, where the ornament reads as completely distinct from its background, is the crest on the stage curtain: a piece of fabric. Compared to Carnegie Hall, the Auditorium's ornamentation has been incorporated into, is secondary to, and supportive of the experience of the overall massing of the space. In Sullivan's terms, it "enchants" the masses with "tones" of "light" and "shade." For him, meaning was conveyed explicitly through the narrative content of the murals. As he stated, "Their purpose is to express, allegorically, the two great rhythms of nature, namely, growth and decadence."[33] In the Auditorium, *the primary character defining formal arrangement comes from the massing as determined by building function*. Completely different from Carnegie Hall, the ornamentation is "subordinate to the general effect of the larger structural masses and subdivisions." In its incorporation it is effectively integral to the plastic modeling of the space.

Wright reinforced this interpretation. In describing his own process he offered a description of Sullivan's efforts at "plasticity." Wright indicated that he worked "to get continuity in the whole, eliminating all constructed features just as Louis Sullivan had eliminated background in his ornament in favour of an integral sense of the whole."[34] By focusing on the background instead of the figure, Wright couched the issue in the inverse of the terms. Sullivan got rid of the autonomous figure and simultaneously the (back)ground, the figure-*on*-the-ground. In this subtle shift Sullivan had illustrated for Wright a paradigmatic example of "of-the-thing-not-on-it." The figure of ornament was incorporated into, that is, "of" the ground. For these two architects, "plastic" meant that the building masses are molded such that the ornamentation is fully incorporated into that massing. Unlike Carnegie Hall, the ornament does not define the overall formal arrangement. The building function does. And the autonomous figural ornament, as a thing-in-itself, while not entirely effaced, has been subordinated and subsumed into the massing. Gone are Carnegie Hall's stylized wreaths and festoons, the denticulated entablature, and engaged composite columns. Gone are the historical references. And with plastic expression, gone is the reading of ornament as the autonomous figure clearly identifiable from the ordered formal array. For Sullivan and Wright, in "plastic decoration" the ornament is "of-the-thing-not-on-it."

The Auditorium was just one of the surprisingly few buildings that Wright believed revealed the "great reach" of the master's genius.[35] The others were the Getty Tomb (Figure 2.3), the Wainwright Building

FIGURE 2.3 *Carrie Eliza Getty Tomb, Graceland Cemetery, Chicago, IL, 1890–1891. Louis H. Sullivan, architect. Richard Nickel, photographer. Richard Nickel Archive, Ryerson & Burnham Archives, The Art Institute of Chicago. Digital File # 201006_119A.9.*

(Figure 2.4), and what Wright characterized with back-handed praise as the "pictorial Transportation Building [(1891–1893)], for what it is worth." All of Sullivan's other buildings were "more or less on these stems" and were in the comparison "relatively inferior."[36] Even though Wright included the Transportation Building, which he admired for its individuality, especially when compared to the other buildings of the fair, he nonetheless dismissed it with that now familiar trope: "picture building."[37] Obviously, for Wright, it did not solve the problem of ornament. But what about the Wainwright? Or the Getty Tomb? Were they "plastic" as well?

We need only to cursorily review them because the evidence is immediately apparent. Even in the extreme variation of building type, from tomb to "skyscraper," the comparisons can be made. The ornamentation in both is without historical precedent. Both are of indeterminate "style." Both are arranged where the ornamentation is in Sullivan's terms, "subordinate to the general effect of the larger structural masses and subdivisions."[38] And in both, virtually all the ornamentation is in Wright's terms, "without background." Except for those anomalous "bases" and "capitals" on the piers of the Wainwright (Figures 2.4 and 2.5), there is no autonomous ornamental figure that has not been subsumed into its ground. On the Getty, any interpretation of the arches as decorative is negated by the reality

FIGURE 2.4 *Historic American Buildings Survey, Creator, Ellis Wainwright, Adler & Sullivan, and Charles K Ramsey.* Wainwright Building, Seventh & Chestnut Streets, Saint Louis, Independent City, MO., *c. 1933. Documentation Compiled After. Photograph by Lester Jones, 1940. (https://www.loc.gov/resource/hhh.mo0297. photos/?sp=2 [accessed September 18, 2018]). Library of Congress, Prints and Photographs Division, HABS. Reproduction number HABS MO, 96-SALU, 49–1.*

of their construction. The tomb is constructed of solid blocks of Bedford limestone. The arches *are* the structural masses to which the ornamentation lends "enchantment of soft tones" and "varied light." Like the Auditorium, Wright would have surely interpreted the ornamentation of these two structures as "plastic" too.

Even though he did not include the Guaranty Building (Figures 2.6 and 2.7) as contributing to Sullivan's oeuvre, Wright did allow that it was "architecture living again."[39] While it may have been derived from the stem of the Wainwright, it is worth reviewing because its ornamentation represents a culmination in the idea of "of-the-thing-not-on-it" or "plastic."[40] Constructed in 1894, the Guaranty is of steel frame construction. Unlike the Wainwright, which is clad in Missouri granite, brown sandstone, brick, and terra-cotta, the Guaranty is clad entirely in one material: the fired clay of terra-cotta.

FIGURE 2.5 *Historic American Buildings Survey, Creator, Ellis Wainwright, Adler & Sullivan, and Charles K Ramsey.* Wainwright Building, Seventh & Chestnut Streets, Saint Louis, Independent City, MO., c. 1933. Documentation Compiled After. Photograph. (*https://www.loc.gov/resource/hhh.mo0297.photos/?sp=8 [accessed September 18, 2018]*). *Library of Congress, Prints and Photographs Division, HABS. Reproduction number HABS MO, 96-SALU, 49–7.*

The stark clarity of just one material fortified the plasticity in its singular massing. Moreover, Sullivan got rid of the articulated attic and cornice by making it all of one carved piece, continuous from the line of the ground to the flaring line at the sky. Like the Monadnock, it too is a cliff of carved, molded, and fired clay, but it is completely alive with ornament. Every surface of its exterior is graven with decoration that is fully incorporated into the building tectonics: the terra-cotta functions as both the weatherproofing and the fireproofing. Except for those unfortunate applied entrance arches, there is virtually no distinguishing between the ornament and its bearer. Fired into the skin, the ornamentation is as bodily integral as freckles, pigmentation, scars, and tattoos. As if witnessing life's electric current, the transparent surface teems with figures coursing up and down its magnificent piers. If removed, the building is flayed of its erethistic skin. This plastic is uncannily vital.

In his efforts to solve the problem of ornament, Sullivan successfully made these significant moves. Foremost was his decision to work in a non-historicist idiom. By 1888, he had already argued against the heedless imitation of historical styles, claiming that "if you would really seek a style, search for it

FIGURE 2.6 *Guaranty Building, exterior, 28 Church Street, Buffalo, c. 1900. Courtesy of the Buffalo History Museum.*

FIGURE 2.7 *Guaranty Building exterior cornice, 2018.* © *James Caulfield.*

not altogether in books, not altogether in history, but search for it rather in the explicit reality of your own inner life and your own outward surroundings."[41] This idea in and of itself was not new. By 1886, many of the leaders of the profession professed the same thing. Recall that at the Western Association of Architects convention, Root had complained about the problem of style, and Sullivan's own partner Dankmar Adler called for a naissance in architecture, the birth of "a new style, the style of America." But Sullivan was one of the earliest to put it into practice. By developing new systems of ornamentation unconstrained by the grammatical requirements of a historical system, he was liberated to design ornament with regard to its formal properties such that he could visually incorporate it into the overall massing of the building. Rather than negotiate whether a cornice should be punctuated with Greek Revival dentils or softened with Egyptian gorge, he negotiated how the ornamentation of his own design lent "enchantment" to the formal and utilitarian requirements of the building. No longer would he need to select willy-nilly from the repository of styles in order to randomly place historically determined decoration on the assembled boxes of the building arrangement to taste. No longer would any given ornament be just as vulnerable to removal and replacement with another from a different era, style, or location. His unprecedented ornamentation was designed for and came from that specific building's requirements. Furthermore, by incorporating it into and having it evolve from the arrangement of the structural masses and subdivisions of the building, he subsumed it within a hierarchical system. Sullivan gave it a formal hierarchy and consequently a formal grammar. He reintegrated the ornamentation into the building architecture and characterized this as "architectural." He made it "of-the-thing."

It is apparent that this was basically a *formal* solution. As such, Sullivan initiated a design shift that would abandon ornament's subjective ideation as understood in the meaning and scholarship of a given historical language/image system, for an objective and empirical ideation in the abstracting language of *form*, or in his terms of "masses" and "subdivisions." He solved the problem by changing the terms. He went from the discourse of styles, Carnegie Hall's Renaissance-Revival, to the discourse of form, the Auditorium's "plastic." It was a deft move that effectively sidestepped the problem. For many, this would become an adequate solution. With his shift from historical narrative to objective form, Sullivan was one of the first to articulate an argument that would inaugurate modernism's pursuit of "pure form." Wright honored this. Sullivan's colleagues in the profession would follow as well.[42] But for him a "formal" solution would never be enough. To sidestep the issue did not solve it.

3

That Object He Became

Two of Sullivan's most important writings were specifically about ornament. Together they begin to clarify his position. The first, the brief essay "Ornament in Architecture," was published when he was thirty-five years old. By that time, he already enjoyed national recognition for his ornamental work. The Auditorium, the Getty Tomb, and the Schiller Building Theater had all been completed and constituted some of the dazzling evidence for his justifiable acclaim. In his built work alone, he had already begun to articulate a philosophy of ornament. The second, the small book, *A System of Architectural Ornament* [*System*], was published in 1924 and delivered to him in the last week of his life. It was the culmination of forty years of experience and the final word on that philosophy. Together both texts provide a fairly consistent picture of Sullivan's attempt to solve the problem of ornament. Because of its more comprehensive scope, I begin with the *System*.

Some may challenge that choice. Architecture historians and scholars have disagreed over its value. David S. Andrew bluntly critiques it. He describes Sullivan's reading of his sources as "sketchy." As a work of exposition, he finds it deficient, claiming that "the sentiment is noble, the ornament is attractive, but how the latter issues from the former ... are matters with which Sullivan chooses not to bother himself."[1] On one hand I have to agree with him. Overwrought, florid, thin, a quick reading suggests the ramblings of a failed, eccentric architect. In contrast, Sullivan scholar, Lauren Weingarden, without specifically referencing Andrew, upends this reading by characterizing the *System* as a cogent piece of expository writing, a "literary treatise," where the drawings "systematically" illustrate the "metaphysical origins and philosophical principles of Sullivan's design procedures."[2] While her characterization may be questionable, she nonetheless provides a valuable contribution to the Sullivan literature. And like her, I have come to see the *System* as a rich trove of his understanding of ornament. But how then are we to interpret it? If we are to take both scholars seriously, as I believe we should, any interpretation requires yet another way of reading.

The *System* is arranged in five sections: a brief "Prelude;" a section entitled "The Inorganic and the Organic;" eight technical plates that graphically illustrate the ideas in ornamentation; another brief section entitled "Interlude: The Doctrine of Parallelism;" and eleven more plates of his lush ornament. It is perhaps not surprising that Sullivan never mentions "sentimentality" at all.[3] While the title of the main essay is "The Inorganic and the Organic," his focus is what he called "man's power."[4] Writing only in terms of "man," Sullivan began with a brief illustration of the human power to create and its relation to the inorganic. He believed that humans have some "innate," "congenital," and "natural" power necessary to generate an organic or living architecture. Emphasizing its importance to our understanding of architecture he concludes that "there can be no genuine understanding of the nature of creative art of any kind, or creative activity of any kind, without a clear vision of man's innate powers and their latent intensity evoked and aroused to action by the power of his desire—which is an emotion, and therefore instinctive."[5]

Sullivan provided a hierarchy of powers by categorizing them into five groups. As if ascending a ladder, they increase in force and moral value. He identified and organized them from the bottom rung to the top as, Group I, "the physical powers;" Group II, "the intellectual group;" Group III, "the emotional group;" Group IV, "the moral group;" and Group V, "the spiritual group." In general terms they reflect the human ability to do physical labor, to reason, to emote, to make moral decisions, and to make sense subjectively of what he calls "Life." As Weingarden illustrates, consistent with his late-nineteenth-century romantic/American transcendentalist stance, Sullivan positioned the physical powers and the intellectual group before and below the emotions, morality, and spirituality. He dismissively suggested that "the people of the world ... exalt Intellect to the rank of fetich."[6] Superior to reason, he upheld the emotional group as "an enormous volcanic complex—the basis of action, especially of spectacular action, private or public, secret or open. It is of *instinct*."[7]

For Sullivan, the supreme exercise of those powers was not political. It was not the control of others that mattered to him, but the making of beautiful things. Similar to the social Darwinists, Herbert Spencer and G. Stanley Hall, both of whom he had read, he described an evolutionary process where "the trail to man's simple powers leads with many windings through the jungle of complexities we call civilization." It culminates in the "modern dream." That telos "(obscured, inarticulate as yet) is to found, on the reality of man and his powers, a civilization befitting him and his powers."[8]

At the culmination of that evolutionary process, both Hall and Spencer envisioned a kind of superior human, one rarified through the winnowing of what Spencer coined "the survival of the fittest." Identified as a man, Hall called him the "cosmic super-man." Spencer dubbed him the "ideal man."[9] As Sullivan climbed up his ladder, he described the various men that occupied each rung: the worker of the physical powers; the scientist of the intellectual group; the emotional man of the emotional group; the philosopher of the moral group; and the "dreamer-man ... the seer, the mystic, the poet, the prophet, the pioneer, the affirmer, the proud adventurer" of the spiritual group. When he finally reached the top we find "to our utter dismay, or utter joy," a man who "is not what our kind for so long had believed him to be and still believes him to be;" for at that highest rung, as "the last veil lifts, the reality-man is found sound to the core, the quintessence of power, the dreamer of dreams, the creator of realities, the greatest of artificers, the *master craftsman*."[10] His emphasized last two words tumble from the ladder like a dead weight crashing through his soaring flight of rhetoric. The apron-clad "master craftsman" is a lesser god, a humble god, no "ideal man," no "cosmic super-man," just the maker of ornament.[11]

—

Though Sullivan presented a seemingly tight, organized, abstracted, and compartmentalized structure of power, he qualified it before he even described it. Calling the grouping a "convenient fiction," he reminds us that "in pursuing such method it is ever to be borne in mind that a living power, not an idealistic abstraction, or nonentity, is to be dealt with."[12] Even though one may intellectually conceive a hierarchy of discrete powers, they must be understood as a more integrated, "interfluent," protean, that is, "living" power. As evidenced in his writing and from the sources he references, Sullivan portrays this power as fully imbricated within the same "living," intellectual, and material practices of his era.

This surely invites questions.

We might begin by asking, how did Sullivan describe his own personal power? How did he understand it? How might it be culturally understood? From the very first page of his autobiography he reveals a surprising strategy. Sullivan wrote it in the third-person singular. While claiming that it gave him more "freedom," it nonetheless manifested in a coincident loss of power.[13] He shifted the subject from the active "I" to someone else, an active "he." Instead of "I did it;" "He did it!" With his very first move Sullivan relinquished his authorial command as subject.

I began chapter two with the story of a dam. It was one of the few childhood tales from the autobiography in which Sullivan described himself autonomously *asserting* himself. It is a story where he claimed some power and authority over and against another: in this case his grandparents, his school, and nature.[14] In most of the other childhood stories he either witnessed others doing something or someone doing something to him. It seems odd then that when he reflected on his accomplishment, he did so in the interrogative. Upon releasing the waters, he did not claim the accomplishment. Rather he *asked* if he had done it. "Had he not built the dam? Was he in high spirits? Had he not built the dam *all by himself*? Had he not planned in advance just what happened?"[15] And when he claimed his authority among the "big strong men" that he so dearly admired, he again asked, "Had he not worked as hard as he had seen big men work? Wasn't he a strong boy for his age?"[16] Regardless of whether his questions were the unintended revelation of his own insecurity, or the intended trope of a rhetorical question, or even the saccharine portrayal of the inquisitive child, they weaken his self-described power.

As he matured, Sullivan described himself as the typical late-nineteenth-century American youth negotiating for some authority. As a boy he was "without desire to plunder" and with no "destructive tendency."[17] But at about age eleven he boasted that "he could lick any boy of his size" and admitted that "sometimes [his] prophecies were verified."[18] In those fights he both won and lost. Apparently they didn't last. In his early teens he referred to them as "former street fights."[19] In the autobiography, they were the only acts of physical aggression by Sullivan. Yes, he liked exercise and boxing, but it is more likely that he saw those activities much like he saw military drill, as "discipline in play."[20] For he despised what the military drill meant. He "had no thought of war other than to loathe it, as the wild dream of madmen who stood safely behind the evil."[21] Similarly, he disliked power as a cultural brute force. When the examiner for his entry into the École des Beaux-Arts noticed his lack of "sympathy" with the ancient Roman Empire, Sullivan responded, "I feel out of touch with a civilization whose glory was based on force."[22]

None of this would seem that remarkable until it is compared with Wright's autobiography. Side by side, the two books reveal a striking difference in tenor and force. Wright's self-portrayal makes Sullivan look downright pacific, as if withdrawn from power.[23] Wright splattered his tale with its lifeblood, boasting of victories in boxing, stabbing, fistfighting, and kicking, even into his sixties.[24] By his account he *always* won.[25] With obvious pride in his strength, authority, and self-assertion, Wright delineated a picture of a man who relished and bragged about his own exercise of physical power.[26] And it is not simply the fact that he lived a more violent life, which he did; it is the way in which he described those fights, in all their graphic violence, that Wright revealed his intention.[27] For him, it was important to convey the impression of his savage power. The reader is *forced* to palpably *feel* Wright's machismo.

"Power" means "the ability to do or effect something," "act upon," like Sullivan's creative power; and it often denotes "physical or mental strength, might or vigor, energy," a "force," and quality of forcefulness. It may also mean "the possession of control or command over others," or, "authority."[28] In the late-nineteenth-century American public sphere, power by definition was most often the culturally determined and imminently contested purview of men. What little power women may have claimed was too often consigned to the domestic, that is, "woman's sphere."[29] Power in public life was a manifestation of gender: who had it, how, when, and where it could be exercised were all culturally determined, segregated, and regulated by sex. This suggests that the differences between Sullivan's and Wright's autobiographies have much to do with their portrayals of gender.

In the generational divide between Sullivan and Wright, we witness the evolution that occurred in the broader culture at large: what Bederman describes as the transition from "manliness" to "masculinity."[30] Wright, in deliberate defiance of those nineteenth-century codes of respectability, and in his defense against the characterized "feminizing" effects of "over-civilization," resorted to the primitive, unrestrained, and savage language of "masculinity."[31] In contrast, Sullivan persisted in using the restrained language of "manliness"—his entire life—long after "masculinity" had overcome it.[32] Though it is apparent that Sullivan understood the cultural forces that precipitated its undermining, and recognized, and at times even decried the alienating effects of "over-civilization," he eschewed the gendered, raw, and primitive power of "masculinity."[33] While power in turn-of-the-century America was contaminated with gender, the power that Sullivan performed was not "masculine."

—

In the *System*, Sullivan outlined the scope of "man's" powers and their importance to self-understanding and the creative act. But what did he believe was their proper deployment? Of the powers alone, how should they be asserted? Through aggression? Since he did not embrace the new masculinity, might it mean that he was stuck in a then outmoded construction of power and gender based on "manliness?" If it was not "masculine," could it be called "feminine?" Or did he actually engage the contemporaneous discourse alternatively?

In addition to those outlined in the *System*, Sullivan focused considerable attention on one other "power." While he endowed "man" with the powers of his hierarchy, he offered "sympathy" as an all-encompassing meta-power that integrated the five groups with each other and with the world. "Man's power to create, is intimately based on his power to *sympathize*."[34] With slight variations, this was a consistent theme over the previous thirty-five years.[35] In his *Kindergarten Chats* (1918) he characterized sympathy as that which "contains, encloses and sets in motion and guides to a definite goal, all that is of human value—all of man's powers and the output of those powers."[36] The idea was critically important because, as indicated, he believed that the institutions of "civilization" had alienated him from himself and from nature. Sympathy restored him to both.

In the *Kindergarten Chats* he elaborated. Perhaps influenced by his reading of Spencer and Alexander Bain, he charted an evolution that commenced with a human being intimately of nature, seen as innocent and good, and whom he called "proto-man."[37] This figure, a kind of noble savage, negotiated his place within the world through "instinct," a generous heart, and *understanding*. As humans evolved into "primitive man," the intellect became more active; it began to dominate. Sullivan cited the Judeo-Christian narrative of the Garden of Eden as an "impressive spiritual allegory" that portrayed the loss of pre-knowledge innocence. "Here began sin: the sin of intellect. Verily he tasted of the fruit of the tree of Knowledge. What a price he since has paid! For when man parted with Instinct ... he parted company with himself, he lost himself."[38] Estranged from nature and himself, this figure, whom Sullivan called "Feudal man," negotiated that alienation through the imposition of "intellect," a selfish brain, and *knowledge*.

In his allegorical anthropogenesis of romantic primitivism, Sullivan effectively traced an evolution where the triumph of reason fractured the human in two.[39] For him, this is the current status of humankind, "merely with new names, new agencies and change of local color."[40] It was the very same condition he feared was happening to himself in his childhood story of the dam. But he offered hope with a culminating figure that he called the "man of democracy," one who is finally returned to full integration. Described as "altruistic" and "beneficent," for Sullivan, that reintegration occurs through "sympathy."

When the young student of the *Kindergarten Chats* asked, "How shall Knowledge and Understanding be reconciled," the wise teacher answered, "There is but one agency, SYMPATHY." When the pupil challenged, "What? So weak a thing as sympathy!" Sullivan averred, "You mean so *great a power* as Sympathy."[41] For Sullivan, sympathy mediates between knowledge and understanding, the brain and the heart, and the intellect and instinct. For the young boy alienated from nature by the driving institutions of late-nineteenth-century civilization, the school and the church, it was through sympathy in the building of a dam that integration was restored.

Today, sympathy is defined as "the quality or state of being affected by the condition of another, with a feeling similar or corresponding to that of the other."[42] Solomon stated that it "is the sharing of feeling or, as a disposition, the ability to share the feelings of others."[43] It is important to note that both definitions situate at least two agents capable of feelings, in a relationship of *shared* affection. As such, the definition is constitutive of one and *another* able to be "affected" by a "condition" or capable of "feeling." Unlike the similar nineteenth-century conception of "empathy," which the late historian Vincent Scully aptly defines as "the physical association by the observer of himself with the *object* viewed [emphasis added]," by definition, sympathy always posits at least two *subjects*.[44]

Sullivan's usage intensifies this notion. For him sympathy becomes a kind of shared *being*. Coming from that same transcendentalist tradition, he credited Whitman, who "beautifully expresses this idea" in the poem "There Was a Child Went Forth."[45]

> THERE was a child went forth every day,
> And the first object he look'd upon, that object he became,
> And that object became part of him for the day or a certain part of the day,
> Or for many years or stretching cycles of years.[46]

The importance of Whitman to Sullivan's thinking has long been recognized. It is perhaps Weingarden in her book *Louis H. Sullivan and a 19th-Century Poetics of Naturalized Architecture* who most thoroughly establishes the poet as Sullivan's literary model for his admittedly heart-felt notions. Relying upon her trenchant historiographical ground suggests that Whitman's conception of sympathy provided an understanding by which Sullivan became that reintegrated or shared being. And Sullivan suggests that Whitman expressed it best in this poem. He was quite taken by it. He often quoted from it in his autobiography.[47] In his essay "The Artistic Use of the Imagination," he referenced it in conjunction with this statement about the artist: "Into all that he sees he enters with sympathy; and in return, all that he sees enters into his being, and becomes and remains a part of him."[48]

We might wonder how literally he meant this. Weingarden suggests that he meant it metaphorically yet concedes that his essay left that interpretation intentionally open-ended.[49] He wrote that it was up to us "to supply what has been left unsaid, to carry on such impulse as there may be as far as [we] can."[50] Throughout his writing Sullivan suggests a literal interpretation.[51] In the *System* he describes sympathy as "the power to receive as well as to give; a power to enter into communion with living and with lifeless things; to enter into a unison with nature's powers and processes; to observe—in a fusion of identities—Life everywhere at work—ceaselessly, silently—abysmal in meaning, mystical in its creative urge in myriad pullulations of identities and their outward forms."[52] For him, what Solomon defined as "sharing of feeling," he understood as "communion," even with lifeless things, "*to receive as well as to give* [emphasis added]." In each case sympathy grants a kind of subjectivity, what he called "identities," to the other. For Sullivan, that meant even "Life." Positing an alternative epistemology to the objectified thing in itself, Sullivan suggests that to be in a world of things means to inhabit not a world of objects, but subjectively, emotively, "in communion" with the rocks themselves, reciprocally. This allowed him to say in the story of the dam that the wooded ravine called to him. "Once found and marked for friendship, it often had called to him in his school—a distant call—he could not come."[53] "Life everywhere at work," sympathy endows subjectivity to the objects around us. The ravine was his friend.

In Sullivan's stories we again hear the echoes of Schiller. While both men believed that the effects of "civilization" alienated humankind from nature, ironically, both believed that *sentimentality* reconciled that alienation. For Sullivan's appeal to *sympathy as one of the tender emotions* is constitutive of the very definition of sentimentality. When he elaborated on its meaning, he even expanded his definition to include the other tender emotions of "compassion" and the capitalized "Love."[54] Even though he did not admit it, the civilized Sullivan effused sentimentally.

—

Sullivan offered an early description of the relationship between sympathy and ornament in his essay "Ornament in Architecture." On one level it can be interpreted in the same formal terms that he understood "plastic." When an ornament seems integral to its bearer, then it is said to be in "sympathy" with the structure. "So, an ornament or scheme of organic decoration befitting a structure composed on broad and massive lines would not be in sympathy with a delicate and dainty one." He described a relationship that is revealed in the contrast between the formal properties of "broad" and "massive," and "delicate" and "dainty." But his usage of the term is more than a trope for a visual condition. For Sullivan, sympathy is some *emotive medium* that as a minimum supports the rational and formal "of-the-thing-not-on-it."

He explained it with a botanical analogy. He wrote that in the same way that "a flower appears amid the leaves of its parent plant,"[55] ornament too must appear "as though by the outworking of some beneficent agency it had come forth from the very substance of the material."[56] He implied that there is some spiritual quality of a building mass, "the spirit of the structure," that is "free to flow into the ornament" much the same way that there is some essential character evinced in the relationship between the plant and its flower, or the pine tree and its needles, or elm tree and its leaves. "An elm leaf would not 'look well' on a pine-tree—a pine-needle seems more 'in keeping.'"[57] Clearly more than formal, not even Darwinian, Sullivan is obviously talking about something else. For he suggests that "if we wish to insure an actual, a poetic unity, the ornament should appear, not as something receiving the spirit of the structure, but as a thing expressing that spirit by virtue of differential growth."[58]

Poetic and highly suggestive, the pine needle/elm leaf analogies are unfortunately predicated on simplistic tautologies. They are not enough.[59] We can turn to the *System* for elaboration but receive little clear expository explication. Sullivan does however provide a link. When he defined sympathy as "a power to enter into communion with living and with lifeless things," he might just as likely have defined it as a "power to enter into communion with organic and inorganic things." In his writing he equates "living" with "organic," and "lifeless" with "inorganic."[60] And it is through the terms "organic" and "inorganic" that he begins to make demonstrable relationships between his conception of sympathy and his drawings of ornamentation.

As already indicated, the title of the primary essay from the *System* is "The Inorganic and the Organic." It is here that Sullivan makes some of his strongest claims. He states, "But nothing is really inorganic to the creative will of man. His spiritual power masters the inorganic and causes it to live in forms which his imagination brings forth from the lifeless, the amorphous." He follows that with, "Thus man in his power brings forth that which hitherto was non-existent;" and a sentence later with, "Thus he commands at will the realm of the organic or living."[61]

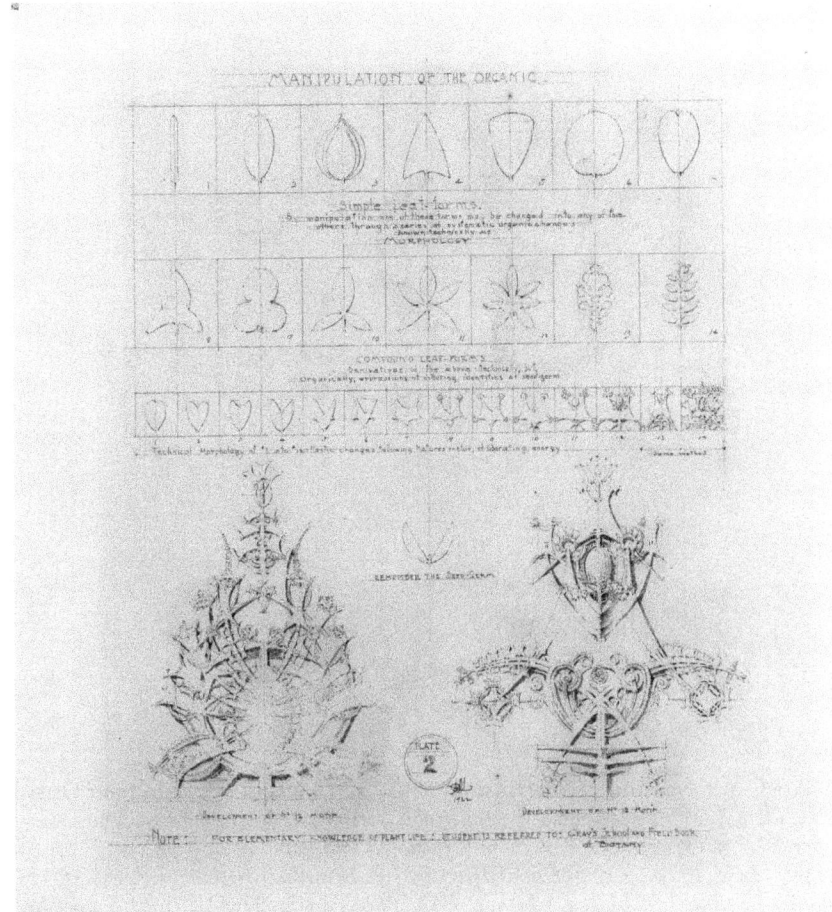

FIGURE 3.1 *Sullivan, Louis Henri (1856–1924)*. System of Architectural Ornament, Plate 2, Manipulation of the Organic. 1922. Graphite on Strathmore paper, 57.7 × 73.5 cm (22 ¾ × 29 in.). Initialed and dated at bottom center of design, "LHS 1922." Commissioned by the Art Institute of Chicago. 1988.15.12. The Art Institute of Chicago, Chicago, USA. Photo credit: The Art Institute of Chicago/Art Resource, NY.

Perhaps the most readily accessible nexus between the text and the drawings, what he calls "plates," occurs on "Plate 2," "Manipulation of the Organic" (Figure 3.1), and "Plate 3," "The Inorganic" (Figure 3.2). On Plate 2, Sullivan illustrated his understanding of the "organic" in the now common interpretation of the biomorphic: shapes isomorphically found in nature and reproduced, much like the digital today, through splines, compound curves, and the parametrics of natural and living matter. In Plate 3 he illustrated the "inorganic" in the equally common interpretation as rational figures generated from the human mind: the geometric shapes of circles, triangles, squares, and polygons.

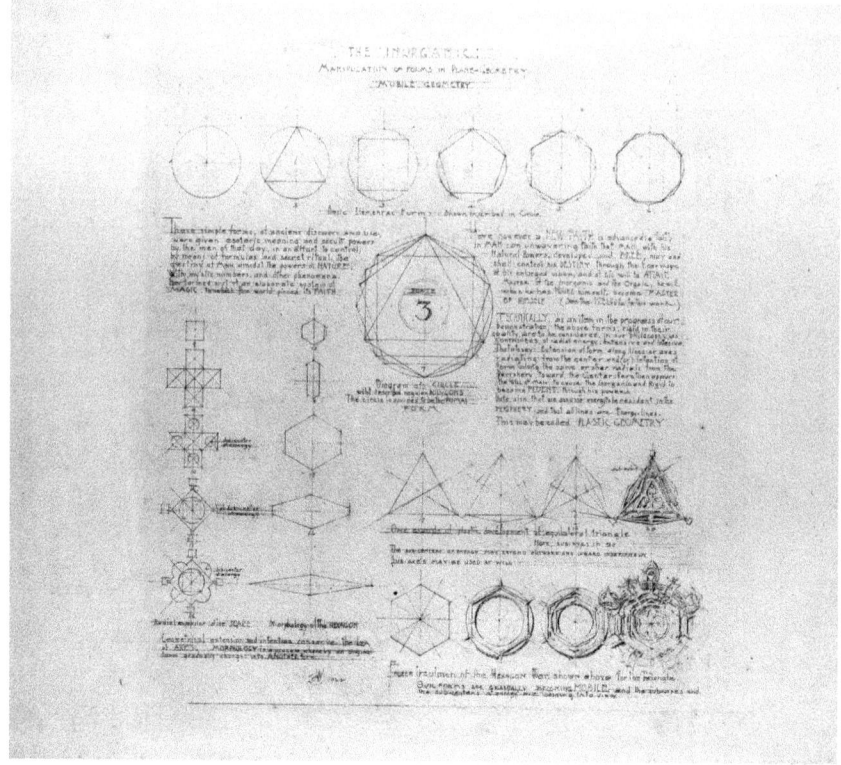

FIGURE 3.2 *Sullivan, Louis Henri (1856–1924). System of Architectural Ornament, Plate 3, Manipulations of Forms in Geometry. 1922. Graphite on Strathmore paper, 57.7 × 73.5 cm (22 ¾ × 29 in.). Initialed and dated at bottom center/left of design, "LHS 1922." Commissioned by the Art Institute of Chicago. 1988.15.12. The Art Institute of Chicago, Chicago, USA. Photo credit: The Art Institute of Chicago/Art Resource, NY.*

In Plate 4 (Figure 3.3) he illustrated their fusion "into a single impulse and expression of man's will." He visually blurred the distinction between the two through a formal synthesis. In a "fusion of identities" the inorganic and the organic are, for Sullivan, in sympathy with each other.

In its simplification this is at best a beginning to an understanding of his intentions. Indeed, Weingarden provides a more thorough analysis of each of the plates. But it is beyond our scope. What is important is the fact that she construes his drawings as *symbolic* of Sullivan's philosophical principles. For her, his ornamentation is a system of visual *symbols*. Consequently, when Sullivan states that the artist "masters the inorganic and causes it to live in forms which his imagination brings forth from the lifeless," we are led to conclude that, at least in his ornamentation, he means this metaphorically. One doesn't really bring forth life from the lifeless.

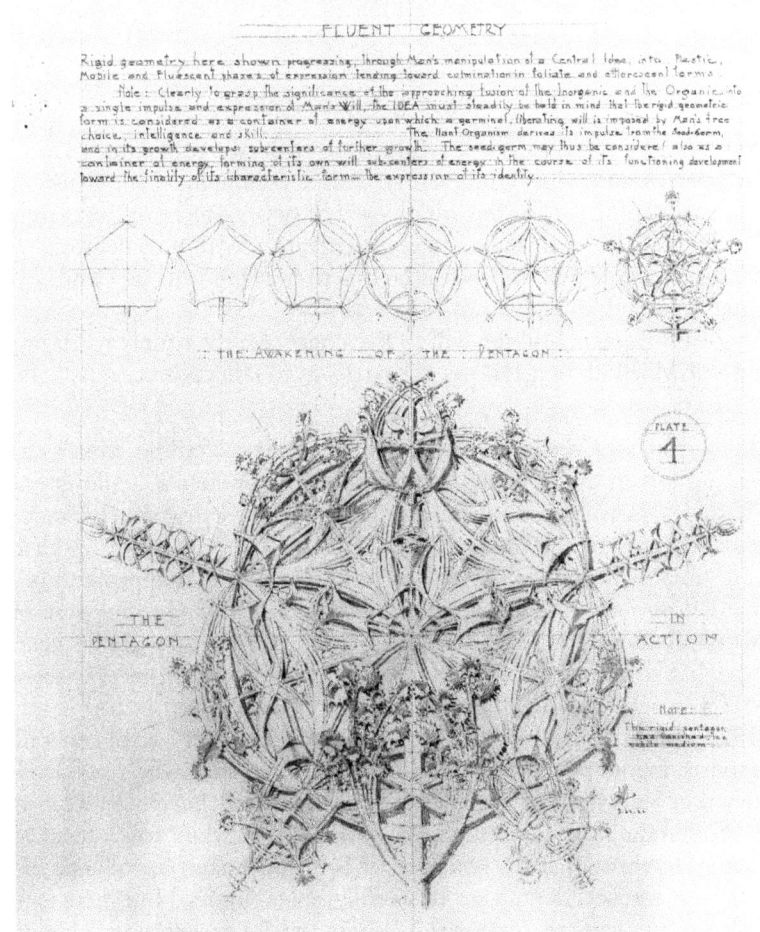

FIGURE 3.3 *Sullivan, Louis Henri (1856–1924). System of Architectural Ornament, Plate 4, Fluent Geometry, 1922. Graphite on Strathmore paper, 57.7 × 73.5 cm (22 ¾ × 29 in.), initialed and dated at bottom right of design, "LHS 2.'22.'22." Commissioned by the Art Institute of Chicago. 1988.15.4. The Art Institute of Chicago, Chicago, USA. Photo credit: The Art Institute of Chicago/Art Resource, NY.*

Though Weingarden calls his process "organic," and the plates symbolic of a kind of "living" ornamentation, in the end they remain just graphite on paper. While this is certainly a valid interpretation, I believe that Sullivan meant more than this.

Sullivan began the *System* with a "Prelude" that starts with a preface he titled "The Germ: The Seat of Power." It is a short text of just three brief paragraphs, none more than two sentences each. Under a sketch of a dicotyledonous seed he wrote:

> The Germ: The Seat of Power
>
> Above is drawn a diagram of a typical seed with two cotyledons. The cotyledons are specialized rudimentary leaves containing a supply of nourishment sufficient for the initial stage of development of the germ.
>
> The Germ is the real thing; the seat of identity. Within its delicate mechanism lies the will to power: the function which is to seek and eventually to find its full expression in form.
>
> The seat of power and the will to live constitute the simple working idea upon which all that follows is based—as to efflorescence.[62]

Andrew dismisses the sentences of the Prelude as falling somewhere "between aphorism and simple description."[63] Its preface is undoubtedly both. With its jarring juxtapositions of "germ," cotyledons, biological analysis, references to the "will to live," and the "will to power"—all of which presumably resolve in the pun of "efflorescence"—it appears to be a syncretic philosophical implausibility.[64] But it had meaning for Sullivan. He had it written before he finished even one drawing for the book. In his heart, he knew what it was about.[65] Because of its importance to him, it seems worthy of a closer look.

By 1923, both the "will to live" and the "will to power" were generally understood as important concepts of Schopenhauer and Nietzsche, respectively. It is likely that Sullivan intended the references. He may have been exposed to an understanding of Schopenhauer's "will to live" while still a teenager in Chicago. He wrote that his good friend John Edelmann introduced him to the "highest transcendentalisms of German metaphysics." But there is no firm evidence that he read *The World as Will and Representation*.[66] He did own a volume of Schopenhauer's *Essays*, and though the essays might not have been specifically about the concept, they probably included editorial comments about it.[67] It is evident that Sullivan had at least a basic knowledge of Schopenhauer's *will*, understanding it as a fundamental reality and foundational to instinctual and nonrational drives. But his somewhat casual joining of the "will to live" with the "will to power" suggests that he was either careless with or not fully cognizant of the subtle differences between the two. After all Nietzsche effectively dismissed the former in *Thus Spoke Zarathustra* when he summarized, "not will to life—but this I teach you—will to power."[68] It seems very unlikely that Sullivan understood ornament in Schopenhauer's rational terms as the object of aesthetic contemplation that could free us from "servitude to the will."[69] His whole intention in his anthropogenesis was to restore the value of pure instinct—evidence of the will itself. Moreover, we need only to recall his hierarchy of powers, where he privileged the nonrational and instinctual drive of the emotions over the reasoning intellect elevated into "fetich." No, it seems much more likely that Sullivan understood ornament in the impassioned terms of Nietzsche's locus of beauty: "Where I must will with all my will."[70]

Sullivan was certainly familiar with Nietzsche's conception of the will and his expression of beauty. In his library, he had what biographers often describe as a "well-worn" copy of *Zarathustra*.[71] In the preface, when Sullivan defined the "will to power" as "the function which is to seek and eventually to find its full expression in form," it is possible that he meant to suggest a sense of the will to power as the overcoming of oneself.[72] By extension, Sullivan's realization of the "full expression in form" could possibly suggest Nietzsche's "Overman." But these remain tenuous connections. For the moment, what is clear is that he referenced both Schopenhauer and Nietzsche in order to link the making of ornament with the drives of the will and consequently with the earliest expressions of humankind: the instincts of "proto-man" himself. And for him, this was more than simply a will to live. In his fundamental interest in power, he seems to have defaulted to a "will to power."

For both Sullivan and Nietzsche, "power" was not the volition of government or military might on the order of Bismarck's German Reich or even physical force.[73] Rather, it was a creative power.[74] For Sullivan, it was the power of the master craftsman and the romantic quest to "know thyself."[75] For Nietzsche, it was also the power to create, but more problematized. For he wrote, "Whatever I create and however much I love it—soon I must oppose it and my love; thus my will wills it."[76] For Nietzsche it was not the static "know thyself," but rather an endless becoming as overcoming, as when "life" said, "I am *that which must always overcome itself*."[77]

For the balance of the *System*, Sullivan regularly wrote about power, occasionally about the will, and less so about life. But never again did he use the phrases "will to live" or "will to power." He only mentioned them in the Prelude. His usage seems to suggest a rather convenient paronomasia that allowed him to place Schopenhauer and Nietzsche, and the will, at the beginning.[78] And it further suggests that Andrew was correct. Philosophically, as expository prose, the Prelude is "sketchy." Even so, I will have to return to it.

—

But what about the "germ?" Twice thereafter Sullivan reminded the reader in the accompanying plates to "remember the seed germ."[79] In the Prelude, he began with it and indicated that it was "the real thing; the seat of identity." With the correlation of "identity" and "individuality" this harkens back to "Ornament in Architecture." There he wrote, "I believe ... that a decorated structure, harmoniously conceived, well considered, cannot be stripped of its system of ornament without destroying its individuality."[80] A decorated building's individuality is revealed through its ornament. By placing that identity within one unique seed germ, he reinforced the analogy between a building and the growth of a plant. In his botanical analogy, the seed germ holds its identity.

Once again, Sullivan is not talking about pure form. "Mere difference in outward form does not constitute individuality. For this a harmonious inner character is necessary."[81] Architectural historian Charles L. Davis II illustrates how this relationship between outward form and inner character suggests that Sullivan was practicing the then-popular "science" of physiognomy.[82] Understood as the revelation of inner "character" through a thing's outward physical characteristics—usually of persons and their faces—Davis suggests that for Sullivan it had direct application in his buildings. He analyzes Sullivan's sketches and writings to illustrate his point. He traces influences from American transcendentalist conceptions of national character and race through his exposure to the principles of physiognomy as a student at MIT and the *École des Beaux-Arts*. He points out that Sullivan's library held several books on the topic to include Johann Caspar Lavater's *Essays on Physiognomy* (1804), Max Nordau's *Degeneration* (1895), and A. E. Willis's *Encyclopædia of Human Nature and Physiognomy*.[83] He clearly establishes that Sullivan was familiar with the conceptual framework of physiognomy and that his drawings and writings suggest that he believed it. Additionally, Davis excavates and illustrates how those beliefs tacitly manifested in divided and disturbing racial beliefs held by Sullivan himself.

Physiognomy posits an essentialist relationship between character and form that over the years has been used in racial and sexual stereotyping, eugenics, and criminology. It was the basis for Cesare Lombroso's notorious claim that he could identify a criminal through a set of facial features that included hawk-like noses, low-sloped foreheads, and shifty bloodshot eyes. Today it seems preposterous that one could conclude, like Willis, that "the affections in brunettes are more steady, constant, enduring, and powerful in nature than in the blonde type" or that a particular shape may determine "the amorous, sensual, talkative and unprincipled eye. Apt to lead a fast life."[84] But physiognomy held such popular influence that even Schopenhauer, in a more constructionist vein, could conclude that "wicked thoughts and worthless efforts gradually set their mask upon the face, especially the eyes."[85] And Sullivan bought the books. In another from his library, that Davis does not mention, the concepts are applied directly to architecture. Irving Pond, in his *The Meaning of Architecture*, explicitly links racial physiognomy with architecture, as *essential* to its meaning. With illustrations more than a little reminiscent of Jacques-François Blondel's 1771 *Cours d'architecture*, Pond draws isomorphic relationships between the "racial characteristics" of a given group of people and the ornament of their buildings (Figure 3.4).[86] And he was the architect for Jane Addams's Hull House.

Even though Sullivan in his writing and drawings does not quite succumb to the fatuity of Willis or the explicit racism of Pond, Davis's argument remains convincing. Consider one other example: Sullivan's description of H. H. Richardson's Marshall Field's Warehouse. In the *Kindergarten Chats* he writes "*that every building you see is the image of a man whom you do not see. That the man is the reality, the building its offspring.*"[87] He

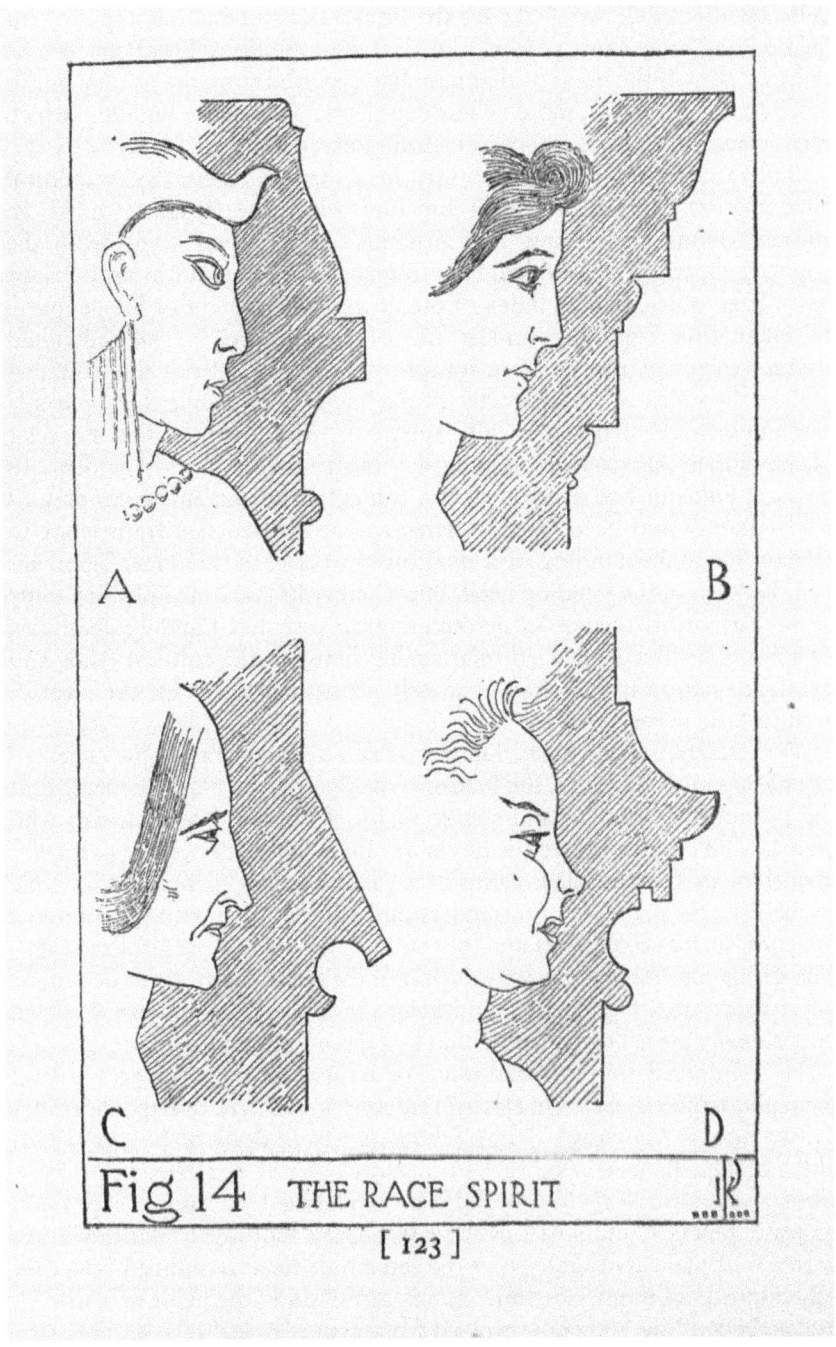

FIGURE 3.4 *Irving K. Pond*, The Meaning of Architecture: An Essay of Constructive Criticism. *Boston: Marshall Jones Company, 1918, 123. Photo by author.*

indicates that while we might see the bricks and stones, "the impulse" for the building came from a "*man*."[88] As if quoting Willis or Schopenhauer, he claims, "Now if the mind of that man has departed from the normal and is more or less perverted, more or less degenerate, so will the building, which is its image, be more or less pervert or degenerate."[89]

Sullivan further understood this in a broader sense as a cultural phenomenon. This was crucial for him who, like Wright, sought an autochthonous architecture and ornament that would come from the young democracy of America. He wrote, "At no time and in no instance has it been other than an index of the flow of the thought of the people—an emanation from the inmost life of the people."[90] The individual characteristics of the building morphology emanate from that "inmost life" as the index of the character of the "man" *and* people that built it.[91] The importance of this is readily apparent, since, for him, the character of the individuality of the building was most realized in its ornament. To be sure, Sullivan had a grasp of the contemporaneous understanding of physiognomy and he utilized its language as a discursive framework to explain his understanding of a relationship between this inner character and the form of the building itself. But whether he construed physiognomy to be a rigorous science in determining an essential building character, or some socially constructed relationship between the cultural ethos and its manifestation in building, or merely a poetic analogy for the creative architect, he never says.

Fortunately, in the *System*, Sullivan relied on more than just the "science" of physiognomy. By using the loaded term, "germ," he placed ornament at the presumed beginning and source of life.[92] For the late Victorian who enjoyed and often confused the recent advances in the sciences (in particular microbiology that revealed realms of *animated* matter theretofore invisible to the eye), the germ was a misunderstood pun meaning both the source of infection such as cold germs and the source of life such as the fertilized egg.[93] The strong interest in the germ was part of the scientific efforts to determine what constituted life, origins, and being. In his use of the term, Sullivan intentionally placed ornament within this discourse, at its genesis.

He reinforced this understanding of nature on the microscopic level throughout the *System*.[94] On Plates 2 (Figure 3.1) and 5, he referred the reader to two books: Asa Gray's *Gray's School and Field Book of Botany* (1874) and Edmund B. Wilson's *The Cell in Development and Heredity* (1896). About Gray's *Book of Botany* Sullivan emphasized its "simple exposition of plant function and structure."[95] There Gray thoroughly illustrated the varieties of plant morphology; at the same time he also outlined how they "functioned" in terms like "how plants grow" and "the plant in action."[96] He explained how the plant evolved from a simple seed to a seedling to a plant. He described how the seed contains embodied energy, the albumen of the seed, as food for the plant to start its life. And he illustrated the cell structure of plants in such fashion that Sullivan would ascertain a specific *functional relationship* between the parts and the whole. For both men, the resultant morphology, the plant's form, is related to its function.

In contrast to Gray, Wilson focused solely on the cellular level. He aimed to explain the relationship between Darwinian evolution and the cells themselves. In the mid-nineteenth century, these fell under two separate fields of study: natural history and "microscopical anatomy."[97] It was not until the 1870s that scientists were beginning to link evolution theory with cell theory. As Wilson summarized, "Through them it became for the first time clearly apparent that the general problems of embryology, heredity, and evolution are indissolubly bound up with those of cell-structure, and can only be fully apprehended in the light of cytological research."[98] Wilson went so far as to determine the exact locus of heredity and evolution within the cell nucleus. While he didn't label it as such, he explored the incipient understanding of DNA, a cataclysmic scientific shift that Sullivan was following.[99] The scientist had determined that the cell's cytoplasm, or protoplasm, is embodied "energy" and that even without a nucleus, "protoplasm is able for a considerable time to liberate energy."[100] In Wilson's terms, "the cell becomes a unit, not merely of structure, but also of function."[101] This meant that the cell, the seed germ, this small structure of nature, contained both the energy and the biological programming to determine individual identity in form. Moreover, they were structurally and functionally related.

For the poetic architect, Gray and Wilson provided a far-reaching and elegant analogy that integrated science, nature, and ornament through the seed germ. But for Sullivan, it was more than analogy. Looking again at Plate 3, he wrote, "Technically, as an item in the progress of our demonstration, the above forms, rigid in their quality, are to be considered in our philosophy as containers of radial energy."[102] And on Plate 5 he wrote, "Any line, straight or curved, may be considered an axis, and therefore a container of energy, and a directrix of power."[103] For Sullivan, this energy was understood in the late-nineteenth-century sense of a pervasive invisible force that had power in both organic things and inorganic things. It was witnessed through the increasingly sophisticated sciences of the different modes of motion such as heat, sound, light, radioactivity, chemical action, electricity, and magnetism; as studied in primitive forms of life and the thresholds between inorganic matter, plant and animal life; as further evidenced in the movements of liquid crystals; and as understood in theories of evolution. The energy could be found in both "living" and "non-living" things, confounding the very definition of, and locus of, life. Consequently, the boundaries between inorganic and organic were permeable. Sullivan's library was full of the latest explorations into these sciences. Like many of his Progressive counterparts, the etiology of energy and life keenly interested him.[104]

In his library Sullivan had Ernst Haeckel's *Riddle of the Universe* (1901) and Charles Godfrey Leland's *The Alternate Sex* (1904), both of which argued, in Leland's words, that "there is no line of demarcation between the organic and inorganic world."[105] Both saw the energy interaction of atoms, that "attraction and repulsion," as evidence of an energy power in all things.[106] And while it blurred the inorganic and organic, it further blurred the physical and psychic. The attraction and repulsion witnessed between atoms, what Haeckel called "affinity" and Leland called "sensivity," led Haeckel to elaborate on the "law of the persistence of force" or what is better known today as the law of "conservation of energy."[107] From this he developed a set of axioms that covered the whole field of organic and inorganic nature. The first stated, "The two fundamental forms of substance, ponderable matter and ether, are not dead and only moved by extrinsic force, but they are endowed with sensation and will (though, naturally, of the lowest grade); they experience an inclination for condensation, a dislike of strain; they strive after the one and struggle against the other."[108] Haeckel indicated, "Every shade of inclination, from complete indifference to the fiercest passion, is exemplified in the chemical relation of the various elements towards each other, just as we find in the psychology of man, and especially in the life of the sexes."[109] He further argued that "this fundamental *unity of affinity in the whole of nature*, from the simplest chemical process to the most complicated love story, was recognized by the great Greek scientist, Empedocles, in the fifth century B.C., in his theory of 'the love and hatred of the elements.'"[110] It manifests in the smallest elemental particle, for even the simplest atom "is not without a rudimentary form of sensation and will, or, as it is better expressed, of feeling (*aesthesis*) and inclination (*tropesis*)—that is, a universal 'soul' of the simplest character."[111] By granting a "will" to what was once considered "dead" matter, Haeckel effectively erased the demarcating line between the organic and inorganic.

Sullivan applied this to ornament. On Plate 3 of the *System* (Figures 3.2 and 3.5), he illustrates lines of energy as "extensive and intensive; that is to say: extension of form along lines or axes radiating from the center and (or) intension of form along the same or other radials from the periphery toward the center."[112] He depicts two "containers of radial energy," one triangular and the other hexagonal, both with the energy radiating outward and inward as if they had "the power to receive as well as to give." Considerably more than the simplistic and distanced symbolism of inorganic/geometric and organic/biomorphic, here ornament *is* an arrangement of vital energy within physical matter organized sympathetically. Literally. It mediates an infinity of energy forces from and to, both the external world and the ornament itself. For Sullivan, Haeckel provided the "science" that enabled him to believe that the making of ornament was an exercise of the creative *will* of man, where "nothing is really inorganic." By the time he wrote *Democracy* he could conclude that there was "no possibility" to "separate thought from the things we call physical. There is no dividing line—no threshold. There are merely phases of consciousness, and we choose to believe that in man consciousness reaches its highest manifestation and power."[113] While Gray and Wilson both offered a biological analogy such that the foundational blocks of identity are physically placed within the

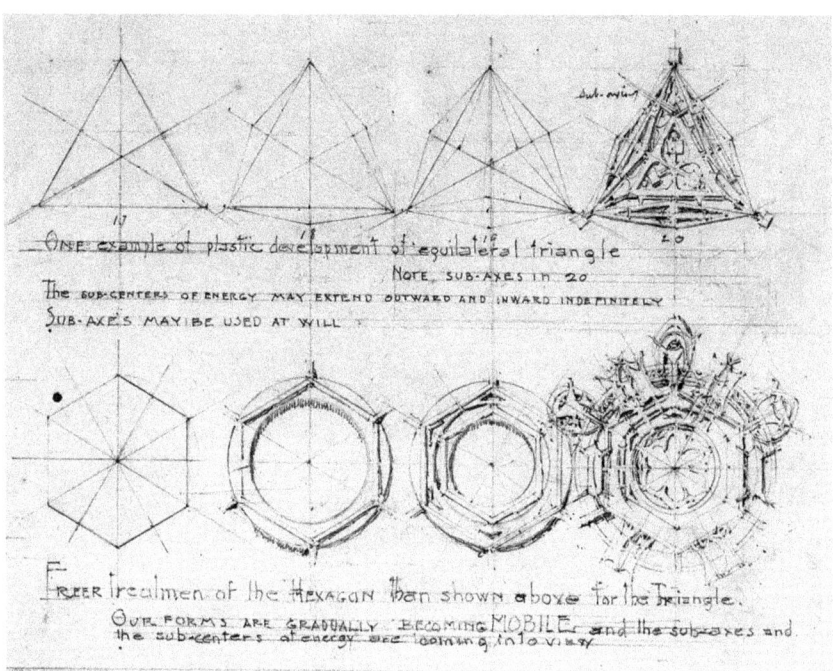

FIGURE 3.5 *Sullivan, Louis Henri (1856–1924). System of Architectural Ornament, Plate 3, Manipulations of Forms in Geometry. 1922. Graphite on Strathmore paper, 57.7 × 73.5 cm (22 ¾ × 29 in.). Initialed and dated at bottom center/left of design, "LHS 1922." Commissioned by the Art Institute of Chicago. 1988.15.12. The Art Institute of Chicago, Chicago, USA. Photo credit: The Art Institute of Chicago/Art Resource, NY.*

latent energy of the seed germ, Haeckel offered the science that translated that individuated energy source homologically into ornament itself. And the reference to both Schopenhauer and Nietzsche placed the creation of ornament at its beginning, in the drive of the will. As that basic human drive, it was the living, individuated, corporeality that mattered to Sullivan. For while the creative choice might be metaphysical, he insisted that "this be taken from the realms of the transcendental and brought into [the] physical, tangible, even psychic reality" of ornament.[114] And that is precisely the point. Of ornament and sympathy, one is a physical, tangible building medium; the other a human inter-relational affection. Yet for Sullivan, *both* mediate between the inorganic and organic, subject and object, and subject and subject; and *both* are constitutive of an inter-relational affection.[115] As the expression of human power made visible, in its highest manifestation, ornament is the organic, physical, and living realization of sympathy.

4

Femininity

Returning to Sullivan's story of the dam, it might be worth considering if and how his understanding of "sympathy" is evidenced within his text. Once he had released the retained waters, in worn-out, blissful, satisfaction, Sullivan rested. "Exhausted with work and delight he lay stretched on his back, in the short grass, looking far up at the spreading branches, glimpsing bits of blue between the leaves, noting how these self-same leaves rustled softly, and twinkled in the sunshine."[1] Quite satisfied in his engineering accomplishment, "he lay stretched on his back, in the short grass." After eating the feast of the child, his Parker House rolls and doughnuts and cookies, and a cup of "warm fragrant milk" from the neighbor's cow, he fell into a deep reverie. Sullivan wrote, "Then he loafed and invited his soul as was written by a big man about the time this proud hydraulic engineer was born. But he did not observe 'a spear of summer grass'; he dreamed."[2]

For his introduction to the dream, Sullivan referenced Whitman, whom he called "a big man about the time this hydraulic engineer was born." He inserted a modified quote from *Leaves of Grass* and the poem "Song of Myself." Like Sullivan, Whitman began with loafing and inviting of the soul:

I loafe and invite my soul,
I lean and loafe at my ease observing a spear of summer grass.[3]

The reference invites many questions. Why did Sullivan insert it here? What did Whitman add to this tale that Sullivan could not or would not, for whatever reason, say? The reference does not add "poetry" given that Sullivan only added shared terms and truncated phrases diminished into prose. Besides a kind of name-dropping, which could have been his intention, the inclusion suggests that it was intended to refer to something from the content of Whitman's poem.[4]

On the most basic level, both Sullivan's tale and Whitman's poem are autobiographical. Both authors describe scenes where they loaf on the grass and invite their souls. Both reference "a spear of summer grass," and both, in their loafing, fall into a deep dreamlike reverie.[5] What follows are dreams of considerably different length (Sullivan's is all of seven lines, Whitman's is eighty-two pages), which nonetheless share striking similarities and a few noteworthy differences.

Sullivan briefly described his daydream:

Vague day dreams they were,—an arising sense, an emotion, a conviction; that united him in spirit with his idols,—with his big strong men who did wonderful things such as digging ditches, building walls, cutting down great trees, cutting with axes, and splitting with maul and wedge for cord wood, driving a span of great work-horses. He adored these men. He felt deeply drawn to them, and close to them. He had seen all these things done. When would he be big and strong too? Could he wait? Must he wait? And thus he dreamed for hours.[6]

Any reader of Sullivan's autobiography will recognize this dream as yet another variation of that often repeated leitmotif of his song of childhood. Watching his father ride the rough sea in a rowboat, the men cutting ice, the moulder, the shoemaker, the farmer, and the shipbuilder: each is another iteration of the beloved, big, strong, working men whom he *adored*.[7] But here, Sullivan condensed the whole host into one dynamic sentence of "digging," "cutting," "splitting," and "driving." In the rapid fire repetition and tacit sentiment of love, it replicates Whitman's catalogs of those whom he loved: the carpenter, deacons, machinist, and "the young fellow [who] drives the express-wagon, (I love him, though I do not know him)."[8] But Whitman was more catholic in his embrace. His entries include the lunatic, prostitute, president, quadroon girl, squaw, and "clean-hair'd Yankee girl;" those who labor, sit, "jeer and wink," men and women, and child; each honored with little more than a rapid line.[9] Sullivan saw these men like the powerful forces of the pent-up waters of his dammed creek: "these crowds of men working, doing many things, all moving at the same time—all urging toward a great end."[10] It suggests Whitman's "urge and urge and urge, / Always the procreant urge of the world."[11] For Sullivan, they "were his beloved strong men, the workers—his idols."[12]

But to this scene, Whitman lustily included what Sullivan, the respectable architect, decorously elided: overt sexual content.[13] When Whitman lay on the grass he wrote,

> *Loafe with me on the grass, loose the stop from your throat,*
> *Not words, not music or rhyme I want, not custom or lecture, not even the best,*
> *Only the lull I like, the hum of your valvèd voice.*

> *I mind how once we lay such a transparent summer morning,*
> *How you settled your head athwart my hips and gently turn'd over upon me,*
> *And parted the shirt from my bosom-bone, and plunged your tongue to my bare-stript heart,*
> *And reach'd till you felt my beard, and reach'd till you held my feet.*
>
> *Swiftly arose and spread around me the peace and knowledge that pass all the argument of the earth,*[14]

Whitman continued with seven more quick, mystical, earthy sentences, each beginning with a breathless "and" like the rhythmic gasps of climax.[15] Described by Michael Orth as "the crucial moment of the entire poem, the creation of the poetic fetus," he considers the "unconventional use of fellatio rather than copulation as the process of conception ... daring, but supremely effective."[16] In the invitation of the soul, Sullivan's power of creation and its poetic progeny are conceived, not as pure acts of imagination, but erotically, in fellatio. The insertion of Whitman sexually colors the daydream. The hydraulic engineer had the "big man" speak for him.[17]

Sullivan may have referenced Whitman's poem to suggest the scene that follows shortly thereafter. In what has been called the "magnificent parable of the twenty-ninth bather," Whitman described a scene of twenty-eight men bathing in the waters by the shore,[18]

> *The beards of the young men glisten'd with wet, it ran from their long hair,*
> *Little streams pass'd all over their bodies.*
>
> *An unseen hand also pass'd over their bodies,*
> *It descended tremblingly from their temples and ribs.*
>
> *The young men float on their backs, their white bellies bulge to the sun, they do not ask who seizes fast to them,*
> *They do not know who puffs and declines with pendant and bending arch,*
> *They do not think whom they souse with spray.*[19]

One is reminded of the scene from Sullivan's autobiography, also at the shore.[20] Sullivan's father stripped, ordered the six-year-old to strip, and threw the boy into the water. After a brief swimming lesson, the father offered a ride to the landing on his shoulders. Sullivan "gloried as he felt beneath him the powerful heave and sink and heave of a fine swimmer, as he grasped his father's hair, and saw the bank approach."[21]

On land, after admiring "his father's hairy chest, his satiny white skin and quick flexible muscles over which the sunshine danced with each movement," Sullivan fell again into a reverie that generated "a new ideal now ... a vision of a company of naked mighty men, with power to do splendid things with their bodies."[22] In many ways this is a touching, ingenuous story; yet it is almost too incestuously intimate in the wet, sensuous grasp, and "heave and sink and heave" of the father's shoulders, that is then followed by the admitted "vision of a company of naked men." With the echoes of shore, water, bathers, wet hair, white skin, the sunshine illuminating the contours of naked male bodies, the two stories encircle each other in overt male sensuality. Sullivan could not have overlooked the comparison.

When Sullivan inserted Whitman's poem as a bridge linking his story of the dam with his daydream, he placed Whitman's sexualized men between his hydraulic engineering story and the recurring dreams of the men that he "adores." There is the overlay and interpenetration of Sullivan the dam builder, Whitman the poet, Sullivan's working men, and Whitman's sexualized men. For Sullivan, this was not only about the asexualized power of work, the power to create. By including Whitman, he was suggesting that this power is an erotic power as well.

But it is a particular relational positioning of power. Notice that when Whitman loafed, he *received* the advances of an unidentified lover. He was held from his beard to his feet. He was penetrated by the tongue of the other to his "bare-stript heart." *He was on his back.* Of the men swimming, someone "seized" them. As erotically charged as all of the tales are, for the men, Whitman and the whole company of twenty-eight bathers, it is a passive eroticism.[23] Whitman and the swimming men are all in the passive role or, in the terms of the nineteenth century, in the "feminine" role. This certainly seems to suggest that Sullivan referenced Whitman to convey this relational understanding consistent with his understanding of "sympathy" where one gives *and receives*. Moreover, in his story of self-assertion *and surrender*, that resolves in "the peace and joy and knowledge that pass all the art and argument of the earth," unbounded from the strictures of convention, it was eroticized.

—

While Sullivan knew the late-nineteenth-century discourse of manliness and masculinity, he did not contribute to it, at least not normatively. As Bederman indicates, turn-of-the-century middle-class men seemed almost obsessed with manhood. Historians point to "the popularity of cowboy novels, the craze for hunting and fishing, and the profusion of 'he-man' rhetoric" as evidence of it.[24] But it is doubtful that Sullivan did much hunting and fishing. And, as already indicated, he did not speak the rhetoric of "masculinity."[25] While his library held the discourse defining "cowboy novels," it also had books that would have challenged any idea of a pure unadulterated masculinity, let alone the essence of the redundant "he-man."[26] Sullivan had books about sex and gender that, in the language of his era, argued that in every man, there is more than a bit of a woman.

He owned three books specifically about sex: Otto Weininger's *Sex and Character* (1906), Patrick Geddes and J. Arthur Thompson's *The Evolution of Sex* (1902), and Leland's *The Alternate Sex*. All three, written in the context of the burgeoning woman's movement, sought to determine a scientific, biological basis for the differences of gender. All three argued for an irrefutable correspondence between anatomy and psyche such that the physical characteristics of a given gender manifested in unique corresponding mental characteristics. They believed that science, and in particular physiology, could in fact determine the relative positioning of power between men and women. Clearly ascribing to a nature-given, essentialist understanding of gender, they all believed that what looked like a woman acted like a woman, and what looked like a man acted like a man. But in Sullivan's library, what it meant to be a man, or a woman, was somewhat more troubled.

Weininger argued strongly for the view that women are by nature inferior.[27] Yet at the same time, he indicated there was no absolute distinction between the sexes. For him, there was no pure male and no pure female. Rather, in the same way that "there are transitional forms between the metals and non-metals, between chemical combinations and mixtures, between animals and plants, between phanerogams and cryptogams, and between mammals and birds," there were only transitional forms between male and female.[28] Surgical anatomy had revealed that in the bodies of both men and women could be found a "rudimentary set of parallels to the organs of the other sex."[29] "There is always a certain persistence of the bisexual character, never a complete disappearance of the characters of the undeveloped sex."[30] Through a set of ratios of the proportion of "male" to "female," or "female" to "male," Weininger developed his "Laws of Sexual Attraction" that explained why two people, to include those of the same sex, are attracted to each other.[31] Those bodies with a higher proportion of characteristics of the opposite sex were more prone to what he called "homo-sexuality."[32] This certainly ran counter to the arguments of those who believed that homosexual behavior was an acquired characteristic or a choice. For Weininger it was physiological. Based on his law, he argued for its decriminalization.[33]

Geddes and Thompson were both eminent British biologists. While today architects know Geddes primarily from his ecological work in planning, both men were known for their holistic interpretation of the sciences. Unlike Weininger, they were the preferred source of contemporaneous feminists because they had argued that "to dispute whether males or females are the higher, is like disputing the relative superiority of animals and plants. Each is higher in its own way, and the two are complementary."[34] However like Weininger, they found mental differences commensurate with physiological differences between the sexes. Now evidenced in cell metabolism and categorized under "intellectual" and "emotional," those differences fell not surprisingly into the usual stereotypes of the era.[35] Those appropriate to this study include the notions that females "have indubitably a larger and more habitual share of the altruistic emotions," and they "excel in constancy of affection and in sympathy."[36] Being those of pity, compassion, and sympathy, the altruistic emotions form a subset of the tender emotions of sentimentality. Sullivan would have read that those emotions, and by extension sentimentality, were biologically "proven" to be female traits.[37]

In *The Alternate* Sex, Leland interpreted the individual strengths of the sexes differently. While he believed that women would always be inferior, he allowed that there were specific traits peculiar to women in which they excelled.[38] And like Weininger, and likewise based on anatomy, he concluded that *"in exact proportion to male developments in women, or the female in man, there is a corresponding masculine or feminine degree of mentality*. This granted, it may be admitted that there must be, in accordance with what there is left of the other sex in all of us, just so much of its mind."[39] This portion of "what there is left" Leland called the "alternate sex." From the man's perspective, i.e., his, it was those attributes of women that were evident in men that most interested him. Leland believed the common stereotypes of his era that "woman in ordinary life thinks and acts less from reason and reflection than man, and much more from emotion and suggestion and first impression."[40] But he claimed further that it was the woman in man that was more familiar with the memory cells of the brain and therefore assisted in memory.[41] She was also the "spirit of the Dream."[42] He concluded that it was the alternate sex in man that provided the "material," "action," and "suggestion" for "Imagination."[43] Obviously, as the purveyor of memory, dreams, and the imagination, the woman in man was a welcome visitor. Leland argued that she should be nurtured because her presence leads to genius. "Great geniuses, men like Goethe, Shakespeare, Shelley, Byron, Darwin, all had the feminine soul very strongly developed in them .... The feminine aid is not genius itself, nor poetry, but it is the Muse which inspires man to make it."[44] And about the disadvantaged men without evidence of the alternate sex, "they rarely produce anything original, or in accordance with Beauty, because they lack Imagination. Now all of Imagination is not due to the inner-woman by any means, but there would be none without her."[45] With the promise of the genius of Goethe, Shakespeare, and Darwin, and her role in dreams and imagination, surely Sullivan would have welcomed that woman into his brain.[46]

The "alternate sex," this "woman in man," this gendered trope, what Leland sometimes called "the Lady of the Brain," is humorous and disturbing.[47] It invites the question: just because these books were in his library, did Sullivan in fact read, much less accept, those authors that promoted homosexuality; claimed that all humans are "bisexual;" and attributed emotion, dreams, and the imagination to the "woman in man"? Moreover, in 1922, during that era of masculinity, did Sullivan, who constructed a system of *powers* based on *sympathy* as the basis of ornament, accept the claim that it is females who "excel" at it?

There are many similarities between the writing of Sullivan and Leland. Both placed dreams and the imagination in a fundamentally anterior relation with reason. Leland stated, "So, as the flower precedes the fruit, Imagination and Poetry precede Reason, and Woman Man."[48] Sullivan "saw that Imagination passes beyond reason and is a consummated act of Instinct— the primal power of Life at work."[49] He too agreed with "sympathy's" feminine roots when he traced its genealogy from the heart. "That from the heart comes forth Sympathy into the open: the subtlest, the tenderest, the most human of emotions; and that of Sympathy is born that child of delight which illumines our pathway, and which we call Imagination."[50] And in his last important essay, "What Is Architecture: A Study in the American People of Today" (1906), we read where he sounded the most like Leland.[51] Here, Sullivan admonished the American people and their architects. After repeating *three times* in succession, that they were in dire need of "great thinkers, real men," he asserted:

> You have not thought deeply enough to know that the heart in you is the woman in man. You have derided your femininity where you have suspected it; whereas you should have known its power, cherished and utilized it, for it is the hidden well-spring of Intuition and Imagination. What can the brain accomplish without these two![52]

Sullivan argued that "real men" "cherish" in their own hearts, the "woman in man." In the language of Leland, the language that he knew and that was available to him, he posited a power that was expressly "feminine." In more than just the spirit of the text, he agreed with Leland—he used the same words. For Sullivan, writing in 1906, femininity was *power*. In 1922, writing in the *System*, he prioritized it such that the "spiritual group" that "sees as in a dream," the dream of woman's purview, and the "emotional group" that "embraces every power of feeling," i.e., of the heart, were both *above* the "intellectual group" or what he called "the cachet of manhood."[53] In an inversion of the prevailing cultural norms that elevated the power of the male over the female and of masculinity over femininity, Sullivan, in his essay on ornament with its ascending ladder of the five groups of "powers," outlined a hierarchy where the powers most associated with women are both "stronger" and higher than those associated with men. If there were any implied contamination of sympathy by "femininity," it mattered not to Sullivan. He "cherished" it.

But clearly the issue is more than femininity. From Whitman to Weininger to Leland and to Sullivan himself, there is from today's perspective an implied subtext of sexuality. What was Sullivan's understanding? Was he not implying it with the inclusion of the erotics of Whitman's poem in the story of the dam? Was that not an implication of homosexuality? How might Sullivan have understood it? Is it even possible to surmise? As to Sullivan's position on Weininger's claim that all humans are "bisexual" or his call for the decriminalization of "homo-sexuality," a few things remain clear. Weininger's use of the term "bisexual" did not have the same meaning it holds for us today. For Weininger it meant that within the human body, sex characteristics of both genders are empirically evidenced.[54] As historian George Chauncey indicates, "At the turn of the century ... *bisexual* referred to individuals who combined the physical and/or psychic attributes of both men and women. A bisexual was not *attracted* to both males and females; a bisexual *was* both male and female."[55] Chauncey also indicates that what is today understood as "homosexuality," as an expression of desire, was then understood as gender "inversion." Like Leland, it was conceptualized as a "third sex" or an "intermediate sex" falling somewhere between men and women. This was a common conception held by some of the leaders in the field.[56]

However, by including Whitman within his story of the dam, it would suggest that Sullivan, like Whitman, was endorsing a broader understanding of sexuality. This is critical when some contemporary scholars argue that Adolf Loos's and Le Corbusier's determinations of ornament as "degenerate" were grounded in homophobia.[57] It should be noted that regarding the cultural understanding of "homosexuality," the differences between Whitman's 1860 and Sullivan's 1922 were profound. In the interim, homosexual behavior had been brought under the regimes of science and medicine, characterized, categorized, and pathologized. As Foucault suggests, in Whitman's time, "The sodomite had been a temporary aberration;" by the time of Sullivan's autobiography, the homosexual was now a "species."[58] "The nineteenth-century homosexual became a personage, a past, a case history, and a childhood, in addition to being a type of life, a life form, and a morphology, with an indiscreet anatomy and possibly a mysterious physiology."[59] With the persistent newspaper publicity of the Oscar Wilde trial of 1895, the threat from that species was in the parlor. In rural America![60] While Sullivan's femininity might be a breach of the code of masculine conduct, homosexuality was a breach of the essence of the man itself.

Beyond the books already described, Sullivan's library offers additional clues of what he probably knew.[61] In it one finds some of what historian Douglass Shand-Tucci calls "telltale signs" of homosexuality: books by or about "Michelangelo, J. A. Symonds ... [and Richard] Wagner."[62] While Wagner is generally not considered to have been homosexual, books about him were often considered just such a sign. Sullivan's library had books on the composer's life, work, and music.[63] Sullivan's love of Wagner was well known. Wright described it as "extravagant worship."[64] He also had additional books about Whitman. He owned one volume of Horace Traubel's (1858–1919) diaries, *With Walt Whitman in Camden* along with Edward Carpenter's *Days with Walt Whitman* (1906).[65] Traubel, whose personal correspondence reveals his "romantic affairs with men," recounts Whitman's warm and affirming correspondence and conversations with and about John Addington Symonds (1840–1895) and Carpenter as well.[66] The latter, whom Chauncey calls the "gay sociologist," or the "gay intellectual," included in his small book the incident where Whitman met Peter Doyle, the man who would be the poet's lover for almost a quarter of a century.[67] It was a "quite romantic" scene, described by Doyle in an interview.[68] Today it is recognized as just another piece of explicit evidence of Whitman's homosexual behavior that for years redactors had distorted to erroneously portray as "homo-social."[69] Carpenter, who expended one whole chapter on the subject of Whitman's sexuality, what he euphemistically titled "Walt Whitman's Children," concluded:

> Whether this large attitude towards sex, this embrace which seems to reach equally to the male and the female, indicates a higher development of humanity than we are accustomed to—a type super-virile, and so far above the ordinary man and woman that it looks upon both with equal eyes; or whether it merely indicates a personal peculiarity; this and many other questions collateral to the subject I have not touched upon.[70]

"Touch upon" he did. After fifteen pages of "telltale" signs, Carpenter disingenuously left it up to the reader to decide.[71]

And finally, in one book alone, there were two of the "telltale" signs combined: Symonds's two-volume biography of Michelangelo. In it, the renowned English poet and cultural historian illustrated how intervening redactors had bowdlerized all the pronouns of Michelangelo's sonnets to erase the suggestion of homosexuality. Symonds restored the original pronouns and Michelangelo's homosexual bent.[72] While there may have been debate whether Michelangelo engaged in homosexual activity, with Symonds' biography Sullivan at least had convincing evidence that the painter of the Sistine Chapel wrote love sonnets to another man.

Clearly, Sullivan knew about homosexuality, was interested in it, and owned a pronounced number of books about it. Indeed, many scholars suggest that he was gay.[73] While historically and socially important, that is not my aim. When Weingarden excavates the influence of Whitman upon Sullivan's architecture, we must ask: does that include the poet's expression of sexuality? Moreover how might that have informed his understanding of sympathy and consequently architecture? Beyond the reading of Whitman's poetry, which as indicated invites considerable interpretation of homosexual content, Sullivan's library, in Carpenter's book, provided first-hand evidence of affirming homosexual behavior on the part of the poet himself.[74] Sullivan's unconditional adulation and repeated references to Whitman suggest his acceptance, if not endorsement, of the behavior.[75] This interpretation is further reinforced by his awareness of Michelangelo's loves as presented by Symonds. And it was upon Michelangelo that he bestowed his highest honor. Of Sullivan's three-day excursion in Rome at the completion of a term at the *École des Beaux-Arts*, he spent *two of them* in the Sistine Chapel, "alone there, almost all the time." Speaking about the experience he wrote,

> Here [Sullivan] communed in the silence with a Super-Man. Here he felt and saw a great Free Spirit. Here he was filled with the awe that stills. Here he came face to face with his first great Adventurer. The first mighty man of Courage. The first man with a Great Voice. The first whose speech was Elemental. The first whose will would not be denied. The first to cry YEA! in thunder tones. The first mighty Craftsman.[76]

Having communed for two full days in silence with frescoes teeming with "a vision of a company of naked mighty men," Sullivan dubbed Michelangelo the *first* master-cum-"mighty"-craftsman.[77] Then, suggesting considerably more than a nonnormative claim of "homosexuality," he continues for another full page and a half in the same gushing, breathless, hagiography and capped it off with another quote from Whitman, the title and first line of "THERE was a child went forth every day."[78] In the intimation of the words that follow, "the first object he look'd upon, that object he became;" and in the next line and the next and the next line after that, the child in endless fusion with a world of "early lilacs," "the Third-month lambs," "the field-sprouts," "the barefoot negro boy and girl," "the schoolmistress," "his own parents," "the blow, the quick loud word, the tight bargain, the crafty lure," "the streets themselves and the façades of houses," a teeming world with "shadows, aureola and mist," together with Whitman *and Sullivan* suggest consubstantiation with the naked mighty men, Michelangelo, and even themselves; for "These became part of that child who went forth every day, and who now goes, and will always go forth every day, / And these become part of him or her that peruses them here."[79] At the very moment that Sullivan identifies Michelangelo as the first master craftsman, at the pinnacle of his hierarchy of powers, he returns us to Whitman. As if needing to remind us yet once again that if we are ever to truly understand architecture, we must understand sympathy; and if we are ever to fully understand sympathy, we must "enter into a unison with nature's powers and processes; to observe—in a fusion of identities." Deliberately constructing an alternative epistemology that transgresses the exclusive categorization of identities, Sullivan offers an emotive and fluid ontology where categorical being dissolves in vital consubstantiation—identities fuse—and they are eroticized.

Historically, in what today can only be seen as harmful, there has been a tradition of interpreting ornamentation as "feminine" and the massing upon which it bears as "masculine."[80] The same interpretations were made about Sullivan's work.[81] Narciso Menocal indicates that even Sullivan believed this. He posits that some of those beliefs came from the master's understanding of Swedenborg's gender "correspondences" and suggests that Sullivan might have learned those from friends, or even Emerson's monograph, "Swedenborg; Or, The Mystic."[82] This interpretation is misleading.

Despite the disturbing generalizations of gender there is no evidence to indicate that Sullivan made such a claim about his ornamentation. To be sure, like most from his era, he used the terms "masculine" and "feminine," and for him their meanings fell within the gender stereotypes of the day. However he rarely applied them as essentialities and never as an exclusive property of a given building component like ornament. Instead he used them as descriptors to emphasize a specific point. At different times he described the characters of American art and architecture as "virile," "effeminate," and "neuter."[83] The context determined the value. Recall that "feminine" was "cherished" too. But in his ornamentation, he remained intentionally vague.[84] Just like the organic and inorganic, with male and female he was not interested in generating a dialectical synthesis that presupposes an exclusive gender binary. Much like Weininger, Leland, and Whitman, he precluded the binary before it was even constituted. And in his architecture, Sullivan constructed a bodily ornament that transcended gender. Indeed, he might have read Emerson's essay, and it is likely that he would have agreed with it. For Emerson *reproved* Swedenborg's categorization of the sexes. As the transcendentalist adjudged, the mystic "pinned his theory to a temporary form:" the gendered body.[85] Emerson suggested a more fluid understanding declaring that "in the spiritual world we change sexes every moment."[86] While Sullivan clearly had an understanding of gender that informed his work, it was not the simplified feminine-ornament/masculine-massing dichotomy. Rather he sought something antecedent to the social constructs that was more nuanced, comprehensive—and more bodily.

At the turn of the century, less than four years after the completion of the Guaranty, there was a marked shift in his ornamentation. While his earlier buildings seemed to move in the direction of a formal solution that he characterized as "plastic," the later works departed from it. The shift is evident in the façade of the Gage building (1898–1900).[87] It persists through all of the important works that followed, especially in the renowned "jewel-box" banks.

There are two broad characteristics of the shift. The first is evidenced in the distillation of building forms into geometric masses simplified into primary rectangular volumes. Like the Auditorium, the massing and its expression were arranged to correspond with the buildings' utilitarian requirements

FIGURE 4.1 *Merchants National Bank, Grinnell, IA, 1913–1914. Louis H. Sullivan, architect. Henry Fuermann and Sons, photographer. Historic Architecture and Landscape Image Collection, Ryerson & Burnham Archives, The Art Institute of Chicago. Digital File # 25419.*

FIGURE 4.2 *Peoples Savings and Loan Association, Sidney, OH, 1916–1918. Louis H. Sullivan, architect. Henry Fuermann and Sons, photographer. Historic Architecture and Landscape Image Collection, Ryerson & Burnham Archives, The Art Institute of Chicago. Digital File # 25419.*

(Figures 4.1–4.2). Except for a few minor anomalies, each volume is bilaterally symmetrical, reinforcing the reading of singular unified units. At the same time, the fenestration has been grouped into large aggregations of carved openings and windows that correspond to "function" and vivify the formal play in the abstracting terms of "solid and void."

All are evidence of Sullivan's continued awareness of, and leadership in, the movement toward the rationalist languages of abstraction, form, and what would become the modernist conception of functionalism. As manifestations of an ever-increasing reliance upon objectifying reason in the construction of an architectural reality, each is evidence, in Harries's terms, of the aesthetic approach.[88]

The second is a flourishing of an extraordinarily robust form of ornamentation that has been *dis-incorporated* from the plastic whole. Unlike the Auditorium, the shift illustrates a trend toward over-scaled ornament that is sharply delineated from its background as autonomous figures. In the same way that one reads the Renaissance Revival colonnade of Carnegie Hall as distinct from its background (Figure 2.1), one clearly reads the terracotta foliated excrescences of the Peoples Savings and Loan as distinct from the brick walls upon which they bear (Figure 4.2). Suggesting "decoration" as opposed to "ornament," Weingarden indicates that in his 1918 review of the bank, the critic Thomas Tallmadge called them "broaches."[89] And it does not take much imagination to see those "trees" of the Home Building Association as nature baked into terra-cotta, detached, and plopped into faux planters (Figure 4.3). Falling somewhere in between the examples of the two theaters, the character defining formal arrangement now comes from *both* the massing as determined by building function *and* the ornamentation.

Clearly for Sullivan, plastic in and of itself was not the solution to the problem. In fact, in his later work, he seems to deliberately defy it. Maybe he had come to see incorporation as expressed in the clever "of-the-thing-not-on-it" as not so important, at least formally. Maybe it was even part of the problem. Perhaps for him, it was precisely in its more tenuous nature that ornamentation is most correct. Recall that "plastic" called for the subordination of details and decoration to masses according to "utilitarian requirements." In its demand of "subordination," "plastic" privileged an aestheticizing of those requirements into formal terms over the more pressing problem of ornament. In the contemporaneous interpretation of Sullivan's own dictum, "form follows function," those same utilitarian requirements became known as building "function." To be sure, Sullivan endorsed this determinist sense of "functionalism." It was constitutive of the first characteristic of his shift in ornamentation. Sullivan led this rationalizing trend. But he knew that it was not a solution unto itself. Moreover, he knew that it should not be privileged over what he considered the greater architectural requirement.

When he wrote the essay, "What Is the Just Subordination of Details to Masses?" recall that Sullivan privileged the "spiritual result" of architecture over any fixed rule. While it might be worthwhile to debate and even posit a

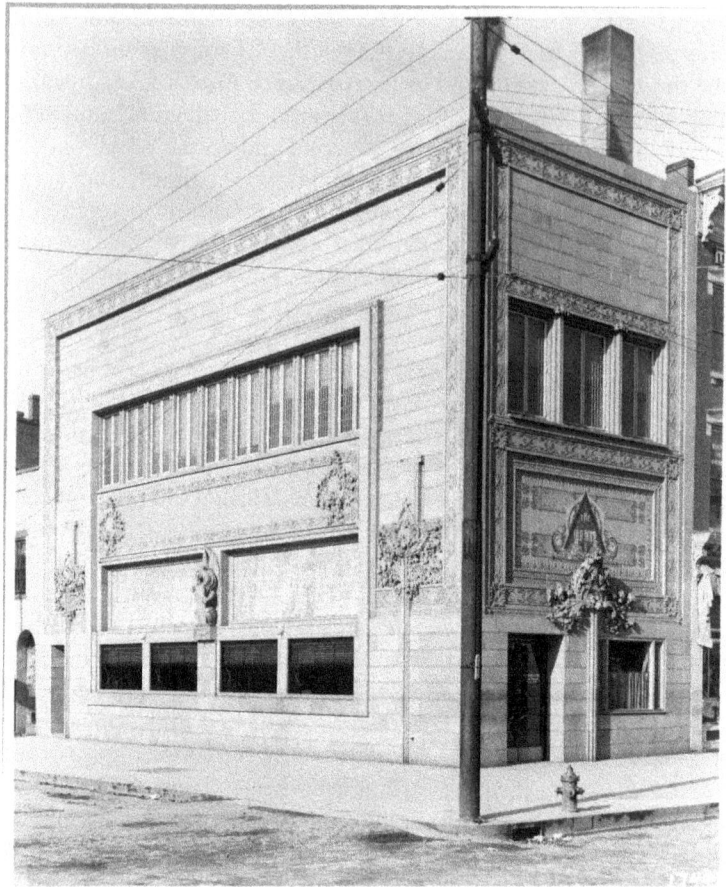

FIGURE 4.3 *Home Building Association Bank, Newark, OH, 1914–1915. Louis H. Sullivan, architect. Henry Fuermann and Sons, photographer. Historic Architecture and Landscape Image Collection, Ryerson & Burnham Archives, The Art Institute of Chicago. Digital File # 25456.*

formal relationship between detail and mass, he argued that "spiritual results precede all other results, and indicate them."[90] Moreover, in the dictum, when he stated "function," he meant something considerably more than just the utilitarian requirements of a building. For him, "form follows function" described a vital organic process where building form proceeded "from one single impulse of desire to express our day and our needs."[91] "Function" was understood as some *character* of "our day:" a *spirit* that presided over the collective daily life. It was the very source of any autochthonous architecture. It was this spirit that he sought to conjure. For him it was the only hope for deliverance from the hegemony of exhausted European image systems of ornament.

Sullivan construed this spirit as an inherent good. He shared in a common late-nineteenth-century utopian vision of the United States as a land of abundance that still disclosed vestigial evidence of primeval nature as good. He believed that the nation was settled under a constitutionally established egalitarian promise of "democracy" that he understood as "beneficent." As allegorically revealed in his anthropogenesis from "proto-man," through "primitive man" and "Feudal man," to the reintegrated "man of democracy," Sullivan posited an American character of democratic optimism that had evolved from, and was reconnected to, this primal garden of innocence.

But this "spirit" was more than just consensus in a secular form of government understood as "democracy." For Sullivan, it was a kind of pantheistic character whom he called the "function of all functions" or more often the "Infinite Creative Spirit."[92] Neither a static ground, nor a being, he suggests a kind of action of all actions.[93] In the *Kindergarten Chats* he equated it with what the student called "God."[94] Coming from his transcendentalist tradition, vividly refined through Whitman's *Democratic Vistas*, he characterized this spirit as the beneficent *spirit* of "Nature" itself.[95] For both Whitman and Sullivan, "democracy" was far more than secular governance; it was the liturgical manifestation of a religion.[96] This spirit was sacred. It was realized through faith. And it was that faith that supported and *vitalized* both men's work.[97]

Privileging this conjuration of spirit over the formal response of "plastic," Sullivan ran counter to the prevailing trend of his era.[98] Despite the fact that he penned its motto, and put it into practice, he knew that alone the rationalist trend would not solve the greater problem of ornament. He recognized that the march toward modernism was an ever more exclusionary trend toward rational purity, and he knew that that would never be enough. For Sullivan, it would be no more than the perpetuation of the reasoned pursuit of "feudal man." Recall that when he reconciled the instinctual and generous heart of "proto-man" characterized as *"understanding,"* with the intellectual and selfish brain of "feudal man" characterized as *"knowledge,"* it occurred through the power of *emotion*. At the culmination of that evolutionary process, the "man of democracy" as the embodiment of "aspirant democracy" was reintegrated through the power of *sympathy*. Privileging *emotion and the spirit*, Sullivan effectively countered the *rationalization and secularization* of the aesthetic approach. For him, the solution to the problem of ornament was to help articulate this spirit. In Harries's terms, the solution was to help articulate a common ethos.

—

To look at his later ornamentation is to witness his final effort to solve the problem. This is the type that he drew in the *System*. It predominates in his best work, especially the banks, and it is the evidence of some of his greatest care and concern. For here Sullivan most deliberately sought to help articulate that ethos. Still organized as a fusion of the "organic" and "inorganic," his biomorphic figuration is formally synthesized with the geometric patterns. While obviously representing the imagery of "Nature," it presents a specific kind of envisioning (Figure 4.4). It is fecund, alluring, sensuous, lush, ripe, abundant, sinuous, and particular. Loosely entwining, each ornament entices the body with the beckoning curls of its vegetative tendrils. It lures with tantalizing seeds, fruits, and flowers. Undeniably mysterious, it is never fully disclosed: it is as if there is always something beyond; lines and figures appear and disappear in the dense foliation. It suggests a kind of endless becoming. In Harries's terms it "embraces time."[99]

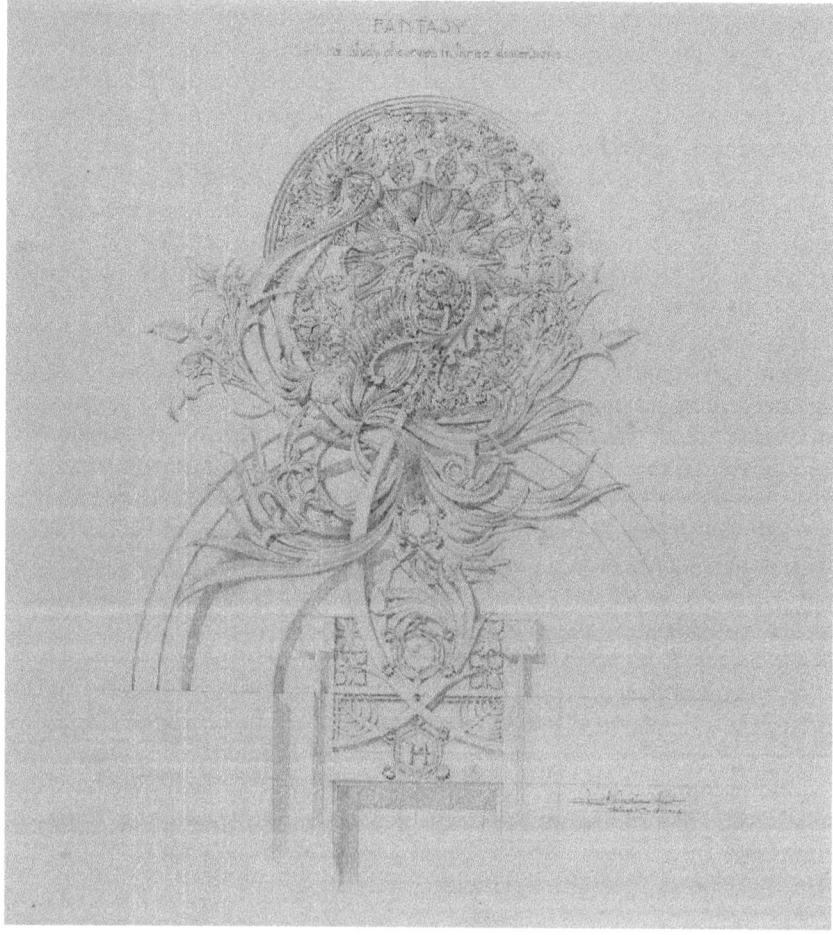

FIGURE 4.4 *Sullivan, Louis Henri (1856–1924). System of Architectural Ornament, Plate 14, Fantasy. 1922. Graphite on Strathmore paper, 57.7 × 73.5 cm (22 ¾ × 29 in.). Signed and dated at bottom right of design, "Louis H. Sullivan fecit Chicago: 7-18-1922." Commissioned by the Art Institute of Chicago. 1988.15.12. The Art Institute of Chicago, Chicago, USA. Photo Credit: The Art Institute of Chicago/Art Resource, NY.*

Simultaneously, most of the "organic" ornamentation is ordered upon the "inorganic" scaffolding of geometry comprised of repeating bilateral symmetries and universal, Platonic figures. Consequently, it likewise suggests a timeless realm of the spirit.[100] Like the Vitruvian Figure that offered Renaissance architects an ideological and religious image linking the finite microcosm of earthbound matter with the infinite macrocosm of God through the numerical proportions of the human body, Sullivan offered an image of nature that likewise linked similar realms. At its most simplistic we may interpret it as Sullivan's ideographic reconciliation of those aforementioned troublesome binaries of inorganic and organic, and subject and object. To those we should now add the body and the spirit, male and female, heterosexual and homosexual, the self and other, the particular and the universal, the finite and the infinite, and understanding and knowledge. Moreover, in this vision Sullivan offered a democratic promise of a beneficent state of nature where all are embodied, all are gendered in whatever terms that might mean, and all are equal. But unlike the Vitruvian figure, Sullivan's iconic ornamentation is not disclosed through the rational figure of *number*. Rather for him, humanity is restored and reconciled with the "Infinite Creative Spirit" of "Nature," through the universal and eternal energy coursing through "Life" *and ornament*.

Sullivan's ornamentation is consequently much more than the ideogram of his ideas. Certainly we may interpret it as the index of his process or as some medium between the man and his world. Yet it is more than that. As ornament, and in particular as Sullivan's beckoning figures, it explicitly *constitutes* the lured and the luring: multiple sexualized subjects who give and receive in the lush abundance of the American garden. It constitutes the feeling subject, *both ways*. Yes, the work feels. Not figuratively, but literally, as the energy of life itself. And while he knows this might never be proven, he understands its truth through an appeal to the emotions. For it is understood and revealed through *an appeal to the tender emotion of sympathy*. For Sullivan, living ornament manifests through sentimentality.

The story of the dam could be interpreted as an allegory of being in the world sympathetically. It is the story of childhood self-assertion *and* surrender that resolved for Sullivan in satisfied loafing and quiescent peace. If only it were that simple. At the conclusion of the story, having dreamed "for hours," Sullivan indicated that "the shadows began to deepen and lengthen; so, satisfied, with a splendid day of work and pondering, he reached home in time for supper." Before the family began their meal, his "Grandmama" said "the usual grace; all heads were bowed as she appealed to her Lord of love to give strength and encouragement and to bestow his blessing upon this small family." Sullivan had mixed feelings about grace. He did not object to "God as a higher member of the family." It was the god of church, "the minister's God, the God of Hell that he disliked and avoided." As he wrote in this childhood expression of love, obeisance, and guilt, "He would have accepted prayer as a necessary evil were it not for the reconciling thought that God seemed to be Grandmama's big strong friend; and what Grandmama loved he knew he ought to love too; even as he loved his own idols—his mighty men."[101]

PART TWO

Frank Lloyd Wright

5

No Damned Sentimentality Either

His mother thought he was too effeminate. Writing many decades after the fact, the son, Frank Lloyd Wright, summarized the signs: he lived through his imagination and preferred reading and drawing and music to playing with the other boys, and with an odd set of scare quotes, he admitted that he liked to "'make things.'"[1] Above all else, he liked to dream by himself. According to Wright, some of it was her fault. After all, she encouraged the dreaming. On top of that, she kept his flowing golden curls way too long. And as if any of this had anything to do with anything, when she read to him, she chose fairy tales and poetry, especially that "sentimental group" of Whittier, Lowell, and Longfellow. Apparently *she* had had enough. In an astonishing admission, Wright declared that she "saw which way her man-child was going. She was wise and decided to change it. And change it she did."[2] Lopping off his curls, she sent him to her brother's farm—to perform manual labor, to make money, to do the things *men* do. And as if positing some cause-and-effect relationship in confirmation of his mother's silly beliefs, Wright characterized the following story as the day he became "a man." "That was a day for him! The day before he had been only a boy on the farm." That day, he was "a man among men." For "to be a man is to do a man's work."[3]

Every summer from his eleventh through his sixteenth year, Wright was sent to work on his Uncle James's farm.[4] Outside the rural town of Spring Green, Wisconsin, it adjoined the productive acreage of his maternal aunts and uncles in their shared ancestral valley.[5] By his fourteenth year he earned the equivalent of a man's pay: $19.00/month plus room, board, and clothes.[6] He milked cows, retrieved the errant pigs, fed and slaughtered chickens, and cleaned up after animals. He hoed fields, baled hay, and reaped grain; it was arduous and, for Wright, unpleasant. He would later say, "It's all pulling tits and shoveling shit."[7] Over time he incorporated the lesson of his Uncle Enos that "work is an adventure that makes strong men and finishes weak ones."[8] But the first year almost "finished" him. The work was too "hard." It was exhausting. He struggled to "add tired to tired and add it again—and add it yet again. And then beginning all over again at the beginning to add it all up some more until it seemed to him he would surely drop."[9] More than once he ran away.

But the boy from downtown Madison, Wisconsin, soon enough learned to enjoy the experience of the country. Irresistibly drawn to its wild beauty and sensuous pleasures, he took visual delight in the chokecherry blooms and the rare white lady slipper, the discovery and taste of wild grapes and strawberries, the trill of birds and frogs. He wrote fondly about it. With telling restraint, he indicated that when he spotted the startling red of a lily across the endless field of tall green meadow grass, it "gave him an emotion."[10] Indeed, it was both inspirational and architectural. For as a boy, he had already read Ruskin. Like the British moralist he developed an unshakable belief in the inherent goodness of "Nature," a belief that became foundational to his understanding of architecture.[11] Over the course of his life he heeded Ruskin's command that "an architect should live as little in cities as a painter. Send him to our hills and let him study there what nature understands by a buttress and what by a dome."[12] As Wright beheld his uncle's lush valley he found that "the trees stood in it all like various, beautiful buildings, of more different kinds than all the architectures of the world. And the boy was some day to learn that the secret of all the human styles in architecture was the same that gave *character* to trees."[13]

As he learned to love the country, he learned to live with its enemies: the skunks, the snakes, the mosquitoes, flies, nettles, and poison ivy; and like the farmer he learned to do everything possible to master the destructive vicissitudes of farm life. "Too dry! Too high! Too low! Too wet! Too hot! Too cold! Too soon! Too late! Drought and Frost—major enemies the farmer must learn to defeat or he will go down like his crops with his animals. Warfare? Comparatively fancy business."[14] Wright fought to become a man. And as he proudly let his reader know, he learned to swear like one too.[15]

On that particular day, Wright was "planking" a field. Driving the two horses Pont (nicknamed for Pontius) and Pilate crosswise over the harrowed ground, Wright stood on wooden planks dragged behind the powerful animals to smooth out the furrows for planting seed. It was the first day he had been entrusted to work alone. In his own way, he was engaged in a kind of architecture. This two-fold superimposition of a human order through and over the soils of the earth must have been supremely satisfying. And as the aspiring architect, Wright embellished his work. He had discovered that many of the tasks on the farm required a repetitive movement that beat their own rhythm. Milking, pitching, hoeing, and binding: each necessitated a repeated body movement that from their unique cadences he generated song. This kinesthetic order was often amplified by a recurrent noise, the squirt of cow's milk in the metal pail, the jingle and clack of machinery, the clopping of hooves, each of which transposed the monotony of humdrum into singsong, into music.

Wright already had extensive exposure to the repertoire of Bach and Beethoven that he had learned from his accomplished father, a preacher and music teacher. He used this as a basis to hum, or whistle, or sing variations stimulated by the rhythms of the work. He found that if he syncopated the audible beat or the body movement, it was made even more interesting. "Work would be better done and no fatigue."[16] Later he would suggest that both folk and sacred dance originated in this way. He intimated that this rhythm might be "the obvious poetry in the mathematics of this universe—maybe."[17] Echoing Sullivan, Wright asserted that it did not come from rational thought as an "idea," believing instead that it came from "instinct" or "whatever it was to suit this naïve release of the within to the work in hand."[18] Unsure even if he should call its source "instinct," yet like Schiller describing it as "naïve," he nonetheless determined an emphasized essentiality that was from "*within himself*." Of this most significant sense of rhythm within he questioned, "'Life' impelling itself to live?"[19]

The morning of planking had gone without incident. After lunch, back on the field, close to four o'clock, as tiredness encroached, the planks caught on a tree stump hidden in the harrowed soil. As the horses continued to pull, the stump gave way in a jolt, catapulting the planks into their heels and the boy onto Pont's rump. Bolting and kicking, the horses sprinted off. Wright grasped the breeching of each horse. Suffering the repeated kicks of the frightened Pont, he knew that if the straps broke, or if he let go, the plankers would go over him. "To hold on and hope nothing would break was the only hope." And from Wright, "there were no cries, no words."[20]

He endured in silence.

No music, no swearing, no screams, no moans, no tears. Another hired hand, Adolph Sprecher, had seen the racing melee and ran to save the boy. He grabbed, missed, and fell. Fortunately the unbalanced load pulled the horses to one side, causing them to run in a wide circle. Sprecher cut them off the second time around, saving the boy "just in time."[21] The lad who had just been "promoted to man's work dropped on the planks and lay there to get the breath back into the body that crazy horse had kicked the breath out of." Sprecher couldn't believe he wasn't seriously hurt. Once Wright finally caught his breath, he pleaded with him not to tell Uncle James—pleaded with him to the extraction of a promise of silence. Wright wanted "to be treated 'like a man.'"[22]

This was of course Wright's story. He chose it for inclusion in his autobiography. He titled the chapter "A Man" with the intention of illustrating what for him was apparently a significant rite of passage: his initiation into manhood.[23] But one may suggest that perhaps this boy's silence betrayed the freeze of abject fear or even cowardice. Or maybe Wright screamed or cried but didn't admit it. It does not matter. This is Wright's construction of what he wanted us to believe, which reveals plenty about what he might have believed. For him, the successful initiation into manhood is met stoically, seemingly without emotion, hardened into silence.

Did it work?

Apparently not.

His initiation was not a singular event. Surprisingly, he describes another—one that his latest biographer, Paul Hendrickson, clearly illustrates is so full of inconsistencies as to suggest multiple fabrications.[24] Yet Wright plows ahead. He has a point to make. As he tells it, at the end of his final summer on the farm, he entered the University of Wisconsin to study engineering. By that time any musical education under the tutelage of his father had been terminated by the son. He had come to believe that "being 'musical' was 'unmanly'" too. He "started in to harden up with the boys."[25] He silenced even his own musical self, that which was essentially "*within himself.*" Then, after one year in college he ran away again. His father and mother had divorced. As the then man of the house he abandoned his impoverished mother and two sisters and caught the train into Chicago. He claims he didn't even leave a note. In order to pay for the trip he pawned his mother's mink collar (the one she had sewn on *his* coat) along with several of his father's books, including a favorite calf-bound copy of Plutarch's *Lives*. Suggesting some significance, Wright noted that the book had "thumbed edges—by the son—at the life of Alcibiades."[26] Repudiating his "education," as if with raised fist and exaggerated heroics, he exclaimed that he was no longer "waiting in the eternal shadows of experience." "In this voluntary break with background," in "the bravery of all Life," he stood "against clear sky—all fear superfluous." Providing the moral to his own story, he concluded with three last lines: "Here say goodbye to 'the boy'. Henceforward, on my own, I am 'I'. The sentimental son of a sentimental mother grown up in the midst of a sentimental family planted on free soil by a grandly sentimental grandfather … the Welsh pioneer [Wright's ellipsis]."[27] Describing yet a *second* initiation into manhood, with this version of self-actualization and the declaration of "'I'" (in quotes), Wright suggests with an emphatic four-fold repetition, that saying goodbye to "'the boy'" (again in quotes), pursuing experience over "'education'" (even more quotes), becoming an architect, and perhaps even choosing Alcibiades, all, had something to do with sentimentality.

—

In the autumn of 1913, long after the planking story and long after he had met, worked for and was fired by Sullivan, Wright received the commission for the Midway Gardens. His client, the "Young Ed Waller," wanted a place to go out, a "beautiful garden resort," a haven to eat and drink, to listen to "good" music, *and dance*.[28] "People up on balconies and all around over the tops of buildings. Light, color, music, movement—a gay place!"[29] Waller insisted that the bar lay "right across a man's path, a manifest temptation."[30]

No inhibitions in these gardens! Enthralling all the senses, including Wright's kinesthetic sense of rhythm, Waller envisioned a paradise of pure pleasure. In a brazen act of daring, the men scheduled the grand opening for May 1, 1914, barely giving themselves seven months for design *and* construction.[31] Wright's spirit "soared."[32]

Exhilarated, it seemed like things might finally be turning around. He was still recovering from his scandalous trip to Europe of 1909–1910. At that time he had abandoned his wife of nineteen years along with their six children, their home, and his thriving architectural practice in Oak Park in order to spend a year in Europe with Mamah Borthwick Cheney (1871–1914)—the wife of Edwin H. Cheney—his clients. It made all the papers. Clients, both existing and potential, were incensed.[33] Wright called their reaction "sentimental." While 1911 was not a bad year, from 1912 through 1914 his workload plummeted. He had only seven income-producing projects.[34] Then from January to May of 1913 he traveled to Japan with Borthwick to buy fine cultural artifacts, especially his much beloved wood-block prints, the *ukiyo-e*.[35] In what had become a passionate avocation, Wright gained wealth, scholarship, and reputation from their sale in the United States.[36] But this trip had been even more successful. While there he cemented the relationships and did some preliminary work for the commission of the Imperial Hotel in Tokyo, surely what would become one of the highest fees of his entire career.[37] In these improving times he raced to complete the Midway Gardens.

Wright summarized his approach. "Most places of the kind I had seen at home or abroad were phantasy developed as a cheap, erotic foolishness. A kind of papier-mâché scene painting. In the Midway Gardens there was to be no eroticism. No damned sentimentality either. There was to be permanent structure."[38] With the expletive he made his emphasis. But what did he mean by it? Was he simply rejecting the pejorative sentimentality with its manifestations in late-nineteenth-century architecture as kitsch? To be sure, that was an intention. But why so adamant? Why "damn?" Was his desire something even more than that?

In his autobiography, there are three general ways that Wright used "sentimentality:" one was to characterize the behavior of the people around him, another himself, and the third as a quality of things, in particular the arts and architecture of his time. In all his writing, the implication was disparaging.

Wright elaborated the most thoroughly and clearly about it in the arts and architecture. Recall that he characterized Gothic architecture as "natural" or "organic" and brashly identified nearly all the architecture that followed as "sentimental." Construing the latter as imitative and empty of meaning, he characterized it as the creation of an emotive "picture" that was devoid of any worthwhile transcendent ideation. In architecture, what he defined as "sentimental" would be understood in today's terms, in the extreme, as kitsch.

But for him it was always a conflicted negativity. Within his personal life he cited numerous examples: sometimes where he was the aggrieved victim of someone else's sentimentality, and more often his own irrational "sentimentality."[39] He fought against himself: his own sentimental nature and, in particular, his vulnerability to love. With surprising candor he admitted to misguided passions, bitter disappointment, and unfathomable hurt: love snatched away in an instant. He knew painfully well the dangers of the tender heart when unrestrained by reason. After one disastrous love, he described it as the blind leading the blind and wondered how it could have happened. He blamed it on "hypocrisy" and labeled it "sentimentality."[40] With the label, he effected a cynical denotation that distanced him from the emotional event. He used it as a way of extricating himself, a kind of safe-guarding against his own vulnerability. He bracketed the behavior as an attempt to control it through reason, yet another kind of sentimental doubling of his own sentimentality. Nonetheless he still loved—willfully—and was often hurt. If, as he suggested, that it is the loss of reason to the extent where one does foolish things, then indeed, Wright was very sentimental. His fight was futile. As his son, John Lloyd, wrote, "He tried to make himself 'Big Bad Bill' to relieve the sentimental pull on his heartstrings."[41] But he rarely succeeded. "I can say without fear of contradiction: 'Big Bad Bill' is just 'Sweet William.'"[42]

Wright repressed those tender emotions with an assertive masculinity. Evinced in the braggadocio and boasting of gory victories in boxing, stabbing, fistfighting, and kicking, he was clearly a voice in what historian Bederman describes as the "new masculinity." Yet it was something more than that. When he exclaimed, "no damned sentimentality," his feelings were in-your-face. With the modifier "damned," the affective content is determined. And Wright does not simply state it. He performed it. As the paradigmatic curse word, "damn" is performative.[43] It is a curse. It simultaneously states, confronts, accuses, and sentences: *"damned sentimentality!"* Often used as a malediction, Wright effectively cursed the objects of his scorn with the pronouncement of "sentimentality."

This exclamation, as an affective outburst and performance, clearly differentiated Wright from Sullivan. Regarding profanity and accounting, Wright wrote that Sullivan "seldom swore and in money matters was immaculate." Of himself, "Seeing only moral no ethical quality in either, I was heedless in both."[44] In his autobiography, "damn" was the expletive of choice. He used it in myriad applications with relish; this during an era when the intentional breach in the code of respectability was confrontational.[45] While today we would hardly call the book scurrilous, in the early 1930s, the word "damn" would have piqued the proper eye, especially in an autobiography.[46] Writing years after the events had occurred, this was not an uncontrolled emotional outburst. "Damn" wasn't just blurted out. It was considered. Wright "swore" for a reason. It was the intentional expression of his confrontation of respectability, a manifestation of his own iconoclasm, and the calculated sign of his constructed masculinity.[47]

Beyond the verbal exclamation, Wright's architectural work evinced the same attitude, and he boasted of it. In the second edition of his autobiography he added an entirely new section, "Book Five: Form." He wrote that the first edition's third section, what he called "Work," should have been preceded with "work-songs." They would have been songs "of our own that is a thing of the militant work-spirit." He called this song the "T-square and triangle verses, a kind of disturbing fife-and-drum corps coming down the street—in a straight-line pattern."[48] Rather disingenuously he claimed that he omitted it from the earlier versions of the autobiography "because the song then seemed, and still does, to be shouting 'damn.'"[49] By 1943 he was less reticent and asked, "Why not? It takes an ego shouting 'damn' to withstand emasculation by such imitative erudition as ours and the 'cultivation' any true ego, upright, is sure to receive at our very best hands."[50]

In both editions Wright privileged the brute force of a physical fight, the assumed raw natural authenticity of the American West, and the physical labor of work over the conciliatory cession of power, the effete artificiality of the East, and the erudition of education. Like Sullivan, he discharged some of his strongest invective against what he called "intellectualism" and "Education." Describing the recent college graduate, he condemned: "This vicarious character is a prematurity and eventually an utter emasculation of soul where the manly ego should be. It is the result of Education that is destined and designed to die on the vine. 'Designed mis-education.'"[51] He preferred the common man like the "wholesome manly Will Rogers" and felt "disgust" for the product of the colleges and "repulsion" for the "specialist:" men he called "effeminate," "impotent," and "less than half-men."[52] While both Sullivan and Wright disliked the effects of education, Sullivan felt it separated him from nature. In this case, Wright felt it separated him from an essential masculinity. And both saw it as symptomatic of over-civilization or what Wright highlighted in quotation marks: "'cultivation.'" In defense, he performed a "militant" ego "shouting damn" as the bulwark of his own masculinity. Supported by his "disturbing fife-and-drum corps," Wright stood and sang a hymn of profanity against "cultivated" "emasculation." Damn!

—

His intentions were not confined solely to his speech. They appeared in his dress as well. But in typical Wright fashion, it gets more complicated. His sartorial flair is often noted because it was so thoroughly outrageous, decidedly "individualist," yet in the end, patently imitated.[53] While living in Oak Park he was described as dressing like the arts and crafts iconoclast Elbert Hubbard (1856–1915), who at times dressed like the father of American iconoclasm, Walt Whitman.[54] The Quaker-style hat, the "wideawake," was a dubious crown that was passed from Whitman to Hubbard to Wright who wore it proudly into the 1950s as a sign of a hundred years' reign of American wideawake iconoclasm.[55] Each of these men in his attire constructed a deliberately self-conscious image as a brand of individualism and social confrontation.[56] In the first critical review of Whitman's *Leaves of Grass*, based on the etching of the frontispiece, the poet was described:

in a garb, half-sailor's, half workingman's, with no superfluous appendage of coat or waistcoat, a "wideawake" perched jauntily on his head, one hand in his pocket and the other on his hip, with a certain air of mild defiance, and an expression of pensive insolence in his face which seems to betoken a consciousness of his mission as the "coming man."[57]

As in the old adage about sailors and swearing, Whitman's etching is the personification of "damn," and it suggests that all three men in their attire made a clear statement as to who they wanted the viewer to believe they were.

But in the language and fashion of the nineteenth century, one could hardly call Wright's dress "masculine." Known for his capes, extravagant bows, flowing scarves, long hair, hats, shoes with lifts, and even his mother's mink collar, Wright's attire was both iconoclastic and effeminate. More like Alcibiades who, according to Plutarch, "wore long purple robes like a woman, which dragged after him as he went through the market-place," Wright simultaneously defended his masculinity while flouting expectations of gender.[58] And he knew what he was doing. He had read Whitman's poetry of questionable sexuality and honored Plutarch's description of Alcibiades. Like his curse and concomitant self-characterization as the most sentimental person he ever knew, Wright's construction was problematic and problematized. But he wore it proudly. Channeling Whitman, Hubbard, and Alcibiades, Wright, in Whitman's words, wanted to "slip like an eel through all blandishments and graspings of conventions."[59]

—

As he started the Midway Gardens, it is not surprising then that Wright, as if exorcising his own personal demons and those of the architecture around him, began with a curse: "no damned sentimentality." While we've come to suspect his sometimes slippery use of the term, the Midway Gardens nonetheless offer the best evidence of what he meant *architecturally*. After all, what does an early-twentieth-century building purged of sentimentality look like, at least according to Wright? Given the adamancy of his assertion, and the fact that he was writing eighteen years after its completion, we can assume that he believed he had succeeded. Consequently, it should evince his solution to the problem of ornament without sentimentality.

The most comprehensive account is Paul Kruty's book, *Frank Lloyd Wright and Midway Gardens*.[60] In it he provides a thorough description—how it came to be built, the pleasure parks that were its predecessors, and why it failed. Though he successfully illustrates how it visually relates to the history of Wright's architecture and the probable influences on the design, he does not fully explain Wright's intentions. He too quickly dismisses why it looked the way that it did, *according to Wright*. Kruty explains that even the best sources about the project tended to rely too heavily on Wright's own retelling. Consequently he analyzes it outside of Wright's explanation. As he put it, his circumspection comes from the fact that "Wright's own account of the building's history, aptly called 'The Tale of Midway Gardens,' has been the principle source of information—and misinformation—for all subsequent accounts."[61] Undoubtedly, the tale contains factual misrepresentations that Kruty assiduously uncovers. But it also contains the one thing that none of the other sources adequately convey, that is, Wright's explicit personal intention for the work, or at least that which he wanted the reader to believe.[62] And it is that intention that reveals his conflict with sentimentality as realized in built form. Given the fact that even the casual reader will recognize that the issue Wright vented most passionately about was "no damned sentimentality," it is telling that none of the sources really addresses it. In his comprehensive 263-page book, Kruty gave it a footnote.[63]

Before he even started working on the Midway Gardens, Wright's repertoire of ornamentation had already undergone a number of permutations. When he began his own practice, his work revealed the influence of his five years working for Sullivan. The Winslow (Figures 5.1–5.2), Heller (1896–1897), and Husser (1899) houses all shared formal properties with the master's efflorescence. Like Adler and Sullivan's Victoria Hotel, the primary ornamentation infilled the frieze of the top-floor window band as a diaper in the shadow of the deep overhanging eaves.[64] And like Sullivan, Wright used geometric, curvilinear, and figural ornamentation to include both realistic foliation and the human figure. For him, his understanding of the master's ornamentation and teaching were a good fit. Both men held a naturalist cosmology. Raised in a household that enthusiastically passed around the books of Emerson, Thoreau, and Ruskin, Wright shared in much of Sullivan's

FIGURE 5.1 *William H. Winslow House, Auvergne Place, River Forest, IL. The Frank Lloyd Wright Foundation Archives (The Museum of Modern Art | Avery Architectural & Fine Arts Library, Columbia University, New York).*

FIGURE 5.2 *Historic American Buildings Survey, Creator, and Frank Lloyd Wright. William H. Winslow House, Auvergne Place, River Forest, Cook County, IL., c. 1933. Documentation Compiled After. Photograph by Richard Nickel, 1965 (https://www.loc.gov/resource/hhh.il0316.photos/?sp=6 [accessed September 18, 2018]). Library of Congress, Prints and Photographs Division, HABS. Reproduction number HABS ILL, 16-RIVFO, 1–6.*

spiritualization of nature.⁶⁵ Constitutional to his self-understanding, the often-capitalized "Nature" was the primary inspirational source in both his architecture and his ornamentation over the duration of his life.

Wright did not liberate himself from the master's influence until he designed the Dana house (1902) where the ornamentation of intersecting chevrons is exuberant, yet utterly devoid of Sullivan's realistically rendered foliation. Gone are the master's curves, let alone his sinuous line. At around the same time, beginning in 1900, Wright began the work that came to define his Prairie style. Being primarily evidenced in his residential work, the style is known for its unornamented simplicity. All the wall surface ornamentation of the previous period had been removed and any decoration that remained occurred almost exclusively in the art-glass windows, laylights, and light fixtures.⁶⁶ Perhaps unwilling or unable to solve the problem of ornament, he avoided it, admitting that "in the matter of decoration the tendency has been to indulge it less and less, in many cases merely providing certain architectural preparation for natural foliage or flowers."⁶⁷ He later wrote that he had learned this "process of elimination of the insignificant" and "simplification" from his appreciation of Japanese art and, in particular, the prints.⁶⁸ While he claimed that he was never influenced by the unornamented Japanese architecture, he was nonetheless by this time fully aware of it. To be sure, historians have convincingly argued that he was influenced by the architecture as well.⁶⁹

The one anomaly from the period is the Coonley Residence (1907). With its large diapers of overlapping squares (Figure 5.3), the ornamentation is no longer consigned to the limitations of the frieze band. Rather, like wrapping paper on boxes, it covers entire surfaces of the articulated volumes of the ensemble. Historians suggest that its influence came from Wright's exposure to the German and Austrian Secessionists at the 1904 World's Fair in St. Louis, Missouri: the Louisiana Purchase Exposition.⁷⁰

From 1900 to 1913, Wright more thoroughly explored the properties of ornament in his nonresidential work. Two important projects of the period, the Unity Temple in Wright's hometown of Oak Park, IL (1906–1909)

FIGURE 5.3 *Avery Coonley Residence, Riverside, IL, 1907. Frank Lloyd Wright, architect. Henry Fuermann, photographer. Historic Architecture and Landscape Image Collection, Ryerson & Burnham Archives, The Art Institute of Chicago. Digital File # 17828.*

FIGURE 5.4 Wright, Frank Lloyd (1867–1959) ©ARS, NY. Unity Temple, Oak Park, IL. Exterior view from the northeast. The Frank Lloyd Wright Foundation. © 2019, The Frank Lloyd Wright Foundation, AZ/Art Resource, NY. All Rights Reserved. Licensed by Artist Rights Society.

(Figure 5.4), and the Larkin Building in Buffalo, NY (1904–1906) (Figure 5.5), prefigure the ornamentation of the Midway Gardens. Even though both were known for their relative lack of decoration, they nonetheless still had ornamental work that came from the foliations of nature. In the preliminary drawings of the temple, Wright revealed those intentions through the transcription of the column capital's realistic leaves into geometric patterns.

Wright knew that his process of abstracting geometric form from nature's realism was an application of the aesthetic concept of "conventionalization."[71] He had defined it in his touching yet elegantly perspicacious essay, "The Japanese Print: An Interpretation." He believed that in the hands of the "true artist," the process was a means to capture some higher truth about the essential nature of the thing represented.[72] He believed the ancient Egyptians had accomplished it with the lotus, the Greeks with the acanthus leaf, and the Japanese with "every natural thing on earth."[73] He wrote,

> If Egypt or Greece had plucked the lotus as it grew and given us a mere imitation of it in stone, the stone forms would have died with the original. In translating, however, its very life-principle into terms of stone well adapted to grace a column capital, the Egyptian artist made it pass through a rarefying spiritual process, whereby its natural character was really intensified and revealed in terms of stone adapted to an architectural

use. The lotus gained thus imperishable significance; for the life-principle in the flower is transmuted in terms of building stone to idealize a need. This is conventionalization.[74]

Understood as a shift from the finite and perishable particularity of that lotus, to the infinite and imperishable universality of the *ideal* of "lotus," with all of it incorporated into the architecture of the building, Wright claimed, "It is reality because it is poetry."[75] While he surely learned the concept from the books he had read, and from his colleagues within the profession, he credited having learned it only from the Japanese *ukiyo-e* prints. For him they were the paradigm of conventionalization.

In his insightful analysis of the now demolished Larkin Building, Jack Quinan asserts that its capitals, like those of the temple's, are more conventionalized patterns derived from realistic foliation.[76] Consistent with the need to adapt those forms for "architectural use," Wright sought an integrating formal response: specific motifs articulated the visual movement of the building such as the "upward thrust of the patterns, and so forth."[77] Of

FIGURE 5.5 *Wright, Frank Lloyd (1867–1959). ©ARS, NY. The Larkin Company Administration Building, exterior. The Frank Lloyd Wright Foundation. © 2019, The Frank Lloyd Wright Foundation, AZ/Art Resource, NY. All Rights Reserved. Licensed by Artist Rights Society.*

the sculptures atop the exterior piers, Quinan made this startling conclusion: "Wright appears more concerned with the formal value of the pier sculptures than with their message."[78] In many cases the messages seem quite secondary. Quinan describes much of the remaining realistic ornamentation in the accepted (and one might suggest clichéd) iconography of the era, where the helmeted male figure holding a torch symbolized "truth," and its female counterpart carrying a caduceus represented "commerce" with a sprig for "peace," and the repeated globes and spheres (Figure 5.5) represented the global intentions of the company along with the sourcing of the materials for its products.[79] All have been incorporated into or conventionalized to conform to the formal/contextual properties of their settings. For Wright, the more formally integrated it was, the more plastic it was—the more "of-the-thing." As to their specific symbolic meanings, he rarely if ever elaborated, at least not in his writing. Beyond a broad conception of "life principle," one might conclude that he hardly even cared.

Finally, only after his first fateful 1909 trip to Europe, where he witnessed firsthand the intense ornamentation of the Secessionists, did ornamentation return to effloresce across broad fields of his work. As will be illustrated, the Midway Gardens therefore are not a departure, but rather a culmination of the ornamental explorations that Wright had taken to that date. And what a culmination it was. Of the different types, Wright had already done some variation of each. But the amount of ornamentation, its profusion across multiple surfaces, the inclusion of sculpture and painting, and the rigor of its application, all to the degree presented, were unprecedented in Wright's work.

—

In Wright's "The Tale of the Midway Gardens" he offered an outline of his thinking. He started with some context from the contemporaneous art world of painting and sculpture.[80] He wrote, "At the time the Midway Gardens were designed, 1913, L' Art Nouveau was dying in France where it originated and gasping wherever else it happened to have 'caught on.' Various experiments in the 'abstract' in painting and sculpture were being made in Europe exciting the aesthetic vanguard and insulting the rank and file."[81] He offered the dying Art Nouveau, that entwining nature style, as the contextual background for the project. Like the "aesthetic vanguard" "insulting the rank and file," Wright determined to make his own personal exclamation of "damn."

He followed with: "But the straight line, itself an abstraction, and the flat plane for its own sake, had characterized my buildings from the first hour I became building-conscious on my own account."[82] Suggesting his childhood exposure to the Froebel "Gifts," those educational "Kindergarten" toys of primary-colored geometric blocks that undoubtedly informed some of his building awareness, he argued that his work in abstraction even predated

FIGURE 5.6 *Thomas Hovenden*. Breaking Home Ties. *1890 (Oil on canvas, 52 ⅛ inches × 6 feet ¼ inches (132.4 × 183.5 cm)). Philadelphia Museum of Art, Gift of Ellen Harrison McMichael in memory of C. Emory McMichael, 1942-60-1.*

the then-current "experiments in the 'abstract'" of the Europeans.[83] With "abstraction" established as his chosen method, Wright interjected one more thought. He offered his assessment of the art that he thought most like its opposite: what he called "realism." He wrote: "Never interested in 'realism', I was already dissatisfied with the realistic element in any building. Like 'Breaking Home Ties' in painting, The Rogers Groups in sculpture, or 'Liberty' covers today, the work of the period was flat on its stomach to the 'realistic.'"[84]

Wright selected two works of popular "art" and a magazine cover for his examples. While *Liberty* magazine was not launched until 1924, a decade after the completion of the Midway Gardens, his choices of painting and sculpture are worthy of a brief review. Both came from the latter half of the nineteenth century and both were extremely popular. Historian Julia Meech-Pekarik tells us that "Breaking Home Ties" (1890) (Figure 5.6) was "the single most popular painting" at the Columbian Exposition of 1893: "The carpet in front of it was literally worn threadbare."[85] And John Rogers made a fortune selling his diminutive plaster sculptures to the end-of-the-century mass market (Figure 5.7).[86] Looking at both, it is obvious that Wright intended to diminish the value of "realism," especially if compared to other American realists of the same period: artists like Winslow Homer, Thomas Eakins, Frederic Remington, or Augustus Saint-Gaudens. In the comparison it becomes clear that both of Wright's choices are *explicitly sentimental* and

FIGURE 5.7 *John Rogers.* Coming to the Parson, *patented 1870, painted plaster. Courtesy of Smithsonian American Art Museum, Gift of John Rogers and Son.*

utterly forgettable. While he didn't say it, for examples of "realism" he chose the extreme of sentimentality, that is, kitsch.

In much the same way that the Europeans were doing it and allegedly before anyone else had thought of it, Wright therefore resorted to "abstraction" to circumvent that presumed risk. For him, that occurred through the abstraction of geometry. He wrote, "I clearly saw my trusty T. square and aspiring triangle as means to the Midway Garden end I had in view. I meant to get back to first principles—pure form in everything."[87] And down the page he added: "Meantime the straight line, square, triangle and circle I had learned to play with in Kindergarten were set to work in this developing sense of abstraction, by now my habit, to characterize the architecture, painting and sculpture of the Midway Gardens."[88] Even the human figure, appearing in the many sculptures across the building site (Figures 6.3–6.6), was to "share in the general geometric gaiety."[89] Called "Cubist" by the press, the sculptures were transformations of the soft flesh of the human body into faceted planes not unlike the then European Cubist work.[90] But for Wright it was "geometric gaiety."

Despite his claims to the contrary, Wright did not come to these ideas exclusively on his own. Only two years prior to the design of the Midway Gardens, he had personally gotten to know some of the leaders of that "vanguard" while he was in Europe. He had been exposed to their work firsthand. In a thorough investigation, Anthony Alofsin traces those influences upon Wright's work. Embracing what would become the modernist sensibility of Primitivism, they believed that an analysis of the arts of "exotic" and "primitive" cultures, those thought to be closer to nature, might lead to something more basic, simple, and pure. In the return to some essence, they hoped they might finally overcome the debased cultural values of the civilized West. In 1910, while still in Europe, for the introduction of his work in the Wasmuth edition, Wright wrote,

> The appreciation of beauty on the part of primitive peoples, Mongolian, Indian, Arab, Egyptian, Greek and Goth, was unerring. Because of this their work is coming home to us to-day in another and truer Renaissance, to open our eyes that we may cut away the dead wood and brush aside the accumulated rubbish of centuries of false education. This Renaissance means a return to simple conventions in harmony with nature. Primarily it is a simplifying process. Then, having learned the spiritual lesson that the East has power to teach the West, we may build upon this basis the more highly developed forms our more highly developed life will need.[91]

Toward the end of his life he would modify the last sentence to read "we may build upon these basic principles."[92] Seeking principles derived from "primitive" cultures, Wright shared in the nascent European Primitivism. Alofsin characterizes his work that evinces this influence as "primitivist." And in much the same way that the Europeans were doing it, Wright resorted to abstraction.

But his evolution into abstractionism had deeper roots than his European exposure. Ten years earlier Wright had participated in and was influenced by the "pure design" movement then cleansing Chicago's turn-of-the-century art and architecture scene.[93] Even though its meaning was debated, there was some consensus among Wright's peers that "pure design" stood for an approach to building that privileged fundamental and presumably universal design principles over historical precedent. But it was more than that. Based heavily on the teachings of the American historian of Japanese art, professor of philosophy and political economy Ernest Fenollosa (1853–1908), it was more fully articulated, and named, by theorists Denman Ross (1853–1935), Arthur Wesley Dow (1857–1922), and Emil Lorch (1870–1963). Historians suggest that Wright was familiar with their work and had probably personally met each of them except Ross.[94] Like their European counterparts, the concept came from an understanding of Asian arts and, in particular, the appreciation of Japanese prints. Ross, who provided the most comprehensive explication of it in his book *A Theory of Pure Design*, defined

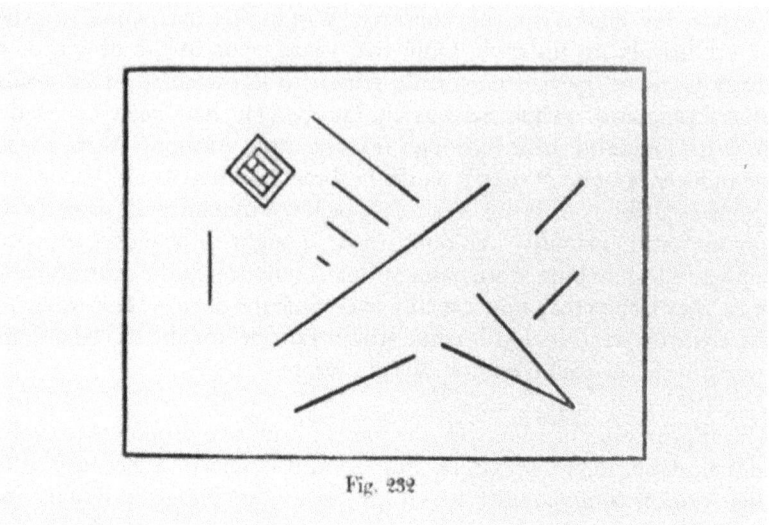

FIGURE 5.8 *Denman W. Ross PhD. A Theory of Pure Design: Harmony, Balance, Rhythm. Boston: Houghton, Mifflin, and Company, 1907, 180. Photo by author.*

it. "By Pure Design I mean simply Order, that is to say, Harmony, Balance, and Rhythm, in lines and spots of paint, in tones, measures, and shapes."[95] Turning from the predominant nineteenth-century focus on historical styles, representation, and the reference to nature—the content of the art itself—pure design focused on composition, material, and technique—the abstracted principles of objectified form. Or in Ross's quaint phrase: "lines and spots of paint." Believing he was elucidating the "principles which underlie the practice," he argued that "being defined and explained, these terms and principles may be known and understood by everybody. They are, so to speak, *the form of the language.*"[96] Working to establish objective criteria, he suggested that his book is "in a sense ... a contribution to Science rather than Art." Quoting Plato he wrote: "'If arithmetic, mensuration, and weighing be taken out of any art, that which remains will not be much.'"[97] Providing an absolute means to appreciate any work of art that would be "understood" by anybody, anywhere, Ross's principles were to be timeless and universal.

As teachers, Dow, Ross, and Lorch had their students perform exercises that illustrated the theory (Figure 5.8). As pure abstractions without referent beyond the compositional exploration, the exercises anticipate the nonobjective art that followed. While Ross refused to see them as anything more than a means to a higher appreciation of representational art, Dow seems to have gone significantly farther. In one exercise he had his students "design a rug with border and centre, the shapes to be *pure inventions, with no reference whatever to nature* [emphasis added]."[98] Apparently he found the method to be sufficient as an art, at least for that of a rug. With the exercise Dow began the shift to "pure invention" as nonobjective art.

Wright's pursuit of "pure form" was consistent with the pursuit of "pure design." Less like Ross and more like Dow, for him it would become the expression of the architecture itself. Over the evolution of his ornamental work there is an apparent shift from his conventionalization of vegetal forms to a kind of total abstraction or, as he put it, "pure form." Unlike the former, which abstracted the figural representations of nature toward geometry, the latter starts with the geometry itself, with just the rectangles, squares, and circles. As a nonobjective art, it was without referent or, in Plato's words, "sufficient to itself."[99] And like the conventionalized foliage of Unity Temple, its motive, or absence thereof, was little more than the resultant formal play as contextualized and incorporated within the building. In his historical survey of Wright's stained glass, Thomas Heinz suggests that manifestations of the conception first appeared in one of the art-glass windows of the Dana House (1903).[100] Designed the year after he had heard Lorch tout the "fundamental and universal principles of [pure] design," the window presents as a totally geometric pattern.[101] Even more than Dow's rug, Wright began to incorporate pure form into some of the ornamental elements of the building. But for him that was not enough. By the time of the Midway Gardens it would become the entire building or, as he said, "pure form in everything."

It is a subtle yet extremely significant shift over the trajectory of his work, a significant and prescient shift in the history of art and architecture. The differences between modernist conceptions of Primitivism, Ross's "pure design," Dow's "pure design," and Wright's "pure form" trace an arc from a method of analysis and interpretation of representational art, to the determination of universal principles supporting that art, to a nonobjective finished product as a fine art and architecture as a self-sufficient presence. As his final defense against sentimentality, Wright removed any referent with its commensurate emotive risks entirely. In its stead he deployed pure geometry. Earlier he had written that it "seemed to hold the surface, give needed contrast, be more architectural; again—less sentimental."[102] As a division of mathematics and construct of human reason, it has an incontrovertible, if self-reflexive certitude, the pure architectural truth that he sought. With his "trusty T. square" firmly in hand, he could have been Plato who upheld "something straight or round and what is constructed out of these with a compass, rule, and square such as plane figures and solids," as things that are "not beautiful in a relative sense, as others are, but are by their very nature forever beautiful by themselves."[103] Plato determined that geometry, because of its "certainty, purity, truth, and what we may call integrity," provided its own "*unmixed*" pleasures that overcame even time. They were "forever beautiful." These were superior to the "mixed" pleasures of the emotions, which were "second rate and inferior"—and temporal.[104] The Platonic understanding of geometry was consistent with Wright's desire to overcome the emotions of sentimentality.

Much like Fenollosa and Dow, Wright's understanding of the pure form of geometry and conventionalization evolved from his interpretation of the Japanese print. Moreover, it was pivotal to his understanding of the Midway Gardens. Recall that about four months prior to starting on the design, he had just returned from a nearly five-month stay in Japan, much of which was spent buying prints. And the year prior in 1912, he had published "The Japanese Print." His understanding of the art was fresh in his mind and part of his current thinking. As if paraphrasing Dow, who defined the principles of composition exemplified in any given work as its "structure," Wright described the print, and all Japanese art regardless of media, as an inherently "structural" art.[105] He asserted that "at the beginning of structure lies always and everywhere geometry."[106] He indicated that the word "structure" is "used to designate an organic form, an organization in a very definite manner of parts or elements into a larger unity—a vital whole. So in design, that element which we call its structure is primarily the pure form."[107] He then made reference to a capitalized "Idea" and indicated that for the Japanese artist, "the forms, for instance, in the pine tree (as of every natural object on earth), the geometry that underlies and constitutes the peculiar pine character of the tree—what Plato meant by the eternal idea—he knows familiarly."[108]

Wright's analogy of "pure form" together with his reference to Plato's "eternal idea" suggests an intentional correlation with a Platonic understanding of being and time. Indeed, Wright even shared some conception with the ancient philosopher's conception of the real. While coming to terms with the purity of geometry and design, and the nature of materials and texture, he concluded that he "knew" "here was reality."[109] After again dismissing "realism" as "subgeometric," he concluded, "Reality is spirit—the essence brooding just behind all aspect. Seize it! And—after all you will see that the pattern of reality is supergeometric, casting a spell or a charm over any geometry, and is such a spell in itself."[110] Closer to the real than mere shadows on the cave, "That is what it means to be an artist—to seize this essence brooding everywhere in everything, just behind aspect." Essential, universal, and timeless, as the intimation of the Platonic ontology of being, structure manifests as those characteristics of the ideal that identify one organic form from another. And for Wright, summoning each was a defense against sentimentality.[111] We need only to recall his solution to "no damned sentimentality:" "There was to be permanent structure."

As his imagination conjured those gardens of pleasure, Wright plotted then three primary strategies as the execration of his curse. (1) He rejected emotive realism in favor of abstraction to lessen the risk of that sentimentality now understood as kitsch. (2) He pushed that abstraction in the direction of geometry as eternal, pure form, without referent, as a defense against the ephemeral, mutable, and "mixed" pleasures of the emotions. (3) Through them he sought to reveal an essential spirit of *his* time, grounded in rational principles and as revealed in the work of "primitive peoples."

Each was a rationally determined step in the removal of the emotions of that sentimentality which had afflicted Western architecture since the Renaissance. And each was a manifestation of "damn."

From the vantage of the twenty-first century, long after those initial strands of modernism had laid the foundations of universal and pure form, it all seems so simplistic and self-evident. But for Wright, it was not that simple. These ideas constituted the apparent defenses that he articulated in writing. But he believed and wrote more than this. At the same time that he fought to repress sentimentality by damnation, he hedged, qualified, and even contradicted his own curse. In Part Three, I look more closely at those contradictions. For now, I focus on what seem to be his primary intentions, particularly as it pertained to his practice of ornament. Those he held to the end of his life.[112]

6

Integral Ornament at Last

Needless to say, Midway Gardens failed to meet the May 1 deadline. But less than two months later, on June 27, 1914, still incomplete, they opened. And to wide acclaim. Kruty described the critical praise, financial success, visitor wonderment, and astounding statistics of its initial run.[1] According to one report more than 200,000 people attended in about three months. Astonished, Kruty repeats, "Two hundred thousand visitors!"[2] By all accounts, the pleasures of the Midway Gardens were more than satisfying.

For the Chicagoan, those pleasures offered a different kind of ornamentation. The project comprised a two- and three-story entertainment venue of poured concrete and structural steel with brick and precast concrete veneers. It included an enclosed, radially symmetrical "Winter Garden" for year-round dining and dancing. Contiguous and to the west was an outdoor, bilaterally symmetrical "Summer Garden" with a "Music Pavilion" for alfresco dining and concerts (Figure 6.1).

FIGURE 6.1 *Midway Gardens, Summer Garden, Chicago, IL, 1913–1914. Frank Lloyd Wright, architect. Henry Fuermann, photographer. Historic Architecture and Landscape Image Collection, Ryerson & Burnham Archives, The Art Institute of Chicago. Digital File # 17845.*

FIGURE 6.2 *Midway Gardens, Chicago, IL, 1913–1914. Frank Lloyd Wright, architect. Henry Fuermann, photographer. Historic Architecture and Landscape Image Collection, Ryerson & Burnham Archives, The Art Institute of Chicago. Digital File # 17860.*

FIGURE 6.3 *Midway Gardens, Chicago, IL, 1913–1914. Frank Lloyd Wright, architect. Henry Fuermann, photographer. Historic Architecture and Landscape Image Collection, Ryerson & Burnham Archives, The Art Institute of Chicago. Digital File # 17861.*

On the exterior the geometric ornamentation wrapped the carefully arranged boxes like the festive gifts at a geometer's birthday (Figure 6.2). The baubles of glittering "electric needles," flower-strewn trellises, gasp-inducing overhangs, and jaunty "sky-frames" (designed to suspend clusters of bubbling spheres), all conspired to effervesce into the enchanted night.[3] As if waving his magic wand, Wright ornamented the cornices at the roofs with pressed metal eaves and incised the concrete copings at the walls with diagonal beats (Figures 6.3 and 6.8). He sprinkled "Dancing Glass" art glass between the chevron-encrusted window mullions, and he cast interwoven diagonal rectangles into the concrete bas-relief balcony rails (Figure 6.8).[4] He lavished the most extensive decoration on the diaper pattern of repeating concrete blocks that fully covered expanses of wall (Figure 6.3).[5]

The interiors were not as heavily ornamented. However they did contain fantastical cast-concrete bas-relief capitals (Figure 6.4). In them Wright converted the life energy of his abstracted, head-bowing human figures into a vitalized matrix of rectangles, squares, triangles, and spheres, which again suggests the influence of his exposure to the Secessionists. The figures emerge from their backgrounds of roiling geometry like Adele Bloch-Bauer from Gustav Klimt's gilded *Portrait of Adele Bloch-Bauer I* (1907) or the two figures in *The Kiss (Lovers)* (1907–1908). There were also wooden bands of concentric squares under the soffits of the balconies. In the corners hung

FIGURE 6.4 *Midway Gardens, Chicago, IL, Detail of Concrete Mural, c. 1914.* The Frank Lloyd Wright Foundation Archives (The Museum of Modern Art | Avery Architectural & Fine Arts Library, Columbia University, New York).

suspended globed lamps, their cords beaded with more wooden spheres, cubes, and tetrahedrons (Figure 6.5).

And throughout the site Wright scattered numerous freestanding sculptural elements, vertical light poles, and the faceted human figures (Figures 6.5–6.6): some of which have been called "sprites."[6] Except for the human figure, all deployed geometry exclusively for their aesthetic expression.[7] Indeed, except for the body, all of it was pure form. In its abundance of Platonic figures as the effusion of "gaiety," it was as if Wright, in kindergarten, were tossing his Froebel cubes, spheres, and pyramids into the air.

FIGURE 6.5 *Midway Gardens, Winter Garden, Chicago, IL, 1913–1914. Frank Lloyd Wright, architect. Henry Fuermann, photographer. Historic Architecture and Landscape Image Collection, Ryerson & Burnham Archives, The Art Institute of Chicago. Digital File # 17852.*

FIGURE 6.6 *Midway Gardens, Summer Garden, Chicago, IL, 1913–1914. Frank Lloyd Wright, architect. Henry Fuermann, photographer. Historic Architecture and Landscape Image Collection, Ryerson & Burnham Archives, The Art Institute of Chicago. Digital File # 17855.*

Consider just one component of that ornamentation. Figure 6.7 illustrates one of the cast-concrete blocks found in the diaper of the walls. Each block measured nominally 18-by-21 inches and each was identical. Being 2¾" thick they were cemented to a structural brick wall in a kind of tile or veneer application.[8] The surface pattern was a bas-relief of seemingly complex rectangular bands that when mortared in place produced a relatively simple series of interlocking vertical and horizontal rectangles (Figure 6.3). The residual space was filled with receding concentric squares. The figure/ground readings are rich and manifold. It took just four blocks to generate the full visual repeat in either direction.[9] Additionally Wright had specified scarlet and green flash glass inserts that were unfortunately dropped when the money ran out.

When compared with the attic frieze of Sullivan's Wainwright Building (Figure 2.5), Wright's intentions are immediately apparent. He removed all semblance of the realistic representation of leaves and he straightened

FIGURE 6.7 Wright, Frank Lloyd (1867–1959) © ARS, NY. Midway Gardens, Cottage Grove Avenue and 60th Street, Chicago, Illinois. Block from Façade, 1913–1914. Cast Concrete, 17 ¾ × 20 ¾ × 2 ¾ in. Gift of Mr. and Mrs. Hal Chalmers and Rexford Battenberg (1972.811). The Art Institute of Chicago, Chicago, USA. Photo credit: The Art Institute of Chicago/Art Resource, NY. © 2019 Frank Lloyd Wright Foundation. All Right Reserved. Licensed by Artist Rights Society.

every sinuous line in favor of explicit, and in this case rectilinear, geometry. The comparison clearly illustrates his intention for pure form. Even though this was just one of the types of ornament found on the project, the same idea applied to all of its other ornamentation except for the human figure.

But as it pertains to sentimentality, the ornamentation of the Midway Gardens went significantly further. Compare the main entrances of the Wainwright (Figure 2.4) with the entrances to the gardens (Figure 6.8).

FIGURE 6.8 *Midway Gardens, Chicago, IL, 1913–1914. Frank Lloyd Wright, architect. Henry Fuermann, photographer. Historic Architecture and Landscape Image Collection, Ryerson & Burnham Archives, The Art Institute of Chicago. Digital File # 17862.*

Sullivan's ornamental frames perform a ceremonial function: they "speak" to the ritual of entering and exiting. They say something about the importance of the building and its users. In contrast, the entrances to Wright's gardens were devoid of overt ornamentation. While the balcony rail overhead and the paired sprites seem to perform this function, they were just some of the many rails and sprites so thoroughly integrated into and arranged around the complex that they would have been inadequate to signify entrance. Instead, Wright wrote that "at the extreme outer corners of the lot toward the main street were set two tall welcoming features, topped by trellises to be covered with vines and flowers, ablaze with light to advertise the entrances to both summer and winter gardens."[10]

For Wright, the signs of entrance were tall volumes that had been fully incorporated into the formal array, trellises with some vegetation, and "light." None were ornament; some were not even building materials. Compared with Sullivan, who always invested his entrances with ornamentation, here, Wright removed it entirely. In so doing he effectively excised the narrative content of entrance from the garden's ornamentation. Instead he opted for a "non-narrative" content sublimated into the form of the building itself, as *pure form*. While the entrance is just one example, in many ways the other ornamentation of the gardens comports with a similar analysis. In the following interpretation of "integral ornament," this should become more apparent. With a simple trick of *placement*, Wright effectively transcribed the remaining ornament into "pure form," both in and of itself, and as contributing to the "purity" of the overall complex. For him, it was no longer sentimental.

—

In the second edition of his autobiography Wright wrote a chapter that he entitled "Integral Ornament at Last." Written in 1943, he articulated the culmination of his philosophy of ornament to date and correlated it with his approach to "organic architecture."[11] It is apparent that his ideas had been germinating as early as the Wasmuth Edition of 1910.[12] As evident in his Prairie houses, they were clearly understood in his heart and his hand as early as 1902.[13] Referring to the late-nineteenth-century problem of ornament, he indicated that for years he eschewed the term "ornament" "to avoid confusion" or "to escape the passing prejudice." Instead, he used the term "pattern."[14] As such, he understood "integral ornament" as a "pattern" that was the "expression of the inner rhythm of Form." It was "founded upon the same organic simplicities as Beethoven's Fifth Symphony, that amazing revolution in tumult and splendor of sound built on four tones based upon a rhythm a child could play on the piano with one finger."[15] Linking the visual abstractions of pattern and rhythm, both realized through repetition, with the audial rhythms of his childhood music from the farm, Wright developed an understanding that was "by instinct at first."[16] He posited that he was defining the very "qualities that make *essential architecture* as distinguished from any mere act of building whatsoever."[17] In his emphasized statement, he placed the essence of architecture within the discourse of integral ornament. And like his childhood music, for Wright, it was "instinctive," "essential," and "*within himself.*"

Included in his description of "integral ornament," Wright outlined two different types. The first he characterized as "*surface qualified by human imagination.*" It approximated that ornament that "adorned" his buildings, that is, in the historical scalar and syntactical relationship of ornament to its bearer.[18] It is that traditional understanding of ornament as a *small* architectural element, seemingly without function, arranged in appropriate places on the surface of a *big* building. As that kind of ornament that appears on the surface of its bearer, visually, it may be "on-the-thing." However Wright, following Sullivan's teaching, worked to make it "of-the-thing." For him, that's what makes it "integral."

While he did not elaborate on it in that chapter, "*surface qualified by human imagination*" was covered in variations throughout his writing to that date. In the previous chapter, he had written about the "*nature-pattern*" of materials that for him was revealed through their "inherent structure."[19] Ornament/pattern was to be in harmony with "nature pattern." A year earlier in his essay, "The Cardboard House" (1931), he articulated this idea. Recall that he suggested that ornament should only come out of the "nature of materials" and their construction techniques. For him the concept goes back at least as far as the Wasmuth editions when he wrote that each material, tool, process, and form had inherent properties—its "nature"—that made it more or less suited for its use.[20] In each case he posits a relationship between the materiality, construction methods, and the form itself.[21] Again, for ornament, the form would be more integral.

In the Midway Gardens, with its limited palette of brick, concrete, and pressed metal, Wright intentionally integrated the ornament into the determined machine processes of fabrication and construction. Much of it done on site with available construction methods, the ornament was poured into the precast concrete blocks and copings, folded into the bent metal cornice, and incised into the art-glass windows. The "nature" or logic of material and construction generated an integral ornament that one might argue was just a slight modification to the shape of the concrete mold, the folds of the bent metal, or the particular cut and the location of glass panes. If one were to remove the ornament of the Midway Gardens, it would mean removing walls, cornices, guardrails, flashing, and windows. In harmony with the nature pattern of materials and construction, ornament was fully integrated into the essence of the building itself. Consistent with the beliefs expressed in his story of first love, Wright developed a "natural" ornament—not "sentimental."

Wright characterized the second type of "integral ornament" as "*imagination giving natural pattern to structure itself.*"[22] Stressing the importance of his idea by repeating and italicizing it, Wright ended with two alternative ways of saying the same thing: "*abstract pattern of structure itself*" and, as if paraphrasing Ruskin, "*structure-pattern made visibly articulate* and seen in the building as it is seen articulate in the structure of the trees or a lily of the fields."[23] He had already articulated this sentiment as early as 1908 when he wrote, "In the main the ornamentation is wrought in the warp and woof of the structure. It is constitutional in the best sense and is felt in the conception of the ground plan."[24] And in the autobiography, pages before he wrote of his intention to have the walls and ceiling blend together to reinforce the quality of a three-dimensional ornamental whole. "Let walls, ceilings, floors become *seen* as component parts of each other, their surfaces flowing into each other. To get continuity in the whole, eliminating all constructed features just as Louis Sullivan had eliminated background in his ornament in favor of an integral sense of the whole."[25] Wright indicated that his understanding had come from Sullivan's illustration of "plastic." As a way of embodying the master's philosophy of nature, Wright transmuted the traditional scalar and syntactical arrangement of ornament on its bearer, as supplement to the building, into the physical structure of the building itself. And he correlated it with his understanding of nature.

> Here the promotion of an idea from the material to the spiritual plane began to have consequences. Conceive now that an entire building might grow up out of conditions as a plant grows up out of soil and yet be free to be itself, [and quoting Sullivan] to "live its own life according to Man's Nature."[26]

Highly suggestive, this requires additional interpretation.

—

In an important essay, contemporary architect and theorist Thomas H. Beeby illustrates how a number of modern architects used ornamental practices to generate the overall formal arrangement of their building designs. He looks specifically at the work of Le Corbusier, Mies van der Rohe, and Wright to make his point. He illustrates how Wright, in the development of an architectural expression distinct from Sullivan's, employed a practice that Beeby characterizes as "ornament structuralized."[27] Essentially he is describing Wright's "*imagination giving natural pattern to structure itself.*" Indeed, as we go forward, for brevity, I use Beeby's phrase instead of Wright's. And for Wright's "*surface qualified by human imagination,*" I abbreviate that to the more prosaic "surface ornament."

Beeby characterizes ornament structuralized as a process where the architect begins,

> with the ornament rather than with construction. The building is conceived as an ornament and built in such a manner that the structure

and method of construction do not dilute the ornamental impact of conception. While programmatic and structural requirements are satisfied, they are secondary to the ornamental manipulation of space, volume and detail.[28]

Beeby carefully and convincingly outlines how Wright, beginning with his Prairie houses, put it into practice. By ordering the plan, to include the location of windows and doors, on a grid much like the geometric scaffolding of Sullivan's ornament, Wright organized the entire structure into a pattern.[29] Complying with the ornamental demands of Sullivan or Owen Jones, he used the mass of the masonry chimney as an organizing "stem." He grouped the windows as "light screens" that formally manifested as large voids, "destroying the house as a closed volume."[30] He utilized flat bands of wood trim as "directrixes of energy" that "radiate from the central spine to the furthest extremity." And as already indicated, with careful manipulation of trim and color he brought the ceilings down onto the walls to "insure visual continuity."[31] Each tactic served to give, in Wright's terms, *natural pattern to structure itself."*

To graphically demonstrate his point, Beeby compares Wright's Unity Temple (Figure 6.9) with the ornament on Plate 4 of Sullivan's *System* (Figure 3.3). He posits that the process of design for both is "clearly analogous."[32] The temple's plan (Figure 6.10) shows that the auditorium is organized by a central square, surrounded by two stories of balconies on three sides with the organ and preacher's "platform" on the fourth. There are four large piers that define the central space, and behind them are flights of stairs in each of the four outside corners.[33] The building section indicates that the centralized square space is the same dimension in height, which defines a perfect cube.

FIGURE 6.9 *Unity Temple, Oak Park, IL, Perspective Sketch. The Frank Lloyd Wright Foundation Archives (The Museum of Modern Art | Avery Architectural & Fine Arts Library, Columbia University, New York).*

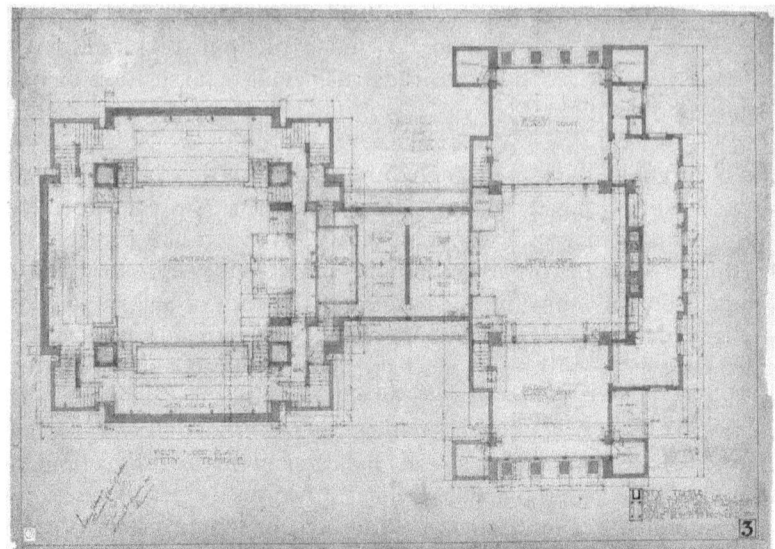

FIGURE 6.10 *Unity Temple, Oak Park, IL, Working Drawing #3, Plan Auditorium Level. The Frank Lloyd Wright Foundation Archives (The Museum of Modern Art | Avery Architectural & Fine Arts Library, Columbia University, New York).*

Beeby illustrates how both men started from simple geometric figures: Sullivan the pentagon, Wright the square (Figure 6.11). They both went through steps that activate the perimeter—Wright by placing the primary void space directly in the center. Beeby correlates Sullivan's corners, as "centers of radial activity," with Wright's stairs at the corners, as concentrating vertical activity.[34] Both men then subdivided the center space according to its "innate geometry."[35] While Beeby does not mention it, both the plan and section of the temple have been laid out on a comprehensive grid system

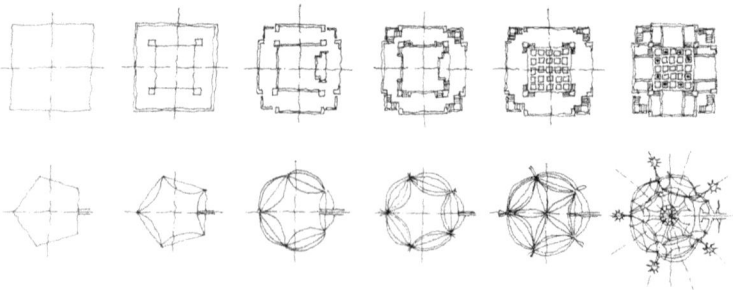

FIGURE 6.11 *"The Grammar of Ornament."* Via III: Ornament. *University of Pennsylvania Fine Arts Press, 1977, Fig. 128. Courtesy of Thomas Beeby, FAIA.*

that patterns the entire ensemble into a rigorous and ornamental order of cubes.[36] Finally, Beeby asserts that the wood trim molding of the temple is equivalent to the foliation of Sullivan's ornament. He writes, "In a sense, the ornamental strips are in direct contrast to the structure since they flow freely throughout the space, independent of the logic of the structure."[37]

Beeby's analysis is accurate and convincing. Yet at the same time, he overlooks two important points. One is the spatial properties represented in Sullivan's ornamentation. We might ask if Beeby's final drawing of Figure 6.11 actually compares with Sullivan's ornament of Plate 4. It's a critical question because the differences reveal the strongest reason for how Wright understood Sullivan's ornament as three dimensional form and space.

Notice that Beeby's drawing illustrates an ornament of two dimensions, while Sullivan's represents three. Sullivan's has visual depth. Looking at Plate 4 again, one might say that it looks like a spherical flower that was slightly compressed under glass and illuminated. Despite its relatively shallow depth, it has extraordinary three-dimensional and spatial complexities.

Returning to the two examples of Sullivan's ornament, Plate 4 from his *System* (Figure 3.3) and again the attic frieze of the Wainwright building (Figure 2.5), it is important to note that both present as bas-reliefs. Plate 4 represents three dimensions; the frieze is in three dimensions; it is molded terra-cotta. Especially noteworthy is that in both cases, there is an implied depth that exceeds the actual depth. On the Wainwright, one could argue that more than a foot of depth is represented in a couple of inches of actual depth, where the stems of the foliation are compressed to fractions of an inch. The frieze presents a physical dimension and represents an even deeper one. In Plate 4, it is impossible to determine the implied depth; the illustration could even be a representation of a city plan, like an aerial photo, with dimensions of hundreds of feet.

With a few simple tricks of drawing, Sullivan conveyed depth. Knowing the specific spatial relationships of the represented figures was essential to the proper logic of the drawing. One had to mentally construct their relative positions in order to correctly draw them. The misapplication of one segment of line would make the drawing illegible. In order to draw Sullivan's ornament, one *had to first conceive of it in three dimensions* (Figures 6.12).

If we return to Unity Temple, the argument is readily apparent. Unlike the foliation of the attic frieze of the Wainwright building, Plate 4's ornamentation is constructed almost entirely of overlapping layers. For ease of illustration I have chosen Plate 17 (Figure 6.13). From it, one may delineate any given layer (Figure 6.14). In total there are well over a dozen clearly identifiable layers to this ornament. It is assumed that the radiating lines of the center square (the middle diagram) interpenetrate the outlying layers adding to the complexity of the spatial organization. Depending on the determined depth of any layer, the sum of the multiple layers could generate an ornament that was perceived as quite deep.

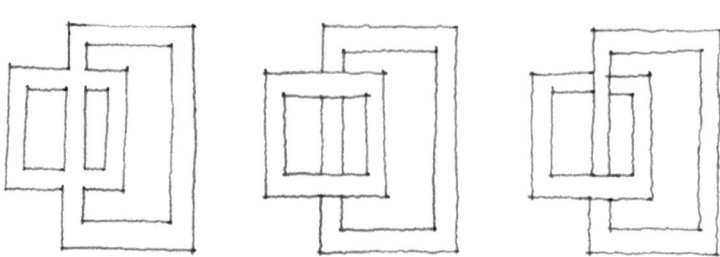

FIGURE 6.12 *Drawing of interlocking figures (drawing by author).*

FIGURE 6.13 *Sullivan, Louis Henri (1856–1934)*. System of Architectural Ornament, *Plate 17, A Geometrical Play-ground. 1922. Graphite on Strathmore Paper, 57.7 × 73.5 cm (22 ¾ × 29 in.). Signed and dated at bottom right of design, "Louis H. Sullivan del: 12/15/22." Commissioned by The Art Institute of Chicago. 1988.15.12. The Art Institute of Chicago, Chicago, USA. Photo credit: The Art Institute of Chicago/Art Resource, NY.*

INTEGRAL ORNAMENT AT LAST 117

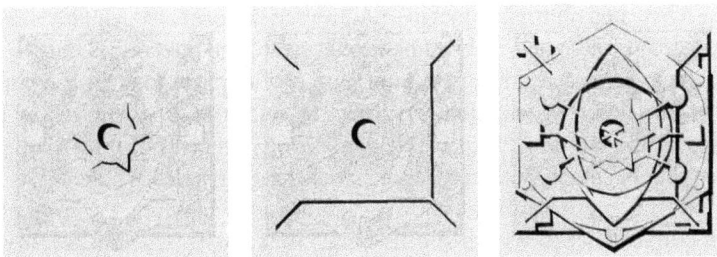

FIGURE 6.14 *Sullivan, Louis Henri (1856–1934)*. System of Architectural Ornament, Plate 17, A Geometrical Play-ground. 1922. Graphite on Strathmore Paper, 57.7 × 73.5 cm (22 ¾ × 29 in.). Signed and dated at bottom right of design, "Louis H. Sullivan del: 12/15/22." Commissioned by The Art Institute of Chicago. 1988.15.12. The Art Institute of Chicago, Chicago, USA. Photo credit: The Art Institute of Chicago/Art Resource, NY. Drawing overlay by author.

It is this spatial quality that transcribes easily into the building. Considering then Unity Temple, each individual floor plan may only be seen as a sequential layer of a complex ornament. The same thinking required to organize the individual layers of Sullivan's three-dimensional ornament is required to organize the plans of Unity Temple. No single floor plan adequately illustrates

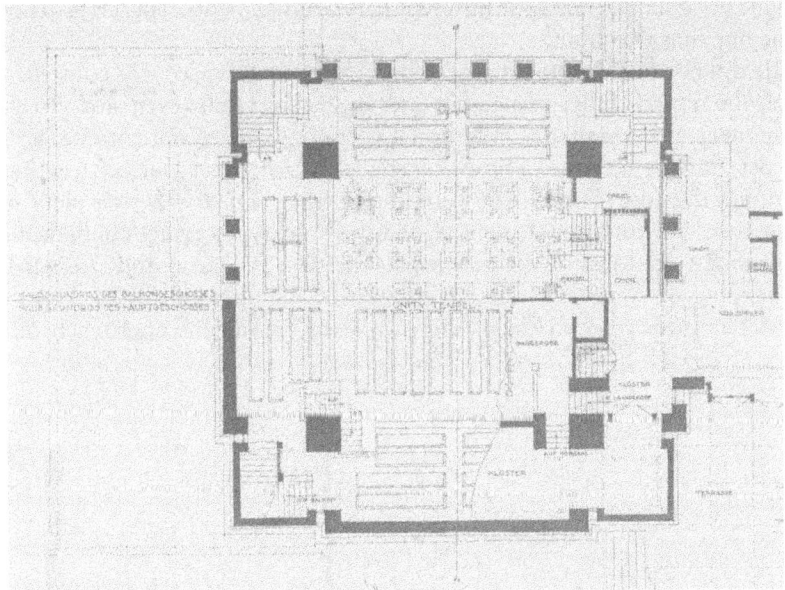

FIGURE 6.15 *Ernst Wasmuth*. Frank Lloyd Wright: Ausgeführte Bauten. Berlin, 1911. Volume 2, Plate LXIV, "Lageplan und Grundriss vom Unity Tempel." Image has been cropped. Avery Architectural & Fine Arts Library, Columbia University.

it. Demonstrably, Wright recognized this and tried to compensate for it in plans where he illustrated multiple floors in one drawing (Figure 6.15). Unlike Sullivan's ornament that is designed to be experienced from one direction, Unity Temple can only be experienced through inhabitation of the spaces that are the building itself. It is consequently inadequate to compare Sullivan's ornament to any given floor plan of the temple.[38] That is like comparing one layer of his ornament to one layer of the temple. Both are fragments of the aggregated whole.

The second point is an issue of representation. In Plate 17, notice how Sullivan conveys depth with just a few lines that illustrate shadows. In some instances it is barely a dusting of line work that outlines the illuminated edge. It doesn't matter whether it is ink or pencil; it is the shadow that adequately defines the figures. With two lines he conveys the illusion of three dimensions (Figure 6.16). With two lines he represents volume and space. Wright understood this intimately. He had been hired by Sullivan based on the merits of his drawing skills. The two men gave the craft considerable importance.[39] With a lifetime of drawing, Wright fundamentally understood the relationship between representation and intention.

Along with the plan, the building section begins to convey some sense of the spatial organization of Unity's ornament. Figure 6.17 is a portion of the longitudinal building section from 1906 and is probably a construction document for the building. Note the arrangement of the wood trim on one of the four piers.[40] Figure 6.18 is a transverse building section from about 1908. It illustrates a different trim configuration on the building piers. Wright designed at least four different trim arrangements. The 1908 version is the one that was built.

He did not finalize the arrangement until after the space was constructed when he could fully experience it, suggesting that even for Wright, "ornament structuralized" was best experienced three dimensionally. On the last drawing he wrote a note that states, "Corner piers surface treatment grouping the four as one." If we compare the trim of the two piers, the 1906 trim is a traditional method. It is arranged in a panel configuration that mimics the form of the pier itself. The trim reiterates and strengthens the reading of "pier." The later trim, in a "C" shape, inflects to the other piers. The piers refer to each other; they are contingent upon each other

FIGURE 6.16 *Drawing representation of three dimensions (drawing by author).*

INTEGRAL ORNAMENT AT LAST 119

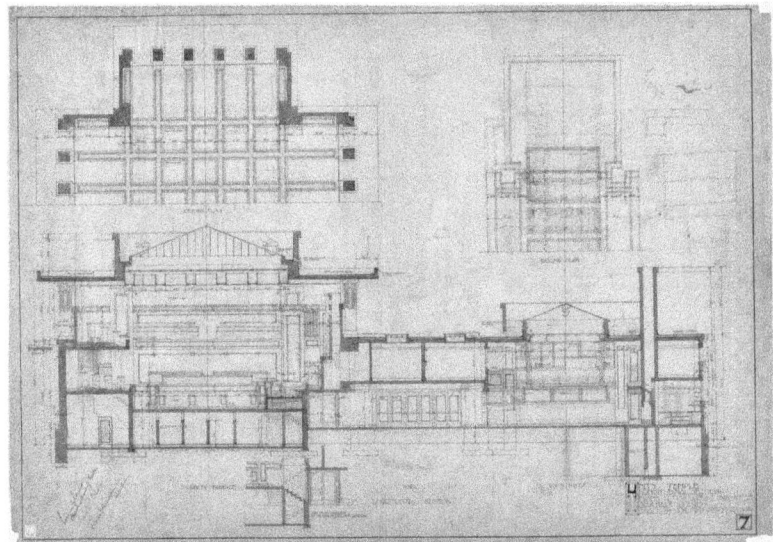

FIGURE 6.17 *Unity Temple, Oak Park, IL, Working Drawing #7, Long Section/ Ceiling Plan. The Frank Lloyd Wright Foundation Archives (The Museum of Modern Art | Avery Architectural & Fine Arts Library, Columbia University, New York).*

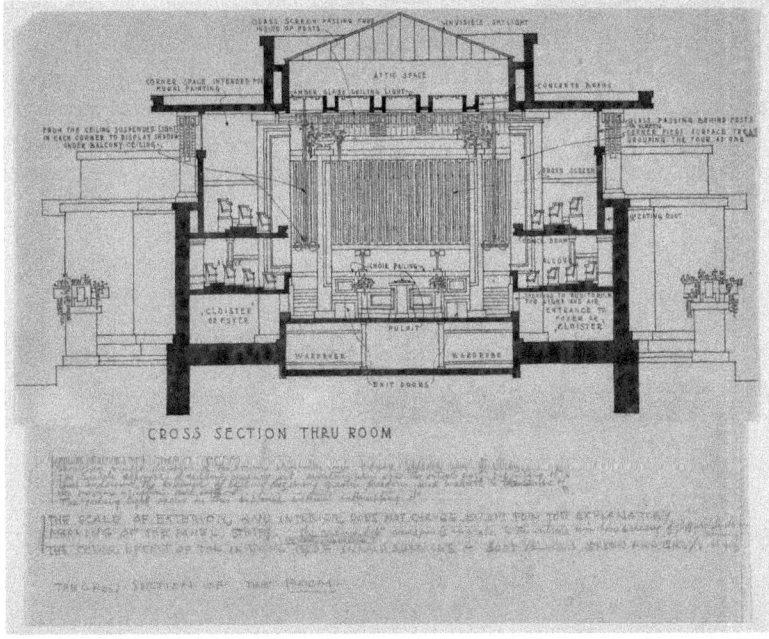

FIGURE 6.18 *Unity Temple, Oak Park, IL, Section with Notes. The Frank Lloyd Wright Foundation Archives (The Museum of Modern Art | Avery Architectural & Fine Arts Library, Columbia University, New York).*

FIGURE 6.19 *Spatial trim diagram (drawing by author).*

and can only be understood as the intentional and unified "grouping." This is an issue of representation. In much the same way that Wright was used to representing a three-dimensional form on paper with just two lines, that is, the backward "L," he created a three dimensional space, with just a few lines, in this case a "C" (Figure 6.19).

The two "C's," the one and its mirror, begin to create an intermediate space—something that would constitute Wright's "grouping the four as one." By a simple and carefully arranged application of a few lines on the piers, Wright transformed it. With wood trim he literally drew a three-dimensional ornament within the space. Anomalous to the overall unit system's gridded order, he created a perfectly useless and essentially decorative elaboration to the "ornament structuralized." Beeby's assertion that they are like the foliation of Sullivan's ornament is accurate. But they are not just decorative lines traced across the ornamental whole. They are generative of another

FIGURE 6.20 *Unity Temple interior, from Pulpit, 2018.* © *James Caulfield.*

whole spatial realm. And too, the piers are no longer to be read as "piers." Unlike the 1906 trim, which reinforced that reading, this trim subverts it. Wright successfully achieved his "grouping" and in the process, the piers are now simply contributing *formal* elements within the overall ornamental composition (Figure 6.20). He transcribed "pier" into "pure form."[41]

Beeby correctly analyzes the relationship between Sullivan's ornament and its realization in Wright's Unity Temple. However it remains incumbent upon us to address Wright's mastery of the *spatial* dimension of Sullivan's ornamentation for a better understanding of his transition to "imagination giving pattern to structure itself."[42] Without it, one risks interpreting just about any artfully arranged radially symmetrical building plan, from any era, as evidence of "ornament structuralized." After all, Beeby's sketch could still be an elaborate nineteenth-century plan. And for Wright, Sullivan's ornamentation was never just a graphic two-dimensional illustration. When

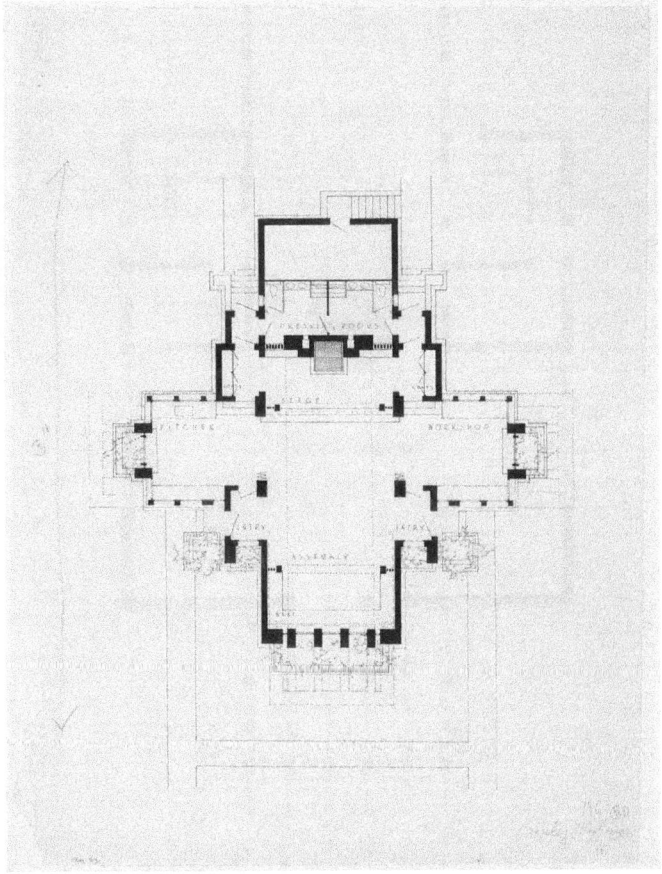

FIGURE 6.21 *Avery Coonley Playhouse, Riverside, IL, floor plan. The Frank Lloyd Wright Foundation Archives (The Museum of Modern Art | Avery Architectural & Fine Arts Library, Columbia University, New York).*

Wright drew it, he knew and *constructed* a dense hypnotically complex virtual world of three dimensions.

Wright's understanding is evident in much of his work of the same period. Compare his floor plan of the "Little Playhouse" for the Coonley Residence (1910) (Figure 6.21) with that of Marion Mahony and Walter Griffin's Nile Club of the same year (Figure 6.22). In the side-by-side juxtaposition, it is readily apparent how radically different Wright's plans were. What makes it that much more curious is the fact that Mahony worked for Wright off and

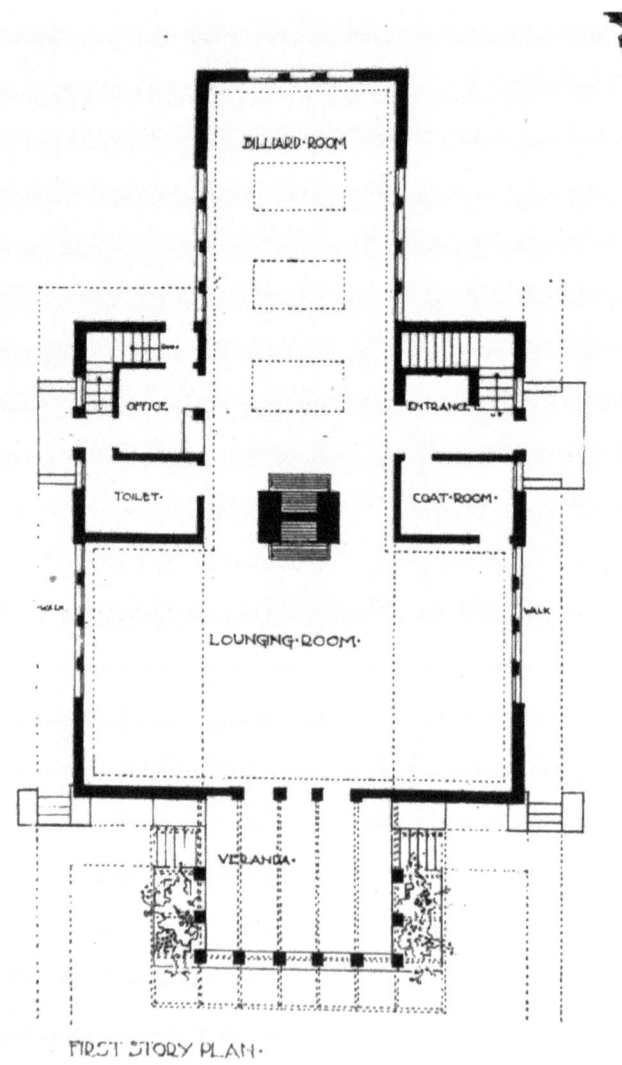

FIGURE 6.22 *Niles Club floor plan. Mahoney, Marion and Griffin, Walter,* The Western Architect. *August 1913. Photo by author.*

on for almost fifteen years before she married Griffin, who also worked for Wright about a third of that time.[43] While there is some flow between the rooms in the Mahony/Griffin plan, the rooms remain discrete, autonomous units. Wright's in comparison are fully interlocked in the superimposition of the organizing and overlapping centralized square.

The simple overlapping of rectangular volumes manifests in endless spatial configurations. Notice the ramifications from the floor plan of the *Gallerie* (Gallery) in the Dana residence (Figure 6.23) and the result in the perspective (Figure 6.24). Wright employs the same spatial understanding of Sullivan's ornament in the articulation of the overlap. Is that transverse beam outlining the ancillary space not like the interlocking elements of Sullivan's ornament? Visually it compares in complexity with Piranesi's *Carceri* series ... or Sullivan's ornament. While today these perspectives are familiar and their formal exploration almost commonplace, during Wright's time they were not. As the Mahony/Griffin plan suggests, the typical late Victorian era room configuration would offer a view of going from discrete room to discrete room, each its own autonomous cell with four walls, a ceiling, and floor, or what Wright called the "box." In contrast, Wright's perspectives

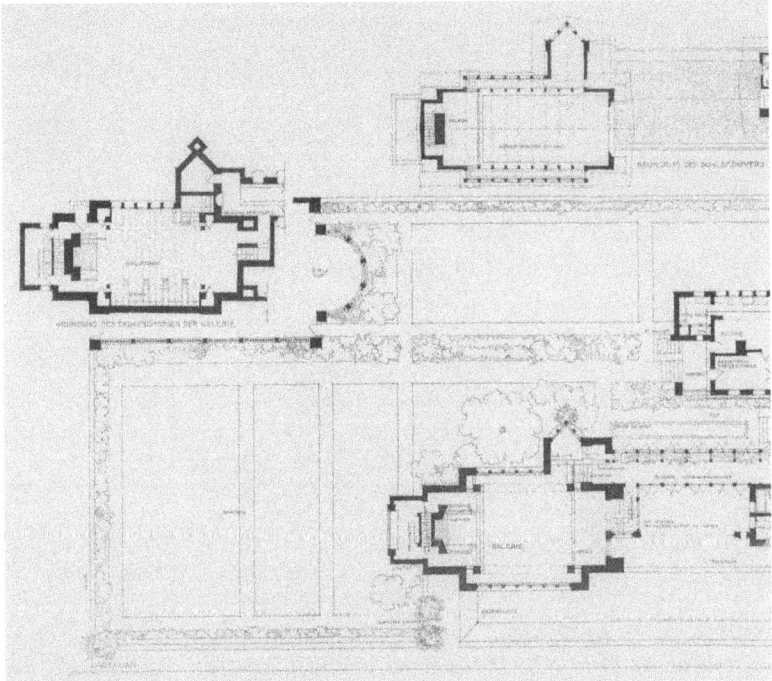

FIGURE 6.23 *Ernst Wasmuth*. Frank Lloyd Wright: Ausgeführte Bauten. *Berlin, 1911. Volume 1, Plate XXXI, "Aussenansicht vom Stadtischen Wohnhause fur Frau Dana, Springfield, Illinois." Image has been cropped. Avery Architectural & Fine Arts Library, Columbia University.*

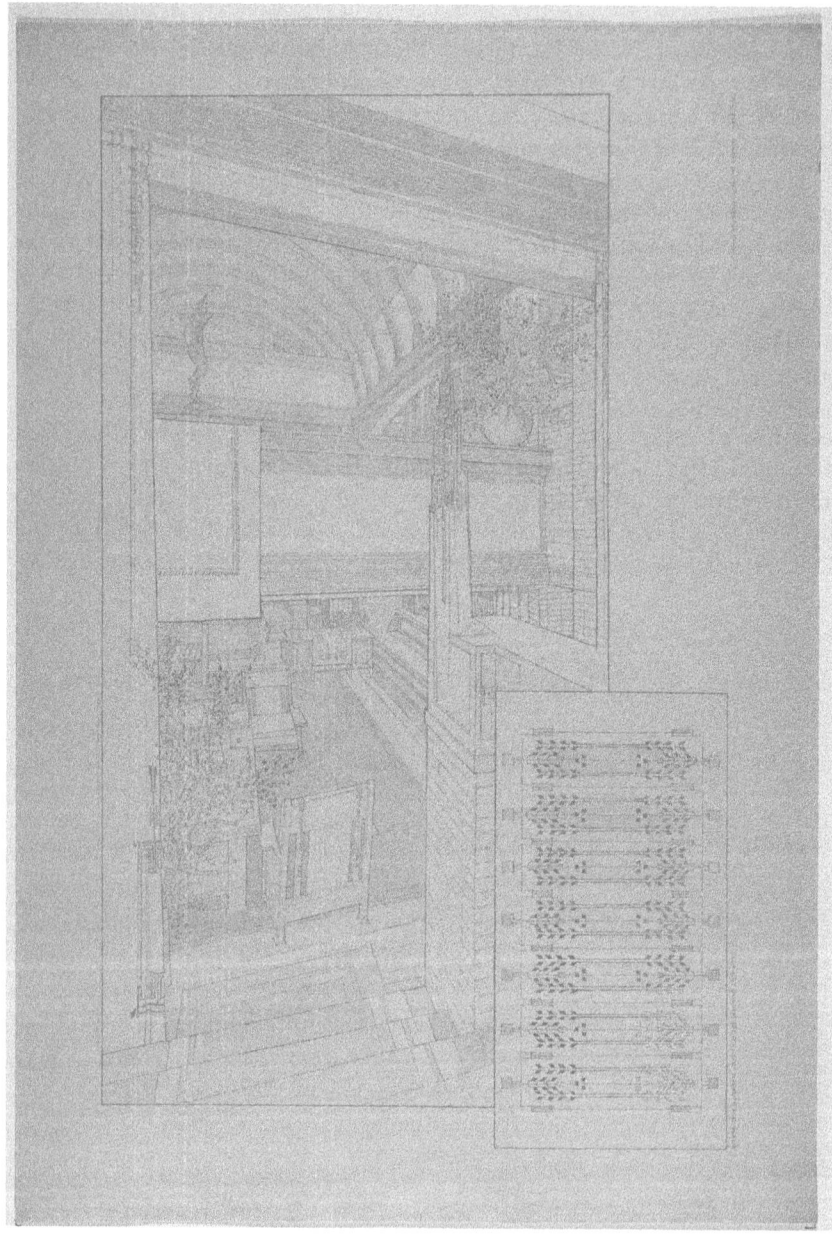

FIGURE 6.24 *Ernst Wasmuth.* Frank Lloyd Wright: Ausgeführte Bauten. *Berlin, 1911. Volume 1, Plate XXXIb, "Inneres des Festhaales for Frau Dana." Avery Architectural & Fine Arts Library, Columbia University.*

illustrate rooms of spatial complexity with interlocking volumes that flow together, as he put it, "to eliminate the room as a box."[44]

I do not mean to re-excavate Wright's development of a new kind of spatial order. His explosion of the box with its roots in Froebel Blocks, and its psychological and functional manifestations for twentieth-century architecture, has long been recognized, analyzed, and thoroughly excavated by previous scholars. No, what is important here is the fact that in addition to those findings, Wright developed a formal arrangement of "organic" architecture that was predicated on his understanding of Sullivan's organic ornament. Moreover, he called it "integral ornament." Wright clearly defined the relationship between organic architecture, ornamentation, and his plans: it was "of the very constitution of the structure." By so doing, he employed a quantum metonymic shift where ornament became structure and structure became ornament. He was in effect using Sullivan's "organic system of ornamentation" to inform his work in the making of an "organic architecture." It is as if the only way he could make that leap was to start with ornament. For Wright knew, like Sullivan, that the two were inextricably interrelated. In so doing, he abandoned neither the philosophy nor the ornament itself. The thread of this extraordinary lineage remains the sinuous line of Sullivan's spatial ornament.

Much like the Unity Temple, the Midway Gardens' "Winter Garden" presented a paradigmatic expression of ornament structuralized. Like the temple, it was organized around a large centralized space with balconies on all four sides and the vertical circulation in the four corners. Instead of the four piers of the temple that pin the ornamental layers together, the Winter Garden had four masonry stair towers that function correspondingly. But the garden pushed the ornamental effect even further. Unlike the temple where each balcony is at the same elevation above the finished floor (Figure 6.20), in the Winter Garden Wright staggered them such that the north and south balconies were one half-story intermediate to the east and west terraces and balconies (Figures 6.5 and 6.25).[45] The "solid" of the exterior walls, with light-screen voids, disappears into the ornamental play. The effect was a swirling array of terraces and balconies cascading around the center dance floor like the folds of a silk ballgown—an evocative and visceral presentation of *giving pattern to structure itself*. But Wright did not intend to evoke the gown. The Winter Garden was one gigantic geometric "ornament"—no narrative, no gown, just "pure form."

That "pure form" revealed itself on the exterior as a complex arrangement of interpenetrating volumes (Figures 6.1–6.3 and 6.8). In order to better "read" them Wright chose two finishes: the diaper pattern and the brick. He assigned a given finish to a given volume. Note how the four tallest towers were completely clad in the brick. They read as solid volumes that are interpenetrated by a series of shorter ones that were clad in the diaper pattern. The surface finish was arrayed across the entire area of all the vertical planes of the given volume, effectively illustrating

FIGURE 6.25 *Midway Gardens, Chicago, Illinois, USA, 1915. Postcard view of one of the interior rooms showing cloth-covered tables and a checked tile floor. Featuring a concert garden, restaurant, and dance hall, the Midway Gardens complex was designed by Frank Lloyd Wright and completed in 1914. It was demolished in 1929. Photo credit: HIP/Art Resource, NY.*

and reinforcing its formal unity and integrity. As they interpenetrate, the different surface treatments of brick and diaper articulated the individual volumes of the overall ornament structuralized. Wright deployed the surface ornament to vivify the articulation of volumetric play as pure form. This manifested in a completely integrated and totally ornamented expression of the entire complex from the largest space as a component of the ornament structuralized to the smallest detail of the smallest surface ornament itself. It was a magnificent tour de force virtually unparalleled in Wright's built work, which makes it all the more surprising. For when Wright most thoroughly renounced sentimentality as his building intention, the resultant project was unprecedented in its proliferation of ornament. Clearly for Wright, ornament, per se, was not the germ of sentimentality.

7

'Like a Man'

Almost two months after its grand opening, Wright was still working feverishly at the Midway Gardens. On Saturday, August 15, 1914, in its festive bar, while eating a late lunch with his son John, he received news. "Taliesin was destroyed by fire."[1] The two men caught the 5:45 train home. As afternoon unfolded into night, he learned that the two warmest loves of his life, Mamah Borthwick Cheney and his home at Taliesin, along with her two children and four of his employees, were forever cooled by an axe, gasoline, and fire-wielding servant. Within two days, all seven were dead. The domestic portion of Taliesin had been burned to the ground. Only his studio survived. As the bereaved struggled to process the magnitude of the incomprehensible horror, Wright focused his attention on Borthwick. He cut down her garden. In a plain box of fresh white pine, he laid her corpse into a bed of flowers, pressed the lid upon them and "fastened home." He then filled the horse-drawn hearse with another whole "mass" of blooms.[2] At the Lloyd-Jones family cemetery, together with his son and two cousins, they lowered her "flower-filled and flower-covered pine box to the bottom of the new-made grave." Asking to be left alone, in the dark, he returned the soil to the waiting earth. Numb, he claimed that "after the first anguish of loss, a kind of black despair seemed to paralyze my imagination in her direction …. The blow was too severe."[3] Biblical in proportion, he broke out in boils.[4]

Out of self-preservation and fear, he went back to work. Claiming he "got no relief in any faith or in any hope," he "could only feel in terms of rebuilding—get relief only by looking toward rebuilding—get relief from a kind of continuous nausea." Ironically denying his own *faith and hope* he immediately rebuilt her memory in Taliesin II. Then over the next ten years he unleashed his creative energy on more iconic buildings: the Imperial Hotel (1913–1923), the Hollyhock House (1916–1920), and the four "textile block" houses (1923–1925). Arising out of the ashes of that gruesome black hole, not surprisingly, even they could not cleanse the stench of smoke, burnt flesh, and death. While renowned for manifold reasons, they too often remained defensive, fortress like, foreboding, and gloomy.[5] On top of that, they added little that was new to Wright's discourse on ornament. Except for one significant turn.

Wright had begun the work on the Imperial Hotel (Figure 7.1) more than a year before the fire. During the trip to Japan with Borthwick he had researched the project, familiarized himself with local materials and methods of construction, and drew sketches in preparation for its schematic design. Commissioned by the Japanese Imperial family together with leaders of the nation's industries, the hotel was to be for foreigners visiting in Tokyo, a kind of liminal space between East and West. Wright responded accordingly. Wright scholar Neil Levine compares the formal order and containment of its Western Beaux-Arts plan to the Eastern Buddhist temple complexes and monasteries of Nara.[6] At the same time he notes a significant atmospheric change that occurred between the initial schemes and those developed after the fire. What was once "lighthearted, joyful, even gay" had become "a sour and ominously solemn mass of brick and lava stone."[7]

Moreover, it feels regressive. As built form, the hotel almost seems to retreat from the Midway Gardens' explicit expression of ornament structuralized. Any formal play of simple interlocking rectangular volumes has now been covered beneath an encompassing Prairie-style roof. Scholars like Levine presume an intentional relationship between the pyramidal mass

FIGURE 7.1 Advertisement for the Imperial Hotel, Tokyo: Main Building Designed by Lloyd Wright. *Japanese, Taishô—early Shôwa era. Leonard A. Lauder Collection of Japanese Postcards. 2002.10943. Photograph © 2020 Museum of Fine Arts, Boston.*

of the building as silhouetted by its roofs and the pyramidal mass of Mt. Fuji. That Japanese symbol of nature's force, the volcano, and talisman of the *ukyio-e*, is echoed in their isomorphic outlines. Levine astutely claims that "Mount Fuji became Wright's totalizing motif. As he developed the design of the building between 1917 and 1919, the form of the hotel, though hardly Japanese in any of its details, came to represent that land as a poetic response to the power of its 'calm mountain God.'"[8] Visible from Tokyo, Fuji formed the deceptively placid backdrop and constant reminder that Wright was building in that great "Ring of Fire:" the Pacific plate's compressing stress earthquake zone. He characterized the process as "building against doomsday."[9] For he knew that "the dreaded force that made the great mountain continually takes its toll of life from this devoted people." Resigned he continued, "Great wave movements go shuddering through the body of their land spasmodically changing all overnight in immense areas. Whole villages disappear. New islands appear as others are lost and all on them. Shores are reversed as mountains are laid low and valleys lifted up. And always flames!" As if recalling Taliesin and Borthwick he summarized, "The terror of it all invariably faces conflagration at the end."[10]

Clearly Wright was no longer in pursuit of anything quite so "pure" in "form." All of the narrative associations of Fuji, "doomsday," and the Japanese land, along with the usual associations of "building," "shelter," "weather," and "protection" that accompany the conception of "roof" (to include the contradicting narratives of Wright's *prairie* roof and the dense *urban* context of Tokyo) confound the unadulterated reading of the self-sufficient presence that "pure form" demands. Indeed, the first impression of the hotel is that of a heavily ornate *building*. Moreover, in the photographs, the excessive surface ornamentation and depths of darkness too often mask the abstract spatial and volumetric play.[11] One might think that Wright was no longer exploring the formal possibilities of ornament structuralized at all.

However, by looking past the foregrounded decoration and roof, the plans and photographs slowly disclose the sensuous complexity of the spatial experience: exteriors of deeply layered interlocking volumes punctuated with strong horizontal and vertical lines of ornamentation (Figures 7.1–7.2); interiors strewn with ribbons of balconies, mezzanines, and bridges, sometimes illuminated with "light screen" clerestories and sometimes framed by the depths of darkness; and low-ceilinged spaces interpenetrating multistoried spaces layered with vistas into the nether regions of the building beyond. According to Cary James who photographed it just before its demolition, "There seems always to be another turning into a farther space; volumes interlock, and short runs of steps lead up to new outlooks. There are constantly changing perspectives of the interior, and through openings at unexpected places come views of the gardens and of the long bedroom wings."[12] As architectural historian Henry-Russell Hitchcock, Jr., described it, the lobby was "an enlarged version of the Midway Gardens interior"[13] (Figure 7.3).

FIGURE 7.2 Wright, Frank Lloyd (1867–1959) © ARS, NY. Imperial Hotel #2 [1509]. Exterior, north entrance, north wing. 1922–1923. Photograph by Henry Fuermann. The Frank Lloyd Wright Foundation. © 2019 Frank Lloyd Wright Foundation, AZ/Art Resource, NY. All Rights Reserved. Licensed by Artist Rights Society.

FIGURE 7.3 Advertisement for the Imperial Hotel, Tokyo: Lobby Designed by Frank Lloyd Wright. *Japanese, Taishô—early Shôwa era.* Leonard A. Lauder Collection of Japanese Postcards. 2002.10952. Photograph © 2020 Museum of Fine Arts, Boston.

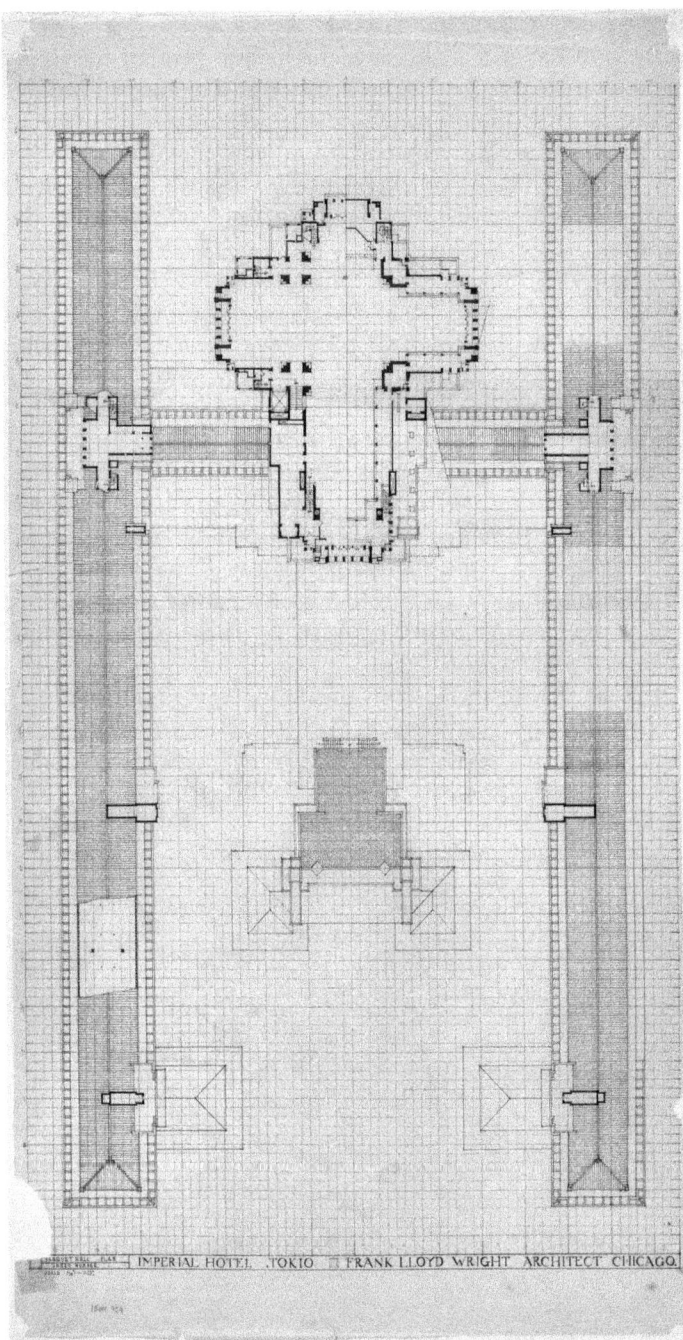

FIGURE 7.4 *Imperial Hotel, Tokyo, Japan. Scheme 2, Banquet Hall Plan. The Frank Lloyd Wright Foundation Archives (The Museum of Modern Art | Avery Architectural & Fine Arts Library, Columbia University, New York).*

The experience of walking through the hotel culminated five stories above grade in a Banquet Hall under the highest peak of the roof.[14] Over its Latin-cross plan (Figure 7.4) and ecclesial longitudinal section, one's eye ascended into the intentionally consecrated ornaments of propitiation under the peak of the roof (Figure 7.5): an epic sacrifice to the inevitable doomsday of Fuji.[15] The entire experience from street to banquet hall was like inhabiting all the sensuality, complexity, and *spirituality* of Sullivan's ornamentation.

In the end, the Imperial Hotel manifested as "imagination giving nature's pattern to structure itself." Wright had not given up on ornament structuralized. But with layers of associative meaning, returning to an architecture of representation entirely unlike the Midway Gardens, the hotel was consequently and *intentionally* not so pure. More like his earlier Prairie-style work where it occurred under an arrangement of cantilevered roofs, there remained however a significant difference. Contextually unlike any of that previous work, the hotel occurred *after* Wright had apprehended the knowledge of the then highest architectural manifestation of objectifying reason and Western thought, that is, pure form. Consequently, he was no longer simply continuing the trajectory of his earlier work. Rather, in an apparent *rejection of the purity of form*, he *consciously returned* to an earlier style of representation.

Not surprisingly, the surface ornamentation was both more traditional and more troubled than that found at the Midway Gardens. Even the choice of material strikes one as regressive. Consistent with his contention that

FIGURE 7.5 Advertisement for the Imperial Hotel, Tokyo: Interior Designed by Frank Lloyd Wright. *Japanese, Taishô era. Leonard A. Lauder Collection of Japanese Postcards. 2002.4664. Photograph © 2020 Museum of Fine Arts, Boston.*

the materials be natural to the site, almost all of the decoration was of a regionally quarried and heavily pocked lava stone, or tuff, called *Oya*. But unlike the gardens, where the ornamentation was integral to the machined processes of manufacture, the hotel's ornamentation reverted to one of the earliest and most primitive techniques of stone construction: it was hand carved, *with an axe*.[16] While all of its patterning is conventionalized and strictly geometric, one immediately recognizes that much of it is positioned in traditional locations, what Bloomer identifies as the edges, openings, and voids where "they might constellate their repertoire of figures."[17]

Like Levine's characterization of the plan as Beaux-Arts, one could say the same about the locations of its ornamentation. Unlike the gardens', the hotel's vertical edges are heavily ornamented as if retracing traditional quoins in lava and light. Voids are framed with ornamental surrounds that speak to ceremonial functions. Primary cornices are heavily accentuated strengthening the reading of both edge and roof. Continuous sill and string courses unify and band the façades, and on the interior mammoth decorative brackets transition between walls and ceilings that reify in stone the building conceptions of "pier," "bracket," and "beam." Finally, Wright completely erased the diaper pattern with its resultant vivification of volumetric play. Gone is the Midway Garden's pure form. In its stead, the ornamentation returned to its more traditional positioning and consequently some unavoidable interpretation of its traditional meanings.

It seems odd that Wright, the self-proclaimed modernist and voice of the "vanguard," would make this return. Having mastered the architecture of pure form, would he not have known better? Did he specifically intend to evoke historical architecture, whether it was Western or Asian? Most historians interpret his uncanny forms as intentional references to earlier cultures, particularly the pre-Columbian Americas and pre-twentieth-century Japan. Alofsin traces the square-within-a-square motif from the Japanese Ichikawa to Europe, America, and back to the hotel. Levine sees the complex profiles with their elaborate decoration as a "masonry analogue" for the more primitive traditional timber framing and bracketing. Nute suggests that the "protective exterior of the Imperial ... may have been subtly echoing the battered earthen wall, or tsuijibei, which surrounds many of the larger temple precincts." Scully compared the hotel's ornamentation to the Midway Gardens and suggested "they may seem more Mayan than Japanese." These interpretations are consistent with an understanding of the work through the modernist lens of Primitivism. While the decoration is geometrical, it has been arranged in such fashion as to suggest narrative associations. Even to the uninitiated its unsettling familiarity feels symbolic and representational. Historians seem intent upon determining the "correct" or "true" referents behind his abstract forms.[18] Though the forms seem to be evidence of Primitivist predilections, recall that Wright denied those influences claiming that he looked to "primitive" cultures not for their manifest forms, but for the "basic principles" that generated them.[19] In either case, whether imitating their built forms or the basic principles upon which those forms were based, the resultant work remains representational.[20]

Wright has gone from the self-sufficient pure form of geometry to a form that is culturally based. And he knew it. He admitted to it. No longer using the phrase "pure form," he conceded that the hotel was the architecture of "Romance."[21] Knowing full well that it ceased to engage the explicit and purely formal display of the Midway Gardens, he admitted that the hotel was a diversion from "the task I had set myself—years ago." Defensively he countered that "to have taken the straight line and flat plane of the machine-age to Japan, regardless of Japanese nature would have been to crucify Japan's best life."[22] Instead he eschewed the demand for purity of form, geometry, and the machine in favor of a contextualized building "wherein the Old was in the New as the New was in the Old."[23] While the ornamentation was still geometric and the ornament structuralized remained, striving to be respectful of Japanese traditions he claimed that "he had taken the straight line and plane there," but he was "regardful."[24]

His motives for this turn are obviously complicated and manifold. While they require more investigation than this study permits, two possible reasons warrant further consideration here. The first suggests that the Imperial Hotel was a personal response to the overriding notion of "doomsday." After the murders and destruction of Taliesin, Wright toiled in the shadow of death for years. At two minutes before noon, on September 1, 1923, as the grand opening ceremony of the hotel was proceeding, his nightmares actualized in the Great Kanto Earthquake. Almost 140,000 lives were lost. Tokyo and Yokohama were leveled. The news of the hotel's survival offered little comfort against the knowledge that it too would never be eternal. The Great Kanto quake was just another reminder of the shadow of Fuji, or the loss of Mamah. The evolution of his work suggests that for Wright, an *abstract conception* of pure form offered little comfort when confronted with the absolute and infinite purity of death.

The second is the obvious fact that Wright was building in Japan. Moreover, he had the experience of living in Japan. From 1916 to 1922, he spent considerably more time there than in the United States. Along with the hotel, he designed thirteen other buildings there.[25] He inhabited the land. Prior to then, most of his work was in Middle America: by contrast a comparatively stable ground of productive soils, and for him, familiar climate. Generally he shared with his clients a similar regional, ideological, and socioeconomic background.[26] Together they shared a Western European heritage with American conceptions of individuality, "common sense," and "democracy."[27] In that regard, they shared some semblance of a common ethos. At the hotel, Wright had to confront not only an alien client, region, and environment, to include a climate that made him physically ill and the "doomsday" of earthquakes, but he had to accommodate a culture that presented a way of being completely different from his Western upbringing.

Compounding these issues was the fact that, at least in Wright's mind, Japanese culture was antecedent to the decadence brought about by the evolution of Western "civilization." Compared to the West, Japan was closer to "Nature as an original source of inspiration."[28] Its people, to include their customs, religions, arts, behaviors, and even their utensils, manifested as the poetic realization of "Nature." Wright construed their culture as an organic, undivided unity or, in his terms, as "natural."[29] His characterization recalls Schiller's conception of the "naïve" where the poet "is" nature. And Wright longed for it. He wanted to be like it. And with the design of the hotel, he believed that he finally had an opportunity to partake of it. As a consequence, he decided that his solution would not be founded upon those manifestations of Western civilization and, in particular, the objectifying reasoning of pure form. Instead he turned to "romance."

Despite his best intentions, any reading of Schiller suggests that Wright's efforts could only be futile. Recall that the eighteenth-century philosopher/poet warned that "once man has passed into the state of civilization and art has laid her hand upon him, that sensuous harmony [of either the naïve poet or the Japanese artist with nature] is withdrawn, and he can now express himself only ... as striving after unity."[30] If Schiller is correct, despite how much Wright may have wished to be like the Japanese artist, for him nature would remain as distant as "*idea* and *object*."[31] Wright must have been aware of that; after all, he *objectified* it into *principles*. He must have *known* that his *interpretation* of Japanese art was an *objectifying analysis*. Though he would likely have denied it, at the hotel, Wright's expression was precisely the same as Schiller's *sentimental* poet. Recall that, distanced from nature, the substance of the work becomes "the elevation of actuality to the ideal or, amounting to the same thing, the *representation of the ideal*" or, in Wright's terms, the representation of "basic principles." While he characterized his approach as "romance," Schiller would have characterized it as "sentimental."[32] And unless he were in some way able to force himself to become "natural," Wright would have had to characterize it as "sentimental" too. Citing his story of first love, he would have to concede that his every effort to *be his conception* of the Japanese artist could only be that "measly external way" or, in his term, "sentimental."

The difference between Schiller's admission and Wright's denial invites a serious question: can one, through an act of will, erase civilization's knowledge from the mind? Or as Wright portrayed himself in his story of first love, can one will oneself into being "natural"? Can one, in Wright's terms, *knowingly* "return to simple conventions in harmony with nature"? Or *objectively* learn "the spiritual lesson that the East has power to teach the West"? Or is every effort to return, as Schiller suggests, just plain sentimental? Wright nonetheless tried. While he was still burdened with his very human response of grief, fear, defensiveness, and gloom, the Imperial Hotel redeemed his troubled spirit through the grace of beauty and sacrifice. As if prepared for Fujiyama's ultimate consummation, with overwrought ornamentation, it was strewn with the flowers of Mamah's casket. Overcoming the objectifying demands of pure form and no damned sentimentality, Wright cut down the gardens, covered the hotel in a mass of ornamentation, and ceded to that inevitability. Calling it "romance," unwittingly, he nurtured his own sentimentality.

—

In September of 1921, and two years prior to the grand opening of the hotel, Wright was absent when the Hollyhock House was declared substantially complete.[33] Too busy sailing back and forth between Japan and the United States, Wright had barely found time to work on it.[34] He had Rudolph Schindler oversee the construction of the project's multiple buildings while his son Lloyd oversaw the landscaping. Stretched impossibly thin by the demands of the hotel, the travel, and the other work he still insisted on taking, neither Wright nor his client, Aline Barnsdall, was happy at the end. She inhabited the house sporadically and within two years of its completion, gave it to the city of Los Angeles for a municipal art center.[35] Situated in Hollywood, California, on the eastern edge of that same Ring of Fire, it mirrored the hotel's western location with its earthquake-prone soils. Still "building against doomsday," Wright returned again to the architecture of "romance."

For ornamentation, the house offered little that was new. Arrayed along the base of the raised attic and scattered across the site were Wright's explicit abstractions of Barnsdall's favorite flower, the Hollyhock. Along with this return to the more familiar and representational conventionalization of vegetal forms is the surprising lack of evidence of the spatial and volumetric organization of ornament structuralized. With an even more traditional plan, the rooms rarely overlap and interlock as witnessed in the hotel's rich spatial play. Consequently, the house offered considerably less of Wright's ornamental explorations. The one anomaly and the home's strongest piece is an exquisite precast concrete bas-relief that Wright placed over the symbolically charged living-room fireplace (Figure 7.6). What seems to be a nonobjective geometric design was revealed by Wright's son Lloyd to be an abstraction depicting Barnsdall as an Indian princess. She is seated on her throne to the left while she overlooks her vast desert lands to the right.[36] The entire fireplace tableau is saturated with signification. Surrounded by a mote of water, its chimney visibly penetrates the roof through a skylight that metaphorically links the four primal elements of water, earth, fire, and air.

Levine poetically constructs a convincing cosmology linking the various elements of the ensemble with Duchamp's *Bride Stripped Bare by Her Bachelors, Even (The Large Glass)* (1915–1923), Navajo sandpaintings, and Brancusi's columnar sculptures such as the *King of Kings* (1920) or the first *Endless Column* (1918).[37] Even though Wright offered no corroboration, historians take multiple readings from the house. They offer virtual unanimity that it refers to the architecture of both the American

FIGURE 7.6 *Hollyhock House fireplace.* Wendingen: Frank Lloyd Wright. C. A. Mees Santpoort Holland, 1925. Photo by author.

southwest Pueblo Indians and pre-Columbian Mexico.[38] As if defining the absolute antithesis of the Midway Garden's *pure* form, Levine characterized it as "a work of pure representation."[39] And Wright was glad to be over it. He reproached himself in writing, "Soon began the gnawing of the old hunger for reality. Romance, I saw as no escape from reality. I had, not yet, descended to make believe. Could I go deeper now?"[40]

After the Hollyhock House and the Imperial Hotel, Wright reverted to his Platonic conception of "reality" by returning to a focus on the machine, standardization, and construction methods in the generation of what, he implied, constituted new building technologies.[41] Returning to his conceptions of the nature of materials and their "nature-pattern," he shifted his attention to the tectonics of the humble concrete block. On his next four projects, the Millard (1923–1924), Storer (1923–1924), Freeman (1924–1925), and Ennis Houses (1924–1925), he developed what he called the "textile block" system. Visually not unlike the diaper-patterned surface ornamentation of the Midway Gardens, Wright pushed the structural properties toward an interwoven system of 16" × 16" precast concrete blocks, poured concrete, and steel reinforcing. But unlike the gardens' veneer, the system was the structural bearing wall itself. Sharing the same decorative properties, the blocks were cast on site in molds that could standardize and replicate any surface pattern imaginable. The system offered seemingly limitless ornamental potential that was even more fully integrated into the physical *structure* of the building. Thoroughly "of-the-thing-not-on-it," Wright had successfully conflated ornament with his metaphorical "structure" of the Platonic "Reality" with the physical "reality" of the building structure itself. He had even more fully integrated the idea and built form into an organic architecture.

Historian Kenneth Frampton characterizes the houses as Wright's attempt to "derive an authentic ornament from the process of fabrication."[42] He sees the tectonics as an adequate poetry unto itself—without referent. He reminds that when doing the Unity Temple, Wright asked, "What shape?" and answered, "Well, the answer lay in what material?"[43] Then, when starting the textile blockhouses, Wright asked, "What form?" and answered, "Well, let the form come. Form would come in time if a sensible, feasible system of building-construction would only come first."[44] Rejecting Hollyhock House's representation and "romance," Wright suggested that he would pursue instead the objectifying practice of building construction, where presumably form would follow in its own due course. Though Levine again sees references to the solid masonry structures of the Spaniards or Native Americans, overall, each house returned to a closer approximation of the pure form of Midway Gardens.[45] Gone are the representational roofs of the Imperial Hotel and its traditional placement of surface ornamentation. Gone are the more traditional plan and the explicit references of the Hollyhock House. Instead each house presents as subtly interlocking, purely rectangular volumes that correspond to their utilitarian purposes. While Wright did not use the expression, they illustrate the determinist understanding of "form follows function." As relatively small and inexpensive houses, the volumes are arranged in picturesque plans of casual asymmetry that nonetheless manage to convey some sense of the ornament structuralized of his earlier Prairie houses. But he did not state that as an intention either.

As "*surface qualified by human imagination*," or surface ornamentation, Wright's utilization of the textile block system seems at times surprisingly careless. Each house deployed its own unique set of strictly geometric patterned blocks, and each individual pattern reveals the hand of a consummate graphic designer. They were arranged with plain-faced blocks in larger patterns of diapers, stripes, checkerboards, edges, and outlines. Pushing the limits of the technology, they are sometimes punctured with glazed lights. In the Millard and Ennis houses there is evidence of a relationship between the arrangement of the decorative blocks and the formal massing of the structures, but it doesn't occur often enough to suggest a clear overriding intention among the four houses. For instance, notice how the patterning of the outside corner of Millard's living room balcony perfectly articulates the exquisite interlocked formal masses (Figure 7.7). But across the remaining volumetric play of its

FIGURE 7.7 *Mrs. George Madison Millard Residence, Pasadena, CA, 1923. Frank Lloyd Wright, architect. Historic Architecture and Landscape Image Collection, Ryerson & Burnham Archives, The Art Institute of Chicago. Digital File # M525580.*

second and third floors, except for the change in pattern on the piers, the patterned blocks simply shrink-wrap everything else in sight. Never does it approach the rigor of the balcony, much less a whole project like the Midway Gardens. Too often the relationship between surface ornament and massing feels casual or sloppy.

A discernable logic or intention seems lacking when confronted with the question of "why?" Why, for example, does the ornamentation of the upper corners of the Freeman house resolve into anomalous chamfering (Figure 7.8)? After all, it shares no formal relationship with anything else and feels sadly meretricious. And the questions continue. Why the partial checkerboard in one location? Or partial diaper in another? Or the stripes? Or the outline? Or no outline?

The seeming lack of rigor is compounded by the specific arrangements of the individual blocks as they were laid in relation to each other. Notice how each block has been designed such that it may be read as a single unit or, when arranged with others, as a more complex design (Figure 7.9). Like the Midway Gardens (Figures 6.3 and 6.7), one simple block takes on multiple figure/ground readings when assembled with four or more.

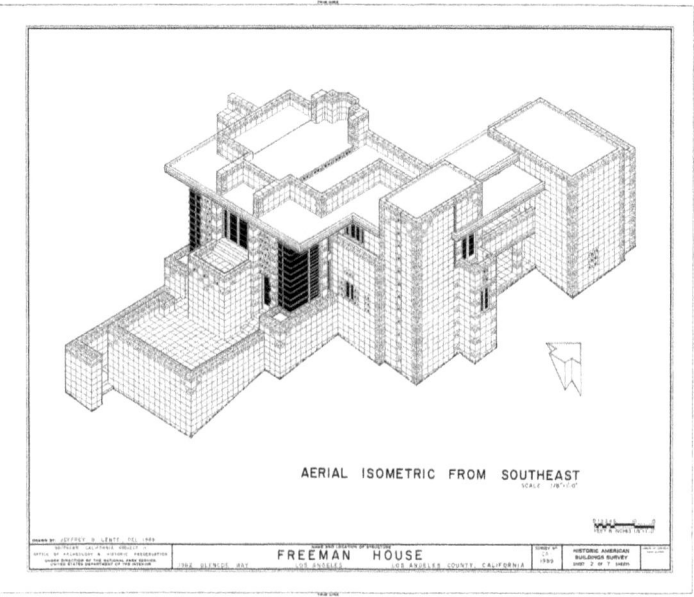

FIGURE 7.8 *Historic American Buildings Survey, Creator, Frank Lloyd Wright, Samuel Freeman, and Rudolph M. Schindler. Samuel Freeman House, Glencoe Way, Los Angeles, Los Angeles County, CA, 1933. Documentation Compiled After. Photograph. https://www.loc.gov/resource/hhh.ca0228.sheet/?sp=2 [accessed September 18, 2018]. Library of Congress, Prints and Photographs Division, HABS. Reproduction number HABS CAL, 19-LOSAN, 62- (sheet 2 of 7).*

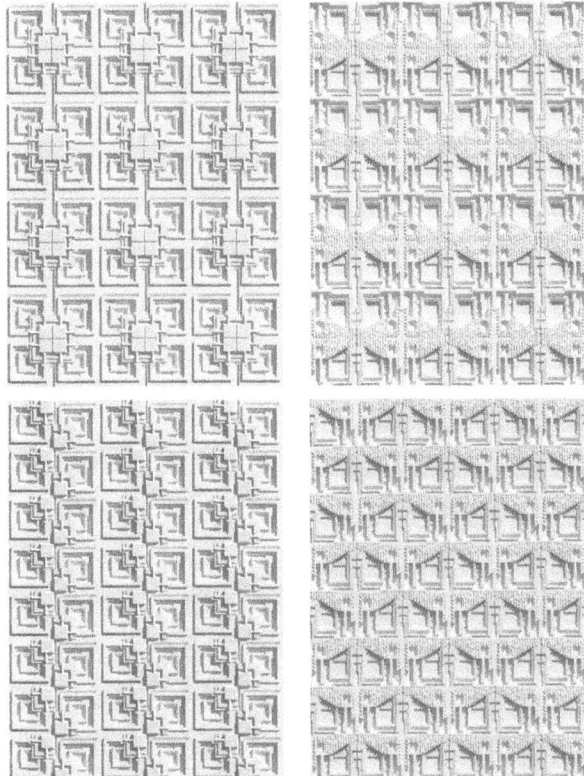

FIGURE 7.9 *Ennis House and Freeman House block detail (drawing by author).*

Curiously, except for the Millard house (with radially symmetrical blocks the argument is moot), Wright failed to capitalize on this potential in any significant way. Instead the blocks have been more often placed to *subvert* that reading (Figure 7.10). Rarely are they in the "correct" and exact groupings of four and more. Wright's intentions, if in fact that's what they were, are at best obscure.[46] We are left with the nagging question of why. Why would he have invested so much attention in the design of the individual blocks, designs that anticipate incorporation into a larger pattern, when he did not utilize it within the broader composition? Why is it that the design of the placement of the blocks pales in the comparison to the design of any given block? Did he no longer care? Too often the arrangement of the patterned blocks suggests a loose hand across the drafting board. It recalls Bloomer's and Harries's distinction between "ornament" and "decoration." It feels decorative, even picturesque. Apparently overlooking his own demands for universal or timeless principles, they appear so arbitrarily placed as to anticipate a different arrangement tomorrow. Ironically, in a system where Wright most thoroughly incorporated his ornamentation into the building

FIGURE 7.10 *Alexander Burran, Photo of Ennis House block detail (2018). Courtesy of Alexander Burran.*

as "of-the-thing-not-on-it," the ornamentation feels least "of-it." He seems to have substituted his interest in the block's tectonics for a conspicuous lack of formal rigor. With such an extraordinary opportunity, it remains even that much more surprising that the ornamentation does not rise to the clarity of idea that was visually witnessed at the Midway Gardens.

Obviously this is just a formal criticism. Even though Wright specifically indicated that the form would follow the building construction, one might suggest that the patterning came from other intentions. The design may refer to some unnamed referent. Perhaps I have misunderstood. Historians continue to see references to Pueblo or Mayan architecture in the designs of the four houses.[47] But even those fail to explain the seemingly casual arrangement of the specific surface patterning. After all, the ornamentation of pre-Columbian architecture was clearly more symbolic and more formally resolved than any of the four houses.

All of this seems to suggest that Wright's interest in solving the problem of ornament was either waning or evolving into another, and as yet unknown, solution that his prodigious creative genius might produce. But the iconic works that followed reveal a conspicuous absence of surface ornamentation. While after the time period of this study, it is worth noting that his best-known later projects like Fallingwater (1935), the first Herbert and Katherine Jacobs House (1936), S. C. Johnson and Son Administration Building (1936) and Research Tower (1944), "Wingspread" (1937), Taliesin West (1937), and the Solomon R. Guggenheim Museum (1956), are all stripped bare. In each of these, instead of any further exploration of surface ornamentation, he pushed even more thoroughly and elaborately the integration of ornamental qualities into the physical structure of the building. From their components of columns, wall systems, or cantilevers, to the formal arrangement of the entire building, each was malleable clay in the hands of his will to ornament. From 1925 until his death, the surface ornamentation that remained on his buildings was simply derivative of his earlier work—and relatively inferior.[48] In his most important works, Wright effectively repressed that component of his practice entirely. The textile blocks were his last significant effort to solve the problem of ornament, as surface ornament, and still keep it. Loaded with untapped potential as the realization of his theoretical intentions, they are uniquely disquieting.

Over the history of Wright's effort to solve the problem, he made significant strides with his supreme examples of conventionalization, pure form—and the removal of surface ornament entirely. With its removal, he illustrated that for him, the articulation of a common ethos need not come from it. Unlike Sullivan who held that the inner character of a building, its identity, and its expression occurred foremost through that medium, for Wright, it might, or it might not. This should never be construed to mean that he did not care. From the very beginnings of his career, Wright strove to be the voice of that ethos. Along with many mid-Western architects, when confronted with the poverty of meaning offered by borrowed European image systems, his primary focus was the development of an American architecture that spoke directly to it. He led in that mission.

Wright believed that Japanese art and architecture provided an exemplary model. He construed their use of conventionalization of form as a mirror to the conventionalization of the society as a whole. Their artists and architects had successfully helped in the articulation of a common ethos. And clearly, for him, just like what he witnessed in the simplified unadorned architecture of Japan, that ethos did not have to be articulated through Sullivan's application of surface ornamentation. It could be in its removal. Recall that even early in his career, the Prairie-style houses were practically devoid of it. And most scholars see those houses as a uniquely American expression. As early as 1910, for his introduction to the Wasmuth edition, Wright wrote that "much ornament in the old sense is not for us yet: we have lost its significance, and I do not believe in adding enrichment merely for the sake of enrichment."[49] But for him, that "yet" came just four years later when he designed the Midway Gardens. To be sure, he regularly returned to solve the problem of ornament. Over the course of his career he developed some of the strongest ornamentation in the history of American architecture. Even though he removed surface ornament from those important buildings of his final phase, over the remainder of his life Wright never denied the conception of "integral ornament." No, even in those later buildings that became ever more naked, they became ever more monumentally ornamental. Even in those buildings where he rejected surface ornamentation in favor of ornament structuralized, he was able to satisfy his drive to ornamentation. No longer tender, he sublimated it into the heroic structure of the building itself.

—

Between the first two editions of his autobiography, when Wright described his planking of the field and his initiation into manhood, he made one almost unnoticeable yet telling erasure. At the conclusion of the tale in the first edition he wrote, "But he always liked best to be sent off alone—to be treated 'like a man.'"[50] In the second edition he wrote, "But he always liked best to be sent off alone—to be treated like a man."[51] The erasure of the quotation marks significantly changes the meaning of the two sentences. What does "'like a man'" mean as compared to "like a man"? Why the quotes? Who or what is being quoted? And why is Wright, the iconoclast, the master of individuality, wanting to be treated *like*, and in fact *imitating*, someone or something else? By the second edition he caught the subtle yet significant distinction and erased the disclosure. At one point he was willing to attribute the qualified sentiment, "like a man," to another source as not his own. It was a way of being "treated" that came from another. It was not something essential to himself. And in the second edition he claimed it as his own. He wanted to be treated *like a man*, in all its individual and dubious authenticity, like the man he "*really*" was.

It might be enough to say that Wright was just quoting the discourse of masculinity of his era. Writing in 1932, telling a fifty-year-old story, he characterized the event as an initiation into manhood. It seems as if it had all the requisite signs: the overcoming of adversity in stoic and heroic style, the indicator that the emotions were controlled by a rational assertion of will. But that is not what happened. Wright did not really overcome adversity. No, he was saved by the hired man. Except for holding on, he really didn't do anything heroic. He merely survived an accident. He even begged the real hero, Sprecher, to collude with his silence.[52] The sum total of his "manhood" was that he worked alone, screwed up, didn't cry, and then managed to survive on the heroism of another. He slew no dragon, saved no damsel, overcame no personal trial. *Wright was the damsel in distress.* After it happened, he was returned to "boyhood" until his uncle deemed him mature enough to try working alone again. Did this really constitute a successful initiation into manhood? For Wright, presumably the proof was that he repressed his emotions of weakness into silence. "There were no cries, no words." The realization of a man might have nothing to do with the success in doing something; it had everything to do with that repression through the successes *and failures* of working alone. Remembering the words of his Uncle Enos, in that agon of "adventure that makes strong men and finishes weak ones," the sign of strength and success that is constitutive of manhood itself is the mastery of emotions, or at least the appearance of it. Wright in his repression was just miming what he thought he was supposed to be. Responding directly to those cultural effects of power, he wanted, as he admitted in the autobiography's first edition, to be *treated* "'like a man.'"

There may be another way to interpret the quotation marks. One might think of Susan Sontag's "Notes on 'Camp.'" She indicates that "camp sees everything in quotation marks. It's not a lamp, but a 'lamp;' not a woman, but a 'woman.'"[53] Now used as scare quotes, Wright is "like a man." For Sontag, "camp is the triumph of the epicene style." As if referencing Sullivan, she characterizes it as "the convertibility of 'man' and 'woman,' 'person' and 'thing.'"[54]

Consider a painting like Cabanel's *Birth of Venus* (Figure 7.11). Once sincerely rendered as sentimental, it was later dubbed kitsch.[55] If someone like Mae West had purchased it in tender affection, and placed it in a position of honor in her outlandish home, it would become camp. It would have gone

FIGURE 7.11 *Cabanel, Alexandre (1823–1889)*. Birth of Venus. *1865. Musee d'Orsay. Photo credit: Scala/Art Resource, NY.*

from a painting, to kitsch, to "a painting." As Wright *portrayed* himself, he had the physical sex characteristics of male with the essentiality of emotion that he feared was "feminine," which he then played as "masculine." In its exaggeration, Wright was a man being a woman, performing a role "like a man." In the exaggerated and *sentimental* posturing against his own tender emotions, Wright had all the subtlety of drag, doubled. As deliberate camp, it would be constitutive of the drag queen, already its own parodic play, playing the male lead, doubly parodic. The multiple confusions of gender are silly, comical, and sad.

Wright's quotation marks reveal like a Freudian slip that he understood his gender expression as something *not* essential to himself. It came from without, socially identified, realized, and constructed. Today, when Judith Butler says that gender is performative and should be understood as an imitation for which there is no original, she suggests that every notion of gender, "like a man," and certainly "'like a man,'" is socially constructed.[56] That is why Wright *had* to erase the quotes. He hated the admission that he was not *essentially* a man. The sign "'like a man'" comes from outside, from another. To be sure, his masculinity, like his fighting, swearing, iconoclasm, was socially constructed and the manifestation of his desire in the repression of his own tender emotions. Like "damn," it was performative.

And his ornament was too. When Sullivan and Wright placed it as the marker of an implied essential identity, Butler would challenge that ornament is always a socially constructed accident for *which there is no original*. Like Kierkegaard's Emmeline who was deluded without a beloved, there never is an *essential* beloved. Its construction is always a multitude of accidents that are only realized through habit, imitation, and repetition.[57] Despite Wright's sad and naïve privileging of the Gothic architect and Japanese artist, there was no essential original unity with "nature." Not even in the twelfth century. Even Schiller recognized this in the naïve poem when he qualified it, with his emphasis, as "the completest possible *imitation of actuality*."[58] Any asseveration to the contrary is just "pure" camp.[59] Ornament is the treatment of a building "like a man," or a "woman," or "whatever," "the triumph of the epicene style," all by necessity, *essentially* in quotes. It is a "lamp."

Certainly Wright at least intuited this. Indeed how often within his texts did he find it necessary to qualify the essential *thing* with quotation marks? Even "Nature."[60] Even himself. He recognized it as an *idea* that humans have conceived and constructed. In that elliptical tautology he neatly packaged it when he heroically declared, "Henceforward, on my own, I am 'I.'" Recall that as the summation of his tale of self-actualization, he transmuted *himself* from the essential "I" to the dubious "'I.'" As much as he desired to determine basic principles and the true essence of things, in the end Wright equivocated over the Platonic notion of being *as truth*. He qualified it with quotation marks. And his awareness only compounded his relationship with both ornament and sentimentality. For if Wright were to cede to the demands of the contemporaneous cultural effects of power that prescribed that he be essentially a "man;" and if there is no essential "man," or "woman," or even "nature;" and if the effusion of the emotions and in particular those tender emotions were construed as "feminine;" then it was *triply* imperative that he repress sentimentality. There is no doubt that Wright was more than willing to engage a practice of ornament. *It just could not be sentimental.*

This study has not pursued an essential understanding of any given artifact's potential for the expression of sentimentality, but rather how Wright considered its expression in his work. But the question remains: can it be determined whether he was rhetorically successful? Has he persuasively argued that the Midway Gardens are without sentimentality? When he indicated that his goal for the gardens was "pure form" without all those references like "missionaries' houses" or "Eastlake," to be assembled in geometric "gaiety," one might ask what "gaiety" is. If as the dictionary suggests that gaiety is a kind of happy excitement or merriment, is that not another kind of feeling as well? Has Wright not substituted one form of emotional expression for another? Absolutely. Furthermore, if one's intentions were to make a building "gay;" make it strictly geometrical as a way of intentionally evacuating all other referent; construct it as one big, festive geometric ornament; toss enough cubes, pyramids, and spheres into the air like confetti, balloons, and the bubbles of champagne for no other reason, one would have a building that was all gaiety, that is all mood, and intentionally nothing else. Like the exquisitely rendered putti over the naked Venus in Cabanel's painting, the exquisitely crafted Midway Gardens were joyously emotive: just gaiety, all affect, no content, fabulous froth—*kitsch*.

But they were not without content, nor were they kitsch. Today the Midway Gardens are academically understood as being firmly seated within the architectural canon, an important contribution to the development of the history of architectural ideas and the rational "science" of Baumgarten's aesthetics. From the strength of their ideation alone they preclude the singular expression of feeling, mood, or atmosphere required of kitsch. When Wright attacked what he called "sentimentality," he grappled with one of the most critical architectural issues of his time: the superficiality of Kierkegaard's "sentimentality," his "picture," and the manifestation of that problem in ornament.

In the entire body of Wright's work, the Midway Gardens were the most fully realized example of "integral ornament" and one of his most important contributions to the architectural idea. They are his masterpiece in the attempt to solve the problem of ornament without removing it entirely. In the development of "integral ornament," Wright effectively strengthened ornament from its own vulnerability and superficiality. He incorporated it into the materiality, tectonics, and construction of the building, and he shifted ornament from its traditional scalar and syntactical arrangement of ornament *on* its bearer to ornament *is* the bearer. In both cases, Wright made it invulnerable by so completely incorporating it, that its removal would result in the destruction of the building itself. In its essentiality, authenticity, and integrity as the brute material of construction, ornament is now as impervious as any building ever was. Compared to its precedents, it is incomparably hard and strong. *Not tender.*

Wright further made a paradigm shift in how the building was experienced and understood. In the intentional erasure of the imitation and realism by which he described the ornament and architecture of the previous 500 years, with all their associative narrative content, he effectively shifted from a subjective narrative structure to an objective abstractive structure. In his uninterrupted pursuit to determine the fundamental principles behind all appearances, he precipitated that shift from Sullivan's affective, inter-relational ornament that gives and receives between subjects to his rational mastery of it as object. And while in the end, he was still willing to call the thing an "ornament," he basically translated the language of ornament from the identification of *things*, like "cartouche," "guilloche," "dentil," and "pilaster," to the language of building abstraction and the *properties of things* like pattern, texture, materiality, and construction tectonics.[61] Severed from meaning and no longer named, ornament is now *that* pattern, *that* texture, *that* material, *that* arrangement. Nameless, effaced, while we may still call it ornament, in today's construction parlance it is more typically called the *detail*. From ornament as "the-thing-in-itself," to "ornament" as "detail," ornament is redefined. And we must surely ask, is it still ornament?

Through each step in the mastery of this heroic adventure to solve the problem, Wright effectively removed the subject, with its attendant messy emotions, from the "manly" pursuit of the work. As basic to his assertion of masculinity, he removed ornament from the more "feminine" realms of language, realism, memory, emotion, and dreams and placed it in the "masculine" domains of rational thought, geometry, abstraction, work, and the building construction itself. And if that were not enough, he magically performed it all with a "masculine" curse: "damned sentimentality." Strangulating that last breath of the tender emotions of sentimentality, he repressed it into silence, for *good*.

Sullivan was sentimental. Wright fought it. There is a kind of sad pathology in Wright's defensive repression and denial. He called himself a sentimentalist and renounced it and that part of himself. His behavior suggests the split within the definition itself. Is sentimentality pejorative or commendatory? Is it as Solomon suggests strictly the appeal to the tender emotions? Or is it the denial of those very same emotions? Those buildings where that appeal is found are often sentimental. Why would we deny it? And perhaps the Midway Gardens were truly sentimental too. About them, Wright's son John wrote, "This romantic building, like the expression he bore, was the mask of a great inner love."[62]

After the Midway Gardens were sold to new owners, Wright wrote,

"They" painted the chaste white concrete sculpture in more irrelevant gaudy colours, stenciled more cheap ornament on top of the integral ornament, wrecked the noble line and perfect balance of the whole. All semblance of the original harmony vanished. Yes, a distinguished beautiful woman dragged to the level of the prostitute is now its true parallel. I often thought, "Why will someone in mercy not give them the final blow and tear them down?"[63]

Anti-German sentiment during the First World War, Prohibition, inadequate funding from its inception, and even Wright's design are just some of the reasons given for the failure of Midway Gardens.[64] In October 1929, on the eve of the Great Depression, they were demolished.

PART THREE

Louis H. Sullivan and Frank Lloyd Wright

8

That Supreme Erotic Adventure of the Mind

Louis H. Sullivan needed someone to draw ornament. It was the late fall of 1887.[1] He was hurrying off to an architect's convention. Deep in the throes of the construction documents for the Chicago Auditorium building (Figure 8.1), he suffered from overwork. He had already been laboring on it for

FIGURE 8.1 *Auditorium Building, Chicago, IL, 1887–1889. Adler and Sullivan, architects. Sullivaniana Collection, Ryerson & Burnham Archives, The Art Institute of Chicago. Digital File #193101.080609–05.*

two years. It was a colossal business. At $3,200,000 it was undoubtedly the most expensive building in the city, and at 110,000 tons, the heaviest and most massive structure in the world.[2] Comprised of a 400-room hotel, a commercial section for 136 offices and stores, its real reason for being and its main claim to fame was its 4,200-seat theater. When completed, it would be the largest permanent concert hall ever built.[3] For Sullivan, the lover of Wagner, it must surely have reminded him of Bayreuth.[4] This was now his chance. But in typical late-nineteenth-century Chicago fashion, his theater was twice as big.[5] Together with his partner Dankmar Adler, he designed the one structure that would best symbolize the recovery of the city once devastated by the Great Fire. In many ways, it was the most important building under construction in the United States.[6] And now, working on the design details of what would become its renowned interiors, Sullivan needed some help.

Frank Lloyd Wright heard about it.

As Wright remembered it, "My heart jumped. I had already formed a high idea of Adler and Sullivan. They were foremost in Chicago. Radical—going strong on independent lines. Burnham and Root their only rivals."[7] Since arriving in the city, Wright had been working primarily for Joseph Lyman Silsbee.[8] But he complained about it. Even as an apprentice he intuited the problem of ornament. Silsbee wasn't solving it but making it worse. With his colleague, Cecil Corwin, he argued about it. Pointing to Chicago's "sentimental" architecture he demanded, "Wasn't Silsbee doing the same thing in the pictures he made, only that he did it as an artist? Silsbee's houses were merely 'arty' then? What thought there was in them was just the same as this?"[9] He had to get out. Soliciting Corwin's encouragement, Wright immediately grabbed some drawings and hurried off to Sullivan's office.

Wright described the first impression of his future *Lieber Meister*. "Mr. Sullivan was a small man immaculately dressed. His outstanding feature his amazing big brown eyes. Took me in at a glance. Everything I felt, even to my most secret thoughts."[10] Wright unrolled his drawings. Sullivan looked them over and asked pointedly, "You know what I want you for, do you?"

Wright answered, "Yes."

"These aren't the kind of drawings I would like to see, but I have no time now. I'll be back Friday morning. Make some drawings of ornament or ornamental details and bring them back then. I want to look at them."

Wright noticed that again Sullivan "looked at me kindly and saw *me*. I was sure of that much."[11] He responded eagerly, "Of course I will."

For Wright, Sullivan's glance *took in everything he felt*. Even his most secret thoughts. In a "glance" of unsettling intimacy evoking the imbalanced power structure of Foucault's "gaze," Wright was laid bare to the core.[12] But he loved it. "Elated," he got back to the office and exclaimed to Corwin, "The job's mine."[13] When asked how he knew, he responded, "How does any one know anything? He *saw*, I tell you, that I can do what he wants done."[14]

How Wright determined that is surely subject to conjecture. Having *failed* to show Sullivan the drawings he wanted to see, Wright apparently based his conclusion on the master's penetrating gaze. Indeed, he had already determined what Sullivan wanted. He concluded, "Making the drawings for him is just a formality."[15] As Wright portrayed it, the relationship was sealed with a "glance."

He nonetheless made the drawings. Working late nights into early mornings with his "T" square and triangle for guidelines, he coaxed his freehand to awaken into Sullivan's efflorescence. That Friday morning he had lots to show.[16] Unrolling his drawings, he showed imitations of Silsbee's ornament. Sullivan thought they were traced. Wright again felt the penetrating gaze "that went clear through."[17] He followed with imitations of Sullivan's own type of ornament that the master conceded were "not half bad." At that moment Sullivan scratched his scalp "with the sharp point of his lead-pencil" and "some white dandruff fell on the drawings." He "blew it off."[18]

Wright continued by showing Gothic improvisations on the ornament of Owen Jones in the *style of Sullivan*.

The master asked, "Owen Jones? Who is he?"

Wright thought he was joking. "You know, 'The Grammar of Ornament.'"

Sullivan looked puzzled, "Anything like Raguenet?"

Wright was forced to admit, "I don't know Raguenet."

Sullivan recovered, "Oh, of course ... I remember the book now. So you are trying to turn Gothic ornaments into my style just to please me, are you?"

"But you see how easy it is to do it."[19]

Immediately Wright knew his mistake. He saw that he had displeased his potential employer and silently conceded that he had reduced the master's ornament "to a mere sentimentality."[20] With his facility for drawing and imitation Wright had diminished Sullivan's ornament—with all of its ideational intention and emotive expression—into an imitable style. Divorced from those intentions Wright's drawings were mere technique. Unthinkingly he had done exactly what his employer Silsbee did. He made an "arty" "picture" with someone else's ornament to get a job, and of course for Wright, that was "sentimentality."

Finally Wright produced drawings of his own design. He described the scene:

> [Sullivan] was immediately interested. Said nothing. He was sitting on a high stool at his draughting board where he had been drawing. After looking them over he made no comment but drew aside the cover sheet from the board. I gasped with delight. "Oh!" I said, "and you asked me to show you mine?" I blushed with shame, felt like a duffer, as indeed I was in the light of this. He seemed to have forgotten me now and went on drawing. I was standing there thinking, if Silsbee's touch was like standing corn waving in the fields, Sullivan's was like the passion vine,—in full bloom.[21]

To Wright, standing there, mulling over his own potential, the master interjected, "You've got the right kind of touch, you'll do."[22] Sullivan agreed to the salary; Wright had the job.

—

In his description of this initial meeting Wright disclosed, perhaps unwittingly, the core beliefs, aspirations, and emotional desires of the two men. From the stare, the gasp, the passion vine, and the "right kind of touch," to their respective ignorance of Jones and Raguenet, and even the dandruff, Wright revealed the incipient love between these two men—and the germ of its demise. As he characterized it, the whole relationship was founded on a stare. One might ask, what kind of stare was *that?* The sexual tension of the scene is palpable. As described, it is the story of two men showing themselves to each other. Wright unrolled his drawings. Then Sullivan, in a gesture of the erotic bedroom, "drew aside the cover sheet" and showed his. Wright gasped! And in a phrase that comes right from the childhood exploration of "playing doctor," he gushed, "Oh! And you asked me to show you mine?" He immediately blushed with shame, a shame so intense he erased any reference of it from the subsequent editions of the autobiography. And he stood and watched Sullivan draw. Here was a man whose *touch* was like the "passion vine, in full bloom."

This might seem like an exaggerated reading, but clearly for Wright, Sullivan's ornament held sexual content. In that often-quoted passage, Wright characterized it as "that supreme erotic adventure of the mind that was his fascinating ornament!"[23] In the first edition of his autobiography, Wright followed that sentence with a paragraph describing Sullivan as the "sensuous master of adventure" with "his back bent over his drawing-board," trancelike, intent on an erotic quest of such extravagant proportion that in the comparison, the great womanizer Casanova and the renowned author of the sexual *double-entendre* Rabelais are described with the same term Wright used to describe himself, as mere "duffers."[24] And poor earthy Boccaccio ranked no higher than a "stable-boy." As Wright described him, Sullivan, in his adventure of ornament, was an even more ardent and carnal sensualist than the most notorious. Not surprisingly, from the subsequent editions, Wright deleted this paragraph too. But it was too late. He had already made clear that he recognized, even exaggerated, the sexual content of Sullivan's ornament. He published it![25]

This reading is almost too easy. It is not Freud's work. In Wright's telling of that first meeting, it has all the puerile subtlety of the schoolyard seduction. Regardless of any "truth" to the story, what did Wright really mean by it? More importantly, what did he intend for the reader to surmise? Given his normally perceptive reasoning, did he actually believe that Sullivan, with his "amazing big brown eyes," in a "*glance*," took in "everything he felt," "even to [his] most secret thoughts?" Did he really expect the reader to believe it? In his recounting, Wright comes off like that caricature of a doe-eyed schoolgirl dreaming in her diary. And he had the audacity to claim that the "glance" occurred three times. Was it not Wright himself who interpreted the stare for us and described himself as fully exposed? Is this not a penetrating stare that pierces the man to his secret heart? If being penetrated is the "feminine" role, was it not Wright who played it and came away elated? Who seduced whom? It was after all Wright who came bearing and baring imitations of Sullivan's alluring ornament as the charms of his seduction. In the end he got the job. He was paid.

All of this suggests a highly unusual self-depiction by Wright who, as the strong, aggressive, and sexually assertive voice of the "new masculinity," portrayed himself as sexualized in the submissive or "feminine" role. Moreover, it sheds a very warm light on what Sullivan meant to him. And finally, it should also be reminded that this was not entirely one way. Unless Wright *completely* fabricated the story, there certainly seems to be something to that "glance."

Unfortunately, we only have Wright's account of the interview. We do not know how Sullivan interpreted it. The way Wright presented it, the master came across as laconic, emotionally withholding. He didn't even comment on the ornamentation of Wright's own design. He simply pulled back the cover sheet, revealed his "ornament," and went back to work. After a few minutes he stated, "You've got the right kind of touch, you'll do." With this apparent reserve, would Sullivan have intimated a sexual subtext to that first meeting? Could he make that admission? Just because Wright understood the master's ornamentation as an "erotic adventure," did Sullivan?

A number of scholars argue for a deflected or sublimated eroticism in Sullivan's work.[26] Circularly, some of that is based on Wright's "supreme erotic adventure" comment. But as Gill pointed out, "Sullivan's unconventional life and unconventional ornament invite unconventional explanations."[27] Despite their interpretations, none provide concrete evidence of the master making an *explicit* sexual reference to his own work or for that matter to anyone else's. Even though I explored how Sullivan endorsed a spectrum of sexuality in Part Two, that does not necessarily mean that he intended *erotic* references within the work itself. The question remains: would *he* have called his ornamental practice a "supreme erotic adventure?"

In the droll conclusion to what Sullivan described as a "metaphysical" presentation, he challenged both his audience and his reader. Speaking to the Chicago Architectural Sketch Club, an organization of mostly younger architects, he stated:

> But, lest you should tend to consider this sort of writing too metaphysical, too fine spun, too unpractical—ornamental rather than useful—I will not leave you till I have laid my finger at the side of my nose in a practical hint:
>
> Let us suppose, then, that I have now before me on this table a collection of drawings containing an original work by each one of you. I tilt back in my chair and examine them leisurely one by one, meanwhile keeping my thoughts entirely to myself.

Being known by your works, it is, of course, the man that I hold in my hand in each case and look secretly into.

How, now, do you suppose I am sizing you up? What, now, do you suppose I am thinking, in each case? What do you think is my estimate of your experiences and your faculties?

Do I understand that my poetic web has caught your practical fly?[28]

And that ended the presentation! In a statement loaded with innuendo, Sullivan claimed that with the drawing it is "the man that I hold in my hand and look secretly into." One has to wonder if Wright was in attendance that evening.[29] For isn't this yet another of Sullivan's "glances?" And this time it is Sullivan who owns it? Perhaps Wright confused the two looks. For a man who can "look secretly into" would it matter whether it was into one's drawings, one's eyes, or one's heart?

Similarly, when Sullivan called Richardson's Marshall Field's Warehouse "a man," one might wonder if he meant the sexualized male.[30] Or did he mean to suggest the asexualized and decorously fig-leafed male of "art?" In a closer reading of that passage, we find that Sullivan described just about everything but the phallus. It remains at most implicit. A few paragraphs later, he wrote, "Therefore I have called it, in a world of barren pettiness, a male; for it sings the song of procreant power."[31] Contrasting the warehouse with the "barren pettiness" of his contemporaries' ("barren" being the term then applied to women incapable of producing offspring), he described it as a man who "sings the song of procreant power." This man is sexually potent. Sullivan alluded to the phallus.

But this turn of phrase, curious to today's ear, invites yet another reference to Whitman. Sullivan again had the poet speak for him. In the poem "From Pent-up Aching Rivers" we read, "From my own voice resonant—singing the phallus, / Singing the song of procreation."[32] Whitman yanks off Sullivan's fig leaf. He *sings* the phallus. When describing Richardson's warehouse, Sullivan was clearly aware that this man *came* with a phallus. By referencing Whitman, Sullivan had again encoded the erotic content within the text. But this time it is in the building. It seems unlikely that he was not aware of the sexual overtones in his design work, when he obviously assigned it in others.[33] Whitman said it for him. In those first two encounters with Wright, it seems even that much more likely that *both* men recognized the sexual potential as they shuffled those eroticized charms of ornament back and forth in front of each other's eyes. And they both knew it was conveyed in a "glance."

All of this might seem like prurient titillation of little value. So what? Moreover, what does it have to do with sentimentality? Yet it is more than just finding the phallus in the ornamental Rorschach. Because sentimentality is defined as an appeal to the *emotions,* it correlates to the *body*. While the exact emotion/body correlation has been long debated, most scholars recognize some mutuality. A racing heart, tears, laughter, sweat, frowns, and smiles are the bodily correlates to specific emotions. Today, most posit a collective interdependence where neither bodily sensation, nor emotion, nor thought can be experienced in absolute isolation.[34] To successfully appeal to the tender emotions is to arouse a *bodily response*.

Sullivan would have understood this. In his library he had Alexander Bain's *The Emotions and the Will*. There he likely read the elaboration of Bain's emphatic position that "Every Feeling has its PHYSICAL SIDE."[35] He also had one of the leading sources in the debate: William James's *The Principles of Psychology*. James took the extreme position and argued with emphatic capital letters that the bodily change experienced in response to a stimulus, "IS" the emotion itself. The experience of an emotion is *only* a physiological state.[36] Today identified as the William James–Carl Lange theory, one might suggest that the appeal to the tender emotions is experienced, or felt, as the appeal to the *tender body*. While James is the extreme, any emotion/body correlation suggests that in sentimentality, the body likewise cedes.

Consequently, when Sullivan engaged a practice of ornamentation through the tender emotion of sympathy, and more generally through sentimentality, he understood that there was a commensurate demand on the body. The sentimental ornament, in its appeal to the tender emotions, in shared subjectivity of giving and receiving, places that demand on the physical, erotic body understood as gendered. It is probable that Wright had some understanding of this as well. It would certainly account for his inner conflict and his vehemence when it came to his own work. For any expression of sentimental ornamentation could only be construed as a *physical* threat to his personal construction of "masculinity."

Given this interpretation, Wright's description of those first two meetings is even that much more surprising. After all, his portrayal was not a disinterested police report but rather a nuanced and edited account of what he wanted the reader to believe had occurred. Clearly, on some level Wright knew that the encounter with Sullivan's ornamentation was sexually loaded. Indeed, he *exaggerated* it. Like Sullivan, he must have understood the master's ornament, *and consequently their embodied relationship*, sympathetically, that is, through the relational positions of to give *and receive*. And he must have known that carried sexual consequences, which put them both in the "feminine" position. For the "man," that meant the locus of risk, anxiety, instability, and weakness. And apparently for Wright, in this instance, that held value.

The cynic could argue that Wright was fine with this if it meant getting a job, just not in his own work. But that doesn't explain why he exaggerated it. Surely he wasn't flaunting some casting-couch prostitution in his autobiography. There must be another reason. To be sure, Wright believed that there was some higher reality that he understood as "truth," for which he was willing to compromise, even to cede, his own "masculinity." And he believed that Sullivan imbibed from that reality. Like his love for the sixteen-year-old Tobin, Wright was willing to defy all "'social'" conventions just to drink from the same cup.³⁷ In this instance, he was more than willing to defy even the social prohibitions of his own gender.

But there must still be another reason. For his portrayal was not that of the noble martyr, the man, forced to sacrifice his cherished masculinity to some higher ideal. In the gendered vernacular of the distasteful task, he didn't "man up," "bite the bullet," "suck it up," and perform the dirty deed for some noble "truth." No, in the physical and sexualized surrender Wright was "elated."

While pondering other possible reasons, I am haunted by his choice of Alcibiades. Recall that when he ran away to Chicago Wright pawned his father's copy of Plutarch's *Lives*. And that from those forty-eight noble lives that included Alexander the Great, Cicero, and Pericles, he had selected just one: Alcibiades. There is something about Wright's relationship with Sullivan that recalls Alcibiades's relationship with that foundational figure of Western philosophy, Socrates. Plutarch described the latter relationship as one of deep, reciprocal love, where the older and wiser Socrates mentored the younger and impetuous Alcibiades. Their love was so renowned that Plutarch considered it to be the most significant factor in Alcibiades's fame.³⁸ We can assume it was the primary reason for inclusion in his book. In its singularity, being loved by Socrates was the one attribute that made Alcibiades unique from those other forty-seven lives. Moreover, it is the most probable reason for Wright's choice in the first place.³⁹ And if Wright identified with Alcibiades, then Sullivan was his Socrates.

But instead of Plutarch's description, I am haunted by Plato's from *The Symposium*. For Plato divulged what Plutarch withheld: the sexual content. While still describing the same relationship, Plato's version recounts Alcibiades's repeated attempts to physically seduce Socrates with the beauty of his "vernal flesh" and "youthful bloom."⁴⁰ He longed to consummate their relationship with his surrender of sex. Like Wright's understanding of Sullivan's interview, Alcibiades understood his relationship with Socrates in sexual terms. Both Wright and Alcibiades described their ingenuous surrender of the tender flesh for proximity to that truth. And both endorsed its value.

To be sure, multiple problems cloud my comparison. Wright cited his choice based on Plutarch's *Lives*, not Plato's *The Symposium*. The two books are not even of the same genre. The former is a comparative analysis of parallel biographies written in order to determine virtue. The latter is a fictional anecdote using real people in order to posit philosophical truth.⁴¹ Moreover, the two seductions do not directly correlate. Alcibiades's manifested through the immediate and dangerous flesh, Wright's through the distanced and mediated ornament and penetrating glances. There is a substantive difference between ceding to the "touch" of an emotion or a glance, and the touch of a man. In each case, Wright could claim that he wasn't referring to Plato's Alcibiades at all—and certainly not to Sullivan's erotic touch of the flesh. But as this chapter unfolds, it should become more and more evident that Wright was familiar with *The Symposium*. More importantly, he actively negotiated with its ideas. Wright not only knew who Plato's characters were; he philosophically negotiated with what they meant. As a way of being in the world, he consciously placed himself in a relative position to Plato, Socrates, and Alcibiades. And despite the physical threat to his own masculinity, he still endorsed his choice, repeatedly, until his death.[42] Obviously these points require additional elaboration to which I shall return. But in his telling of this surprising, erotically charged encounter, Wright, at a minimum, like Alcibiades, suggests that in approaching truth there remains some value in the erotic surrender of the flesh. And in that, he was "elated."

—

It makes sense that for this interview Wright showed Sullivan the work of his current and potential employers. But of all the designers and practitioners of late-nineteenth-century Victorian ornamentation, why did he choose Jones? In the confusion that followed, Sullivan at first admitted that he did not know him. Then Wright was forced to admit that he did not know Raguenet. Did Sullivan truly not know Jones, or had he just momentarily forgotten him? How are we to account for their respective ignorance or forgetfulness? Was Sullivan dissembling? Or Wright? Moreover, why would Wright admit to any professional ignorance in his autobiography?

At the most basic, for these two proud men, their admissions disclose their respective educations. Sullivan studied architecture at M.I.T. and, in 1874, spent a year in Paris at what was then the West's premiere school of architecture, the *École des Beaux-Arts*.[43] In its classically based program with a focus on the architecture of ancient Greece and Rome, he would have studied ornamental theory. Raguenet's work on ornament was published in Paris in 1872 and would have been known as local and current. In contrast, Wright never attended a school of architecture. He took a couple of classes at the University of Wisconsin, Madison, none of which, according to university records, included ornamental theory.[44] In fact, Wright admitted that he found Jones's *The Grammar of Ornament* (1856 or 1865) in the most unlikely of places: in the library of his Uncle Jenkin's church.[45]

It might have just been circumstance and luck that the two men referenced these two masters of ornamentation. Wright had only discovered Jones that year. He might have known no other.[46] But Sullivan certainly knew others and he chose Raguenet. The differences between the two ornamentalists reveal much about the differences between the two architects. Sullivan had a copy of Raguenet's *Matériaux & Documents D'Architecture Classés par Ordre Alphabétique* (1872). In 1909, he owned almost 250 volumes on architecture, of which over a quarter were in French, another 18 percent in German, and the balance primarily in English.[47] A large number of these were pattern books for ornament.[48] But from today's perspective, it is surprising that Sullivan, the architect whose renown was predicated heavily on his extraordinary ornamentation, owned few of the most seminal works from the century. There was no Semper, Riegl, Ruskin, Dresser, *or Jones*.⁴⁹ Yet there was a copy of Jones in Uncle Jenk's church.

The Raguenet is a sourcebook of etchings (Figure 8.2), most of them drawn by the author, of ornamented architectural elements. Organized by type or function, they are categorized under such headings as *Console* (console), *Balustre* (baluster), *Applique* (applique), *Chapiteau* (capital), and so on. Although the book claims to be arranged alphabetically, it is not. There is no explanatory text. Style as an organizing category was apparently unimportant. Each entry is identified with an exact street address or location.⁵⁰ In many ways it presents as a quaint vestige of Schiller's "naïve," with all the finitude of actual, individual ornaments, each from its own unique locale, as if they had come from the life traditions of that place. But all the ornaments shown are stylizations and variations of earlier styles. They refer to some earlier ornamentation. They may seem to be exemplary of Schiller's "sentimental." But there is no apparent reflection upon the style or meaning of each ornament. Whatever "*representation of the ideal*" remains anybody's guess. Organized as arbitrarily as an alphabet, with no explanatory text, each piece of decoration is presented as divorced from its life traditions. As such, any ideal or meaning comes from a shallow formal play as it relates to function. This shape is for a console; that one is for a baluster. The assemblage in the parlance of the day was based on what Wright called "the shallow hokum of taste."⁵¹ Thus, any baluster could be arranged with any other ornament, so long as it still functioned as a baluster.

FIGURE 8.2 *A. Raguenet,* Matériaux & Documents d'Architecture Classés par Ordre Aphabétique, *1872, 3. Photo by author.*

Raguenet's *Matériaux* was therefore typical of Wright's understanding of the problem of ornament: the debased "reiteration of restatements by classic column, entablature and pediment." It is evidence of that late romantic "sentimentality," which is laden with those tender emotions yet severed from any suitable object or ideation: it is the empty emotional attitude of Emmeline's "first love"—or kitsch. And this was Sullivan's reference.

In contrast Jones (Figure 8.3) presents a completely different approach. He believed that nineteenth-century architects should not be copying the imagery of historic ornamentation but instead be learning the principles that generated it. As he stated, "The principles discoverable in the works of the

FIGURE 8.3 *Owen Jones*, The Grammar of Ornament. *New York: J. W. Bouton, 1880, plate LXXXI. Photo by author.*

past belong to us; not so the results. It is taking the end for the means."⁵² As if in direct rebuttal to Raguenet, Jones included pages of written text to establish and clarify those principles. As such, he believed that he could posit value within the ornament itself. His solution was a rational analysis of each ornament based on objectifying reason.

While his text worked to relate the ornamentation within its cultural and formal context, the plates as visual taxonomy exaggerated the abstractive quality of his work. Within any given plate, there is no visual cue to indicate the given ornament's context. Without referring to the legend, the viewer might not know if it is from a pilaster, or a soffit, or a frieze.⁵³ Like images taken through a microscope, each conveys as much understanding of any vital organic architecture as carbon atoms do of the human body. This alienation is exacerbated by the grammatically and materially incorrect juxtaposition of one ornament against another, where a stone sculpture is adjacent to a bronze gate, adjacent to ivory diptychs, next to bronze doors, all on the same plate that might yet be next to a plate of painted borders from pottery shards.⁵⁴ Moreover, Jones's disproportionate inclusion of the diaper pattern, with its boundless open fields, compounds the a-contextualization, dematerialization, and abstraction. Graphically, as compared to Raguenet, the net result is a generalized presentation that foregrounds analysis, abstraction, pattern, visual complexity, and texture over the realistic, material, three-dimensional presentation of ornament in situ. And this was Wright's reference. Writing forty-five years after his first discovery of the *Grammar of Ornament*, he still honored it by proudly recalling that he had traced one-hundred onionskin sheets from it. This should come as no surprise. For anyone like Wright, who sought principles as the determination of that "essence brooding just behind all aspect," Jones was the perfect find. Wright pronounced the first five propositions as "dead right."⁵⁵

It was more than just luck that Wright found the *Grammar of Ornament*. Had he discovered Raguenet we probably would have never known. For Wright believed he had found in Jones a formative solution to the problem of ornament. In contrast, Raguenet was the problem. In the recounting of that meeting with Sullivan, it is evident that Wright would not have even wanted to be known as familiar with Raguenet. He believed he had found in Jones an incremental step in the mastery of the problem and he was already pursuing it.

The odd thing is Sullivan's response—especially since contemporary historiographers assert that he too *was influenced by Jones*.⁵⁶ If that were the case, had he indeed just momentarily forgotten him? Or in this telling had Wright distorted the facts? Or is it possible that for Sullivan, Raguenet was simply more important than Jones? With the advantage of history's hindsight, and the fallacy of oversimplifying in order to construct a simplified trajectory, it is easy to dismiss Raguenet as part of the problem of ornament and praise Jones as instrumental to a "solution." But looking again at the comparison between their respective plates, one might ask to which Sullivan gave his heart—and to which his mind? Privileging the emotions over reason, it seems very likely that, much like his purchasing of de Kock, Sullivan preferred to overlook the risk of kitsch for that occasional sigh or tear. To be sure, Raguenet was part of the problem, but for Sullivan, Jones was not the solution.

—

But what about that dandruff? Why after forty-five years, fifty-nine years, and still again after seventy years, did Wright both remember and decide to include, in all three editions of his autobiography, the embarrassing scene of Sullivan scratching his head?[57] It is such an ugly, unflattering, and seemingly insignificant incident where Sullivan, with the instrument of his craft, *his pencil*, scratched his dead skin onto Wright's drawings. It is certainly something that Wright could have left out. We might wish that he had. But apparently, for him, it had the quality of what Kierkegaard called an "occasion," that "little accidental external circumstance" that captivates enough of one's attention to tie reality with an idea and back again.[58] This unpleasant occasion troubled Wright, but he did not explain why. Citing just the circumstance, he did not offer the idea.

Perhaps, consciously or not, Wright understood that between Sullivan and himself, their respective modes of being in the world could actually be illustrated with something as occasional and repulsive as the dead skin from the scalp. Writing many years after Sullivan's death, perhaps Wright recalled the "dust" of the master himself, those desiccated remains of the corporeal man that mediated between the vital, subjective, and organic person he loved, and the lifeless, objective, and inorganic substance of brute matter, atomized into dust. He might have been subconsciously thinking of Sullivan's *System*, where the master wrote that "nothing is really inorganic to the creative will of man"[59] and that to "be taken from the realms of the transcendental and brought into physical, tangible, even psychic reality, requires that the spirit of man breathe upon ideas the breath of his living powers."[60] Perhaps as he showed his drawings that day, Wright feared and recognized that his imitations of Sullivan's ornament as perceived by the master were nothing more than a rational exercise, like dead skin from the reasoning head, unworthy of the full-blooded haptic skin of the tender body.

While they might look the same, Wright knew there was a difference between the master's "ornament" and ornament, and the master's "dust" and dust. He feared and understood that even if he were to produce perfect imitations of Sullivan's style, like images of a heretofore undiscovered Sullivan, it would not be enough. For he knew that the problem of late-nineteenth-century ornamentation was not that it was poorly drawn or that it lacked technique or craft. Rather, it was the "idea" that generated the imitation that offended.

Schiller had warned of this before the nineteenth century had even begun. When describing the pleasant feeling experienced in the presence of the "modest flower, a stream, a mossy stone, the chirping of birds," he suggested that it is not the objects themselves that are pleasing, but "an idea represented by them which we love in them."[61] For illustration he offered an exact duplicate of the "modest flower," an imitation by which the viewer could not distinguish between the two. He argued that the "discovery" that one was an imitation "would completely destroy the feeling of which we spoke."[62] Writing in 1795, Schiller raised the same thorny moral issues that challenge today's New Materialist, especially as found in the contemporary capabilities of material and biological duplication. If there were a fully duplicated clone of the beloved, to whom would the heart belong? We have an "idea" about both the original and the imitation that determines how we feel about each. It is Schiller's notion of this idea that distinguishes between a bone fragment and a relic; the perfect copy of a Renoir and its original; blood and "blood;" the soil at Mecca, and "Mecca." Or dust and Sullivan's dandruff. This begins to explain the feeling of disdain that both Sullivan and Wright felt for the nineteenth-century imitations of the twelfth-century Gothic cathedral. The perfect replica of Chartres would have been laughable to the architects. This suggests ontological questions about what constitutes authentic, original, natural, and essential, as different from imitation, copy, artificial, and constructed. But it remains something more. For the two architects, their interest in the difference between ornament and the master's "ornament" was not entirely disinterested.

In a musing footnote Schiller remarked that he was not the first to reflect upon this phenomenon. As far as he knew, it was Kant who offered a similar example: an exact imitation of the beautiful song of the nightingale.[63] Schiller made this arch comment about the cool rationalist. "Anyone who has learned to admire the author only as a great thinker will be pleased here to come upon a trace of his heart."[64] Schiller correctly identified the source of the concern. For while it was the *idea* of the original that mattered, it really only mattered to the *heart*. In the end, to the empirical eye there is no difference between the bone and the relic, the soil of Mecca and "Mecca," or ornament and "ornament." But there is to the heart. When Wright and Sullivan honored the "idea" of the original as compared to the copy, theirs was not a *disinterested analysis of an idea*, but a *feeling about the idea*, a type of *sentire in mente*. They were being *sentimental*.

When Wright showed nearly exact replicas of Sullivan's ornament, and admitted "how easy it is to do it," the master was displeased.[65] And Wright in an uncanny, unintentional *double-entendre* admitted that he had unwittingly "reduced" the master's ornament to "a mere sentimentality." Writing in 1932, Wright knew that Sullivan believed that ornament "requires that the spirit of man breathe upon ideas the breath of his living powers that they stand forth, created in his image, in the image of his wish and will."[66] Wright knew that his spurious *imitations*, even if they were *exact replicas* of the master's, were unworthy of Sullivan's life-giving *pneuma*. In ugly, painful, bitter irony, Sullivan mimetically *drew*, and then *blew*, his own dead skin across the surface of Wright's drawings. And by placing it in all three editions of his autobiography, Wright simultaneously admitted and erased the idea of the occasion. For he was unable to master that "dust." Doubly embarrassing, it haunted his memory and intruded into the autobiography like an unwelcome cloudy daemon.

—

> But I had, from the first, seen a different side of [Sullivan], as I felt I would. He always loved to talk and I would often stay after dark in the offices in the upper stories of the great tower of the Auditorium looking out over Lake Michigan, or over the lighted city. Sometimes he would keep on talking, seeming to have forgotten me—keep on until late at night.[67]
>
> I meant to write not as the disciple I never was, nor the pupil he never wanted, but write as the capable workman who understood (that is to say, loved) the man he served—a man who loved him in return.[68]

It was not long after Wright started working for Sullivan that he was up galloping with the master in that "supreme erotic adventure of the mind that was his ornament." Wright fondly recalled, "How often have I held the Master's cloak and sword while he adventured into the realm within to win his mistress. While he wooed the mistress I would woo the maid. Those days!"[69] With obvious affection and nostalgia, Wright portrayed the two architects as lusty musketeers in erotic pursuit of a shared love that Wright personified as "mistress" and "maid." Their issue was none other than the conception of Sullivan's ornament. For the two men together, that exciting and productive adventure lasted over five years, an unparalleled period for the history of American architecture.[70] When Henry-Russell Hitchcock crowned Richardson, Sullivan, and Wright as that "great triumvirate of American architects," it should always be foregrounded that from 1887 to 1893 Wright worked for Sullivan.[71] It was under the *Lieber Meister's* tutelage that Wright learned the art of building and construction that presaged the twentieth-century modern architecture that followed, and much of that can be attributed to Sullivan.[72]

While Wright worked for him, the master radically reconceived the idea of the skyscraper. Like puppeteers from the top of their own Auditorium tower, Sullivan and his partner Adler lifted up some of the first steel-frame skyscrapers in the world: the Schiller Building (1890–1892), the Wainwright Building (1890–1892) (Figure 2.4), the Union Trust Building (1892–1893), and the Chicago Stock Exchange (1893–1894) (Figure 8.4)—all within that five-year period.[73] As such, they conjured some of the first images of how a skyscraper should look. As Claude Bragdon stated, "Sullivan has the

FIGURE 8.4 *Chicago Stock Exchange Building, 1892–1894. Adler and Sullivan, architects. Barnum and Barnum/Commercial Photographic Company/J. W. Taylor, photographer. Richard Nickel Archive, Ryerson & Burnham Archives, The Art Institute of Chicago. Digital File # 201006_157A.233.*

distinction of having been, perhaps, the first squarely to face the expressional problem of the steel-framed skyscraper." Sullivan admitted they were tall and formally expressed it. The idea was so radical that the moment he threw down the incomplete sketch of the Wainwright Building, with a mere three bays outlined, Wright immediately "sensed what had happened."[74] It was an idea so prescient that it has dominated the conception of the skyscraper ever since. And all of it, to the chagrin of those mid-twentieth-century scholars, historiographers, and critics wanting to trace a simplified arc of modernism, was covered in ornament.

Even more importantly, it was during that same brief period that Sullivan formulated his most seminal ideas. He published over a dozen of his principal essays, to include "The Artistic Use of the Imagination" (1889), "The High Building Question" (1891), and his first important treatise on ornament: "Ornament in Architecture" (1892). During Wright's first year of employment, Sullivan wrote "Style" (1888), the essay in which he laid claim to architecture's potential to make visible the aspirations of the young American democracy.[75] That essay proved so foundational that Louis Mumford claimed he was "the first American architect to think consciously of his relations with civilization."[76] And only shortly after he fired Wright, Sullivan published what Twombly calls his "most influential essay:" "The Tall Office Building Artistically Considered" (1896).[77] Here, for the first time, he articulated the modernist dictum that would be recited in architecture books, schools, and offices for the next one hundred years: "form follows function."[78] And Wright learned all of it directly from the master.

Sullivan sat at Wright's drafting table, teaching, advising, offering counsel—singing Wagner. Before construction of the Auditorium was complete, they had already moved into the top two floors of its seventeen-story tower (Figure 8.1).[79] By design their offices sat next to each other. Together they shared an endless view over Lake Michigan. Facing east, these two geometers of nature surely tracked the lambent circle of the rising moon as it reflected off the lake's ink-black plane. Alone in that well-proportioned tower of Sullivan's fertile imagination, late at night, abetted by Wagner's seductive modulations, the two ascended higher and higher over each more earth-shattering idea. They wooed mistress and maid. It must have been heady. As evidence, Wright described the opening of the Auditorium as a phenomenal success, "the greatest outpouring of Chicago's most important and best," a fortnight of opera with "Adalina Patti—incredibly famous then—and a long line of better than star-musicians like the Italian Tamagno."[80] President Harrison too. Enthralled, he proclaimed: "From now forward the fame of Louis H. Sullivan was secure."[81] As he traced and retraced the master's ornament, he succumbed to the scintillating allure of his brilliance.

How many of those moonrises, reflected in that lake, prompted Sullivan to remember Daniel Burnham's divulgement, "See! Louis, how beautiful the moon is, now, overhead, how tender. Something in her beauty suggests tears to me."[82]

Indeed.

Wright's aspirations had been met in Sullivan's fame, consummated in late night talks and serenades. In Sullivan, in love, Wright, like Alcibiades, had found his Socrates, except for the Wagner. Believing he could understand the master's "extravagant worship," he knew he could not share it. He felt the music "too sentimental if not sensual."[83] Consciously he repressed the gratification of the emotions and the flesh. The love between them soon foundered on the *threat* of sentimentality. When Sullivan read portions of his "Essay on Inspiration," Wright responded, "I thought it a kind of 'baying at the moon.' Again—too sentimental." In panicked defense he protested, "I never liked his writing in those early days. Challenged again by sentimentality. Yes, here was this inimical quality showing even in him. What had been suspicion now began to ripen into rebellion against sentimentality in general."[84]

9

Ornament Purely as Such

Sullivan's "Essay on Inspiration," a long prose poem, covered the transcendental themes close to his heart: the eternal rhythms of nature as begotten and returned through the cycles of life and death, what he called "growth" and "decadence." In it he suggests that for inspiration, the artist should attune the rhythms of the work with those eternal rhythms.[1] Sullivan sought that attunement in his own work. Recall that these were the themes of the murals in the Auditorium theater.

Written in 1886, the same year that he first came across Whitman's *Leaves of Grass*, the "essay" again suggests the influence of America's poet on the "lyric poet—no functionalist."[2] Sullivan had read his poem that year to the Western Association of Architects, and as Twombly put it, "his audience was stunned."[3] He was never asked to address the association again. Undeterred, he rewrote it and expanded it several times over the course of his life. The themes were simply that important to him. But unlike Whitman's, Sullivan's poem is overripe, stilted with "thee" and "thou," turgid with "delirium" and "trembling." One must search for its huge themes rendered vulnerably thin beneath a thick lacquer of sap. In its emotive fervor it is however not inconsistent with his work, and yes, in both the pejorative and commendatory senses, the "Essay on Inspiration" is sentimental.[4]

This was not the first time that Wright characterized Sullivan's work as "sentimental." As much as he admired, respected, and loved the master, he believed Sullivan's ornamental work was too. Couching it in the terms of "sensuous efflorescence," Wright described how he would slowly "corrupt" it.[5]

> Whenever the Master would rely upon me I would mingle his sensuous efflorescence with some geometric design, because I could do nothing else so well. And, too, that way of working to me seemed to hold the surface, give needed contrast, be more architectural; again—less sentimental. But I couldn't say this to him and I wasn't sure.[6]

Between the lines of this quote Wright made a rare admission. When he conceded "I could do nothing else so well," he was being uncharacteristically humble. He admitted that Sullivan could do something that he could not. When he compared the master's ornament with his, Wright could only approximate it, through geometry, a mere portion of the master's effusion. His humility reveals that his understanding of Sullivan's ornament, like his understanding of sentimentality in general, was conflicted and complicated. Even though he characterized and subsequently denounced it as sentimental, he nonetheless greatly admired some inherent quality that it had. He was humbled by it.

While it is clear that Wright interpreted Sullivan's ornament to exhibit sensuous content as a kind of carnal beauty that he qualified as "erotic," he also understood it as the embodiment of a higher ideal that came from the core principles and beliefs of the Master himself. He wrote, "I see his richest individual quality and his sense of principle more clearly articulate by him in that feature of his work that was his sensuous ornament."[7] He believed that Sullivan's "loyalty to principle was remarkable as a vision when all around him poisonous cultural mists hung low, to obscure or blight any bright hope of any finer beauty in the matter of this world."[8] Suggesting that Sullivan's principles raised his ornament to a "finer beauty" than the mere carnal, Wright understood it as having "personal, appealing charm. So very like and so very much—his own."[9] Similar to Sullivan's physiognomic understanding of ornament as revealing a building's "inner character" and "individuality," Wright compared it to "the wondrous smile upon his face."[10] He described it in the terms of a love that he conflated with his love for the man himself. He suggested that it mediates between a carnal love and a higher love of principle, a kind of love of the good. In his argument he was able to conclude that "the capacity for love—ardent, true, poetic—was great in him, as his system of ornament in itself, alone, would prove."[11]

Wright's portrayal of Sullivan's ornament as evidence of a "finer" or spiritual beauty, and as the object of love, mirrors the understanding of love and beauty as portrayed by Socrates in Plato's *The Symposium*. While the participants of the symposium each offered their own encomium to Eros, the Greek god of love, it was Socrates who posited beauty as the object of love, with its etiology in the human desire for immortality.[12] In Socratic terms, eros is understood as the desire for timeless being. Citing the wisdom of Diotima, a fictional Mantinaean woman, Socrates recounted her metaphoric ladder of love. He described an ascent from the carnal beauty of the body, through the beauty of the soul, then practices and laws, the various branches of knowledge, that culminated in the contemplation of that metaphysical or spiritual beauty, "the Beautiful" itself.[13] That "Beauty," in its eternality, "neither comes to be nor perishes, nor has it growth nor diminution."[14] Existing "in itself alone by itself, single in nature forever," it is shared by all other physical things that are beautiful and perishable.[15] And it is that "Beauty," removed from finite reality that we are called to contemplate.

For there, at the top of the ladder, Diotima rhetorically asked, "Are you not convinced ... that there alone it will befall him, in seeing the Beautiful with that by which it is visible, to beget, not images of virtue, because he does not touch an image, but true virtue, because he touches the truth?" For there "it is given to him to become dear to god, and if any other among men is immortal, he is too."[16]

Suggesting that the master had ascended that ladder to a "finer beauty," Wright granted Sullivan's ornament a place in eternity when he wrote, "His ornament, as he did it, will be cherished long because no one in ancient or modern times has had the quality to produce out of himself such a gracious, beautiful response, so lovely a smile evoked by love of Beauty."[17] Sullivan's other architectural work will not last, but his ornament will. "Yes, my great master's works, as to form, except his ornament as something, *sui generis*, precious in itself, will die with him. It is no great matter."[18] As if paraphrasing Socrates, Wright suggested that Sullivan's love of the capitalized, that is, spiritual "Beauty," as realized in his ornament, attained immortality. If we were to construe that love of "principle" as a love of the good, the comparison is evident and complete. By describing Sullivan's adventure of ornament as the love of the good that manifests as the beautiful, and by granting it fulfillment as immortal, Wright situated and *deemed it successful* within the terms of Plato's discourse.

To be sure, that discourse has been so foundational, pervasive, and comprehensive to Western thought that Wright may have simply rehashed its abridged and diminished cultural manifestations. Perhaps this comparison is insufficient to suggest that he was intentionally and consciously referring to *The Symposium*. But Wright referred to the Platonic themes often enough to suggest that he enjoyed some familiarity with the text. He regularly juxtaposed its most important themes: love, beauty, truth, the good, and immortality.[19] While these too could have been the clichéd cant of the late-nineteenth-century Chicago architect's office, it seems more likely, given his claim that he read "Socrates," with his application of it in the description of Sullivan's ornament, and his fairly regular summation of its themes, that he had more than just a secondhand understanding of it. And if that is not enough, at the conclusion of his own encomium of Sullivan's work, Wright, as another symposiast reclining on his couch, warned aspiring architects to answer to their own individuality. For "Eros is a fickle god and hard to please."[20] With this additional correspondence, Wright added his voice to the collective encomia and placed Sullivan's ornament firmly within the Platonic discourse of beauty. But even more than that, he found Sullivan's ornament, and the man himself, *beautiful*.[21]

Why then did he corrupt it? Can a work be both beautiful as good and sentimental as bad? Did Wright think Sullivan's ornament was both, and he corrupted only its sentimentality? Might he have only corrupted a chosen manifestation of sentimentality, say that of the pejorative definitions, like kitsch? Did he intend to suggest that Sullivan's ornament expressed that which Harries indicates "does not so much arouse love or desire, but their simulacrum?" Given his affirmation within the Platonic construct of love and a "finer beauty," it is impossible that he understood it in those terms.[22] This love was no simulacrum. Wright knew and had just described it as much more than that. Certainly he saw Sullivan's work as emotional; perhaps it was too much so. But he would never characterize it as evidence of addiction "to indulgence in superficial emotion." Clearly he did not mean to characterize it as kitsch. His desire to make an ornament less sentimental than Sullivan's again suggests that he corrupted specific qualities of what he understood the term to mean, *other than kitsch*. And again, we confront Wright's difficulty with the *tender* emotions.

Even though Wright in his own misprision corrupted Sullivan's ornament, he nonetheless honored it. In perhaps the highest honor, he believed that Sullivan had successfully solved the problem of ornament. Rhetorically Wright asked,

> Do you realize that here [in Sullivan's ornament] is no body of culture evolving through centuries of time a scheme and "style" of plastic expression but an Individual working away in the poetry-crushing environment of a more cruel materialism than any seen since the days of the brutal Romans? An individual who, in this, evoked the goddess that whole civilizations strove for centuries to win—and wooed her with this charming interior smile—all on his own in his brief lifetime.[23]

In what amounts to very rare praise, Wright effectively interpreted Sullivan's ornament and the man himself as beautiful in the terms of Plato's *Symposium*. Sullivan had individually solved the problem of ornament that had plagued the late-nineteenth-century architect. For Wright, with a reassignment of Eros's gender, had determined that Sullivan successfully wooed "the goddess" and had done it "with this charming interior smile."[24] In Sullivan, Wright found his Socrates. And like the *Symposium*'s Alcibiades, Wright did not sing his encomium to Eros but to Socrates, that is, to Sullivan himself.

But this is certainly unexpected. Why would Wright, who *knew* Sullivan, portray the master's ornament in the Socratic and contemplative, indeed disembodied terms of love, the Beautiful, and abstract truth? That seems like the last way that Sullivan, along with Casanova, Rabelais, and Boccaccio, would have understood it.[25] Moreover, how did Wright see himself in all this? If he portrayed Sullivan as Socrates, was he again portraying himself as Alcibiades?

"And suddenly, there was a loud knocking at the courtyard door as of revelers."

With that, into the symposium, along with a flute-girl and "certain others of his followers," crashed a drunken Alcibiades. "Crowned with a bushy wreath of ivy and violets and a multitude of fillets," he gushed in love for

Socrates.²⁶ Smitten, he exclaimed how his heart leapt and tears flowed upon hearing the beauty of the philosopher's words.²⁷ Anguished, he recounted his repeated and unsuccessful attempts to physically seduce the man. He admitted to a shame that came from a grave inner conflict over his inability to reciprocally love a man who understood the object of love to be the spiritual quest of the good. For he felt that the only currency he could offer was the beauty of earthly things: his noble status, fame, conquest, and handsome flesh. He believed that the ideal consummation of his love would be—in sex. Unlike Socrates who argued rationally through education, reason, and ascetic contemplation, Alcibiades argued passionately through experience, the image, emotional desire, and the flesh. And surprisingly, Socrates tacitly conceded that the drunken interloper, as if providing yet another legitimate encomium, had spoken the truth.²⁸

What could Wright possibly have intended by his comparison? Could it be that he was just projecting his hunger for the mentorship and love of his own Socrates upon Sullivan? Was he turning Sullivan into the Socratic lover of that "finer beauty" in order that he might drink from that font of wisdom? Was he consequently willing to be the loving Alcibiades in order to attain it? To include the sex? In elation?²⁹ Was he hoping that Sullivan, the mortal, might be the contemplative lover who ascended Diotima's ladder above the flesh to the rational study of the "Beautiful" itself, "and if any other among men is immortal, he is too?"³⁰ Was Wright suggesting that Sullivan, with his back bent over his drafting board, contemplated the eternal Ideal of Platonic Forms? In pursuit of the good? In pursuit of truth? Did he need to believe that Sullivan was "dear to god?"

In love, the answer is probably yes.

Or might it have been that this was this the only way that Wright knew how to interpret his master and his work? Perhaps the Socratic view was how Wright placed *himself* within the world. Perhaps he wasn't Alcibiades at all. He simply projected *his* worldview onto Sullivan's earthly existence. He simply could not understand the "real" man.

—

While there are similarities between the Socratic idealized pursuit of the Beautiful and the master's earthly pursuit, Sullivan was no Platonist. Consider just his notion of truth. Yes, Sullivan contemplated an insensible inner world where one, in the words of Socrates, might "touch" the "truth." It was Sullivan's regularly expressed desire to understand "his inner and his outer world."³¹ He repeated variations of it so often that it occurs almost to the degree of Wright's obsessional ruminations over "sentimentality." He sought "the mystic spirit" that "might prove the key to turn a lock in a door within a wall which shut out the truth he was seeking—the truth which might dissolve for him the mystery that lay behind appearances."³² Penetrating through the image, behind appearances, Sullivan almost sounds like the Platonic lover of the beautiful who "does not touch an image, but true virtue, because he touches the truth."

But his truth was something altogether different. Sullivan called "abstract truth" a "mirage."[33] We know that he closely read *Thus Spoke Zarathustra;* and as evidenced throughout his writing, he agreed with Nietzsche's assessment that our truths are little more than the manifestations of our "will to power."[34] In the *Kindergarten Chats* he posits truth as an "infinite unfolding, unnumbered beginnings and expanding rebeginnings—truth out of luminous truth."[35] Careful to clarify it as a metaphysical distinction, he qualified it as "becoming." In *Democracy*, he rejected the Platonic legacy as it had evolved through Kant's notions of "pure reason," the "thing-in-itself," and what Sullivan characterized as the dualism of "mind" and "Cosmos."[36] Recall that he claimed that there was "no possibility" to "separate thought from the things we call physical. There is no dividing line—no threshold. There are merely phases of consciousness, and we choose to believe that in man consciousness reaches its highest manifestation and power."[37] And unlike Plato's notion of truth as expressed in the noumenal, unchanging, and eternal Forms, Sullivan sought a phenomenal truth that "lies everywhere." It "reveals itself where least expected." It is "manifold." It "appears in contradictions, in similitudes, in paradoxes."[38] Compared to transcendent truth, "the wayside weeds shame it. The real moonlight makes of it a will-o-the-wisp."[39] Indeed, he probably chuckled, twice, when he read Nietzsche's commandment that "we shall call every truth false which is not accompanied by at least one laugh."[40]

In terms that he regularly interchanged, sometimes calling it "reality," "life," or "nature," his truth manifested through the senses. It was much closer to a Romantic notion of the truth, that is, the truth that Schiller assigned to nature itself.[41] And like Schiller, Sullivan understood "civilization's" triumph of reason as one magnificent veil, as that which alienated humans from that natural truth. Sullivan in his cry for the awakening of "Plain Men!" and the "complete dissolution of the present scheme or plan of civilization" called for the "removal of all veils, which these have hung up to hide behind—All of them veils of words and ceremonials; of forms, customs and procedures."[42] For the architect of civilization, the great veils could only *seem* ample. Like the veil of appearances, they hid the "truth" that Sullivan was actively seeking.

Notice that Sullivan included "words" as part of the problem.[43] Similar to veils, he called them "masks" and understood them as impediments to that truth of reality. "Habit has accustomed you to this company of masks, beautiful some of them, repellent others, but you seldom draw aside a word-mask to see, for yourselves, the countenance of reality which it may both reveal and conceal."[44] He admitted that of "words in themselves he had come to form a passing aversion, since he had noted their tendency to eclipse the vibrant values of immediate reality. Therefore he preferred to think and feel and contemplate without the use of words."[45] In what he admitted was "for fun, for 'practice'" he engaged in a kind of apophatic meditation, a realm of pure affect, or *being* without words.[46] Repeating himself he wrote, "Indeed, one of his favorite pastimes was deliberately to think and feel and contemplate without the use of words, to create thus a wordless universe, with himself, silent, at the center of it all."[47]

Historian T. J. Jackson Lears indicates that this type of exercise was an example of a much broader late-nineteenth-century cultural interest in a variety of modes of access to alternate states of being, like dream, hypnosis, and trance.[48] Lears characterizes it as a kind of fin-de-siècle desire to withdraw. He describes it as "the desire to abandon autonomous selfhood and sink into a passive state of boundless union with all being."[49] He calls it the "contemplative mode" and sums it up as the "antimodern cult of inner experience" and the "lure of the premodern unconscious." As if describing Sullivan, Lears notes, "For many fin-de-siècle seekers, the contemplative mode promised refuge from the endless dualism of Victorian culture—subject and object, free will and determinism, mastery and submission—in a boundless union of self with all being."[50] While it is clear that Sullivan had many reasons for engaging it, Lears suggests that two of the most important sources were the paradigmatic naïve poet Goethe, in his call to "Live in the All," and the American transcendentalist Emerson, with his references to Oriental mysticism, Western idealism, and the deification of nature.[51] Again as if caricaturizing Sullivan, Lears sardonically describes it as the "union with the unconscious life of maples and ferns."[52] As "abandonment," an "unconscious," "passive," feeling, a kind of last ditch withdrawal from the grinding, evolutionary, late-nineteenth-century march of civilization, Lears sees it as "the 'feminine' side of the newly dominant achievement ethos [that] promised liberation from the systematic morality of the male bourgeoisie."[53] An escape from "civilization," it was the return to the premodern, the naïve, and it too was contaminated with gender.

In his *Civilization and Its Discontents* (1930), Freud wrote about the practice, giving it academic and medical authority—and a name. He called it the "oceanic feeling."[54] Originally understood as a means to religious enlightenment, Freud, the rational scientist, basically dismissed it. He admitted in self-centered, unscientific antipathy that "I cannot discover this 'oceanic feeling' in myself. It is not easy to deal scientifically with feelings."[55] From his Western, rationalist, ethnocentric vantage, Freud could not imagine a religious source that did not spring from the strongest of childhood needs, what he identified as "the need for a father's protection."[56] Viewing religion's generation through his own patriarchal and "scientific" lens, completely overlooking the oceanic feeling's shared root in the eastern half of the world's religious practices, and the possibility of maternal "protection," Freud categorically dismissed the oceanic feelings as "something like the restoration of limitless narcissism."[57]

Despite the questionable science, one might still give credence to Freud's final assessment. For he certainly invites these questions: Might the oceanic feeling be in fact just the indulgence of one's own limitless, that is, solipsistic narcissism? And is this not the same criticism of sentimentality in general? How different is Freud's categorization from the narcissistic emotional expression of Emmeline's "first love" beyond scope? How different is the oceanic feeling's engagement of a practice of endless feeling without words, from the extreme of Solomon's "emotional self-indulgence" and "an emotion for its own sake," both of which are the essential criticisms of sentimentality in general?[58] Freud might go further and ask how much Sullivan's escape into the "oceanic feeling," his tolerance of kitsch, the reading of de Kock, the appeal of Raguenet, and even his drinking were not just escapist mechanisms to indulge his own narcissism? Through Freud's clinical eye, despite its distorted biases, there is something almost legitimate in the critique and unseemly in the practice. Sullivan's indulgence in the oceanic feeling and sentimentality in general will always be vulnerable to the dissecting eye of reason.

But Sullivan was obviously not suggesting that architects withdraw into an eternal bliss of oceanic feeling. Perhaps in defensive anticipation of the criticism, he admitted it was "for fun, 'for practice.'" Yet it is clear that he tried to come to some understanding of the relationship between the human constructs of meaning, words, transcendence, and architecture, and his notions of reality, matter, immanence, and ornament. As if challenging any Cartesian ontology grounded in thought, his practice raises the question: Can one *be* without *articulated* thought, that is, without words? And what role might ornament play in *being*?

Sullivan offered poetry in lieu of the reasoning words of prose, exposition, logic, and philosophical dialectic.[59] He offered the poetics of art over objectifying reason, an aesthetic truth over a discursive truth, Nietzsche over Plato. He suggested that "poetry" brings us closer to reality, that "real-real of his diaphanous longings," than one can attain with words alone.

> Consider, now, poetry as apart from words and as resident in things, in thoughts, in acts. For if you persist in regarding print or language as the only readable or hearable things—you must, indeed, remain dull interpreters of the voices of Nature, and of the acts and thoughts of the men of the present and the past, in their varied, but fundamentally alike activities.[60]

He circumscribed words in the same way that he qualified mathematics, logic, and abstract truth. When he called abstract truth a "mirage," his concern was that it was a "working of the intellect detached from reality—therefore detached from life."[61] And "it was against what he deemed the impertinence of rigid logic that he rebelled, for once we assume an abstraction to be real, he thought, we lose our anchorage which is in the real."[62] Counter to a Platonic conception of the real, more like that of his contemporaries, the American Pragmatists, Sullivan needed that sensuous reality.

In his essay "What Is Architecture?: Study in the American People Today," Sullivan challenges his commonsensical reader to the value of poetry. Defending it over prose, he writes, "You say that poetry deals only with metaphor and figures of speech. What is your daily talk but metaphor and figures of speech! Every word, genuinely used, is a picture; whether used in conversation or in literary production. Mental life, indeed physical life, is almost entirely a matter of eyesight."[63] One hears the echoes of Nietzsche's famous argument where words are "arbitrary differentiations," "the copy in sound of a nerve stimulus," "transferred into an image: first metaphor." And "truths are illusions about which one has forgotten that this is what they are; metaphors which are worn out and without sensuous powers ...." And the abstract concept is "merely the residue of a metaphor."[64] Both men warned of the inadequacy of any language that has been removed from reality to convey something like abstract truth. Like Sullivan who argued that "habit has accustomed" us to this "company of masks," Nietzsche suggested that "after long usage" truths seem "fixed, canonical, and binding."[65] For both men, *repetition* offered a comforting yet unreliable mask in the reification of "truth." Sullivan argued instead for poetry, which "properly understood, means the most highly efficient form of mental eyesight. That is to say, it is that power of seeing and doing which reveals to Man's inner self the fullness and the subtle power of Life."[66]

Harries warns against the seduction of Nietzsche's famous quote. He writes, "How good this sounds! Science is moved into the vicinity of art, but is it not poorer, having traded colorful pictures for pale concepts? Also more dishonest, more ignorant, since it refuses to acknowledge that its reality is only the product of an artistic creating?"[67] In the substitution of poetry for objectifying reason, Harries implies that one might fail to recognize and value the success of science. And he further suggests that "it would be irresponsible not to affirm the liberating potential of objectifying reason."[68]

But Sullivan would have agreed. For one could not really argue that his intention was to usurp science with art. As revealed in his work, his library, and his writing, it is clear that he tried to apprehend reality through the lens of science as well.[69] With his partner, Adler, who did the engineering in the Auditorium, the two architects designed what would then have been the most technologically sophisticated theater in the world.[70] His library held multiple books of science and engineering above and beyond his ninety-six volumes of the popular *Van Nostrand Science Series*. And recall that the only two citations in his *System*, in jarring juxtaposition to the mystical imagery of the illustrated ornament, were Asa Gray's *School and Field Book of Botany*, and Edmund B. Wilson's *The Cell in Development and Heredity*, two foundational science books at the turn into the twentieth century.[71]

As if to explain the juxtaposition, in the last section of the *System* Sullivan provided a brief explanatory text, what he called "Interlude: The Doctrine of Parallelism." Here he claimed that it might just seem as if science and art are separate "parallel" activities that, in the Euclidian sense of the word, may never intersect. He countered with what he called "parallelism," a mystic domain where art, science, and philosophy "fuse as it were into a single vital impulse." He posited that the "theme is therefore exploited analytically and synthetically, differentially and integrally with the object ever in view of so humanizing of science that it energizes art and so exhibiting the masterful fluency of art that it in turn illuminates science."[72] While Sullivan learned, utilized, paid for, and participated in the rapid and voracious hunger for the truths of science, he recognized that in his ornament and in his architecture, as in life itself, they cannot and will not fully address the nature of love, the spiritual questions of myth, or the common ethos. Just like an insular life of poetry or "colorful pictures," to live an insular life through the clear monocular lens of science is an impoverished life. While he honored science he understood its limitations. To overcome them, he offered a realm where science "energizes" art and art "illuminates" science. For the student of architecture, it is evident in the synthesis of ornamentation and technology in his Auditorium.

In architecture that truth best materialized in his ornament, or as Wright aptly characterized it, Sullivan's "own soul's philosophy incarnate."[73] Understood poetically, it manifested "as apart from words and as resident in things, in thoughts, in acts." Or in ornament. As a variation of "of-the-thing-not-on-it," to be resident *in* things meant considerably more than the formal understanding of "plastic." Reconsider his solution to the problem. Recall that he abandoned historical imitation in the hopes of founding an autochthonous system of ornamentation that might help to articulate the common ethos of the young American nation. For him this was accomplished through faith in a kind of pantheistic character that he called the "Infinite Creative Spirit" or the "function of all functions." Specific to the nation, it was a *spiritual/poetic* articulation that he characterized under the expansive rubric, "democracy." Recognizing that the conception was vulnerable to the critical demands of objectifying reason, Sullivan privileged the expression of the emotions over rational thought. Consequently, unlike Wright, he continued to utilize *both* a rationally conceived image system of geometry and abstraction, *and* an emotive realism with alluring sensuality. For Sullivan, that emotional expression had to be foregrounded despite the fact that he knew that it held consequences for the body. Indeed, he intentionally doubled its corporeality. He knowingly purposed his ornament to be both the carnal image of an invisible truth and an emotional stimulus that would trigger a bodily reaction. Furthermore, he knew that that reaction entailed the erotic and gendered body with all of its commensurate cultural demands of propriety and "masculinity." Nonetheless he regularly referenced the erotic subtext at the same time that he "cherished" its potential for "femininity."

All of this was essential to sustain his need for the sympathetic and bodily exchange of *to give and to receive.*

Each of these significant moves stemmed from that philosophical core, and each might have seemed to be enough to solve the problem of ornament. But by the end of the nineteenth century, Sullivan knew better. Neither alone nor in total were any of these adequate solutions. He was no fool.[74] He knew that it would never be enough to simply declare that *he* had finally articulated a common ethos, that it had magically emerged in *his* ornamentation, and that everyone had to believe in it. For Sullivan knew that in an industrial and enlightened era, when the gains of "civilization" were measured through technological advancement and rational thought, the essential "truth" of *any* object, that is, its ontology in and of itself and in relation to all else, was properly determined by objectifying reason. Regardless of how hard anyone might try, the mute, brute matter of ornament could never be more than just *objectified* matter manipulated into an *image*. It could never be "living." For that to change, ornament's fundamental truth, *and the truth of the matter that made it*, had to be reconsidered.

And that was Sullivan's primary intention in his *System*. Recall that there, on the *first* page of his *final* document on ornamentation, in the "Prelude," the text collapsed under the withering demands for clarity and logic. As prose, it failed to stand up to the rigors of proper exposition. It was just too sketchy. But if we were to reinterpret it in Sullivan's more privileged parlance of poetry, as a kind of prose poem, it deserves another look. Moreover, we now have a broader framework within which to interpret it.

When Sullivan referenced both Schopenhauer's "will to live" and Nietzsche's "will to power," he identified the source of ornament as coming from an instinctual and nonverbal drive as the expression of the will. But like the oceanic feeling, still fully embodied as a kind of *embodied will*, this ornament must be construed as antipodal to Schopenhauer's desire to be delivered from "servitude to the will." Instead, based heavily on his close reading of *Zarathustra*, Sullivan must have understood it in the terms of Nietzsche's question about the locus of beauty: "Where is beauty? Where I must will with all my will; where I want to love and perish that an image may not remain a mere image. Loving and perishing: that has rhymed for eternities. The will to love, that is to be willing also to die."[75]

Willing with all his will, Nietzsche posits a conception whereby the objectified matter utilized in the construction of an image, like ornament, no longer remains "a mere image." Situated at the melting point where the warmth of love dissolves any last defense against the will to live, he fully cedes to that eternity without words, the infinite nothingness of death. He contends that acts of will, to power, to love, *and to perish*, transmute the fundamental truth of matter as such.[76] In so doing he offered a wholly different conception of beauty, being, *and time*, from that which Plato posited in *The Symposium*. He privileged the particular, ephemeral emotions as effusions of the individual will over the universal, eternal ideals as the contemplations of rational thought. Overcoming the desire for immortality, Sullivan must also *will to die*. And then ornament may not remain a mere image.

Harries provides some context. He reminds us that "not only are we humans vulnerable and mortal, but we know of our mortality, know that all that now is and all that still awaits us will some day be past."[77] Acknowledging Nietzsche, he posits "a will to power in human beings coupled with the recognition that we never have enough power to secure our existence, that we are subject to time, vulnerable and mortal."[78] And he reminds us that Nietzsche characterized the typical human response as the "will's ill will against time."[79] The Platonic dream of "forever" is evidence of that "ill will." At the revealed nexus of our individual finite reality and intuited sense of infinity realized through the seemingly unchanging human spirit, Harries situates a desire for immortality and its correlate, what he alliteratively calls the "terror of time." He speaks of what he calls a "perennial Platonism:" that recurring expression through the history of art and architecture of the Platonic desire for "forever," where the conception of beauty is understood "in opposition to time."[80] In contrast, Nietzsche suggests that beauty will-fully cedes to it. Pointing directly at Plato, he dismisses Socratic "contemplation" of the beautiful with a gendered characterization as "emasculated leers."[81] Instead, he embraced both time *and death*.

When Sullivan read *Zarathustra*, this particular passage must have resonated as more than important—and more than vaguely familiar. Ten years earlier he had already surrendered his heart to Whitman's *Leaves of Grass*.[82] There the poet described his "Leaves," his poetry, or as Whitman might have construed Nietzsche's terms, his *image*, as "tomb-leaves, body-leaves, growing up above me, above death."[83] Similarly to Nietzsche, Whitman, in his "Calamus 2," correlated his art with beauty, love, and death. He reflected that those very leaves "are very beautiful to me, you faint-tinged roots—you make me think of Death, / Death is beautiful from you—(what indeed is beautiful, except Death and Love?)" In his own way, Whitman, like Nietzsche, held that the image is essentially transformed through the will to perish. "Indeed, O Death, I think now these leaves mean precisely the same as you mean;" and later, "That you beyond them, come forth to remain, the real reality." Like the will to perish, Whitman claimed, "Through me shall the words be said to make death exhilarating, Give me your tone therefore, O Death, that I may accord with it."[84]

Sullivan read both men—and he concurred.

It was only shortly after he had read the *Leaves*, yet still before *Zarathustra*, that he had composed his "Essay on Inspiration." Adding to this collective *amor fati*, he too sang "To death then, hear a hymn."[85] Like Whitman's "accord," Sullivan sought to reconcile his art with that "sweet oblivion."[86] For inspiration he suggested that the artist cede to death through "languorous compassion."[87] He aligned himself, and his architecture, with the rhythms of nature: death, birth, life, and death; and that alignment occurred through what he characterized as the "inscrutable" "serenity" that comes "with the help of exquisitely vital sympathy."[88] He, like Whitman and Nietzsche, each in his own way, embraced the temporality of time and the infinity of death. And each suggested that the locus of his art fell at the nexus of the will to the tender emotions (Nietzsche's love, Whitman's love, and Sullivan's compassion and sympathy of which he said "You may even call it Love.") and the will to die.[89] There, finally, at the very effusion of three of the tender emotions of *sentimentality*, "an image may not remain a mere image" and ornament may not remain mere objectified matter.

From his "well-worn" copies of *Leaves of Grass* and *Zarathustra*, Sullivan partook of this alternative ontology. He understood it through Nietzsche's conception of the will to power. It is most evident in the Prelude. Even when his subject was the seemingly inert matter of ornament, he began with a living organism, the seed germ. More than a curious poetic trope, from the beginning he insisted that ornament is alive. When describing this source of life, he stated that "the Germ is the real thing; the seat of identity. Within its delicate mechanism lies the will to power: the function which is to seek and eventually to find its full expression in form." In these two pivotal sentences, Sullivan poetically summarized his thesis and his affirmation of Nietzsche. No longer are we to understand "function" in the architectural and determinist terms of "utilitarian requirement." More like that by which a thing perpetually becomes, recall that it is a spiritual character, the "function of all functions," the "Infinite Spirit," that which manifests ultimately into a particular form, *or ornament*. And here its locus is "the seat of identity." With a colon, he completely qualified that "function" as the "will to power." Positing a final and absolute break from being, he offered instead Nietzsche's endless overcoming of the will, or becoming, as an alternative to the ontology of ornament as such.

For the balance of the *System*, Sullivan continued to expound upon this alternative truth. His poetic essay "The Inorganic and the Organic," what he called a "brief, *impressionistic* sketch [emphasis added]," can now be seen as consistent with this exploration. Having rejected the mind/world dualism of Kant with its privileged position of the human mind from within that duality, Sullivan, after Whitman, dismantled the rigid hierarchical relations between humans and objects, and objects and objects, in favor of a kind of consubstantiation with all things. By placing himself in the world sympathetically, he inhabited it, not objectively but reciprocally, emotively, as between subjects. Ontologically, all objects, while still individuated, remain on an equal footing: a world of collective animation and subjectivity. More than simply changing definitions, he posits an alternative way of being. Moreover, in each case, the definitive locus of life itself is blurred, particularly in ornament.

Inhabiting the world subjectively, as between subject and subjects, Sullivan found ornament as the architectural medium for its highest realization. It effectively mediates between the living, willing, individuated subject, that is the human, and the visible and invisible world beyond.

Accessed not through the prose of reason but through the poetry of the imagination, it is a world that transgresses transcendental truth with an immanent and paradoxical truth. Sullivan's ornament is a vibrant realm without words, a living ornament where dust is no longer dust. In his fluid poetics of protean individuality and subjectivity, like the charmed jewelry, underwear, notes, slippers, or muffler that remain after the loss of the beloved, or perhaps even the patterns in their dust, ornament offers a weak *lifeline* between this evanescent world of meaning, significance, and *logos*, and another of raw immanence, animality, and affect—that oceanic world of water in water, unknowing, life and death. Ornament wills subjectivity. In the simplest and most naïve way, in its constitution of the subject, Sullivan breathed life. It doesn't matter. In the oscillation between the two he constituted that electric frisson of life and death, and he *knew* it. In the naïve yet optimistic molding of earth's expectant dust, Sullivan transubstantiated it.

—

Wright's portrayal of Sullivan raised the question of whether he actually saw the master. Or did he blind himself to the truth of the man because he so much wanted the counsel and love of his own teacher of wisdom, that is, his own Socrates? Consider that it was Wright who provided us with the description of their first meeting. From the penetrating glance, the erotic subtext, the confusion between Raguenet and Jones, and the embarrassing issue of dandruff, Wright, whether he was conscious of it or not, certainly saw Sullivan. He just could not be him. He understood the master's mode of being in the world as approaching a truth that he longed for. It manifested in what he called a "finer beauty." He knew it was within himself, the most sentimental person he ever knew. But he repressed it.

Even though he willingly characterized Sullivan's ornament in terms of beauty, Wright was not so quick to characterize his own work in those terms. He admitted to a personal difficulty with it. He alluded that some of that difficulty came from his family upbringing. With startling capitalization that again suggests Plato's spiritual "Beauty," he wrote that his "family did not so well know the truth of BEAUTY. These valley-folk feared beauty, seeing in it a probable snare for unwary feet, and making the straight way their own feet might mark in the snow less admirable in their own sight and as an example for irresponsible youth."[90]

Wright was making at least two references here. For his family, stout descendants of New England Puritanism, an obvious "snare for unwary feet" would have been the carnal beauty of the flesh. But he used the phrase "in the snow" to qualify that notion with a secondary reference. He was referring to the childhood story from the very first page of his autobiography. There he described a scene where, on the morning of a new-fallen snow, as a boy of nine he was taken for a walk with another of his mother's brothers. Uncle

John had determined to show the lad "how to go!"[91] Tracking a perfectly straight line, the two ascended the sloping fields. Mitten in glove they climbed until Wright, overcome by the seductive beauty of the "naked" weeds to his left and to his right, their "sharp shadows laced in blue arabesque beneath," broke free.[92] On his own, he ran merrily behind, drawing a "wavering, searching, heedful line" from one bronze, "pod-topped" weed to the tall golden lines of another. In his arms, he gathered huge bejeweled clusters of "beads on stems and then beads and tassels on more stems." He was enraptured by their beauty. When he proudly caught up to his uncle at the summit, he was met with a frown of reproach. The uncle turned and pointed to his own arrow straight track through the snow. The two then looked at the nephew's track that "embroidered" the straight line "like some free, engaging vine as it ran back and forth across it." The uncle pointed at it with "gentle reproof."[93] "Uncle John's meaning was plain—NEITHER TO RIGHT NOR TO THE LEFT, BUT STRAIGHT IS THE WAY."[94] Wright returned his gaze to his armful of weeds, his "treasure." He was "troubled." He knew "something was left out."[95]

Wright offered this story as the "Prelude" to his autobiography. It is rich in affective content. The boy is described as "eager," "trembling," "flushed," "glowing," "troubled," and "shamed." His line is "wavering," "searching," and "heedful." In contrast, the uncle is "fixed," "intent," "possessed," "strong," "satisfied," "stern," and "purposeful." His line is "straight," "mindful," and "heedless." Here Wright laid the groundwork for an argument that permeates the entire autobiography. When he stated that beauty might make "the straight way their own feet might mark in the snow less admirable in their own sight," he illustrated more than the reproof of succumbing to the lure of erotic beauty. It was the reproof of experiential beauty in general. The straight line was "how to go!" In this story Wright graphically sketched the difference between his Uncle John's understanding of beauty and his own childlike understanding as the difference between the long straight ascending line and the meandering sinuous line. And like Sullivan's comparison with transcendent truth, even "the wayside weeds shame it."

At the conclusion of the first edition of his autobiography, Wright offered a "Postlude" where, like the covers of his book, he reflected back upon that walk in the snow. There on the last page, he finally answered what that "something" was that was "left out."[96] Calling it "the order of change," and a "natural order," he described it, still with some qualified uncertainty, as "well loved" and "the principle, or is it the very quality of life itself—vaguely felt by the boy as 'left out' in the early lesson." And "so far as change is by law of natural growth, change is beneficent. Organic change is not chance. No menace." The 66-year-old Wright, looking back over his finite life, sought to reconcile himself with the infinity of death. He calmly reflected, "Our life on earth should be blessed, not antagonized by this beneficence of natural growth ... death a crisis of growth [his ellipsis]." In words that could have been written by Sullivan (both men used the term "growth" interchangeably for "life"), with the themes of life and death consistent with a natural and therefore beneficent order, Wright offered the vicissitudes of "Life," to include death, as the alternative to changeless "abstract truth." He wrote, "Life has been as it will be, a changing test of eternal principle."[97] In words that echo a phrase he attributed to Plato, "the eternal idea of the thing," Wright posited the meander of "Life" against the straight line of the Platonic "eternal principle."[98] While he did not explicitly state it, his implied message was clear. As his mode of being, Wright constructed a worldview that upheld an "order of change," to include ephemeral experience and its finality, death, over the Platonic eternal truth.[99] Rejecting the eternal and disembodied spiritual Beauty delineated by Socrates in *The Symposium*, Wright ceded to the mortality of the flesh as "organic" and therefore "beneficent" "change." Moreover, he equated it graphically with the meandering sinuous line.

Like Plato, Wright explicitly posited a correspondence between geometry and time where the former is construed to be in opposition to the latter. In contrast, the meander embraces time. This idea, that geometry approximates a timeless world of the spirit, has endured across the history of Western art and architecture. Harries characterizes it as another manifestation of "perennial Platonism," with its correlate, the "terror of time."[100] He indicates that it "surfaces again and again in the course of the history of art and architecture." After doggedly interrogating its persistence he concludes that "we are dealing here with aesthetic preferences that cannot be dismissed as just another fashion. The appeal of the language of geometry transcends particularities of time and of place. [...] The very temporality of our existence endows geometric forms with their special aura."[101]

Even if one were to challenge Harries's argument, he leaves us with this nagging question: Where did Wright really stand in all of this? In his ornamentation up to and through the Midway Gardens, with its progressive evolution away from the free-form line of realism, to abstraction, to geometry, and pure form, we should ask again, was Wright after that "timeless realm of the spirit?" What about after the gardens? Did he then, as stated in his Postlude, seek an "order of change" as manifested in the meander? Or was it something other than this binary suggests?

As Wright has repeatedly shown, for him, things are never that simple. In "The Japanese Print," written *before* he started the Midway Gardens, he indicated:

> Geometry is the grammar, so to speak of the form. It is its architectural principle. But there is a psychic correlation between the geometry of form and our associated ideas which constitutes its symbolic value. There resides always a certain "spell-power" in any geometric form which seems more or less a mystery, and is, as we say, the soul of the thing.[102]

He added that any geometric form carries associative content that has the potential to "suggest certain human ideas, moods and sentiments—

as for instance: the circle, infinity; the triangle, structural unity; the spire, aspiration; the spiral, organic progress; the square, integrity." These "ideas, moods and sentiments" as both ideational *and emotive content* are constitutive of this "spell-power."[103] For Wright, the Japanese artist was the master at both grasping "underneath" for the geometry of the form and evoking the "spell-power" of the geometry itself.[104] This power he called "psychic" or "psychological," and he again linked it back to Western thought with "what Plato called (with reason, we see, psychological if not metaphysical) the 'eternal idea of the thing.'"[105]

Wright's conflation of Platonic thought with a Japanese mastery of "spell power" is problematic.[106] For one, his geometry no longer strives for purity. Wright intentionally "mixed" it with the "sentiments," *the emotions*. Conversely, how might Japanese artists have understood his characterization of their work as the "eternal idea of the thing," that is, through a Platonic understanding of being and time? The question is critical due to the fact that at the end of the nineteenth century most scholars recognized that traditional Japanese conceptions differed widely from Plato's. Wright's contemporary, the Japanese philosopher Kitarō Nishida (1870–1945), compared the two and made some telling conclusions. While my summary that follows is based on Nishida's, both suffer gross cultural generalizations and oversimplification. I include them only to frame Wright's intentions and the problems that arise when synthesizing the two different conceptions.

Nishida summarized that unlike the "Greeks," who addressed the problem of "being" through objective reason, the "special characteristic" of the Japanese "consisted of being an emotional culture."[107] He described it as "a culture of pure feeling" and noted that emotions "can be thought to be predominantly temporal in sensibility." They have "a temporal flow."[108] Consequently, traditional Japanese culture "did not look to the eternal beyond. It moved immanently from thing to thing, without transcending time." Neither of being nor becoming, it conceived the "ground of the world" "in the direction of its temporal determination."[109] For Nishida, that "entails the idea of nothingness," that is, "non-being."[110] He stated that when time is understood as

> the determination of absolute non-being or nothingness, it must be linear; it must move from instant to instant. Here a true "momentalism" can be conceived. Time must always be considered from the present—that is, from the moving present, the self-determining present. This is precisely the reason that it can be regarded as the determination of non-being.[111]

While it seemed as if he privileged a Platonic notion, Wright simultaneously seemed to have synthesized some Japanese notions as well. For even beyond the inclusion of the emotion-contaminated "spell power," it is clear that, at least later in his life, his "order of change" was less Platonic than Japanese. Additionally, while reflecting back upon his turbulent life, he wrote,

> Day by day I enjoy more the eternity that is now. At last I am realizing that eternity *is* now. And that eternity only divides yesterday from tomorrow. It is now as though the mind itself at times were some kind of recording film in endless reel, to go on perfecting and projecting pictures endlessly, seldom if ever the same as the moment changes.[112]

As if looking at an infinity of discrete *moments*, Wright offered a film analogy that suggests the Japanese conception of time, "a true 'momentalism,'" where "time must always be considered from the present."

Wright followed his conception with two additional sentences: "But the same scene and scheme may show itself from infinitely varying angles as the point of view changes if informing principle, the *impulse* living in it all, stays in place. Else the impotence of confusion, the chaos of madness: vain imprisonment in the Past."[113] To his variation Wright again added some essential and stable "informing principle," an eternal "*impulse* living in it all" that "stays in place." Despite his seeming desire for a Japanese "momentalism" and its predicate nonbeing, he maintained a kind of ground of all being. With its multiple contradictions, one can only smile at his unwittingly ironic defense against "chaos," "confusion," and "madness." With still more irony, we might say that Wright portrayed a Platonic understanding of the thing through geometry that is both universal and eternal ... for *the moment*. As if intuiting the incommensurability of the Platonic conception of being and time, and the ephemeral reality of "Life," Wright sought to reconcile the two through the emotions of "spell power" and a Japanese understanding of "momentalism" and nonbeing. And despite the leaps of logic, I am unable to categorically dismiss his position. Indeed, it has a poetic ring of paradoxical truth.

While Wright was working on the Imperial Hotel, the Japanese ambassador to the United States gave him a copy of Kakuzo Okakura's delicate exegesis of the tea ceremony, *The Book of Tea*.[114] With its brief introduction into the Chinese mystical philosophy of Taoism and the Japanese meditation of Zen, Okakura offered an alternative to the Platonic conception of truth and a way to perhaps better understand Wright's comments. In his descriptions of Taoism and the writings of Lao Tzŭ, Okakura introduced them by saying, "They spoke in paradoxes, for they were afraid of uttering half-truths."[115] After elaborating on a philosophy that generally privileged the relative over the absolute, he offered what might be construed as a variation of Wright's "eternity is now." For, "It is in us that God meets with Nature, and yesterday parts from to-morrow. The Present is the moving Infinity, the legitimate sphere of the Relative. Relativity seeks Adjustment; Adjustment is Art. The art of life lies in a constant readjustment to our surroundings."[116]

For Wright, these words must have surely resonated. It has long been recognized that he had an extraordinary ability to integrate and synthesize the ideas, imagery, and work of others into his architecture. As if coming from the Freudian realm of dreams, historian Vincent Scully astutely characterized it as "condensation."[117] Commensurate with that ability was an eye-popping way of qualifying, or simply overlooking, the fallacies and contradictions in his arguments. He hedged his positions, ignored the facts, and walked away from his lies, all in the tenacious, and by all indications *sincere* pursuit of what he believed was some greater "truth."[118] While he regularly and substantively engaged the Platonic themes at the limits of reason, Wright danced across the pesky incommensurables of their logical limits. Nonetheless, in his necessarily finite work he made declarations, *for now*, and then moved on. In all fairness, we might remind ourselves that Wright's medium was not the singular logic of philosophy but the manifold poetry of architecture. And as evinced in his work, we must also concede to its convincing power. Whether we like it or not, seductively swirling through the fractured geometry of those Midway Gardens of pleasure, convolutes the apparition, "eternity is now."[119]

In the end, for truth, *for principles*, Wright posited a Platonic conception through paradox as fractured haiku.

Even though he condensed his Western heritage with his Eastern experience, he nonetheless privileged Japan. Consistent with his understanding of Japanese culture and its architecture as still grounded in autochthonous, viable, life traditions, and his derogation of the contemporaneous West because it was not, he believed that the Japanese artist held a more organic, comprehensive, and intuited grasp of the relationship between an ideal in geometry and nature itself. Coming from his Japanese understanding and his own sentimentality, he recognized that that grasp was realized through the emotions.

In a particularly poignant conclusion to "The Japanese Print," Wright summarized: "Let me illustrate once more. To know a thing, what we can really call knowing, a man must first love the thing, which means that he can sympathize vividly with it."[120] As if he were again referring to *The Symposium* and Plato's "eternal idea of the thing," Wright argued that in order to truly know it, in Plato's terms, to "touch truth," we must begin with the drive of love. Suggesting a conflation with the influence of Sullivan, he added: "which means that he can sympathize vividly with it."[121] Returning to a closer reading of the essay reveals his repeated emphasis upon sympathy as the necessary antecedent to some knowledge of the thing itself.[122] Together with love, these two emotions constitute the very medium through which one accesses that knowledge. Eschewing any understanding of eternality and truth, which is accessed solely through rational thought, he argued in favor of bridging the infinite transcendent idea of the *thing* with the finite ephemeral reality of the quotidian *things* of "Life" through an effusion of love and sympathy. Hoping to overcome the leaps of his logic and warrant the paradox, *he appealed to the weak and ceding tender emotions*. As such, Wright essentially argued that the ontology of the thing, as a construct of knowledge, indeed, as proximity to truth itself, occurs through "sentimentality" in the commendatory sense. Relying on his Japanese understanding for that reconciliation, he ceded to his own sentimental nature. His inner conflict plays out beautifully in this elegant essay while it simultaneously suggests a deep insight into the understanding of being.

But as evidenced in his practice of ornament, at least for the duration of the time period of this study, it becomes more and more apparent that Wright would not or could not cede to the tender emotions of love and sympathy. *Especially love.* Though he initially might have endorsed their appeal in his essay, his contemporaneous ornament belies the feeling. His later writing does too. For Wright grew to share his family's difficulty with the love of beauty. Despite his claim that he embroidered the meander across the snow and ceded to an order of change, as the adult-architect he proudly drafted his Uncle John's righteous straight line. He relied on his "trusty T. square and aspiring triangle," for an ornamentation of abstraction and geometry. As much as he waxed reflective about the meandering vicissitudes of "life," in the evolution of that practice he increasingly opted for the reductive Socratic rectitude of geometry.[123] Whatever tender spells its power evoked, he checked by his continued repression of sentimentality, in both the pejorative and commendatory senses.

In a strange statement made about the rearing of his children, he disclosed his difficulty with the sentimental love for the beautiful. He wrote that "the 'father' in the architect took the children's future to heart in that I wanted them to grow up in beautiful surroundings. I intended them all to be infected by 'a love for the beautiful.' I then called it so in spite of growing prejudice against the sentimental."[124]

Overlooking the fact that the gender specific "'father'" is in quotation marks, and Wright's questionable performance of the role is again qualified, his increasingly negative feelings are evident in his claim of a "growing prejudice against the sentimental." Also placing "'a love for the beautiful'" in quotation marks, he indicated that he had "then called it so," suggesting that by the time he wrote his autobiography he no longer did. In this terse statement Wright *recognizes the correlation between sentimentality and the Platonic discourse of love and beauty, and admits to silencing it precisely because of that correlation*. With the shared basis in the tender emotion of love, he offered a very qualified understanding of "beauty" as something less than desirable. The "love" of beauty was too close to the "love" of sentimentality. Moreover, he revealed his ambivalence by qualifying that "love" as something that "infects."

At the same time that Wright described Sullivan's ornament as successful in the Platonic terms of love and beauty, in his growing prejudice against sentimentality, he progressively separated the two within his own work. It would almost be enough to suggest that he learned this from his family. But he was also participating in what Harries identifies as another aspect of the aesthetic approach: the divorce of love from beauty. Recall that the approach posits an "ideal of the art-work as an autonomous aesthetic object, serving neither church, nor state, nor love, serving only art."[125] In *The Broken Frame* (1989), Harries tracks the divorce from its foundations in *The Symposium*, through Baumgarten (who saw the beautiful "as sensible perfection"), Kant (who saw "the beautiful as object of an entirely disinterested satisfaction"), and again in Schopenhauer (who saw the beautiful as "the object of pure knowing").[126] Each was an incremental step of purification ever more grounded in reason. Each further repressed the emotion of love, consequently severing it from beauty. And Wright shared in it. Recall that when he sought to overcome the sentimentality of the popular late-nineteenth-century realism, he cited for his examples works of kitsch: "Breaking Home Ties" and the Rogers Group. He responded by resorting to abstraction, geometry, and pure form to effectively repress the excessive and empty effusion of love. Attuned to the tenor of the times, he compared himself to the European artistic vanguard, claiming he led the way. When he repressed that love and severed it from beauty, he knew he was participating in the broader aesthetic movement. And while he didn't call it as such, in architecture, he *led* the "aesthetic approach."

If we consider his ornamentation one last time, we find that so much of his intention complied with its demands. While he, like Sullivan, erased any hint of that reflective, sentimental ornamentation that imitated previous historical styles, Wright went so much further. In his first and most obvious move, he privileged abstraction and geometry over Sullivan's perpetuation of realism with its sinuous line. Commensurate with its removal, Wright effectively erased that language of ornament that was expressed in the identification of things. He replaced it with the language of abstracted form and the properties of things. And while he never completely removed narrative content from his ornament, he thoroughly mastered the command for "of-the-thing-not-on-it" in the development of his "integral ornament." In his most comprehensive move, he thoroughly incorporated ornament into the materiality, techniques, and construction of the building, and he executed the radical shift from "structure ornamented" to "ornament structuralized." Ornament went from its traditional scalar and syntactical arrangement *on* its bearer to *is* the bearer. And finally, in his most iconic works from the latter half of his career he took the then radical step and removed all surface ornamentation entirely.

With each choice he strengthened the measurable, verifiable purification of objectifying reason. Far more consistent with a Platonic ontology, he privileged the eternal, universal, and transcendent truths of the mind as grounded in rational "principles" over the temporal carnal body, the dangerous irrational emotions, and the unprovable spirit. As if listening to Kant, Schopenhauer, and the European vanguard, Wright leaned evermore toward the object of an entirely disinterested satisfaction and pure knowing. He removed the finite and individual story in favor of the infinite and transcendent idea. Each choice was an incremental shift from a subjective narrative content to an objective abstractive content, and each was instrumental in repressing and severing love from beauty. By leading that vanguard, he ceded to the demands of the aesthetic approach.

Consonant with his own internalized demands, he simultaneously capitulated to his Puritan family, the reality principle, and his own sense of guilt. As if responding to the social requirements of a constructed masculinity, the terror of time, and the erotic adventure in *his* mind, Wright the adult, in submissive compliance with Uncle John's admonition, followed the tracks of the arrow-straight line. He repressed the "shamed" emotions of his childhood for the "fixed," "intent," "possessed," "strong," "satisfied," "stern," "straight," "mindful," "heedless," and "purposeful" reasoning of the adult. He conflated the demands of *both* the broader aesthetic approach and his own upbringing. Finally able to overcome Sullivan's hungry and interested gaze of desire, he effectively mastered the problem of ornament by resolving it into its universal "purity." Metaphorically, Wright took the few remains of his master, the individual man whom he loved, his dandruff, his "dust," and turned it into its universal components: protein molecules and carbon atoms. Love evanesced in a cloud of just dust.

And Wright knew it. He knew, just as Harries would warn many years later, that in choosing reason, ornament could not rise to the status of the autonomous art object brought about by the aesthetic approach. It could not be a self-sufficient presence. By definition, ornament must serve its bearer. In his attempt to thereby save it from its assured death caused by its essential illogicality, Wright took a 180-degree turn and fully incorporated it *into* its bearer. It was a deft and fatal move. For we must surely ask again and again: when ornament went from a *thing* to "*of-the-thing*-not-on-it," what changes were wrought in its ontological status? When it went from ornament as a thing to "ornament" as the properties of things, from ornament to materiality and construction, and from ornament to ornament bearer, was it really still ornament?

Returning once again to the introductory essay that Wright wrote for the Wasmuth publication, one finds an uncanny and correctly described "ornament" as unique and different from his description of "integral ornament." Immediately after his first definition of ornament structuralized, he wrote: "What ornamentation may be found added purely as such in this structure is thus a makeshift or confession of weakness or failure. Where the warp and woof of the fabric do not yield sufficient incident or variety, it is seldom patched on. Tenderness has often to be sacrificed to integrity."[127]

Wright suggested that there is another type of ornamentation: that which is "added purely as such." Different from "integral ornament," which is "conceived in the organic sense," this second type is *added* to the structure *purely* as *ornament in and of itself*, suggesting a kind of "pure application" of "pure ornament." And unlike integral ornament, which Wright showed to be strong and fully integrated into the building, he found pure ornament to be a "confession of weakness or failure" and that it was therefore "seldom patched on." Recalling the ornamentation of the Imperial Hotel or the Hollyhock House, for Wright, it was better to be "sacrificed." He then made a metonymic shift and called it "tenderness." As if expiating the god of reason he concluded that "tenderness has often to be sacrificed to integrity." Ornament, purely as such, is sacrificed. And we face that same question: Is "integral ornament" the same as *pure* ornament? Or, is "integral ornament" still ornament? Avoiding another semantic shift, Wright essentially said no to both. They are two different *things*. In the turn to "integral ornament," he removed pure ornament, effectively killing it. In his terms, ornament, purely as such, is the tender detail sacrificed on the altar of reason.

—

As pathetic as Wright's ornament "purely as such" sounds, Sullivan must have agreed with the characterization, particularly the "confession of weakness or failure." And surely he recognized it in his own work. For if one were to evaluate Sullivan's ornamentation in *rational* terms, especially when compared to Wright's, it *is* a "confession of weakness or a failure." And Sullivan knew that too. In contrast to Wright's objectifying shift, Sullivan's ornament, while still based on Haeckel, Gray, Wilson, and the sciences, is a much more intentional, alchemical, vitalizing, emotive effusion of the individual will that is unavoidably incommensurable. Despite Sullivan's rhetoric, it was surely evident even to him that every empirical test will reveal that the attic frieze of the Wainwright Building (Figure 2.5) is still terracotta, just burnt clay, just dust. And every logical analysis of his ornament must eventually confront that threshold where the master disappears into that inner world foreclosed to reason. His ornament always falls beyond and outside the discourse of pure reason. It is always contingent, peripheral, and excess to the pursuit of pure knowledge. While it can be appreciated for many reasons, it will always be recognized as a *rational weakness* and a *logical failure*. And in a roundabout way, that was obviously his point. For he recognized that the immanence of that inner world, linked with sensuous reality, still disclosed an eternally veiled and unknowable realm inhabited by the gods of immortality, truth, and the good. Rather than the self-blinkering and sad poverty of postponing or forgetting as necessitated by objectifying reason, Sullivan reconciled himself to that realm—*now*. While he knew that as a simple breach of logic he could not cede to the illogicality of his ornament through reason, he could through the emotions. He knew too that it could only occur through a specific subset of the emotions, that is, those of *cession*, those of weakness, those that willfully surrender to the inherent irrationality, illogic, and demands of the heart—the *tender* emotions of sentimentality.

In architecture, a construct inescapably of reason and artifice, that particular cession occurs through the flawed mode of sentimentality. As that state of "feeling in idea," sentimentality conjoins the tender emotions in thought and reconciles that thought to its own irrationality. And in architecture ornament is its purest condensation. This is ornament, or in Wright's term, ornament "purely as such." Through sentimentality, Sullivan reconciled himself to that realm in an immense sacrifice of time, material, energy, and cost that would be comparable to the most religiously devoted, all the while knowing and hence admitting to its rational impossibility. It is the admission, or in Wright's liturgical terms, the "confession," of its own inadequacy. In order to partake, one must confess to that inadequacy. Pure ornament is simultaneously the recognition of some incommensurable belief, the admission of its incommensurability, and the confession of its failure while nonetheless squandering time, energy, and money in the reconciliation of that belief through the heart. Pure ornament confesses, sacrifices, and redeems through the offering of the tender emotions. In a double-edged misreading of Wright's own statement, Sullivan too, would say yes, "Tenderness has often to be sacrificed to integrity." It is the very character of pure ornament itself. But unlike Wright's reasoned sacrifice that killed it, Sullivan's pathetic sacrifice, at the very embrace of the *will to love* and the *will to perish*, like the "purest" of religious sacrifice, transubstantiated it. Now revitalized, ornament purely as such is never dust but incommensurable "dust."

And Wright knew *all* of this too. After all, he defined it for us. When he developed integral ornament, his primary intention was to overcome sentimentality. If he was as successful as he believed, then it follows, in his terms, that the definitive quality of ornament "purely as such" is its inherent sentimentality. Indeed, he called it "tenderness." When he identified the tender emotions of love and sympathy as the medium to the knowledge of the thing itself, he likewise identified them as the medium to ornament as well. But his inner conflicts prohibited him. He had to kill it. While the two architects made radically different interpretations of ornamentation, they both understood that the practice is always a sentimental practice. For it is only through the appeal to the tender emotions that we can even begin to understand the transubstantiation of brute matter. Otherwise it is just decoration—or burnt clay.

This would certainly seem to imply that of the two, from their ornamental work alone, Sullivan had better helped to articulate a common ethos. To be sure, they both believed that they had.[128] But was he in fact successful? Criticized as idiosyncratic and too individualistic his ornamentation raises questions as to what constitutes a *common* ethos, especially in a democracy that celebrates the unique *individual*.[129] With no majority religious faith and no aristocracy crowned by the gods, who or what establishes commonality in a plurality? Referencing Nietzsche, Lukács, and Broch, Harries raises serious doubts for that potential under the contemporary Western politics and economics of democracy and capitalism. He indicates: "Inseparable from the ethical function of ornament is its essentially public character. If it is to articulate the ethos of a society, ornament may not be the property of an individual or a particular group. Like ordinary language, it must be shared by the society in its entirety."[130] Was it enough that Sullivan was just another expression in what was basically a highly individualistic American understanding of "democracy," what Whitman called "perfect individualism?"[131] Like Sullivan's skepticism of language itself, is it simply reified through repetition by others? Does that still honor all individuals? Can we determine his success? How would we even *know*? Or is it only determined through *feeling*? Indeed, are we, today, not also at risk of evaluating everything through the lens of the aesthetic approach? Must we not be sentimental to even share in an ethos? Does that sharing not also require surrendering to our own unknowing? Is it not an act of faith? Or love? Or sympathy?

On the opening night of the Auditorium theater, Sullivan's ornamentation was resoundingly praised, suggesting perhaps a common language. It became so recognizable and renowned that the adjective "Sullivanesque" has been used ever since.[132] But that same ornamentation didn't last much longer than its creator. As a commonality, it is evident in the work of a few stalwart disciples like Purcell and Elmslie. But their firm folded even before Sullivan's death. For his ornamentation was soon overrun by the relentless march of the progress of reason and the aesthetic approach. Did it fail to articulate that common ethos? Or was it just too emotional, too feminine, too erotic, too individualistic, or as Wright suggested just too sentimental for the twentieth-century American?

10

Epilogue: When We Are Dead

The year Sullivan fired Wright, the United States suffered the worst economic depression it had ever experienced: the Panic of 1893. In that singularly inauspicious moment, Wright was forced to start his own firm. Yet somehow he managed to thrive. Before being fired, he had already furtively developed a small circle of clients. Having learned well the lessons from his own Socrates, he grew a flourishing practice that within the next seventeen years produced buildings that the esteemed critic Ada Louise Huxtable would claim "stand as icons of American architecture even if Wright had never done anything else."[1] By 1910, he had designed and built the Unity Temple and the Larkin Building, as well as most of his prairie style houses, including the Robie, the Coonley, and the Darwin D. Martin houses. His work received regular and wide publication in the architectural journals along with coverage in popular magazines like *Ladies' Home Journal*. But it was the publication of his monographs, *Ausgeführte Bauten und Entwürfe von Frank Lloyd Wright* (1910) and the subsequent *Frank Lloyd Wright: Ausgeführte Bauten* (1911), both published by Verlag Ernst Wasmuth A. G., Berlin, illustrating his most important buildings with their convincing power and overwhelming prescience, that secured Wright's international fame and influence forever.[2] The foundations had been laid in the making of that great edifice, what Huxtable called "that extraordinary man who was arguably America's greatest architect," Frank Lloyd Wright himself.[3] At age forty-three, his immortality was accomplished, and though he lived another forty-nine years and continued to produce important work, he would never again have a period of such intense and influential productivity.[4] In the following fourteen years—until Sullivan's death—he would expand on this reputation with the completion of the Midway Gardens, the Imperial Hotel, and the California textile block houses. But within that latter period, the number of projects per year significantly decreased.

The office of Adler and Sullivan did not endure the Panic as well. Its workload plummeted. In 1895, no new projects came into the office at all.[5] On July 11, having found more lucrative employment with Crane elevator, the fifty-one-year-old Adler dissolved the partnership. He died five years later. Without Adler, Sullivan's workload never fully recovered. During the time the two men had worked together, in just the fifteen years from 1880 to 1895, they had designed more than one hundred buildings, many of them huge with very profitable commissions. In the remaining thirty years of his life, Sullivan would design no more than twenty buildings, most of them by comparison pitiably small with proportionately low commissions.[6] In twice the amount of time, he had half the amount of work, and that work paid considerably less per project. With long periods of no work whatsoever, it was grotesquely unsustainable.

Sullivan is often described as a tragic character. He was a gifted architect whom even Wright characterized as a genius, who nonetheless failed.[7] He experienced all the promise of early success, even international fame, but he never recovered from the economic depression. And he continued to live on, suffering through another twenty-five years in which to decline and die. Biographers attribute the failure to multiple reasons: lack of business acumen, the loss of Adler's professional and social connections, some kind of personal disintegration, his misunderstanding of power, his alcoholism, and even his sexuality. Some believed he was simply out of touch with what the people wanted. Maybe it was his ornament. Maybe he was just too sentimental. By all accounts, after the dissolution of the partnership, he suffered a fairly consistent and steady decline of fortunes through the auction of all his household goods, the divorce and abandonment by his wife of just ten years, the sale of his vacation home and last piece of property in Ocean Springs, Mississippi, and the move down to the Warner Hotel.

Probably his dire poverty prompted him to call Wright that day in 1918. While it was enough to revive their friendship, it did not resolve his financial and personal crisis.[8] By 1924, when the young émigré Viennese architect, Richard Neutra, in Chicago, in homage, asked about meeting Sullivan and publishing the *Kindergarten Chats,* he was resoundingly rebuffed. "They all laughed at me. Sullivan? They asked,—isn't he that old drunkard? He's a pauper now, and is being supported by his friends; each one pitches in five dollars a month. I guess he's living in a run-down tenement or 'hotel' on Warner Avenue, around Thirty-fifth Street or so."[9]

—

Wright visited the Warner Hotel on that grim Sunday of April 13, 1924.[10] He knew the end was near. That was only the worst of his woes. He too was suffering a nightmarish personal and professional drought. He had been consigned to the margins of the profession in what his biographer Smith described as "the architect's seeming impotence."[11] Since that initial fertile period, Wright's ability to acquire work had been thwarted by fourteen years of bad publicity engendered by his own repeated affronts to early-twentieth-century respectability. The nation did not know how to handle the precocious architect who spent months abroad, first with one mistress, Borthwick, and then repeatedly over the next seven years with another, Miriam Noel (1869–1930). Unable to prevent it, he helplessly fed salacious copy to a self-righteous press that was quick to remind readers that Wright was still married to Catherine (1871–1959) with whom he shared six children. In defense, he made disastrous, condescending, statements to reporters.[12] It was all too much. Quite simply, the "nation looked upon him as a pariah."[13]

Unable to get work, he was losing his first and "true" love, architecture. Moreover, he never seemed to fully recover from Borthwick's murder.[14] In November 1922, after thirteen years of trying, he finally secured the divorce from Catherine. His mother, with whom he shared an unusually close yet strangely complicated love, died three months later. And his last tempestuous love, Noel, addled with morphine addiction and psychic fragility, would leave him within a matter of days.[15] Surely he saw that coming. Bereft of love and any prospects for significant work, Wright faced a bitter, cold, darkness.[16]

And the *Lieber Meister's* death.

It was the last full day of Sullivan's life. Just a couple of days prior, he had finally received the rushed copies of his *Autobiography of an Idea* and his *System of Architectural Ornament*.[17] As Wright told it, the autobiography lay on the table beside the bed. He had propped Sullivan up and put his overcoat around the dying man. Sullivan looked over at the book. Wright recalled the scene:

> "There it is, Frank." I was sitting by him, my arm around him to keep him warm and steady him. I could feel every vertebra in his backbone as I rubbed my hand up and down his back to comfort him. I could feel his heart pounding. His heart, the physician said, was twice its natural size owing to the coffee and bromide he had become addicted to.
> "Give me the book! The first copy to you. A pencil!" He tried to raise his arm to take the pencil; he couldn't lift it. Gave it up with an attempt at a smile.[18]

With that last "attempt at a smile," that "wondrous" smile that Wright saw in Sullivan's ornament, the evidence of his "charming interior smile" with which he had successfully wooed "the goddess that whole civilizations strove for centuries to win," Sullivan conceded defeat. Wright entwined the dying man within his arms and the arms of his overcoat. It was not just mutual need that held the two together. And it was more than the warmth of the other's body when there was no one else available. For these two masters of the world of their specific making, it had come to the point where that same world now centripetally immured them within the cheap walls of the Warner Hotel. Sullivan, dying, had used up all other options. Virtually penniless, friendless, loveless, he had no choice. As hard as he had tried, he could be nowhere else. And Wright had to be there too. For when they had first met, the master's "glance" took in everything he felt, "even his most secret thoughts." Already thinking his entire being was laid bare, Sullivan was the one man with whom he had nothing to hide. Wright could finally be the most sentimental person he ever knew. He could willfully cede to the tender emotions, including adoration.

And now he felt Sullivan's heart, "twice its natural size," marking its time, pumping between the tensioned bars of its ribcage, awaiting its freedom in one last exhausted, metaphorical burst. In the mutual recognition of each other's heart, this is where they had to be. If this didn't matter, what would? For both men had left such littered trails of personal destruction in the monomaniacal pursuit of architecture that without this there would be no legacy of meaningful social intercourse whatsoever. Sullivan would die without love. To assume that their passion for architecture did not come from a social need would be mistaken. And to eternally and hermetically sublimate that need in architecture's "arid" field was untenable.[19] Surely, they were both more *men* than that. Yet still! Not for the *proof* of love, nor the appeal to love, nor the reflection of love, but for love itself. At its purest and most naïve!

Wright loved Sullivan.

His *Lieber Meister*.

And Sullivan loved Wright.

On the nightstand, the autobiography remained. Together with the *System* it comprised the last luminous leaves of Sullivan's immortality, the ornaments of his oblation of grace, the index of his blissful cession to the terror of time, and the evidence of his own sentimentality. Like Homer's and Hesiod's, the master's immortality was secure.[20] And there Sullivan and Wright sat, pathetically supporting each other in anticipation of the inexorable end.

—

Before Socrates drank from that poisoned cup, surrounded by his already mourning friends, he put his feet on the ground and allayed their grief with this explanation of his poise.[21] "I am afraid that other people do not realize that the one aim of those who practice philosophy in the proper manner is to practice for dying and death."[22] The *one* aim. As every elenchus in the Socratic Method is dialectically deduced, as the first and last question of pure knowledge are posited, there remains the intractable question of death. Plato told us that Socrates's philosophical telos, as the desire for wisdom and the mastery of a universal, pure knowledge, was realized and challenged by that confrontation with our own mortality. For Socrates, it was only when the soul left the body that it could truly come to know the eternal idea in its incomprehensible infinity. He believed that "if we are ever to have pure knowledge, we must escape from the body and observe things in themselves with the soul by itself. It seems likely that we shall, only then, when we are dead, attain that which we desire and of which we claim to be lovers, namely wisdom."[23] Death is the threshold to the full revelation of pure knowledge, the thing-in-itself, wisdom, and truth. In the meantime we wait, and contemplate. Plato effectively postponed reconciliation with our mortality.

Recall that in *The Symposium*, Socrates suggested that a basic human drive is for immortality. In contradistinction to the ultimate reconciliation that would occur in death, we have an inherent desire to live forever. He suggested that it is through the begetting of children, the making of art, or fame as "immortal glory" that we believe we can attain a qualified immortality. But these are said to be only the lower mysteries of love. Alternatively, the contemplation of the Beautiful while still alive is the closest we may come to the gods, to immortality, *to truth*. Once again for Socrates, the ideal is a disembodied contemplation, "pure, unalloyed, unmixed, not full of human flesh and colors, and the many other kinds of nonsense that attach to mortality."[24] As such, it too is incommensurable, because we are, after all, always full of human flesh. And consequently it too is a postponement. The whole Socratic construct privileges thought over the body and postponement over gratification. Socratic beauty is just *a promise* of redemption from the terror of time.

Sullivan did not postpone. While sometimes drawn with too sketchy a hand, but sharing Socrates's ultimate aim nonetheless, the telos of his project could be summarized as a desire for wisdom that *reconciles* life with death. Harmonizing Whitman's exhilaration of death with Nietzsche's will to perish, Sullivan sang his gloriously sentimental hymn of "overwhelming sympathy." Understood as "the power to receive as well as to give," sympathy enabled the mortal architect to "enter into communion with living and with lifeless things; to enter into unison with nature's powers and processes; to observe—in a fusion of identities—Life everywhere at work." No longer objectively observing things in alien exteriority, he construed each through collective subjectivity where the divisions between "soul" and "thing," subject and object, and even life and death are reconciled in a fusion of identities. Overcoming the Socratic ontology with its lifetime of dry, postponing, disembodied contemplation to "practice for dying and death," Sullivan attuned his breathing, emotive, full-blooded, and sensuous self to nature's eternal rhythms of life and death—sentimentally—in sympathy. No longer construing the desiccated dust of expired humanity as mere objectified dust, or even the brute matter of an image as mere image, he overcame the objectification of the thing such that now even ornament is no longer mere ornament.

And Wright did not want to postpone either. When he offered that "shamed" child who traced the living meander through death's cold snow as a "changing test of eternal principle," where death was just another "crisis of growth," Wright revealed that he too, like his *Lieber Meister*, wanted with all his heart to reconcile those two great rhythms of nature. Through multiple attempts he eschewed disembodied Socratic contemplation in favor of bridging the mortal body with a more qualified experiential and emotive "truth." With his exaggeration of the erotic content of that first meeting with Sullivan; his subliminal recognition of the master's dandruff; his embrace of the order of change; his geometry qualified with emotive spell power; his Japanese conceptions of paradox, non-being and time; and even his repeated scare quotes, Wright revealed his recognition of the impossibility of ever truly knowing the thing in itself as an absolute, pure, and eternal truth in a finite world. In each attempt, he posited an alternative understanding of some proximate truth. To be sure, when Wright expressed the desire "to know a thing, what we really call knowing," he shared in Socrates's telos. But unlike the ancient philosopher who awaited death's revelation of "pure knowledge," Wright, like Sullivan, reconciled to our temporality through a contaminated emotive "knowledge"—for now. As he put it, to know the thing "a man must first love the thing, which means that he can sympathize vividly with it." Like Schiller, who reconciled "actuality as a limit" and the "idea as infinitude" through the tender emotions of sentimentality, Wright reconciled the finitude of the thing with the knowledge of its infinite ideal through an appeal to sympathy and love. He too defaulted to sentimentality. Moreover, determined to have that reconciliation now, he knew that it must occur through the living flesh. Conflating the love of carnal beauty with the love of that finer beauty, he, like Sullivan, *sympathetically, and erotically, ceded his own body.* And he was "elated." Wright wasn't Socrates—but Alcibiades. Driven to the threshold of madness by his love of truth, he, like that ancient Athenian, reconciled himself to its impossibility by embracing the flesh as embodied experience, emotional desire, and the image—as ornament.[25]

Wright wrote that after the death of Sullivan, the death of his mother, and the destruction and loss of "three beloved homes," he, as the sufferer of the inescapable temporality of "Life," built yet again. "Now the fourth home built by my own hands, a new home built out of a battered and punished but still sentimental self in the same quest—Life!"[26] For Wright, in the act of building, it was the *sentimental self* who persisted and believed in this quest. Despite life's battering and punishing inflictions, that self, that is, the one who loves and believes, cedes to the inevitability of life and death. The sentimental self is tender: tender to the battering and punishment, tender to the demands of the heart, tender to the finitude of life, and tender to the unknowable infinitude of transcendence as revealed through death.

Sullivan and Wright *both* suggest that weak sentimentality is the emotional strength that enables us to persist when the rational self confronts its limits. At the inevitable vanishing point of objectifying reason, we are all sentimental. Indeed, unlike Plato's postponement until after death, even more than just a palliative against the terror of time, sentimentality, in its appeal to the tender emotions, *reconciles* us to that "battering," now. As the appeal to pity, sympathy, fondness, adoration, compassion, and love, it is much like Sullivan's smile, the gift of grace. Bridging feeling and thought, *sentire in mente* is the emotive medium of irrational discourses: like faith, death, *and ornament*. Even though he verbally banished its application from his practice, surely Wright understood that he relied on it there too. For even he, in the design of his "integral ornament," ultimately had to cross that insuperable chasm between the finite reality of his built construction and the infinitude of his transcendent ideation. And despite all his protestations to the contrary, surely Wright knew that the supreme ornamentation of the Midway Gardens was sentimental too.

—

Between the first two editions of his autobiography, Wright made another revealing edit. In the *second* edition, he confided this about Sullivan's muffler, "I should have liked to keep the warm muffler he had worn about his neck. But—what use? He was gone!"[27] After Sullivan's death, Wright wanted that muffler. It was his heart's wish. But as if searching for a justifying function, he coldly asked, "what use?"

Why did he want it anyway? Would he actually wear it? If he wrapped that muffler around his bare neck, would he conjure Sullivan's? Was he longing to marry the topography of musculature from Sullivan's neck, the bulge of Adam's apple, the impressions left in the scarf of the sinews and arteries that coursed the lifeblood of the Master's genius, with the contours of his own? Could that warm scarf, like an efflorescing tendril of the Master's ornament, re-entwine, as the realization of a wish, the two men around the tender flesh of their conjoined necks? Or, was he just asking for the warmth of scarf to fend off death's chill? Surely, it is something even more than these. For Wright knew that Sullivan believed that the man, the child who *went forth*, that is Sullivan himself, *was the muffler*.

But, he couldn't buy it. Wright knew better. Or so he thought. In the *first* and more candid edition of his autobiography, he disclosed a more fragile, emotional, grieving, and conflicted self that he struggled to control and would later elide from the subsequent editions. Revealing in its repeated ellipses of apparent self-editing and repression—the revelation of his failed attempts to control his emotions—Wright could not hide what he truly believed. Reason must repress emotion. In the end, he pathetically rejected the warm muffler in favor of Eden's cold-blooded serpent whose promise of knowledge exposed the meaning of naked flesh, the poverty of thought, and the intractability of death. Wright admitted, "I should have liked to keep the warm muffler he had worn about his neck ... But ... sentimentality. What use? He was gone!"[28]

NOTES

Preface

1. *The New York Times*, April 16, 1924, 23; Mervyn D. Kaufman, *Father of Skyscrapers: A Biography of Louis Sullivan* (Boston: Little, Brown and Company, 1969), 158; Hugh Morrison, *Louis Sullivan: Prophet of Modern Architecture* (New York: W. W. Norton & Company, 1998).
2. Frank Lloyd Wright, *An Autobiography* (London: Longmans, Green and Company, 1932), 106–7; Brendan Gill, *Many Masks: A Life of Frank Lloyd Wright* (New York: G. Putnam's Sons, 1987), 100. Most sources rely on Wright's account. According to him, against company policy, he began moonlighting. He developed his own clients and worked on his own buildings outside of the firm of Adler and Sullivan. Gill suggests that both men were actually ready for the split and points out that it is unclear who really initiated it. His most convincing argument suggests that it may actually have been caused by Wright's embezzlement of some of Sullivan's personal funds.
3. Wright, *An Autobiography* (1932), 260; 262. Wright acknowledged that they had a reconciliation of sorts in late summer of 1914, but then they did not meet again for another seven years.
4. Gill, *Many Masks*, 63–4.
5. Louis Sullivan, "Ornament in Architecture," *Louis Sullivan: The Public Papers*, ed. Robert Twombly (Chicago: The University of Chicago Press, 1988), 80.
6. Frank Lloyd Wright, "The Ethics of Ornament," *The Prairie School Review* IV, no. 1 (First Quarter 1967): 16.
7. Wright, *An Autobiography* (1932), 201.
8. Antoine Picon, "Ornament and Its Users: From the Vitruvian Tradition to the Digital Age," in *Histories of Ornament: From Global to Local*, ed. Gülru Necipoğlu and Alina Payne (Princeton: Princeton University Press, 2016), 10. Picon makes an important distinction between emotion and affect, particularly as it impacts the relationship between the observer and the object of ornament. However, this is a case study about two architects from a specific time period when that distinction is rarely or inconsistently made. I rely therefore on Teresa Brennan's summation when she states, "There is no reason to challenge the idea that emotions are basically synonymous with affects." Theresa Brennan, *The Transmission of Affect* (Ithaca: Cornell University Press, 2004), 5–6.
9. One might argue that for Sullivan, sentimentality wasn't worth mentioning at all. But how does that square with Wright's adamancy, especially when the two men were so close? Clearly, Sullivan wasn't ignorant to the discourse. Foucault states that "there is no binary division to be made between what one says and what one does not say; we must try to determine the different ways of not saying such things …. […] There is not one but many silences, and they are

an integral part of the strategies that underline and permeate discourses." My aim is to uncover Sullivan's "different ways of not saying such things." Michel Foucault, *The History of Sexuality Volume I: An Introduction*, trans. Alan Sheridan (New York: Vintage Books, 1990), 27.

10 Sigmund Freud and Josef Breuer, *Studies on Hysteria*, trans. James Strachey in collaboration with Anna Freud (New York: Basic Books, Inc., 1957), 17.

Chapter 1

1   Wright could possibly have been twenty-one. He was not clear what time of year this story occurred.
2   Wright, *An Autobiography* (1932), 85–6.
3   Wright, *An Autobiography* (1932), 85–7.
4   Wright, *An Autobiography* (1932), 87–8.
5   Wright, *An Autobiography* (1932), 87; Wright, *An Autobiography* (New York: Duell, Sloan and Pearce, 1943), 88.
6   Wright, *An Autobiography* (1932), 88.
7   Wright, *An Autobiography* (1943), 89. I quote from the second edition because Wright cleaned up some sloppy syntax from the first. Unfortunately, he also cleaned up his penchant for qualifying quotation marks.
8   Wright, *An Autobiography* (1932), 84–8.
9   Wright, *An Autobiography* (1932), 102. Wright wrote that he was nineteen when he told Sullivan that Tobin was seventeen.
10 When they first met, Kitty was sixteen. Unless they met in the spring of that year, Wright was already twenty. Wright, *An Autobiography* (1932), 76; 102; 108. Wright's accounting in his autobiography is inconsistent. Later he claimed that on the day they were married he was almost twenty-one and Tobin was seventeen. By all reputable accounts Wright was born on June 8, 1867, and Tobin was born on March 25, 1871. The difference in age was three years, nine months, and seventeen days. They were married on June 1, 1889. Tobin had just turned eighteen; Wright would turn twenty-two in a week. Paul Hendrickson, *Plagued by Fire: The Dreams and Furies of Frank Lloyd Wright* (New York: Alfred A. Knopf, 2019), 25; 139. Secrest, *Frank Lloyd Wright*, 96, 102. Gill, *Many Masks*, 23. Robert Twombly, *Frank Lloyd Wright: His Life and Architecture* (New York: John Wiley & Sons, Inc., 1979), 4; 25.
11 Gill, *Many Masks*, 80.
12 *The Compact Oxford English Dictionary*, 2nd edition, s. v. "sentiment," "sentimentality." The dictionary offers a definition that states that in generalized usage, "sentiment" may mean "refined and tender emotion; exercise or manifestation of 'sensibility'; emotional reflection or meditation; appeal to the tender emotions in literature or art." And like "sentimentality" it recognizes the semantic shift and adds, "Now chiefly in derisive use, conveying an imputation of either insincerity or mawkishness." The first phrase might imply a raw expression of emotion unencumbered by thought.
13 Wright's autobiography was not the first time that Wright distinguished between "sentiment" and "sentimentality." In 1901 he wrote, "The whole sentiment of early craft degenerated to a sentimentality having no longer decent significance nor commercial integrity." Describing the Japanese print, he wrote,

"Chaste and delicate, it has taught that healthy and wholesome sentiment has nothing in common with sentimentality, nor sensuous feeling with banal sensuality." Frank Lloyd Wright, "The Art and Craft of the Machine," *Frank Lloyd Wright: Writings and Buildings*, ed. Edgar Kaufmann and Ben Raeburn (New York: A Meridian Book, New American Library, 1960), 57. Frank Lloyd Wright, *The Japanese Print: An Interpretation* (1912; repr., New York: Horizon Press, 1967), 28.

14 Friedrich von Schiller, *Naïve and Sentimental Poetry and on the Sublime: Two Essays*, trans. Julius A. Elias (New York: Frederick Ungar Publishing Co., 1966), 113. Used by permission of Bloomsbury Publishing, Plc.
15 Schiller, *Naïve and Sentimental Poetry*, 110.
16 Schiller, *Naïve and Sentimental Poetry*, 111.
17 Schiller, *Naïve and Sentimental Poetry*, 112.
18 For a good summary of the evolution of conceptions of nature, see the introductory essays in Diana Balmori and Joel Sanders, *Groundwork: Between Landscape and Architecture* (New York: The Monacelli Press, 2011), 12–45.
19 Schiller, *Naïve and Sentimental Poetry*, 105.
20 Schiller, *Naïve and Sentimental Poetry*, 111.
21 Schiller, *Naïve and Sentimental Poetry*, 111.
22 Schiller, *Naïve and Sentimental Poetry*, 111–12.
23 Schiller, *Naïve and Sentimental Poetry*, 116.
24 Schiller, *Naïve and Sentimental Poetry*, 116.
25 Schiller, *Naïve and Sentimental Poetry*, 113.
26 For a good summary of those debates, see Balmori and Sanders, *Groundwork*, 12–45.
27 Frank Lloyd Wright, *Genius and the Mobocracy* (New York: Duell, Sloan and Pearce, 1949), XI; XIII. Wright, *An Autobiography* (1932), 136, 227. Wright, *An Autobiography* (1943), 336. Wright's antidote to this sentimentality was to build what he called a "natural house." He offered both Taliesin I and Hollyhock House as examples.
28 Schiller, *Naïve and Sentimental Poetry*, 111; Wright, "The Art and Craft of the Machine," 57. Wright, *Genius and the Mobocracy*, XI.
29 Wright, "The Art and Craft of the Machine," 57. Wright presented multiple versions of this idea. It should be noted that in *Genius and the Mobocracy* he specifically excluded the later Greeks and the Romans from his chosen builders of a natural form of architecture. He did not mention this particular exclusion in "The Art and Craft of the Machine."
30 Wright, *An Autobiography* (1932), 350.
31 Wright, "The Art and Craft of the Machine," 57.
32 With each of these questions it is imperative to be considering a *style* and not a *building in a style*. It is the same difference as that between the infinite ideal of children and the actual finite child. A style already represents some ideal.
33 I am not referring to some effect of a style, like deep shadows, delicate proportions, or ethereal light effects. Nor am I referring to the feeling that a given style might elicit. Again, this is only about the imitation of a style based on the ideals it is presumed to represent.
34 Wright, *An Autobiography* (1932), 80–1; 88; 154; 350–2. Wright, *An Autobiography* (1943), 360.

35 Søren Kierkegaard, *Either/Or*, Vol. I, trans. David F. Swenson and Lillian Marvin Swenson (Garden City, NY: Anchor Books, 1959), 453, fn. 1. Kierkegaard only identifies the dramatist as "Scribe." In his notes, Howard A. Johnson indicates that Augustin Eugène Scribe (1791–1861) was a French dramatist and that Heiberg's translation of his comedy, *The First Love*, was published in 1832. Scribe is probably better known today for his opera libretti to include works for Meyerbeer, Donizetti, and Verdi.
36 Kierkegaard, *Either/Or*, 247.
37 Kierkegaard, *Either/Or*, 252.
38 Kierkegaard, *Either/Or*, 254.
39 Arnold Wolff, *The Cologne Cathedral*, 2nd edition, trans. Margret Maranuk-Rohmeder (Köln [Cologne]: Verlag Kölner Dom, 1999), 23.
40 Arthur Schopenhauer, *The World as Will and Representation*, Vol. 2, trans. E. F. J. Payne (New York: Dover Publications, 1969), 418.
41 Wright, *An Autobiography* (1932), 350. Ironically Wright considered the "Cathedral of Cologne" an example of a living architecture, when "architecture was the great writing of mankind." Given his other arguments we might infer that he was not familiar with its nineteenth-century completion. See Frank Lloyd Wright, *Modern Architecture: Being the Kahn Lectures for 1930*, with a new introduction by Neil Levine (Princeton: Princeton University Press, 2008), 56.
42 Wright, "Roots," *Frank Lloyd Wright: Writings and Buildings*, ed. Edgar Kaufmann and Ben Raeburn (New York: New American Library, A Meridian Book, 1960), 19–20.
43 Sullivan used the same trope of death when referring to classical architecture and its styles. He called it a "cemetery of orders and of styles." Louis H. Sullivan, *The Autobiography of an Idea* (1924; repr., New York: Dover Publications, 1956), 189.
44 Architecture critic Montgomery Schuyler (1843–1914) had made the exact same argument about Gothic and Renaissance architecture in 1891. However as early as the 1830s, men like Horatio Greenough and James Fennimore Cooper were making similar arguments for an American architecture. Schuyler, *American Architecture and Other Writings*, 58–9. See also Joseph R. Tebben, *The Old Home: Louis Sullivan's Newark Bank* (Granville, OH: The McDonald & Woodward Publishing Company, 2014), 63–4. Vincent J. Scully, Jr., *The Shingle Style and the Stick Style: Architectural Theory and Design from Downing to the Origins of Wright* (1955; repr., New Haven: Yale University Press, 1971), xxiii–xxiv.
45 Sherman Paul, *Louis Sullivan: An Architect in American Thought* (Englewood Cliffs, NJ: Prentice-Hall, 1962), 26.
46 Paul, *Louis Sullivan*, 26. Sullivan would make a similar argument indicating that architects should "cease to regard [architecture] under the artificial classification of styles," but rather as "a product and index of the thought of the people of the time and place." Louis Sullivan, "What Is Architecture? A Study in the American People of Today," *Louis Sullivan: The Public Papers*, ed. Robert Twombly (Chicago: The University of Chicago Press, 1988), 177–8.
47 Wright, *An Autobiography* (1932), 80–1.
48 Wright, *An Autobiography* (1932), 80; 88; 240; 330.
49 The courthouse is a relatively late example of the style. I use it here simply because it is a prime example of the problem. Wright was particularly aware of the courthouse because it had just been completed while he was writing his autobiography.

50 Sometimes called "Classical Revival." When so designated, it must then be distinguished from the eighteenth-century "Classical Revival" period by calling the earlier, "Early Classical Revival." In either case there were two distinctly different periods of "Classical Revival" and the courthouse was the latter.
51 Wright, *Modern Architecture*, 57.
52 Wright, *Genius and the Mobocracy*, XII. Regarding Wright's intentions in his use of the word "picture," see also "The City," from the Kahn Lectures. Wright, *Modern Architecture*, 112. Wright, *An Autobiography* (1932), 268. Wright described the architecture of the World's Columbian Exposition as a "pseudo-classic collection of picture-building" and even Sullivan's Transportation Building as "the pictorial Transportation Building for what it was worth."
53 Karsten Harries, *Between Nihilism and Faith: A Commentary on Either/Or* (Berlin: Walter de Gruyter, GmbH & Co., 2010), 88.
54 Harries, *Between Nihilism and Faith*, 88.
55 Karsten Harries, *The Meaning of Modern Art: A Philosophical Interpretation* (Evanston, IL: Northwestern University Press, 1968), 79.
56 Robert C. Solomon, *In Defense of Sentimentality* (Oxford: Oxford University Press, 2004), 5.
57 Charles Paul de Kock, *Edmond and His Cousin*, trans. Edith Mary Norris (Boston: The Frederick J. Quinby Co., 1904).
58 Sullivan's set was published in 1904.
59 Solomon, *In Defense of Sentimentality*, 5.
60 Solomon, *In Defense of Sentimentality*, 4.
61 Depending on the viewer, Michelangelo's *Pieta* might or might not be kitsch. But it certainly appeals to the tender emotions.
62 Solomon, *In Defense of Sentimentality*, 241–52.
63 Solomon, *In Defense of Sentimentality*, 252.
64 Solomon goes so far as to defend kitsch for the cause of ethics. The chapter section title is "'Thank Heaven for Little Girls'; or, In Defense of Kitsch." Solomon, *In Defense of Sentimentality*, 252.
65 Wright, *An Autobiography* (1932), 63.
66 Louis Sullivan, "Development of Construction," *Louis Sullivan: The Public Papers*, ed. Robert Twombly (Chicago: The University of Chicago Press, 1988), 177–8, 214.
67 *Chicago Encyclopedia*, s. v. "Economic Geography." www.encyclopedia.chicagohistory.org/pages/409.html
68 Chicago incorporated in 1837 with a population of about 4,000. In just fifty-three years its population had doubled 126 times.
69 Marvin Trachtenberg and Isabelle Hyman, *Architecture: From Pre-history to Post-modernism/the Western Tradition* (New York: Harry N. Abrams, Inc., 1986), 496.
70 One was not simply from France; one was French, meaning a member of the "French race."
71 Here "immigrants" means that they were either born abroad (most from Europe) or were the children of parents who were born abroad. *Chicago Encyclopedia*, "Demography."
72 Delores Hayden, *The Grand Domestic Revolution: A History of Feminist Designs for American Homes, Neighborhoods and Cities* (Cambridge, MA: MIT Press, 1982), 153.

73 Hayden, *The Grand Domestic Revolution*, 153.
74 For a social critique of the presentation of American "civilization" in the *World's Columbian Exposition*, with its sordid racial, class, and gender underbelly, see Gail Bederman, *Manliness & Civilization: A Cultural History of Gender and Race in the United States, 1880–1917* (Chicago: University of Chicago Press, 1995), 31–41; Robert C. Allen, *Horrible Prettiness: Burlesque and American Culture* (Chapel Hill: University of North Carolina Press, 1991), 226; and Robert W. Rydell, *All the World's a Fair: Visions of Empire at American International Expositions, 1876–1916* (Chicago: University of Chicago Press, 1984), 61–2; 65.
75 Upton Sinclair, *The Jungle* (New York: Penguin Books, 2006), xxvi.
76 For comparable arguments see also Jackson Lears, *Rebirth of a Nation: The Making of North America, 1877–1920* (New York: HarperCollins Publishers, 2009); Thomas C. Leonard, *Illiberal Reformers: Race, Eugenics & American Economics in the Progressive Era* (Princeton: Princeton University Press, 2016).
77 Bederman, *Manliness & Civilization*, 25.
78 Bederman, *Manliness & Civilization*, 25.
79 Bederman, *Manliness & Civilization*, 18.
80 Bederman, *Manliness & Civilization*, 18.
81 Bederman, *Manliness & Civilization*, 17.
82 Bederman, *Manliness & Civilization*, 19.
83 Bederman, *Manliness & Civilization*, 218.
84 Bederman, *Manliness & Civilization*, 37.
85 Solomon, *In Defense of Sentimentality*, 6.
86 Wright's latest biographer, Paul Hendrickson, in his particularly thorough investigation of some of the peripheral characters to Wright's story, tracks Jones's sordid evolution from progressive preacher's son to the "most morally repugnant character in this book—by far." Hendrickson, *Plagued by Fire*, 244.
87 I have intentionally placed "riot" within quotes. Hendrickson clarifies: it "wasn't a riot; it was a race massacre, a kind of instant and unplanned pogrom" that left hundreds dead and "upward of nine thousand" black Tulsans homeless in a night of "torching and looting and killing." Hendrickson, *Plagued by Fire*, 248–9.
88 Secrest, *Frank Lloyd Wright*, 86–7.
89 Sullivan was not alone in his early admiration of Spencer. Author of the evolutionary concept of "survival of the fittest," Richard Hofstadter indicated that even "James, Royce, Dewey, Bowne, Harris, Howison, and McCosh,—had to reckon with Spencer at some time." According to Hofstadter, Emerson called him a "stock writer." William James said that Spencer "is the philosopher whom those who have no other philosopher can appreciate." Like Sullivan, James was initially quite taken with Spencer's worldview. And like Sullivan, yet long before, he also came to reject it. See Richard Hofstadter, *Social Darwinism in American Thought*, Rev. ed., 3rd printing (New York: George Braziller, Inc., 1969), 32; 33; 219, n.2.
90 Bederman, *Manliness & Civilization*, 35.
91 Bederman, *Manliness & Civilization*, 35.
92 Solomon, *In Defense of Sentimentality*, 9. Though he regularly included it throughout his book, Solomon did not include "love" as one of the tender emotions: a curious omission given the *OED*'s emphasis of the "tender emotions, especially those of love."

93   OED, s. v. "ornament."
94   Kent Bloomer, *The Nature of Ornament: Rhythm and Metamorphosis in Architecture* (New York: W. W. Norton & Company, 2000), 26.
95   OED, s. v. "ornament."
96   Wright, *Modern Architecture*, 79. Even Le Corbusier made the distinction, again privileging "ornament." See Thomas Beeby, "The Grammar of Ornament/Ornament as Grammar," *Via III, Ornament*, ed. Stephen Kieran (Philadelphia: University of Pennsylvania, Fine Arts, 1977), 13.
97   Bloomer, *The Nature of Ornament*, 12.
98   Bloomer, *The Nature of Ornament*, 12.
99   Bloomer, *The Nature of Ornament*, 35.
100 Bloomer, *The Nature of Ornament*, 26.
101 Wright, "Roots," 19–20.
102 Wright, "Roots," 25.
103 Sullivan and Wright were certainly not unique in their pursuit. In Chicago alone, their colleagues George Maher, Irving Pond, and John Root had all developed individual solutions to the problem. And throughout the West, Art Nouveau, Vienna Secessionist, Jugendstil, and Art Deco were all styles that worked to revitalize ornament within the industrialized culture.
104 Alfred Barr, Jr., Henry-Russell Hitchcock, Jr., Philip Johnson and Lewis Mumford, *Modern Architects* (New York: Museum of Modern Art and W. W. Norton & Company, 1932). This, the *International Exhibition* catalogue identified the four most important leaders as Walter Gropius, Le Corbusier, J. J. P. Oud, and Mies van der Rohe.
105 Karsten Harries, *The Ethical Function of Architecture* (Cambridge, MA: MIT Press, 1997), 4.
106 Harries, *The Ethical Function of Architecture*, 154.
107 Harries, *The Ethical Function of Architecture*, 4.
108 Wright, "The Art and Craft of the Machine," 57.
109 Harries, *The Ethical Function of Architecture*, 21. Harries begins with Baumgarten's first coining of the term "aesthetics" and its categorization as a branch of philosophy.
110 Karsten Harries, *The Broken Frame: Three Lectures* (Washington, DC: The Catholic University of America Press, 1989), xi.
111 Harries, *The Ethical Function of Architecture*, 26. Harries indicates that this is Kant's understanding.
112 Wright, "The Art and Craft of the Machine," 57–8. Wright, recalling Victor Hugo's familiar declaration that "the book will kill the edifice," blamed it on Gutenberg's invention of the printing press and claimed that "human thought discovers a mode of perpetuating itself, not only more resisting than architecture, but still more simple and easy."
113 Wright, "The Art and Craft of the Machine," 58.
114 Wright, *Modern Architecture*, 54. John Root, *The Meanings of Architecture: Buildings and Writings of John Wellborn Root*, collected by Donald Hoffmann (New York: Horizon Press, 1967), 22. Wright was certainly not the first to articulate these sentiments, especially in Chicago. His professional colleagues John Root and Irving Pond both denounced the movement toward art for art's sake, and both characterized it as "decadent." See also Pond, *The Meaning of Architecture: An Essay in Constructive Criticism* (Boston: Marshall Jones

Company, 1918), 68; 71. Pond went so far as to call the Corinthian column "decadent" and evidence of a "new-born love of ornament for ornament's sake."
115 Harries, *The Ethical Function of Architecture*, 55.
116 Harries, *The Ethical Function of Architecture*, 48.
117 Harries, *The Ethical Function of Architecture*, 28.
118 Harries, *The Broken Frame*, 50.
119 Harries, *The Broken Frame*, 50.

Chapter 2

1 Sullivan, *The Autobiography of an Idea*, 54.
2 Sullivan, *The Autobiography of an Idea*, 54.
3 Sullivan, *The Autobiography of an Idea*, 54.
4 Sullivan, *The Autobiography of an Idea*, 41. Now Wakefield Massachusetts.
5 Sullivan, *The Autobiography of an Idea*, 53.
6 Sullivan, *The Autobiography of an Idea*, 51.
7 Louis Sullivan, "Emotional Architecture as Compared with Intellectual," *Louis Sullivan: The Public Papers*, ed. Robert Twombly (Chicago: The University of Chicago Press, 1988), 95.
8 Sullivan, *The Autobiography of an Idea*, 52.
9 As noted in Chapter 1, Schiller indicated that the naïve poet "is" nature; the sentimental poet "will seek her."
10 Sullivan, "Emotional Architecture," 99.
11 Sullivan, *The Autobiography of an Idea*, 55.
12 Sullivan, *The Autobiography of an Idea*, 56.
13 Sullivan, *The Autobiography of an Idea*, 55. Sullivan's autobiography is full of examples of his ingenuous expression of thrilled emotion. Sullivan describes himself as exceedingly emotional. Sullivan, *The Autobiography of an Idea*, 41.
14 Wright, *Genius and Mobocracy*, 61. It is not clear whether Sullivan ever used the expression.
15 Wright, *Genius and Mobocracy*, 62.
16 Louis Sullivan, "Ornament in Architecture," *Louis Sullivan: The Public Papers*, ed. Robert Twombly (Chicago: The University of Chicago Press, 1988), 82.
17 Louis Sullivan, "The Tall Office Building Artistically Considered (1896)," *Louis Sullivan: The Public Papers*, ed. Robert Twombly (Chicago: The University of Chicago Press, 1988), 111.
18 Sullivan refers to the elm leaf and pine needle as being "in keeping" with, respectively, the elm and pine trees. And Wright was fascinated with the peacock that to him seemed "introduced for love of beauty—ornament?" Sullivan, "Ornament in Architecture," 83. Wright, *An Autobiography* (1932), 43.
19 Wright, *An Autobiography* (1932), 266–7.
20 Louis Sullivan, "Plastic and Color Decoration of the Auditorium," *Louis Sullivan: The Public Papers*, ed. Robert Twombly (Chicago: The University of Chicago Press, 1988), 73–4; Wright, *An Autobiography* (1932), 266.
21 Wright, *An Autobiography* (1943), 108. I use the 1943 edition because of its concision.
22 The first example in the *OED* dates from 1598.

23 Gustav Flaubert, *A Sentimental Education: The Story of a Young Man*, Translated with an Introduction by Douglas Parmeé (Oxford: Oxford University Press, 2000), 129.
24 Pond, *The Meaning of Architecture*, 199.
25 Wright, *An Autobiography* (1932), 145–8. Wright, *Modern Architecture*, 17; 30; 72–3. Wright used the term much more frequently in his writing than Sullivan. The discerning reader can begin to tease out his intended meanings from these few examples.
26 Wright, *An Autobiography* (1943), 146.
27 Wright, *An Autobiography* (1932), 267.
28 Wright, *An Autobiography* (1932), 267.
29 Sullivan, "Plastic and Color Decoration," 74.
30 Louis Sullivan, "What Is the Just Subordination, in Architectural Design, of Details to Mass?" *Louis Sullivan, The Public Papers*, ed. Robert Twombly (Chicago: The University of Chicago Press, 1988), 32.
31 Sullivan, "What Is the Just Subordination?" 32; 33; 35.
32 Tuthill had hired Adler and Sullivan to consult on the acoustics.
33 Sullivan, "Plastic and Color Decoration," 75.
34 Wright, *An Autobiography* (1943), 147. Wright completely rewrote this chapter in this, the second edition of the autobiography, with a more thorough definition of "plastic."
35 Wright, *An Autobiography* (1932), 268.
36 Wright, *An Autobiography* (1932), 268.
37 Wright, *An Autobiography* (1932), 268.
38 Sullivan construed those "subdivisions" to be also based on building function. In the Wainwright, the attic story of restrooms, barbershop, and mechanical equipment was functionally different from the office floors below and consequently given a different exterior treatment. Montgomery Schuyler criticized the Guaranty Building because it failed to make that distinction. Schuyler, *American Architecture*, 187.
39 Wright, *An Autobiography* (1932), 267–8.
40 Schuyler, *American Architecture*, 187. Schuyler wrote, "The designer has in this respect fully availed himself of the plasticity of his enclosing material."
41 Louis Sullivan, "Style," *Louis Sullivan: The Public Papers*, ed. Robert Twombly (Chicago: The University of Chicago Press, 1988), 52.
42 Jonathon Massey, *Crystal and Arabesque: Claude Bragdon, Ornament, and Modern Architecture* (Pittsburgh: University of Pittsburgh Press, 2009), 2–5; George W. Maher, "A Plea for an Indigenous Art," *Architectural Record* 21 (June 1907): 433; Pond, *The Meaning of Architecture*, 197. Maher and Pond were colleagues of Sullivan in Chicago. Bragdon was an acquaintance and known follower of Sullivan's work. While still based on some associative narrative content, George Maher's "motif rhythm theory" and Claude Bragdon's universal "form-language" offered solutions to the problem of ornament—not from their narrative content, but, as their titles suggest, from the language of form. Irving Pond's "idealized interpretation of the inhering structural forces," though not as explicit in its characterization, was still determined primarily through a reading of form.

Chapter 3

1. David S. Andrew, *Louis Sullivan and the Polemics of Modern Architecture: The Present against the Past* (Chicago: University of Illinois Press, 1985), 27.
2. Lauren S. Weingarden, "Louis Sullivan's *System of Architectural Ornament*," *Louis H. Sullivan: A System of Architectural Ornament* (New York: Rizzoli, 1990), 11. Weingarden includes Andrew in her bibliography but does not mention him in her text.
3. As indicated, Sullivan rarely used the word.
4. For Sullivan, late in his career, power was almost a fixation. In essays that seemingly had little to do with the topic he would nonetheless expound upon it. See, for example, Louis Sullivan, "The Chicago Tribune Competition," *Louis Sullivan: The Public Papers*, ed. Robert Twombly (Chicago: The University of Chicago Press, 1988), 224–32; Louis Sullivan, "Concerning the Imperial Hotel Tokyo, Japan," *Louis Sullivan: The Public Papers*, ed. Robert Twombly (Chicago: The University of Chicago Press, 1988), 244–51.
5. Louis H. Sullivan, *A System of Architectural Ornament According with a Philosophy of Man's Powers*, 1924 (New York: The Eakins Press, 1967), not paginated.
6. Sullivan, *A System of Architectural Ornament*, not paginated.
7. Sullivan, *A System of Architectural Ornament*, not paginated.
8. Sullivan, *A System of Architectural Ornament*, not paginated. Sullivan had Hall's *Adolescence* in his library. G. Stanley Hall, *Adolescence: Its Psychology and Its Relations to Physiology, Anthropology, Sociology, Sex, Crime, Religion and Education*, Vol. 1 (New York: D. Appleton and Company, 1904). For the contents of Sullivan's library, see Williams, Barker & Severn Co., *Catalogue at Auction: Household Effects, Library, Oriental Rugs, Paintings, Etc. of Mr. Louis Sullivan* (Chicago: Ryerson & Burnham Archives, Art Institute of Chicago, Accession # 1931.1, 1909), item 148. Frank Lloyd Wright indicated that Sullivan was greatly influenced by Spencer and that he gave Wright a copy to read. Perhaps having given Wright his copy, there was no Spencer in the auction catalog. Wright, *An Autobiography* (1932), 102.
9. Hofstadter, *Social Darwinism in American Thought*, 40. Bederman, *Manliness & Civilization*, 105–8. Herbert Spencer, *The Data of Ethics* (New York: A. L. Burt Company, n.d.), 327–31.
10. Sullivan, *A System of Architectural Ornament*, not paginated.
11. Sullivan might have been influenced by two other sources from his library. Edward Carpenter in his *Days with Walt Whitman* described Whitman as the "master-workman," "the workman, the normal (or 'average') man," "the man who deals with materials and wins his living from them," and the man who uses his medium "with the same directness and mastery that he uses towards life." In words that would have appealed to Sullivan, Carpenter concluded: "Hence a new era of literature—a literature appealing to all who deal with life directly, and know what it is." This "average" "master-workman" is something quite different from Spencer and Hall's "ideal man" and "cosmic super-man." Another probable source, identified by Weingarden, is Nietzsche's *Thus Spoke Zarathustra* and the idea of the "overman." Edward Carpenter, *Days with Walt Whitman: With Some Notes on His Life and Work* (1906; repr., London: George Allen & Unwin Ltd., 1921), 105. Weingarden, "Louis Sullivan's *System of Architectural Ornament*," 14.

12 Sullivan, *A System of Architectural Ornament*, not paginated.
13 Sherman Paul, *Louis Sullivan: An Architect in American Thought* (Englewood Cliffs, NJ: Prentice Hall, 1962), 133. Paul referenced Sullivan's letter to Charles Whitaker (the editor of the *Journal* of the American Institute of Architects), January 28, 1922 (Burnham Library). There Sullivan indicated that he wrote it in the third person "because it permitted him greater freedom."
14 It was not until he was about eleven that he mentioned the fights (see below). But they were only generally described and they lacked the attention to specific detail that the earlier memories evoked.
15 Sullivan, *The Autobiography of an Idea*, 55.
16 Sullivan, *The Autobiography of an Idea*, 55.
17 Sullivan, *The Autobiography of an Idea*, 37; 63.
18 Sullivan, *The Autobiography of an Idea*, 105.
19 Sullivan, *The Autobiography of an Idea*, 135.
20 Sullivan, *The Autobiography of an Idea*, 183.
21 Sullivan, *The Autobiography of an Idea*, 183.
22 Sullivan, *The Autobiography of an Idea*, 231.
23 In an interview with Mike Wallace, Wright described himself as a pacifist. Frank Lloyd Wright and Mike Wallace, *The Mike Wallace Interview*, September 1, 1957, and September 28, 1957. http://www.hrc.utexas.edu/multimedia/video/2008/wallace/wright_frank_lloyd.html [accessed April 19, 2013].
24 Wright, *An Autobiography* (1932), 98–9; 101–2; 122. (1943), 432–3.
25 Wright fails to mention the fight with his own son where according to Cadwell, "John Lloyd knifed by Wright himself during their salary dispute, the father's lunges exhausted only when the son beat him unconscious on the stone floor." Michael Cadwell, *Strange Details* (Cambridge, MA: MIT Press, 2007), 79.
26 In one example, Wright splashed in the gore and victory of a fight (that he initiated) with "Ottenheimer," a coworker in the office of Adler and Sullivan. In defense, Ottenheimer stabbed Wright. Wright finally prevailed with the whack of the full swing of his T-square on the exposed flesh of Ottenhemer's neck. "The cross-head snapped off and flew clear down the length of the room." Ottenheimer "wilted, slowly, into a senseless heap on the floor like a sail going down." Wright reveled in the fact that *he* had been dangerously wounded. "My shoes were full of blood." Wright, *An Autobiography* (1932), 101.
27 Wright's violence erupted even into his family life. Friedland and Zellman describe a disturbing scene of his unleashed physical fury against his wife Olgivanna and stepdaughter Svetlana, as witnessed by his daughter Iovanna. Roger Friedland and Harold Zellman, *The Fellowship: The Untold Story of Frank Lloyd Wright & the Taliesin Fellowship* (New York: Harper Perennial, 2007), 204–5.
28 *OED*, s. v. "power."
29 Delores Hayden, *Redesigning the American Dream: The Future of Housing, Work and Family Life* (New York: W. W. Norton & Company, 2002), 225. With the "stock phrases" "woman's place is in the home," and "What's a nice girl like you doing in a place like this?" Dolores Hayden illustrates how "both attitudes are linked to a set of nineteenth-century beliefs about female passivity and propriety in the domestic setting ('woman's sphere') versus male combativeness and aggression in the public setting ('man's world')."

30 Bederman, *Manliness & Civilization*, 16–23. For comparable arguments, see also Lears, *Rebirth of a Nation* and Leonard, *Illiberal Reformers*.
31 Wright used the term "manliness" all of one time in his autobiography. He described Lewis Mumford as follows: "With the essential manliness and nobility seen in the man as seen in his work he made no attempt to be apologetic or conciliatory." Wright qualified the "nobility" of manliness with a presumably more "masculine" refusal to apologize or conciliate. See Wright, *An Autobiography* (1943), 352.
32 In the *Kindergarten Chats* for example there are numerous instances when Sullivan uses "manliness" in the prescribed fashion. It occurs multiple times throughout his writings. Twombly, after a description of Sullivan the person, concludes, "He was in short, with a few notable exceptions [his drinking, excessive work habits and the occasional loss of temper], a stern Victorian gentleman of the old school, an obvious credit to his profession." Louis H. Sullivan, *Kindergarten Chats and Other Writings* (1918; repr., New York: Dover Publications, 1979), 28; 30; 74; 77; 132; 141. Robert C. Twombly, *Louis Sullivan: His Life and Work* (Chicago: University of Chicago Press, 1986), 215–16.
33 Sullivan's library was the well-stocked library of the turn-of-the-century Progressive. The auction catalogue lists 274 entries for books, many of which were multiple volumes, such that the entire library comprised more than 900 volumes. It was full of the leading voices of the cultural issues of the day to include Jane Addams, Patrick Geddes, G. Stanley Hall, Lafcadio Hearn, C. Hanford Henderson, William James, Rudyard Kipling, Charles Godfrey Leland, Henry Davenport Northrop, Frederic Remington, Upton Sinclair, John Spargo, Oscar Lovell Triggs, Mark Twain, Thorstein Veblen, and Otto Weininger. Williams, Barker & Severn, *Catalogue at Auction*, not paginated.
34 Sullivan, *A System of Architectural Ornament*, not paginated.
35 Sullivan, "Ornament in Architecture," 82. Sullivan, "What Is the Just Subordination?" 31; 35.
36 Sullivan, *Kindergarten Chats*, 149.
37 Alexander Bain, *The Emotions and the Will* (1875; repr., Whitefish, MT: Kessinger Legacy Reprints, n.d.), 124–5. Another book from Sullivan's library, Bain indicates that "the Tender Emotion, in all its outgoings of sociable regards, is one of the first, if not *the* first, of human emotions. It surpasses every other life interest." Referencing Spencer, who holds "the central fact of Benevolent regards," Bain adds the following: "What is not so apparent is that this is a primary fact of the constitution, due to a chance variation, and perpetuating itself by the great advantage conferred by it in the struggle for life."
38 Sullivan, *Kindergarten Chats*, 148.
39 This was a compelling idea for Sullivan. In *Democracy* he offered a different version where he suggested it was Zoroaster that "split man's life through the center as with a glittering axe, and That Which is One, fell asunder." Louis H. Sullivan, *Democracy: A Man-search*, intro. Elaine Hedges (Detroit: Wayne State University Press, 1961), 26.
40 Sullivan, *Kindergarten Chats*, 148.
41 Sullivan, *Kindergarten Chats*, 149.
42 *OED*, s.v. "sympathy."

43 Solomon, *In Defense of Sentimentality*, 51.
44 Vincent Scully, "Louis Sullivan's Architectural Ornament," *Perspecta 5: The Yale Architectural Journal*, ed. Edwin Close, II (New Haven: School of Architecture, Yale University, 1959), 74.
45 Sullivan, "The Artistic Use of the Imagination (1899)," *Louis Sullivan: The Public Papers*, ed. Robert Twombly (Chicago: The University of Chicago Press, 1988), 66.
46 Whitman, *Leaves of Grass* (Philadelphia: Rees Welsh & Co., 1882), 221. This is Sullivan's personal edition (signed and marked up by him) that is currently in the archives of the Library of Congress. His library also contained the 1860 edition as cited in the auction catalogue.
47 Sullivan, *The Autobiography of an Idea*, 25; 37; 40; 61; 236.
48 Sullivan, "The Artistic Use of the Imagination," 66.
49 Lauren Weingarden, *Louis H. Sullivan and a 19th-Century Poetics of Naturalized Architecture* (Burlington, VT: Ashgate Publishing Company, 2009), 234.
50 Sullivan, "The Artistic Use of the Imagination," 67. Weingarden, *Louis H. Sullivan and a 19th-Century Poetics*, 234.
51 Recent studies in ornament, affect, and new materialisms all provide avenues by which we might take Sullivan literally. See, for instance, Antoine Picon, "Ornament and Its Users: From the Vitruvian Tradition to the Digital Age," *Histories of Ornament: From Global to Local*, ed. Gülru Necipoğlu and Alina Payne (Princeton and Oxford: Princeton University Press, 2016), 16; Lars Spuybroek, *The Sympathy of Things: Ruskin and the Ecology of Design* (Rotterdam: V2_Publishing, 2011), 148; 183.
52 Sullivan, *A System of Architectural Ornament*, not paginated. Sullivan restates this idea in his autobiography. Sullivan, *The Autobiography of an Idea*, 269.
53 Sullivan, *The Autobiography of an Idea*, 54.
54 Sullivan, *Kindergarten Chats*, 149.
55 Sullivan, "Ornament in Architecture," 83.
56 Sullivan, "Ornament in Architecture," 83.
57 Sullivan, "Ornament in Architecture," 83.
58 Sullivan, "Ornament in Architecture," 83.
59 Philip Johnson provides one of the more insightful yet scathing critiques of Sullivan's analogies. Philip Johnson, "Is Sullivan the Father of Functionalism?" *Art News* 55, no. 8 (December 1956): 45.
60 Sullivan, *A System of Architectural Ornament*, not paginated.
61 Sullivan, *A System of Architectural Ornament*, not paginated. This was not the first time that Sullivan would make similar claims. See also Sullivan, *Democracy*, 382. Sullivan, "What Is the Just Subordination?" 32.
62 Sullivan, *A System of Architectural Ornament*, not paginated.
63 Andrew, *Louis Sullivan and the Polemics of Modern Architecture*, 32; 35. Andrew, after five pages of carping about Sullivan's "aping," "use," and "reliance," upon the metaphysics of Kant, Schopenhauer, and Nietzsche, together with the democratic idealism of Whitman, concludes that "Sullivan's reading of Whitman was evidently sketchy, as was his reading of everyone else."
64 Apparently Weingarden did not have issue with it. While she does not specifically address what Sullivan might have meant by "the seat of identity," "the will to power," "the seat of power" or "the will to live," she does trace a

genealogy of Sullivan's transformation of the seed-germ to Ruskin's pictorial transformations of "natural facts." Once again, she suggests that we are to construe Sullivan's transformations as symbolic, at different times calling them a "model," "paradigm," "metaphor," or "analogy." Weingarden, "Louis Sullivan's *System of Architectural Ornament*," 13–15; 18–20.

65 Twombly, *Louis Sullivan: His Life and Work*, 437.
66 Sullivan, *The Autobiography of an Idea*, 206. In the Lotos Club notebook, Sullivan listed books that he read that are not found in his library. There is no reference to Schopenhauer, much less *The World as Will and Representation* here either. See Louis Sullivan, *Lotos Club Notebook* found in the Avery Architectural and Fine Arts Library, Columbia University, New York, 190.
67 Williams, Barker & Severn, "Catalogue at Auction." There were a couple of different volumes of Schopenhauer's *Essays* published within the time frame of Sullivan's library. However, there is not enough information in the auction catalog to know which publication. But it is possible that the editor of his volume included some information about the will. For instance, in two *Essays* appropriate to the period, both being T. Bailey Saunders translations, Saunders included a brief summary of *The World as Will and Representation*. Sullivan could have developed an elementary understanding of it from them. Arthur Schopenhauer, *The Essays of Arthur Schopenhauer*, trans. T. Bailey Saunders (New York: Willey Book Company, n.d.), iii–vii; and Arthur Schopenhauer, *Essays of Arthur Schopenhauer*, trans. T. Bailey Saunders (New York: A. L. Burt Company, n.d.), iii–xxii. Andrew, *Louis Sullivan and the Polemics*, 33.
68 Friedrich Nietzsche, *Thus Spoke Zarathustra*, *The Portable Nietzsche*, ed. and trans. Walter Kaufmann (New York: Penguin Books, 1976), 227.
69 Schopenhauer, *The World as Will and Representation*, 1:180.
70 Nietzsche, *Thus Spoke Zarathustra*, 235.
71 Morrison, *Louis Sullivan*, 225. Elaine Hedges, Introduction to *Democracy* by Louis H. Sullivan, xiv. Andrew, *Louis Sullivan and the Polemics of Modern Architecture*, 33. Both Hedges and Andrew cite Morrison as their source. Andrew also cites other sources.
72 Nietzsche, *Thus Spoke Zarathustra*, 170; 227.
73 Walter Kaufmann, *Nietzsche: Philosopher, Psychologist, Antichrist*, 3rd edition (Princeton: Princeton University Press, 1968), 198; 202.
74 Sullivan, *Democracy*, 216; 381–3. Sullivan, *Kindergarten Chats*, 166.
75 Peter Gay describes the study of the self as a "core ideal" of romanticism. In an apt play of Sullivan's themes, he writes, "Victorian moderns outstripped their precursors by escalating the search for the inner man—and woman—and converting it as much as possible into a dependable discipline, in a word to be objective about subjectivity." Peter Gay, *Why the Romantics Matter* (New Haven and London: Yale University Press, 2015), 22.
76 Nietzsche, *Thus Spoke Zarathustra*, 227.
77 Nietzsche, *Thus Spoke Zarathustra*, 227
78 Sullivan did get caught up in his words. At one point he wrote that "man" "has the power to will—it is one of his many powers." Sullivan, *A System of Architectural Ornament*, "The Inorganic and the Organic," not paginated.
79 Sullivan, *A System of Architectural Ornament*, Pl. 2 & Pl. 5.
80 Sullivan, "Ornament in Architecture," 81.
81 Sullivan, "Ornament in Architecture," 83.

82 Charles L. Davis II, "Louis Sullivan and the Physiognomic Translation of American Character," *Journal of the Society of Architectural Historians* 76, no. 1 (March 2017): 63–81, https://jsah.ucpress.edu/content/76/1/63.full.pdf+html [accessed September 11, 2019].
83 Some of the other books in Sullivan's library that cover physiognomy that Davis does not mention are Patrick Geddes and J. Arthur Thompson, *The Evolution of Sex* (1889); Charles Godfrey Leland, *The Alternate Sex* (1904); Otto Weininger, *Sex & Character* [n.d.]; and G. Stanley Hall, *Adolescence* (1904).
84 A. E. Willis, *Encyclopædia of Human Nature and Physiognomy* (Chicago: Loomis and Company, Publishers, 1889), 44.
85 Friedrich Schopenhauer, "On Physiognomy," *Essays*, trans. T. Bailey Saunders (New York: Willey Book Company, n.d.), 70. As previously indicated, it is not clear which of Schopenhauer's essays were in Sullivan's library.
86 Pond, *The Meaning of Architecture*, 221–4. For the Blondel I am indebted to Antoine Picon in his essay, "Ornament and Its Users: From the Vitruvian Tradition to the Digital Age," and Vittoria De Palma in her essay "A Natural History of Ornament" both in *Histories of Ornament: From Global to Local*, ed. Gülru Necipoğlu and Alina Payne (Princeton: Princeton University Press, 2016), 12 and 32.
87 Sullivan, *Kindergarten Chats*, 24.
88 Sullivan, *Kindergarten Chats*, 24.
89 Sullivan, *Kindergarten Chats*, 24. In the startling slip from adjective to noun—or could it be a verb?—one might wish to ponder a building that is "more or less pervert."
90 Louis Sullivan, "What Is Architecture?" 177. As Davis asserts, Sullivan believed that his "buildings operated as physical embodiments of national characteristics." Davis, "Louis Sullivan and the Physiognomic Translation," 63.
91 Andrew suggests that Sullivan overlooked a self-contradiction within his argument: that while he believed the "beliefs of a society are clearly manifested in the buildings it raises," he also believed that the late-nineteenth-century "architecture of the United States was in fact not the true representative of democratic 'thought.'" It seems more likely that Sullivan would have recognized this contradiction and believed that the over-civilizing aspects of the architecture profession, especially from those architects educated in Europe, had perverted the buildings that were being built and that it took architects like Sullivan and Wright to reveal their folly. Andrew, *Louis Sullivan and the Polemics of Modern Architecture*, 19.
92 Sullivan believed in the inner character of a building to the degree that its ornament should "be determined at the very beginning of the design." Sullivan, "Ornament in Architecture," 82.
93 George Frederick Drinka, M. D., *The Birth of Neurosis: Myth, Malady, and the Victorians* (New York: Simon and Schuster, 1984), 72. Drinka illustrated the confusion. It was believed that from the germ of a fertilized egg, an infected mother would deliver both the child and her infections, such as syphilis, tuberculosis, and the vitamin deficiencies of rickets and pellagra.
94 In the intervening years between his essay "Ornament in Architecture," and *A System of Architectural Ornament*, as evidenced by his library alone, Sullivan had done additional research on the scientific study of nature.
95 Sullivan, *A System of Architectural Ornament*, Plate 5, not paginated.

96 Asa Gray, *Gray's School and Field Book of Botany* (New York: Ivison Blakeman and Company, 1878), 138–42; 157–66. Gray's argument and language would have informed how Sullivan might have understood a given relationship between form and function, and the development of his dictum, "form ever follows function."
97 Edmund B. Wilson, PhD, *The Cell in Development and Inheritance* (New York: The Macmillan Company, 1911), 2.
98 Wilson, *The Cell in Development and Inheritance*, 6.
99 Wilson's *The Cell in Development and Inheritance* was first published in 1896 at about the time Sullivan was finishing the Guaranty Building. The book was of such importance that Wilson regularly updated the data to match the current science through multiple editions until 1953. I refer to the 1911 edition.
100 Wilson, *The Cell in Development and Inheritance*, 358.
101 Wilson, *The Cell in Development and Inheritance*, 6.
102 Sullivan, *A System of Architectural Ornament*, Plate 3, not paginated.
103 Sullivan, *A System of Architectural Ornament*, Plate 5, not paginated.
104 As indicated, besides the individual volumes on these sciences, Sullivan also had ninety-six volumes of the Van Nostrand Science Series.
105 Charles Godfrey Leland, *The Alternate Sex or the Female Intellect in Man, and the Masculine in Woman* (London: William Rider & Son, Ltd., 1904), vi.
106 Ernst Haeckel, *Riddle of the Universe at the Close of the Nineteenth Century*, trans. Joseph McCabe (New York: Harper & Brothers Publishers, 1901), 20–1. Haeckel credits his shared beliefs and indebtedness to Goethe. Sullivan had a five-volume set of Goethe's *Werke*, in German, that may have reinforced Haeckel's arguments.
107 Haeckel, *The Riddle of the Universe*, 212.
108 Haeckel, *The Riddle of the Universe*, 220.
109 Haeckel, *The Riddle of the Universe*, 224.
110 Haeckel, *The Riddle of the Universe*, 224.
111 Haeckel, *The Riddle of the Universe*, 225.
112 Sullivan, *A System of Architectural Ornament*, Plate 3, not paginated.
113 Sullivan, *Democracy*, 382.
114 Sullivan, *A System of Architectural Ornament*, Plate 5, not paginated.
115 For Sullivan the importance of the loss of demarcation between subjectivity and objectivity, and its source in Whitman, cannot be overemphasized. As an idea it recurs throughout his writing. Sullivan, *The Autobiography of an Idea*, 25; 37; 40; 61; 236. Sullivan, "Emotional Architecture as Compared with Intellectual," 92–3. Sullivan, *Kindergarten Chats*, 99.

Chapter 4

1 Sullivan, *The Autobiography of an Idea*, 55–6.
2 Sullivan, *The Autobiography of an Idea*, 56.
3 Whitman, *Leaves of Grass*, 29. These are the fourth and fifth lines of the poem. The first through the third are the famous beginning, "I CELEBRATE myself, and sing myself, / And what I assume you shall assume, / For every atom belonging to me as good belongs to you." Whitman's shared atom is consistent with Sullivan's sympathy.

4   As a kind of name-dropping, Sullivan might simply be saying that he is aligning his work with Whitman's. This too would be consistent with the thesis.
5   Whitman observed the spear of grass. Sullivan "did not." While Sullivan referred to it, he simultaneously denied it. Robert Atwan, in his thorough analysis of the poem, offers numerous interpretations for the grass and suggests that it is the same Calamus grass that would provide the title for the frequently homoerotic poems of the "Calamus" section of *Leaves of Grass*. The shape of the grass suggests phallic imagery. That symbolism is further reinforced with the "spear." Perhaps Sullivan understood the symbolism and thought it inappropriate for his childhood dream. Robert Atwan, "Observing a Spear of Summer Grass," *The Kenyon Review*, New Series 12, no. 2 Impure Form (Spring 1990): 17–19; 21–2; 24.
6   Sullivan, *The Autobiography of an Idea*, 56.
7   Sullivan, *The Autobiography of an Idea*, 23; 34; 68; 68–9; 69–70; 86. Sullivan placed himself in relation to these men in the terms of another of sentimentality's tender emotions: "adoration." It was not unique to this story. In variations of adoration, including worship, honor, and idolization, this general power relationship with men appears throughout *The Autobiography of an Idea*, 57; 68; 69; 85; 86; 101; 247. Solomon, *In Defense of Sentimentality*, 9.
8   Whitman, "Walt Whitman," *Leaves of Grass*, 40.
9   Whitman, *Leaves of Grass*, 39–41.
10 Sullivan, *The Autobiography of an Idea*, 86.
11 Whitman, *Leaves of Grass*, 30.
12 Sullivan, *The Autobiography of an Idea*, 86.
13 Atwan, "Observing a Spear of Summer Grass," 17–22. Atwan offers additional analysis of the symbolism of the poem.
14 Whitman, *Leaves of Grass*, 32. Juan A. Herrero Brasas indicates that scholars from William James to George Carpenter, Roger Asselineau, Richard Maurice Bucke, and Gay Wilson Allen see this passage as indicative of a mystical experience. Some go so far as to suggest that Whitman's writing is strictly metaphorical as an expression of the ineffable and that it is not to be construed as literally erotic at all. How much these interpretations were a part of the effort to sanitize Whitman's poetry and in particular the homoerotics is beyond the scope of this study. Suffice it to say that I agree with Schmidgall who at the end of his review of Herrero Brasas's book quotes Whitman's "energetic paean" to Horace. "Sex: sex: sex: whether you sing or make a machine, or go to the North Pole, or love your mother, or build a house, or black shoes, or anything—anything at all—it's sex, sex, sex: sex is the root of all." Juan A. Herrero Brasas, *Walt Whitman's Mystical Ethics of Comradeship: Homosexuality and the Marginality of Friendship at the Crossroads of Modernity* (Albany: State University of New York Press, 2010), 34, 36, 38, 40. Gary Schmidgall, "Herrero Brasas, Juan A. Walt Whitman's Mystical Ethics of Comradeship: Homosexuality and the Marginality of Friendship at the Crossroads of Modernity [review]," *Walt Whitman Quarterly Review* 28, no. 1 (2010): 74.
15 Whitman, *Leaves of Grass*, 32–3.
16 Edwin Haviland Miller, ed., *Walt Whitman's "Song of Myself:" A Mosaic of Interpretations* (Iowa City: University of Iowa Press, 1989), 65. In this collection of critical interpretations, Miller includes Michael Orth's (1968) comments and critique.

17 Sullivan's circumspection is understandable. From today's perspective, it is difficult to imagine, but Whitman was severely censured for the sexual content of his work. According to Geoffrey Saunders Schramm, the *New York Times* wrote of the 1860 edition of *Leaves of Grass* (the edition Sullivan owned), "If possible, he is more reckless and vulgar than in his two former publications." When his employer at the Department of the Interior found a copy in his desk, Whitman was fired. The 1881 edition was banned in Boston as obscene literature. Geoffrey Saunders Schramm, "Whitman's Lifelong Endeavor: *Leaves of Grass* at 150" (The Walt Whitman Archive: http://www.whitmanarchive.org/about/articles/anc.00007.html [accessed October 20, 2013]), 3.
18 Miller, ed., *Walt Whitman's "Song of Myself,"* 74. Sculley Bradley (1939) made this comment.
19 Whitman, *Leaves of Grass*, 37.
20 Sullivan, *The Autobiography of an idea*, 78. On the Atlantic coast in Newburyport, MA, Sullivan used the term the "sea."
21 Sullivan, *The Autobiography of an Idea*, 79.
22 Sullivan, *The Autobiography of an Idea*, 79.
23 Miller, ed., *Walt Whitman's "Song of Myself,"* 67. Albert Gelpi describes it is "a bearded body in the woman's position."
24 Bederman, *Manliness & Civilization*, 10–11.
25 In his autobiography, Sullivan described just one scene where he went hunting. He was fourteen. When the hunting party got to their destination, "a sumptuous lake," Sullivan walked to the edge and shot his gun—at nothing. "This display was too dramatic, even for Louis. Once was enough." He was so emotionally shaken he had to leave the group to recover. Sullivan, *The Autobiography of an Idea*, 153–4. See also, Robert Twombly who debunks the myth of Sullivan's "male prowess" as the "rugged individualist." See Twombly, *Louis Sullivan*, 356.
26 Williams, Barker & Severn Co., "Catalogue at Auction," not paginated. Sullivan's library included Frederick Remington's *Pony Tracks* (1895); Mark Twain's *Roughing It* (1888); Henry Davenport Northrop's *Indian Massacre's* (1891); Rudyard Kipling's *From Sea to Sea* (1899); Walter Dwight Wilcox's *Camping in the Canadian Rockies* (1896); Meriwether Lewis's, *History of the Expedition under the Command of Lewis and Clark* (1893); A. W. Greeley, *Arctic: Three Years of Arctic Service* (1886): all books that traced the end-of-the-century lineaments of manhood.
27 Otto Weininger, *Sex and Character* (New York: G. P. Putnam's Sons, n.d.), 252. Weininger wrote, "However degraded a man may be, he is immeasurably above the most superior woman."
28 Weininger, *Sex and Character*, 2–3.
29 Weininger, *Sex and Character*, 6.
30 Weininger, *Sex and Character*, 5.
31 Weininger, *Sex and Character*, 29.
32 Weininger, *Sex and Character*, 45–6.
33 Weininger, *Sex and Character*, 51.
34 Patrick Geddes and J. Arthur Thompson, *The Evolution of Sex* (1889; repr., Ann Arbor: University Microfilms International, 1983), 289. A rather dubious endorsement for women's equality, Geddes and Thompson based these findings on the study of evolution. They would make their position quite clear

regarding women's suffrage when they wrote, "What was decided among the prehistoric Protozoa cannot be annulled by Act of Parliament." Geddes and Thompson, *The Evolution of Sex*, 267. See also Bederman, *Manliness & Civilization*, 153.
35 Geddes, *The Evolution of Sex*, 267. For Geddes and Thompson, "males are more active, energetic, eager, passionate, and variable," "and are very frequently the leaders in evolutionary progress." Females "are more passive, conservative, sluggish, and stable" "and tend rather to preserve the constancy and integrity of the species." "The more active males, with a consequently wider range of experience, may have bigger brains and more intelligence; but the females, especially as mothers, have indubitably a larger and more habitual share of the altruistic emotions. The males being usually stronger have greater independence and courage; the females excel in constancy of affection and in sympathy."
36 Geddes, *The Evolution of Sex*, 271.
37 Obviously Sullivan was aware of the association. He characterized the "feminine" as "intuitive sympathy, tact, suavity and grace." Sullivan, *Kindergarten Chats*, 23.
38 Leland, *The Alternate Sex*, 4–6. Later in the book, having illustrated the strengths of women, he stated that "there is small difference indeed as to which is the Superior Sex in the transaction—which ye may all reason out everyone his or her own way, drawing everyone his or her own conclusions." Leland, *The Alternate Sex*, 77.
39 Leland, *The Alternate Sex*, 35.
40 Leland, *The Alternate Sex*, 62.
41 Leland, *The Alternate Sex*, 65.
42 Leland, *The Alternate Sex*, 62.
43 Leland, *The Alternate Sex*, 68.
44 Leland, *The Alternate Sex*, 41.
45 Leland, *The Alternate Sex*, 42.
46 It is likely that Sullivan would have agreed with at least three of Leland's choices for genius: Goethe, Darwin, and Shakespeare. Sullivan had seven volumes of Goethe and a volume of *Shakespeare's Works* in his library. In his contribution to the *Lotos Club Notebook* he states that he read Charles Darwin's *The Descent of Man*, Vol. I, in October of 1875. He would have been nineteen years old. See *Lotos Club Notebook*, Avery Library, Avery Classics, Columbia University, NY, not paginated. Williams, Barker & Severn, *Catalogue at Auction*, not paginated.
47 Leland, *The Alternate Sex*, 33.
48 Leland, *The Alternate Sex*, 73.
49 Sullivan, *The Autobiography of an Idea*, 236.
50 Sullivan, *Kindergarten Chats*, 133.
51 "With the exception of his books," Robert Twombly calls this essay Sullivan's "last major theoretical work." Twombly, *Louis Sullivan: The Public Papers*, 174.
52 Sullivan, "What Is Architecture," 187; 190. More authors cite Sullivan's essay of twenty years earlier, "Characteristics of American Architecture" (1885), where he deplored an American architecture that was not "virile." Suggesting that he was asking for a more "masculine" architecture, he assessed the contemporaneous architecture as having a "marvelous instinct," and "stubborn

common sense," but as if hidden behind a veil of American Romanticism it was like the emasculated Hercules at the foot of Omphale. Sullivan called for the awakening of an authentic power in the making of a distinctly American architecture. Louis H. Sullivan, "Characteristics of American Architecture," *Louis Sullivan: The Public Papers*, ed. Robert Twombly (Chicago/London: The University of Chicago Press, 1988), 4–5. Narciso G. Menocal, *Architecture as Nature: The Transcendentalist Idea of Louis Sullivan* (Madison: The University of Wisconsin Press, 1981), 17. Paul, *Louis Sullivan*, 32–5.

53 Sullivan, *A System of Architectural Ornament*, not paginated. Sullivan, *The Autobiography of an Idea*, 176.
54 Weininger, *Sex and Character*, 5; 45–52.
55 George Chauncey, *Gay New York: Gender, Urban Culture and the Makings of the Gay Male World, 1890–1940* (New York: Basic Books, 1994), 49.
56 Chauncey, *Gay New York*, 48–9.
57 John Potvin indicates that both he and Beatriz Colomina share this view. John Potvin, *Bachelors of a Different Sort: Queer Aesthetics, Material Culture and the Modern Interior in Britain* (Manchester: Manchester University Press, 2014), 225.
58 Foucault, *The History of Sexuality*, 43.
59 Foucault, *The History of Sexuality*, 43.
60 Even the small-town Illinois newspapers, to include Wright's *The Oak Park Vindicator*, covered the Oscar Wilde trial and its aftermath. The case was so well known that the name "Oscar Wilde" became code for transgressive sexual behavior. *The Edwardsville Intelligencer* cites the case of a doctor charged with having an orgy with young men as an "Oscar Wilde case of our own." Even Wright was vulnerable to the accusation. After a neighbor called him "queer" to the visiting Martin brothers, Darwin Martin in a letter to Elbert Hubbard came to his defense stating that "he is no Oscar Wilde." *The Oak Park Vindicator*, June 14, 1895. *The Alton Weekly Telegraph*, April 11, 1895. *Decatur Daily Republican*, June 12, 1895. *The Edwardsville Intelligencer*, June 11, 1895. Jack Quinan, *Frank Lloyd Wright's Martin House: Architecture as Portraiture* (New York: Princeton Architectural Press, 2004), 28–9.
61 In addition to those listed, the library also included Max Nordau's *Degeneration* that outlined the decadence, with hints to the sexual "decadence," in fin-de-siècle France. Having lived in Paris from 1874 to 1875, Sullivan would have been able to put Nordau's account in some relative perspective. Nordau's critique of Wagner would have precluded Sullivan's agreement with the denouncement of "degeneration." Moreover, Nordau's comparison of Henrik Ibsen with Richard Wagner might partially account for Sullivan's having the two-volume set of Ibsen's plays. Max Nordau, *Degeneration* (New York: D. Appleton and Company, 1895), 13.
62 Douglass Shand-Tucci, *The Crimson Letter: Harvard, Homosexuality, and the Shaping of American Culture* (New York: St. Martin's Press, 2003), 146. Shand-Tucci was describing the "telltale signs" that he found in a library from about 1912. Chauncey offers similar "telltale signs" and indicates that within gay folklore of 1890–1940, the "heroic figures" from the past who they claimed were "gay" included Michelangelo, Shakespeare, Walt Whitman, Oscar Wilde, and Julius Caesar. Chauncey, *Gay New York*, 283.

63 Julien, *Richard Wagner: Sa Vie et Ses Oeuvres*; Nohl, *Life of Wagner*; and Upton, *The Standard Operas*, of which the most pages were devoted to Wagner. The library also included fourteen volumes of what were identified as "Oratorios, etc." Williams, Baker & Severn, *Catalogue at Auction*, not paginated.
64 Wright, *An Autobiography* (1932), 101.
65 It is unclear which of the three published volumes Sullivan owned: 1905, 1908, or 1914. Given that he auctioned his library in 1909, and unless the 1908 volume was a gift, it seems likely that he owned the first volume that covered the dates March 28 to July 14, 1888. However it should be noted that Sullivan is mentioned in the *third* volume. Traubel wrote that Whitman had saved a letter that Sullivan sent him and Traubel read it and recorded it. Whitman responded, "'Ain't that catchin'? It sounds like something good that comes along on the wind for them as know enough to suck in. I'd say that feller's some shucks himself: whatever he does I'll bet he does big: he writes as if he reached way round things and encircled them. He's an architect or something; and he's a man for sure." Horace Traubel, *With Walt Whitman in Camden (November 1, 1888—January 20, 1889)* (1914; repr., New York: Rowman and Littlefield, Inc., 1961), 25–6.
66 Chauncey, *Gay New York*, 107; 144; 231. Carpenter was known for his positive portrayal of and advocacy for homosexuality and homosexuals, whom he called "Uranians," in a number of treatises and books, to include *Love's Coming of Age*. Any close reading of Traubel's diaries discloses numerous telltale signs. For Traubel's sexuality see Herrero Brasas, *Walt Whitman's Mystical Ethics*, 152.
67 Rodger Streitmatter, *Outlaw Marriages: The Hidden Histories of Fifteen Extraordinary Same-sex Couples* (Boston: Beacon Press, 2012), 1. Carpenter says the relationship lasted ten years. Carpenter, *Days with Walt Whitman*, 149.
68 Carpenter, *Days with Walt Whitman*, 148.
69 Whitman's homosexual behavior is so generally accepted today that his claim that he fathered six children is characterized as one of literature's great fabled lies. Schmidgall, *Walt Whitman: A Gay Life*, 74. Herrero Brasas, *Walt Whitman's Mystical Ethics*, 14, 89, 144. See also Michael Warner, ed., *The Portable Walt Whitman* (New York: Penguin Books, 2003), xxvii.
70 Carpenter, *Days with Walt Whitman*, 151–2.
71 "Disingenuous" because of Carpenter's advocacy for "Uranians." Late in his life he recounted to Gavin Arthur that he had had a sexual encounter with Whitman during one of his visits. See Arnie Kantrowitz, "Edward Carpenter," *Walt Whitman: An Encyclopedia*, http://www.whitmanarchive.org/criticism/current/encyclopedia/index.html [accessed February 6, 2014].
72 John Addington Symonds, *The Life of Michelangelo Buonarroti*, Vol. 2 (London: John C. Nimmo, 1893), 93–179.
73 A number of sources raise the possibility of Sullivan having been a homosexual, but none can cite concrete evidence. Twombly, *Louis Sullivan: His Life & Work*, 398–406; Jennifer Bloomer, "D'Or," *Sexuality and Space*, ed. Beatriz Colomina (New York: Princeton Architectural Press, 1992), 170–2; Timothy Rohan, "Rendering the Surface: Paul Rudolph's Art and Architecture Building at Yale," *Grey Room* 01 (Fall 2000): 97. Of the love between men, most authors recognize the strong bond of love between Sullivan and Wright, and some note its sexual overtones. Gill, *Many Masks*, 63. Wright states

that of "smoking," "drinking," "whoring," Sullivan "practiced them in their many forms to a dreadful extreme." Wright, *Genius and Mobocracy*, 40–1. Yet Twombly states "that rumors of his rogue male posture cannot be substantiated, and that his romantic interest in women was sporadic enough to be virtually nonexistent." Twombly, *Louis Sullivan: His Life & Work*, 356. Perhaps the most convincing suggestion of homosexual behavior comes from Philip Johnson's surprising allegation in *Art News*, where he cites "the sex troubles" as another reason for Sullivan's downfall. Johnson, who later publicly admitted to his own homosexuality, would have been privy to the extensive, underground network of identity information of who was and who wasn't that was necessary for both survival and love within the homosexual community. While Johnson's statement is highly suggestive, it is still vague enough to be inconclusive. Johnson, "Is Sullivan the Father of Functionalism?" 45.
74 Both editions of Sullivan's *Leaves of Grass*, 1860 and 1881, included the explicitly homoerotic "Calamus" poems.
75 For known references made to the poetry of Whitman's *Leaves of Grass* in his autobiography, see Sullivan, *The Autobiography of an Idea*, 25; 37; 40; 56; 61; 236.
76 Sullivan, *The Autobiography of an Idea*, 234.
77 Sullivan, *The Autobiography of an Idea*, 207–8; 234. Sullivan dubbed Wagner the other "master craftsman" in only slightly less passionate terms. Whitman is the only other person he speaks of in the same laudatory terms but he never explicitly refers to him as the "master craftsman" or "mighty craftsman."
78 Sullivan, *The Autobiography of an Idea*, 236.
79 Whitman, *Leaves of Grass* (1882), 282–4. Walt Whitman, *Leaves of Grass 1860: The 150th Anniversary Facsimile Edition* (Iowa City: University of Iowa Press, 2009), 223. I include the 1860 edition (facsimile) because it adds the final phrase, "And these become part of him or her that peruses them here." All other phrases quoted are from the 1882 edition.
80 Determining the characteristics of anything as "feminine" or "masculine" is problematic. By definition it presupposes an insufficient and dangerous generality regarding the properties of gender. It has no more merit than defining building characteristics based on race. We cannot, and consequently should not, make generalizations regarding what is an essential property of "woman" in order to determine what is "feminine," nor "man" in order to determine "masculine." Archaic terms, any usage of "feminine" and "masculine" must be accordingly qualified and contextualized.
81 Menocal, *Architecture as Nature*, 31. Twombly, *Louis Sullivan: His Life and Work*, 401. Lewis Mumford, *The Brown Decades: A Study of the Arts in America 1865–1895* (1931; repr., New York: Dover Publications, 1971), 68.
82 Menocal, *Architecture as Nature*, 24–5.
83 Sullivan, *The Public Papers*, 4; 5; 190. Sullivan, *The Autobiography of an Idea*, 326. Sometimes Sullivan was describing the architects, and sometimes their buildings, and sometimes the arts in general.
84 Like his response to an interviewer regarding the style of the ornamentation of Hooley's Theater, Sullivan probably would have responded similarly regarding gender: "The vaguer you are in such matters the better I shall be pleased." Louis Sullivan, "*From* Hooley's New Theater," *The Public Papers*, ed. Robert Twombly (Chicago: The University of Chicago Press, 1988), 2.

85 Ralph Waldo Emerson, "Swedenborg; Or, The Mystic," *Representative Men. Seven Lectures* (Cambridge, MA: The Riverside Press, 1884), 123.
86 Emerson, *Representative Men*, 124.
87 I mention the Gage Building here to indicate the time frame when the shift is first evident. The work that Sullivan did was just the design of the façade. The overall massing to include the arrangement of solid and void was predetermined before Sullivan became actively involved.
88 To be sure, from the twenty-first-century perspective the volumes might not appear so abstracted. But any reading of the contemporaneous critics gives some idea of how they were perceived. For example the particularly astute and culturally attuned critic Montgomery Schuyler complained that the People's Savings Bank of Cedar Rapids, Iowa, needed a cornice of some sort to alleviate the building's otherwise "absolute plainness." Weingarden reminds us that he also criticized the Peoples Savings Bank for its "shocking starkness." Montgomery Schuyler, *American Architecture and Other Writings*, ed. William H. Jordy and Ralph Coe (1961; repr., New York: Atheneum, 1964), 306–7. Lauren S. Weingarden, *Louis H. Sullivan: The Banks* (Cambridge, MA: MIT Press, 1987), 63.
89 Weingarden, *The Banks*, 113.
90 Sullivan, "What Is the Just Subordination?" 33–4. In this six-page essay Sullivan spends all of a paragraph specifically on the formal relationship between details and mass (p. 32). The balance of the essay primarily covers the "spiritual result."
91 Sullivan, *Kindergarten Chats*, 160.
92 At different times Sullivan called this spirit the "Infinite Creative Spirit," "Infinite Spirit," "Eternal Spirit," "Spirit of the Universe," and "Spirit." He also called it the "Function of all functions." Sullivan, *Kindergarten Chats*, 43; 45; 46, 97; 99; 140. Sullivan, "What Is the Just Subordination?" 34. Sullivan, "Emotional Architecture," 94. Louis Sullivan, "Essay on Inspiration," *Louis Sullivan: The Public Papers*, ed. Robert Twombly (Chicago: The University of Chicago Press, 1988), 21; 24. Louis Sullivan, "The Young Man in Architecture," *Louis Sullivan: The Public Papers*, ed. Robert Twombly (Chicago: The University of Chicago Press, 1988), 137.
93 *OED*, s. v. "function." The *OED* defines "function" as an "action."
94 Sullivan, *Kindergarten Chats*, 46.
95 Sullivan, *Kindergarten Chats*, 46; 99.
96 Sullivan, "What Is Architecture?" 195. Walt Whitman, "Democratic Vistas," *Walt Whitman: Prose Works 1892, Volume II, Collect and Other Prose*, ed. Floyd Stovall (New York: New York University Press, 1964), 381–2; 398. Herrero Brasas questions whether Whitman's poetry is a religious doctrine or an ethical code. He argues that because Whitman never formulated a systematic doctrine, nor did his disciples try to indoctrinate others with systematic theological beliefs, then it must be an ethical code. Herrero Brasas, *Walt Whitman's Mystical Ethics*, 31.
97 Sullivan asked, "Could ever there have been, can there ever be a question, that any art may live at any time? He who asks it, it may be, is well advised, but he has surely little faith;—and without faith, what are we all,—but zeros?" Whitman said this about his *Leaves of Grass*. "I think the Leaves the most religious book among books: crammed full of faith. What would the Leaves be without faith? An empty vessel: faith is its very substance, balance—its

one article of assent—its one item of assurance." Louis Sullivan, "May Not Architecture Again Become a Living Art?" *Louis Sullivan: The Public Papers*, ed. Robert Twombly (Chicago: The University of Chicago Press, 1988), 115. Horace Traubel, *With Walt Whitman in Camden (March 28—July 14, 1888)* (1905; repr., New York: Rowman and Littlefield, Inc., 1961), 372.
98 Mumford clearly articulates the deterministic functionalism of modernism and criticizes Sullivan's invocation of a "spiritual function." Mumford, *The Brown Decades*, 69–70.
99 Harries, *The Ethical Function of Architecture*, 228. I address this more fully in Chapter 9.
100 Harries, *The Ethical Function of Architecture*, 228.
101 Sullivan, *The Autobiography of an Idea*, 57.

Chapter 5

1 Wright, *An Autobiography* (1932), 14.
2 Wright, *An Autobiography* (1932), 14.
3 Wright, *An Autobiography* (1932), 37.
4 Wright's mother, weeping, sent the boy to her brother James Lloyd Jones's farm for the summers. Gill suggests that the mother, "alarmed by what she took to be the rather girlish delicacy of her son's preoccupations," held an ulterior motive that was consistent with her cutting off his golden curls: to "strengthen and harden" the young Wright. Friedland and Zellman similarly indicate that "Manhood did not come easily to Frank Lloyd Wright." Along with the aforementioned "indicators," they cite the story where the young Wright, upon seeing a plow about to cut through a field of daisies, "threw himself in the way of the plow and wept." Wright, *An Autobiography* (1932), 16. Gill, *Many Masks*, 46–8. Friedland, *The Fellowship*, 6–7.
5 Secrest indicates that at one time the family collectively held 1,800 acres of land in the valley. Secrest, *Frank Lloyd Wright*, 37.
6 Wright, *An Autobiography* (1932), 40.
7 Gill, *Many Masks*, 48.
8 Wright, *An Autobiography* (1932), 19. His mother's younger brother.
9 Wright, *An Autobiography* (1932), 16.
10 Wright, *An Autobiography* (1932), 24.
11 As a boy, Wright read Ruskin's *The Seven Lamps of Architecture*, a gift from his Aunts Nell and Jane. Wright, *An Autobiography* (1932), 31.
12 John Ruskin, *The Seven Lamps of Architecture* (New York: The Noonday Press, 1974), 99.
13 Wright, *An Autobiography* (1932), 25.
14 Wright, *An Autobiography* (1943), 46.
15 Wright, *An Autobiography* (1932), 41.
16 Wright, *An Autobiography* (1932), 40.
17 Wright, *An Autobiography* (1932), 39.
18 Wright, *An Autobiography* (1932), 40.
19 Wright, *An Autobiography* (1932), 40.
20 Wright, *An Autobiography* (1932), 38.

21 Wright, *An Autobiography* (1932), 38.
22 Wright, *An Autobiography* (1932), 38.
23 In the first edition of the autobiography Wright did not break this section out into a separate chapter. In the second edition he did, and it is that edition in which he entitled it "A Man." Wright, *An Autobiography* (1943), 38.
24 Through school transcripts, church records, fraternity house records, correspondence with his mother, and even opera house schedules, Hendrickson constructs a more likely sequence of events that indicates Wright made two trips to Chicago and that his family knew he was going. Moreover, he suggests that Wright appropriated much of his story from Harland Garland's novel, *Rose of Dutcher's Coolly*. Hendrickson, *Plagued by Fire*, 36–53.
25 Wright, *An Autobiography* (1932), 33. While it is apparent, at least from the comments of Uncle Enos, that his uncles equated farm work with masculinity, Gill suggests that some of the equation of music with femininity came from his mother. See Gill, *Many Masks*, 46.
26 Wright, *An Autobiography* (1932), 59.
27 Wright, *An Autobiography* (1932), 60.
28 Waller was the son of the successful real estate developer, Edward Carson Waller, another of Wright's clients.
29 Wright, *An Autobiography* (1932), 178.
30 Wright, *An Autobiography* (1932), 180.
31 Paul Kruty, *Frank Lloyd Wright and Midway Gardens* (Urbana: University of Illinois Press, 1998), 28.
32 John Lloyd Wright, *My Father, Frank Lloyd Wright* (1946; repr., New York: Dover Publications, 1992), 71.
33 Gill indicates the scandal made the front page of the Chicago Tribune. Huxtable elaborates. And it was not just the Chicago papers. Wright's son read about it in the San Diego papers. For a good example of the impact on a personal level, Quinan quotes from a letter from William Martin to his brother Darwin that his wife "refused to be seen with [Wright] in the auto." Gill, *Many Masks*, 204. Ada Louise Huxtable, *Frank Lloyd Wright: A Life* (2004; repr., New York: Penguin Books, 2008), 108. John Lloyd Wright, *My Father*, 63. Quinan, *Frank Lloyd Wright's Martin House*, 209–10.
34 Robert Twombly, *Frank Lloyd Wright: His Life and His Architecture* (New York: John Wiley & Sons, 1979), 145.
35 Mamah Borthwick Cheney reverted to her maiden name after her divorce from Edwin Cheney.
36 Wright was able to finance much of the bad accounting of his architectural practice and the financial tragedies of his personal life through his prints. By his own account, on the trip to Japan in 1922, he bought $125,000 worth of prints that were worth more than a million dollars in the United States. Wright, *An Autobiography* (1943), 526.
37 Most recent sources debunk Wright's story about a Japanese commission touring the world to find the perfect building and hence the ideal architect for the design of the Imperial Hotel. See Gill, *Many Masks*, 224–5; Twombly, *Frank Lloyd Wright: His Life and His Architecture*, 151–2; Secrest, *Frank Lloyd Wright: A Biography*, 214.
38 Wright, *An Autobiography* (1943), 181.

39 In each case, Wright dismissed his opponent with the *ad hominem* accusation of "sentimentality." Because of the frequency and usage in relation to the things that he wanted, it might seem like Wright wielded it as a cudgel to traduce all those who prevented him from having his way. However the apparent power of sentimentality to Wright within his own personal story, even within the few quotes made here, precludes that interpretation.
40 Wright, *An Autobiography* (1932), 201.
41 John Lloyd Wright, *My Father Frank Lloyd Wright*, 56.
42 John Lloyd Wright, *My Father Frank Lloyd Wright*, 57. See also page 59 for another example of Wright's vulnerable "heartstrings." Even his apprentices commented on Wright's tender nature. Edgar Tafel, *Apprentice to Genius: Years with Frank Lloyd Wright* (New York: McGraw-Hill Book Company, 1979), 68.
43 J. L. Austin, *How to Do Things with Words: The William James Lectures Delivered at Harvard University in 1955* (Eastford, CT: Martino Fine Books, 2018), 6. British philosopher of language, Austin (1911–1960) illustrated that any curse is performative.
44 Wright, *Genius and the Mobocracy*, 40–1.
45 Wright, *An Autobiography* (1932), 87; 99; 183; 263. Wright, *An Autobiography* (1943), 109; 379; 432; 433; 461; 471; 488; 498.
46 While profanity occasionally appeared in the arts as the emotional outbursts from the mouths of others, e.g., Rhett Butler's infamous "damn" was 1939, it was rare indeed when it was exclaimed by the reflective autobiographer.
47 Talking with Horace Traubel, Whitman stated, "Some day you will be writing about me: be sure to write about me honest: whatever you do do not prettify me: include all the hells and damns." Whitman insisted on maintaining that image even after the grave. Traubel, *With Walt Whitman in Camden (March 28—July 14, 1888)*, 398.
48 A T-square and a triangle were the primary tools for drawing perpendicular, horizontal, and vertical lines.
49 Wright, *An Autobiography* (1943), 379. In 1932, in the first edition of his autobiography Wright was willing to write "damn'd sentimentality." But it was only in 1943, in the second edition, that he opened up and admitted that his whole architectural practice shouted "damn."
50 Wright, *An Autobiography* (1943), 379.
51 Wright, *An Autobiography* (1943), 458.
52 Wright, *An Autobiography* (1943), 400–1; 462.
53 Richard Neutra, *Life and Shape* (1962; repr., Los Angeles: Atara Press, 2009), 185; John Lloyd Wright, *My Father Frank Lloyd Wright*, 94; Alan Hess, *Frank Lloyd Wright: The Houses* (New York: Rizzoli International Publications, 2005), 217, and numerous examples from his biographers. Even Wright himself comments about it, *An Autobiography* (1932), 56; 59; 96.
54 Secrest indicates that Wright and Hubbard were also dressing like the Scottish architect, Charles Rennie Mackintosh, who was wearing the same "black satin bow, dashingly tied at the neck, that was de rigueur for the artist," of that time. On the night of October 8, 1910, after spending over a year in Europe, where one might imagine him to have acquired a modicum of *continental* flair, Wright returned to Oak Park dressed like the Quaker Oats man. Secrest, *Frank Lloyd Wright*, 158; 205. William R. Drennan, *Death in a Prairie House: Frank Lloyd*

Wright and the Taliesin Murders (Madison, WI: Terrace Books, University of Wisconsin Press, 2007), 31; 57.

55 Huxtable calls it the "porkpie" hat, which has a smaller brim. See Huxtable, *Frank Lloyd Wright*, 41 and 220.
56 Whitman had chosen the etching, made from a photo, for the frontispiece of his 1855 edition of *Leaves of Grass*. Fifty-five years later, Hubbard had chosen his etching, same pose, same dress without the wideawake (too much of a giveaway), also made from a photo, as the frontispiece for his book of stories, *The Mintage*. From photo to etching to frontispiece, these were thoroughly considered images. It should also be noted that the wideawake was typical of Quaker attire and probably worn as a symbol of pacifism by all three men.
57 Jeff Solomon, "How Whitman Seduced Us with a Photograph," *The Gay and Lesbian Review* 17, no. 4 (July–August 2010): 43. Jeff Solomon is quoting Charles Henry Dana of *The New York Daily Tribune*, July 23, 1855.
58 Plutarch, *Plutarch's Lives of Themistocles, Pericles, Aristides, Alcibiades and Coriolanus, Demosthenes and Cicero, Cæsar and Antony*, The Harvard Classics, Charles W. Eliot, LL. D., ed., translation called Dryden's Corrected and revised by Arthur Hugh Clough (New York: P. F. Collier & Son Company, 1909), 119. Plutarch also offered Alcibiades's shield and the modifications he made to his boat as evidence of effeminacy.
59 Walt Whitman, *The Uncollected Poetry and Prose of Walt Whitman* ed. Emory Holloway (Garden City, NY: Doubleday Page and Company, 1921), 83.
60 For the scholar, Wright's Midway Gardens are frustrating. For all their significance as one of Wright's most important projects, they are also one of the most poorly documented. Kruty's account is the most thorough analysis. See Kruty, *Frank Lloyd Wright and Midway Gardens*, 37–59, for the demise of Midway Gardens and p. 126 for the probable role of Wright's son, John, in the photographing of the building.
61 Kruty, *Frank Lloyd Wright and Midway Gardens*, 3. Kruty's compelling analysis demolishes Wright's implication that the building complex had been designed over a weekend. Wright had written that "the thing had simply shaken itself out of my sleeve. In a remarkably short time there it was on paper—in color." Through a careful examination of a confusing sequence of four schemes, Kruty demonstrates that it had taken about as many months to design. The "Tale of Midway Gardens" is found in Wright's autobiography, Wright, *An Autobiography* (1932), 178–88.
62 Most sources focus primarily on the story of Midway Gardens and Wright's life with some critical assessment of the architecture of the building. See Norris Kelly Smith, *Frank Lloyd Wright: A Study in Architectural Content* (Englewood Cliffs, NJ: Prentice-Hall, 1966), 108–9; Gill, *Many Masks*, 228 and 257; and Twombly, *Frank Lloyd Wright: His Life and His Architecture*, 152–4. The better sources put the architecture in a broader context of architectural history and scholarship. See Henry-Russell Hitchcock, Jr., *In the Nature of Materials, 1887–1941, The Buildings of Frank Lloyd Wright* (New York: Duell, Sloan and Pearce, 1942), 62–4; and Henry Russell Hitchcock, Jr., *Modern Architecture: Romanticism and Reintegration* (New York: Payson & Clarke, Ltd., 1929), 115. Note that Hitchcock's criticism of the "Cubism" of the Midway Gardens warms over time. Also, the catalog for "The Midway Gardens" exhibition at the University of Chicago offers three pages of narrative; a statement from

Alphonso Iannelli, the sculptor; a letter from John Lloyd Wright, Wright's son and the project superintendent, to Iannelli; and three quotes from Wright himself from his well-known writings; none of which significantly alter the understanding of the project, nor address Wright's concern for sentimentality.

63 Kruty, *Frank Lloyd Wright and Midway Gardens*, 209, n. 51.
64 The Victoria Hotel was completed in 1893, the year Wright was fired from Adler and Sullivan. Certainly Wright was familiar with the building and may have worked on its design.
65 Wright, *An Autobiography* (1932), 15; 31. Wright tells us that while living in Weymouth, Massachusetts, his mother sent the books of Channing, Emerson, Theodore Parker, and Thoreau to her family back in Spring Green Wisconsin. While Wright claims he was just three years old, biographers indicate that he lived in Weymouth from ages 7–10. Robert C. Twombly, *Frank Lloyd Wright: An Interpretive Biography* (New York: Harper & Row, Publishers, 1973), 9. Secrest, *Frank Lloyd Wright*, 55.
66 With combinations of clear and colored glass often set in varying widths and thicknesses of came, Wright's art glass evolved into elaborate works of art: one typical-sized casement sash in the Darwin Martin House (1904) has over 750 individual pieces of glass set in copper came. Additionally the Joseph J. Husser House (1899), the Darwin Martin House, and the much later Charles Ennis House (1924—not a Prairie-style home) had decorative glass mosaic surrounds around their fireplaces. Each depicted a stylized wisteria vine in bloom. Thomas A. Heinz, *Frank Lloyd Wright's Stained Glass & Lightscreens* (Salt Lake City: Gibbs Smith, Publisher, 2000), 52–3. Quinan, *Frank Lloyd Wright's Martin House*, 116.
67 Frank Lloyd Wright, "In the Cause of Architecture," *Frank Lloyd Wright: Collected Writings*, ed. Bruce Pfeiffer (New York: Rizzoli International Publications, 1992), 1:95.
68 Wright, *The Japanese Print*, 20–1.
69 Kevin Nute makes a convincing argument for the influence of Japanese architecture on Wright's work. Kevin Nute, *Frank Lloyd Wright and Japan: The Role of Traditional Japanese Art and Architecture in the Work of Frank Lloyd Wright* (New York: Van Nostrand Reinhold, 1993). Wright's apprentice Edgar Tafel likewise cites the influence. Tafel, *Apprentice to Genius*, 46–7.
70 Kruty, *Frank Lloyd Wright and Midway Gardens*, 189; 214. Anthony Alofsin, *Frank Lloyd Wright, The Lost Years, 1910–1922: A Study of Influence* (1993; repr., Chicago: University of Chicago Press, 2009), 12–16. Wright evinced his enthusiasm for the fair by his encouragement of his Oak Park staff to attend.
71 Alofsin, *Frank Lloyd Wright: The Lost Years*, 120. Alofsin traces Wright's understanding of the concept as coming from an English line articulated by Owen Jones and William Morris and a French line by Viollet-le-Duc and Victore Ruprich-Robert. It was understood and practiced by Wright's contemporaries in the profession, including Richardson, Root, Silsbee, and Sullivan. And as Alofsin thoroughly outlines, Wright's understanding flourished by his later exposure to the Austrian and German Secessionist's interest in it. Another earlier source for Wright's understanding may have come directly from his reading of Ruskin. Weingarden in her genealogy of Sullivan's influences traces his understanding of conventionalization back to Ruskin's illustration of the principle in *The Seven Lamps of Architecture*. As indicated, Wright had read *The Seven Lamps* as a boy. Weingarden, *Louis H. Sullivan and a 19th-century Poetics*, 53 and 103.

72 Wright, *The Japanese Print*, 66.
73 Wright, *The Japanese Print*, 67.
74 Wright, *The Japanese Print*, 67.
75 Wright, *The Japanese Print*, 67.
76 Jack Quinan, *Frank Lloyd Wright's Larkin Building: Myth and Fact* (Cambridge, MA: MIT Press, 1987), 92, fn. 8.
77 Quinan, *Frank Lloyd Wright's Larkin Building*, 92.
78 Quinan, *Frank Lloyd Wright's Larkin Building*, 89.
79 Quinan, *Frank Lloyd Wright's Larkin Building*, 96.
80 That in itself being an indication of how Wright saw the project: it was to be a work of art that contributed to the history of ideas.
81 Wright, *An Autobiography* (1932), 181–2.
82 Wright, *An Autobiography* (1932), 182. Typically and defensively, Wright maintained that all his ideas bubbled up from the wellspring of his own innate genius, or better still from the magical depth of his, and only his, endless sleeve. And furthermore, he thought of it first.
83 Wright, *An Autobiography* (1932), 11–12. Wright held to the importance of this "Kindergarten training" through to the end of his career. See, Frank Lloyd Wright, "New Architecture: Principles," *Frank Lloyd Wright: Writings and Buildings*, ed. Edgar Kaufmann and Ben Raeburn (New York: A Meridian Book, New American Library, 1960), 306.
84 Wright, *An Autobiography* (1932), 182. This was not the first time that Wright disparaged "realism," particularly in relation to ornament. Twenty-three years earlier he had already written that "with birds and flowers on hats, fruit pieces on the wall, imitation or realism in any form, ornamentation in art goes to the ground." Wright, "The Ethics of Ornament," 17.
85 Julia Meech-Pekarik, "Frank Lloyd Wright's Other Passion," *The Nature of Frank Lloyd Wright*, ed. Carol R. Bolon, Robert S. Nelson, and Linda Seidel (Chicago: The University of Chicago Press, 1988), 126. It may also be the popularity of both works that accounts for Wright's vehemence. Earlier he mentions both works in similar terms in "The Japanese Print." Wright, "The Japanese Print," 32.
86 "Coming to the Parson" (patented 1870) was the highest selling work in Rogers's history. It sold over 8,000 copies.
87 Wright, *An Autobiography* (1932), 182.
88 Wright, *An Autobiography* (1943), 181. I cite the 1943 edition because here Wright references the kindergarten training. H. Allen Brooks makes the astute observation that Wright did not equate the Froebel lesson of his kindergarten training to his buildings until after he became exposed to the concepts of pure design. H. Allen Brooks, *The Prairie School: Frank Lloyd Wright and His Midwest Contemporaries* (Toronto: University of Toronto Press, 1972), 40.
89 Wright, *An Autobiography* (1932), 183.
90 Kruty, *Frank Lloyd Wright and Midway Gardens*, 148. Wright was in Japan when the much-publicized and highly influential "Armory Show of 1913" came to Chicago. The show covered the avant-garde of Europe's art scene and included Duchamp's "Nude Descending a Staircase No. 2" and Braque's "Violin and Candlestick," two of the definitive works of cubism. When Wright returned to Chicago, just after the show left for Boston, it was the talk of the town.

91 Frank Lloyd Wright, *Studies and Executed Buildings by Frank Lloyd Wright* (1910; Wasmuth; repr., New York: Rizzoli International Publications, 1990), 10.
92 Frank Lloyd Wright, "The Sovereignty of the Individual," *Frank Lloyd Wright: Writings and Buildings*, ed. Edgar Kaufmann and Ben Raeburn (New York: A Meridian Book/New American Library, 1974), 84; 88. For his introduction to an exhibition at Palazzo Strozzi, Florence, Italy, 1951, Wright modified the preface to the Wasmuth edition.
93 Brooks outlines Wright's relationship and role in the pure design movement. David Van Zanten describes Wright's relationship with the Chicago Architectural Club and its role in the pure design movement. He also covers his attendance and role at the two conventions of the Architectural League of America where the topic was discussed. Wright mentioned "pure design" as part of his ruminations while working on the Unity Temple. Brooks, *The Prairie School*, 37–40. David Van Zanten, "Schooling the Prairie School: Wright's Early Style as a Communicable System," *The Nature of Frank Lloyd Wright*, ed. Carol R. Bolon, Robert S. Nelson, and Linda Seidel (Chicago: The University of Chicago Press, 1988), 73–5. Donald Leslie Johnson, *On Frank Lloyd Wright's Concrete Adobe: Irving Gill, Rudolph Schindler and the American Southwest* (Surrey, England: Ashgate Publishing Limited, 2013), 85–6. Wright, *An Autobiography* (1932), 159.
94 Marie Frank, *Denman Ross and American Design Theory* (Hanover: University Press of New England, 2011), 211. Frank cites Wright's attendance at one of Lorch's lectures to the Chicago Architectural Club. Kevin Nute outlines some of the mutual associations between Wright, Dow, Lorch, and Ross, as well as the connections and probable meeting with Fenollosa. Nute, *Frank Lloyd Wright and Japan*, 24–6; 86–7.
95 Denman W. Ross, *A Theory of Pure Design: Harmony, Balance, Rhythm* (New York: Peter Smith, 1933), 5.
96 Ross, *A Theory of Pure Design*, v.
97 Ross, *A Theory of Pure Design*, v–vi. Ross was quoting Plato's *Philebus* where Socrates is the speaker, paragraph 55. Ross did not cite which translation. The Dorothea Frede translation reads: "If someone were to take away all counting, measuring, and weighing from the arts and crafts, the rest might be said to be worthless." Plato, "Philebus," *Plato: Complete Works*, ed. John M. Cooper (Indianapolis: Hackett Publishing Company, 1997), 445.
98 Arthur W. Dow, *Composition: A Series of Exercises Selected from a New System of Art Education*, 4th edition (New York: The Baker and Taylor Company, 1902), 42. By the thirteenth edition Dow had removed the phrase "with no reference whatever to nature." Arthur Wesley Dow, *Composition: A Series of Exercises in Art Structure for the Use of Students and Teachers*, 13th edition (N.D.; repr., Berkeley: University of California Press, 1997), 127.
99 Plato, "Philebus," 443.
100 Heinz, *Frank Lloyd Wright's Stained Glass*, 6.
101 Emil Lorch, "Some Considerations upon the Study of Architectural Design," *The Inland Architect and News Record* 37, no. 5 (June 1901): 35. *Inland Architect* published the paper Lorch gave at the third annual convention of the Architectural League of America in Philadelphia, May 24, 1901. In that paper Lorch referenced the content of the paper that he gave to the Chicago Architectural Club, the one that Wright attended on March 4, 1901. Marie

Frank elaborates on the potential multiple overlapping connections with Lorch, Ross, and Dow. See Frank, *Denman Ross and American Design Theory*, 210–13.

102 Wright, *An Autobiography* (1932), 102.
103 Plato, "Philebus," 441.
104 Plato, "Philebus," 448; 449. Plato specifically refers to the emotions on page 440.
105 Dow, *Compositions*, 13th edition, 64; 98. Wright, *The Japanese Print*, 15.
106 Wright, *The Japanese Print*, 15.
107 Wright, *The Japanese Print*, 15. Note that this Japanese idea of "organic" is not inconsistent with Wright's typical usage.
108 Wright, *The Japanese Print*, 15–17.
109 Wright, *An Autobiography* (1943), 157.
110 Wright, *An Autobiography* (1943), 157.
111 Wright, *An Autobiography* (1943), 157. The 1932 version is less fleshed out and a little too sketchy. Wright, *An Autobiography* (1932), 159–60. These ideas wove through Wright's thinking, at first tentatively. Earlier, while working on the Unity Temple (1905–1908) he questioned this quoted phrase: "'design is abstraction of nature-elements in purely geometric terms'—that is what we ought to call pure design?" Shifting to the Temple's materiality, and gaining confidence in his thinking, he conflated the geometry of "nature pattern" with the materiality of "nature-texture" and suggested that both "often approach conventionalization, or the abstract, to such a degree as to be superlative means ready to the designer's hand to qualify, stimulate, and enrich his own efforts." Wright would continue to espouse these same ideas in 1930. Wright, *Modern Architecture: Being the Kahn Lectures for 1930*, 27.
112 Meech-Pekarik cites a letter she received from Curtis Besinger who described Wright's "print parties" of the 1940s and 1950s. In his eighties and nineties Wright still spoke in terms of "ideas" or "principles" derived from Japanese prints and how they were the basis of his work. Meech-Pekarik, "Frank Lloyd Wright's Other Passion," 143.

Chapter 6

1 Kruty, *Frank Lloyd Wright and Midway Gardens*, 37–41.
2 Kruty, *Frank Lloyd Wright and Midway Gardens*, 40.
3 Wright, *An Autobiography* (1932), 186. Wright called the rectangular frames over the roofs "sky frames." Different schemes illustrate various arrangements of suspended spheres and vegetation from the frames. The clusters of suspended spheres were never installed. For a period of time, single spheres were suspended within the frames.
4 Kruty, *Frank Lloyd Wright and Midway Gardens*, 132.
5 And that didn't even include the brilliantly colored flash-glass inlays, additional garlands of vines and flowers, mature trees, and the multitude of various-sized "gay colored balloons" that popped from the peaks of the "electric needles" and towers—all of which were excised when the money ran out.
6 Kruty, *Frank Lloyd Wright and Midway Gardens*, 139–140. Generally all the figures of the Midway Gardens are today referred to as "sprites." Kruty indicates that "there is nowhere a record of Wright's identifications of these

figures at this time" (140). Later in his autobiography Wright stated, "The human figure? Sprites of these geometrical forms themselves." Wright, *An Autobiography* (1932), 183. Wright didn't really improve the clarity in later editions when he wrote, "The human figure? Well, the sprites of these geometrical forms themselves: they might come in to play and share in the general geometric gaiety." Wright, *An Autobiography* (1943), 181.

7   For Wright it was very important that the figures were rendered in abstraction and not "realism." When the Midway Gardens opened, the critics called them "Cubist." Their faceted planes reinforced that reading. As has already been indicated, Kruty clearly outlines the impact of the Armory show on Chicago. He writes, "Cubism especially was mentioned almost daily in Chicago newspapers. The fascination with Cubism was so widespread that cartoonists used any excuse to draw faceted figures." See Kruty, *Frank Lloyd Wright and Midway Gardens*, 148.

8   Johnson, *On Frank Lloyd Wright's Concrete Adobe*, 110.

9   Kruty indicates that the two small intermediate and raised rectangles falling between the bands were "black" and "attached," evidently not poured as part of the block itself. Kruty, *Frank Lloyd Wright and Midway Gardens*, 128.

10 Wright, *An Autobiography* (1932), 180.

11 Wright, *An Autobiography* (1943), 346–8. Wright included much of the first edition content about "integral ornament" into the second, but I reference the second because it is more comprehensive.

12 Wright, *Studies and Executed Buildings* (Wasmuth), 14.

13 It is already in evidence in the Susan Lawrence Dana House, designed in 1902, and full blown in the Darwin Martin House of 1903.

14 Wright, *An Autobiography* (1943), 347.

15 Wright, *An Autobiography* (1943), 347–8.

16 Wright, *An Autobiography* (1943), 146.

17 Wright, *An Autobiography* (1943), 347.

18 Wright, *An Autobiography* (1943), 347.

19 Wright, *An Autobiography* (1943), 344–5.

20 Wright, *Studies and Executed Buildings* (Wasmuth), 14.

21 Wright, "Prairie Architecture," *Frank Lloyd Wright: Writings and Buildings*, ed. Edgar Kaufmann and Ben Raeburn (New York: A Meridian Book/New American Library, 1974), 46–7. Wright, *Modern Architecture: Being the Kahn Lectures for 1930*, 74. He offered, for example, that "geometrical or straight lines were natural to the machinery at work in the building trades then." This is a little disingenuous given Wright's preference for the "T" square and triangle, when the scroll saw was also a readily available machine. Wright also pointed out that Sullivan, in contrast, designed his ornament with the consideration of the ornament first and then did whatever was necessary to find and force the materials that could construct it. Wright, *Genius and the Mobocracy*, 58; 60. It is in fact just as likely that Sullivan contributed to Wright's development of these ideas. See, for instance, Sullivan's essay of 1887 where he wrote "that the materials of construction should largely determine the special form of details." Sullivan, "What Is the Just Subordination?" 32.

22 Wright, *An Autobiography* (1943), 347.

23 Wright, *An Autobiography* (1943), 347.

24 Wright, "In the Cause of Architecture," 95.

25 Wright, *An Autobiography* (1943), 146–7.
26 Wright, *An Autobiography* (1943), 147.
27 Beeby, "The Grammar of Ornament," 13. Beeby gets the expression from a lecture given by Robert Kerr to the Royal Institute of British Architects in 1869. Kerr established four categories by which a building is "ornamented." They are "structure ornamented," "structure ornamentalized," "ornament structuralized," and "ornament constructed."
28 Beeby, "The Grammar of Ornament," 13.
29 Frank Lloyd Wright, "In the Cause of Architecture: The Third Dimension," *The Work of Frank Lloyd Wright: Wendingen* (1925; repr., no city: Bramhall House, 1965), 57. Wright called this organizing grid the "unit system." He utilized it in most of his work. On the Hollyhock House he used it to order the plan of the house together with the plan of the trees across the entire 36-acre site.
30 Wright, *An Autobiography* (1932), 139.
31 Beeby, "The Grammar of Ornament," 20.
32 Beeby, "The Grammar of Ornament," 20.
33 The walls and exterior columns, and their ornamentation, were all cast-in-place concrete that was washed clean after the forms were removed, exposing the gravel aggregate. Wright claimed that it would look like coarse granite. The ornamentation was fully integrated into the material and art of construction. In the same way columns are poured, the ornament was as well.
34 Beeby, "The Grammar of Ornament," 21.
35 Beeby, "The Grammar of Ornament," 21.
36 Joseph M. Siry, *Unity Temple: Frank Lloyd Wright and Architecture for Liberal Religion* (Cambridge: Cambridge University Press, 1996), 120–1.
37 Beeby, "The Grammar of Ornament," 21.
38 Beeby recognizes this problem by the fact that he never illustrates just a floor plan. Each of his plans is some composite of different floor plans and the reflected ceiling plan.
39 Wright, *Genius and the Mobocracy*, 55. Wright indicates that Sullivan would say, "*Take care of the terminals, Wright. The rest will take care of itself.*" For Sullivan and Wright, in a good drawing, the terminus of a line is clear and firm. Where there is an intersection with another line it should be emphatic, often by an extension of the lines beyond the intersection.
40 In Figure 3.24, the pier on the left is confusing because there is an intermediate pier to the foreground of the main structural pier in discussion. See the floor plans.
41 For an alternative interpretation of this trim see H. Allen Brooks, "Frank Lloyd Wright and the Destruction of the Box," *Journal of the Society of Architectural Historians* 38, no. 1 (March 1979): 10. http://olli.illinois.edu/downloads/courses/Spring%202016/Architecture%20of%20Frank%20Lloyd%20Wright/Destruction_of_the_Box_FLW.pdf [accessed April 6, 2016]. More interested in how Wright explodes the box, Brooks illustrates how this application of trim also subverts the reading of "corner."
42 I do not doubt that Beeby understands this as well. He simply did not address it.
43 Johnson, *On Frank Lloyd Wright's Concrete Adobe*, 66. Brooks, *The Prairie School*, 79.
44 Wright, "Prairie Architecture," 45.

45 The staggered multiple levels were of such complexity that the accomplished builder, Paul Mueller, required additional circulation drawings just to figure out the stair and elevation changes.

Chapter 7

1 Wright, *An Autobiography* (1932), 188. This story hardly needs retelling. From multiple biographies, including one that focuses primarily on the event, to historical fiction, to opera, one might think that all that needed to be said has been said—or sung. However, recently Paul Hendrickson sleuths even more information about that day (and in particular about the murderer himself) that contributes significantly to the Wright archive. I nonetheless begin with Wright's words and follow with those that are consistent with the record.
2 Wright, *An Autobiography* (1932), 189.
3 Wright, *An Autobiography* (1932), 190.
4 Wright, *An Autobiography* (1932), 191.
5 Neil Levine described the Imperial Hotel and Hollyhock House as "regressive and defensive" and the Millard house as "closed and contained." Gill described Hollyhock House as a "Mayan fortress," "forbidding," and "grim." Scully describes the hotel as "oppressive, weighing down." Neil Levine, *The Architecture of Frank Lloyd Wright* (Princeton, Princeton University Press, 1996), 114; 119; 154. Gill, *Many Masks*, 252. Vincent Scully, Jr., *Frank Lloyd Wright* (New York: George Braziller, Inc., 1960), 23.
6 Levine, *The Architecture of Frank Lloyd Wright*, 115.
7 Levine, *The Architecture of Frank Lloyd Wright*, 119.
8 Levine, *The Architecture of Frank Lloyd Wright*, 121.
9 Wright, *An Autobiography* (1932), 213. In the second edition of his autobiography, Wright added "building against doomsday" to the title of his account of the Imperial Hotel.
10 Wright, *An Autobiography* (1932), 213.
11 Hitchcock, *In the Nature of Materials*, figures 231 and 232. A problem that all contemporary scholars face is the fact that the building was demolished in 1968. Only a fragment of the whole has been preserved. The remaining drawings, small models, and photographs are inadequate to fully convey the overall spatial quality. As Hitchcock explains, "Those who have not seen the vast, richly decorated public rooms of the Hotel find them hard to understand in photographs." The best three-dimensional representations of the interiors, the photographs, generally illustrate spaces where the massive ornamentation blocks the views into and through the interlocking volumetric and ornamental play. The surface ornament seems to compete with the sense of ornament structuralized. Admittedly, this manifestation is less likely to happen in actual space with the turning head and animated eye, but whether one may have been able to sense the ornament structuralized is in doubt. After all, the evaluation of the Midway Gardens was performed only through drawings and photos, and there it is readily apparent, even in just two photos (Figures 6.1–6.2).
12 Cary James, *The Imperial Hotel: Frank Lloyd Wright and the Architecture of Unity* (Rutland, Vermont: Charles E. Tuttle Company, 1968), 16.

13 Hitchcock, *In the Nature of Materials*, figure 232.
14 Unlike James, who concluded that the experience of the hotel is "limitless and unending; there is no certain point to be called beginning; there is no ending either," I cannot overlook the formal center of the banquet hall as an "ending." It is generated by the symmetry, the primary axes, the ascension from the street level, the circulation routes, the relative scale of the spaces, and the functional hierarchies of the spaces. Based on my experience of the building limited to texts, photos, and drawings, formally there certainly seems to be a termination under the peak of the highest hip roof. James, *The Imperial Hotel*, 16.
15 All of the early photographs of the space show the ceiling of the transept disappearing into darkness. Those photos where it is visible are obviously illuminated by additional lighting.
16 A quarry was bought in Nikko, today about two hours north of Tokyo, specifically for the stone. As Wright stated, the American crew tried in vain to get the stonecutters to use contemporary equipment, which "was soon buried beneath the chips that flew from their busy stone-axes." Wright, *An Autobiography* (1932), 217.
17 Bloomer, *The Nature of Ornament*, 38–9. See also Alofsin, *Frank Lloyd Wright: The Lost Years*, 202.
18 Alofsin, *Frank Lloyd Wright: The Lost Years*, 204. Levine, *The Architecture of Frank Lloyd Wright*, 120. Nute, *Frank Lloyd Wright and Japan*, 153–4. Scully, *Frank Lloyd Wright*, 23.
19 I believe this characterization of Wright's understanding of his work was even stronger than he admitted. Writing twenty years after his death, Wright's apprentice from 1932 to 1941, Edgar Tafel wrote that "Beauty, to Mr. Wright was not a matter of taste. It was neither relative nor subject to the fluctuations of history or culture. Beauty was everlasting, an absolute quality existing in a 'realm of essences.' Only the object or characteristic that reflected these essences could be called beautiful. Mr. Wright's concept reflected the platonic belief in the eternal idea, centered around the acknowledgement of universal principles, perfect forms, preexisting and unchanging essences of all things, material and abstract." Tafel then went on to illustrate how Wright developed these same ideas from the Japanese print. Siry makes a compelling argument linking Wright's ideology and the desire to establish "principles" to his religious background and the theological debates of the Western Unitarian Conference in the 1880s. Tafel, *Apprentice to Genius*, 100–1. Siry, *Unity Temple*, 217–18.
20 Like all things Wright, even this is not that simple. Nute provides this noteworthy quote from Antonin Raymond, one of his assistants on the project. "After a year of the work on the hotel I became quite bored. The principal cause of this was the endless repetition of Wright's mannerisms, his grammar, as he called it, to which I could add nothing and which seemed to me so devoid of content, particularly in Japan." Nute continues, "In fact, Wright appears to have regarded his 'organic' decorative forms as being their own content; that is, as aesthetically pleasing in themselves without reference to any external concept at all. Rather like notes in a musical composition, these forms were apparently seen as having no objective meaning beyond their relationship to each other and to the organic whole of which they were a part." Nute, *Frank Lloyd Wright and Japan*, 154–5.
21 Wright, *An Autobiography* (1932), 224.
22 Wright, *An Autobiography* (1932), 224.

23 Wright, *An Autobiography* (1932), 225.
24 Wright, *An Autobiography* (1932), 224. Bruce Pfeiffer quotes Wright's response when asked why he did not make the hotel more "modern." "The answer is that there was a tradition there worthy of respect and I felt it my duty as well as my privilege to make the building belong to them so far as I might." Frank Lloyd Wright, *Frank Lloyd Wright: Preliminary Studies, 1889–1916*, ed. Yukio Futagawa, text Bruce Pfeiffer (Tokyo: A. D. A. Edita, 1985), 140.
25 These totals do not include the three-month trip Wright spent in Japan with his first wife (1905), nor the four-month trip to Japan with Borthwick (1913). Wright designed fourteen buildings for sites in Japan, of which six were built. Of those built, there were the hotel, a school, and residences.
26 Wright constructed one project in Montecito, California: the George C. Stewart Residence (1909), where he simply relocated the Midwestern Prairie-style house to the Pacific coast.
27 Wright, "In the Cause of Architecture," 90. H. Allen Brooks indicates that in 1908 Wright described his early clients as follows: "I found them chiefly among American men of business with unspoiled instincts and ideals. A man of this type usually has the faculty of judging for himself. He has rather liked the 'idea' and much of the encouragement of this work receives come straight from him because the 'common sense' of the thing appeals to him." H. Allen Brooks, *The Prairie School*, 16.
28 Wright, *The Japanese Print*, 66. Wright was writing about the Western "we" when he wrote, "It is so now more than ever before because we are further removed from Nature as an original source of inspiration." The implication was that Japanese artists were closer.
29 Wright, *The Japanese Print*, 68.
30 Schiller, *Naïve and Sentimental Poetry*, 111.
31 Schiller, *Naïve and Sentimental Poetry*, 105.
32 Wright's nostalgia for a Japanese architecture that was closer to nature may recall Heidegger's longing for the Black Forest farmhouse and authentic dwelling. We would do well to listen to Harries who warns that "such farmhouses lie irrecoverably behind us." Harries, *The Ethical Function of Architecture*, 166.
33 Kathryn Smith, *Frank Lloyd Wright, Hollyhock House and Olive Hill: Buildings and Projects for Aline Barnsdall* (New York: Rizzoli International Publications, Inc., 1992), 160.
34 Among the other projects from this time period, Wright did two that are recognized as significant contributions to his repertoire of ornament: the A. D. German Warehouse (1915–1920) in Richland Center, Wisconsin, and the Frederick C. Bogk Residence (1916) in Milwaukee. Both are remarkable as simple boxlike structures with intense concentrations of precast concrete ornamentation. Much more so than the Imperial Hotel, in both cases the ornamentation clearly references pre-Columbian designs. Scully defines the earlier warehouse as Wright's "first clearly *overt* use of such forms [emphasis added]." Scully, *Frank Lloyd Wright*, 24.
35 Levine, *The Architecture of Frank Lloyd Wright*, 147.
36 In two separate personal interviews (Kathryn Smith, May 1974, and Levine, August 1976), Lloyd Wright conveyed basically the same story to both historians. Kathryn Smith, *Frank Lloyd Wright, Hollyhock House and*

Olive Hill: Buildings and Projects for Aline Barnsdall (New York: Rizzoli International Publications, Inc., 1992), 128, fn. 37. Levine, *The Architecture of Frank Lloyd Wright*, 142, fn. 88.
37 Levine, *The Architecture of Frank Lloyd Wright*, 144.
38 Levine, *The Architecture of Frank Lloyd Wright*, 139–40. See Johnson, *On Frank Lloyd Wright's Concrete Adobe*, 125, fn. 20 and fn. 21 for a comprehensive list of sources from Scully, Gill, Secrest, and Twombly.
39 Levine, *The Architecture of Frank Lloyd Wright*, 147.
40 Wright, *An Autobiography* (1932), 235.
41 Johnson adequately illustrates that Wright was not the first to develop what he called the "textile block" system. Walter and Marion Griffin had invented a similar system they called "knitlock" almost seven years prior, and his own son, Lloyd Wright would follow with a system he called "knit-block." But there is no doubt that Wright pushed the decorative properties farther than his precursors. Johnson, *On Frank Lloyd Wright's Concrete Adobe*, 73–81.
42 Kenneth Frampton, *Studies in Tectonic Culture: The Poetics of Construction in Nineteenth and Twentieth Century Architecture* (Cambridge, MA and London: MIT Press, 1995), 101.
43 Frampton, *Studies in Tectonic Culture*, 106.
44 Wright, *An Autobiography* (1932), 235.
45 Levine, *The Architecture of Frank Lloyd Wright*, 152.
46 Siry astutely notes that the seemingly random arrangement of Unity Temple's art-glass laylights have been arranged to suggest one of Wright's favorite analogies of weaving. The ceiling offers sufficient repetition and clarity of design to determine a very subtle yet overriding pattern that could certainly suggest a textile. But if that's the intention on the houses—a likely possibility with "textile" blocks—it doesn't work. The specific arrangement of the design does not elicit that reading. Nor would it explain why Wright changed the arrangement in different locations on the same house. Siry, *Unity Temple*, 176.
47 Scully evocatively characterized the Ennis house claiming it "surmounts its California hilltop like a temple from Tikal before excavation of its base, and it rides across the city of Los Angeles like some avenging phantom from the pre-Columbian past." Vincent Scully, *Architecture: The Natural and the Manmade* (New York: St. Martin's Press, 1991), 344–5.
48 Some of Wright's houses after 1925 continue to show vestiges of his earlier explorations in ornament. Typically, it occurs on the exterior cornices and on the interior decorative cutout screens found in the clerestory windows, casework, and recessed lighting. See, for example, the following houses in Hess, *Frank Lloyd Wright: The Houses*: Rosenbaum House (1939), 280; 282–3; Pope Leighey House (1939), 284–289; Weltzheimer House (1947), 298–9; Ray Brandes House (1952), 312–16; Frank Sander House (1952), 337; John and Catherine Christian House (1954), 356. See also the work that Wright did for Florida Southern College.
49 Wright, *Studies and Executed Buildings* (Wasmuth), 14.
50 Wright, *An Autobiography* (1932), 38.
51 Wright, *An Autobiography* (1943), 39. Like the second edition, the third was published without the quotation marks. Wright, *An Autobiography* (1977), 58.
52 Ignoring his promise, Sprecher told Wright's Uncle James about the incident.

53 Susan Sontag, "Notes on 'Camp'," *Against Interpretation and Other Essays* (New York: Picador; Farrar, Straus and Giroux, 1966), 280.
54 Sontag, "Notes on 'Camp,'" 280. While beyond the topic of this thesis, Sontag illustrates the relationship between sentimentality, kitsch, and camp. And like the roots of the demise of sentimentality, Sontag places the genesis of twentieth-century camp in the eighteenth century and suggests that there is more than just a shared beginning. While sentimentality is ever more reviled, camp is ever more celebrated. Isn't A's elevation of Scribe's mediocre play to great art as comedy an exercise in camp? And Wright's seriously sentimental and exaggerated posing against sentimentality can only put a tender smile on the contemporary visage. It's "pure camp." See footnote on "pure camp" below.
55 Harries offers a detailed analysis illustrating how Cabanel's multiple clichés prevent any true encounter with a work of art. Characterizing it as kitsch, he says "it is merely a stimulus to evoke a mood." Harries, *The Meaning of Modern Art*, 79.
56 Judith Butler, "Imitation and Gender Insubordination," *The Lesbian and Gay Studies Reader*, ed. Henry Abelove et. al. (New York: Routledge, 1993), 313.
57 Judith Butler, *Bodies That Matter: On the Discursive Limits of "Sex"* (New York: Routledge, 1993), 9. See also Sara Ahmed, *The Cultural Politics of Emotion* (New York: Routledge, 2004), 12.
58 Schiller, *Naïve and Sentimental Poetry*, 111.
59 Sontag, "Notes on Camp," 282; 283; 293. Sontag distinguishes between "pure Camp" and what she calls "deliberate Camp." In a categorization that echoes Schiller, Sontag defines pure camp as "naïve," as compared to deliberate camp, "which knows itself to be Camp." "In naïve, or pure, Camp, the essential element is seriousness, a seriousness that fails." And Sontag reminds us that "camp is tender feeling."
60 Wright, *Modern Architecture: Being the Kahn Lectures*, 60. It was no mistake when Wright indicated that "organic architecture" "will be as much 'Nature' as we are ourselves natural." He offered a very qualified version of "Nature," particularly when capitalized and in quotes.
61 Recall that for a while, Wright did not use the word "ornament," preferring instead "pattern" "to avoid confusion or timely prejudice." Wright, *An Autobiography* (1932), 358.
62 Wright, *My Father, Frank Lloyd Wright*, 73.
63 Wright, *An Autobiography* (1943), 192.
64 Kruty offers an extensive analysis. See Kruty, *Frank Lloyd Wright and Midway Gardens*, 19–59.

Chapter 8

1 Different biographers offer different dates for when Wright first met Sullivan. Twombly, writing in 1973, suggests that it was after November 1887. Writing later, in 1979 he suggests it could be as late as 1889. In his biography of Sullivan (1986), Twombly suggests it was probably early 1888, *Louis Sullivan: His Life and Work*, 173. Gill writing in 1987 suggests 1887. Secrest does not give a date but one can infer from her other dates that it was late 1887/early

1888. It should be noted that Wright wrote that at their first meeting Sullivan was just getting ready to go to the St. Louis, Architect's Convention, Wight, *An Autobiography* (1932), 89. Could that have been the meeting of the Western Association of Architects that met in Cincinnati on November 16 and 17, 1887? Was Wright mistaken about the location? For my purposes here, I am using Friday, November 18, 1887, as the date. Robert Twombly, *Frank Lloyd Wright: An Interpretive Biography*, 20. Twombly, *Frank Lloyd Wright: His Life and Architecture*, 19. Gill, *Many Masks*, 58–9; 75. *The Inland Architect and News Record*, December 1887, 75.
2 Richard Nickel and Aaron Siskind cite the cost at $3.145 million. Sullivan, writing more than twenty-six years after its completion, cites the cost at $3.5 million. Garczynski, writing for the promotional material of its opening, cites the cost at "almost $3,500,000." Twombly, *Louis Sullivan: His Life and Work*, 161. Richard Nickel and Aaron Siskind, *The Complete Architecture of Adler & Sullivan* (Chicago: The Richard Nickel Committee, 2010), 362. Sullivan, "Development of Construction," 216. Edward Garczynski, *Auditorium* (New York: Exhibit Publishing Co., 1890), 71.
3 Twombly, *Louis Sullivan: His Life and Work*, 161.
4 It was just twelve years prior that the opera composer had acted as the "architect" for his own renowned *Festspielhaus* by appropriating plans from an unasked Gottfried Semper.
5 Wagner's *Festspielhaus* at Bayreuth seats 1,925. Sullivan satirized the tendency in late-nineteenth-century Chicago to promote bigness. See Sullivan, *The Autobiography of an Idea*, 200.
6 Twombly, *Louis Sullivan: His Life and Work*, 190.
7 Wright, *An Autobiography* (1932), 89.
8 The facts of Wright's first foray into Chicago are the hidden gems of the historian's quest. Most likely, Wright lied about his age, when he left Madison, how long he went without employment, and how he got his first job. Hendrickson provides probably the most thorough account. All accounts agree that he went to Chicago and got his first job in Silsbee's office. Hendrickson, *Plagued by Fire*, 36–53.
9 Wright, *An Autobiography* (1943), 76.
10 Wright, *An Autobiography* (1932), 89.
11 Wright, *An Autobiography* (1932), 89. Between the editions, Wright waffled almost dizzily on the italicized emphasis. In the first edition it is on "me." In the later edition the emphasis is on "saw." Wright, *An Autobiography* (1943), 90.
12 Michel Foucault, *Discipline and Punish: The Birth of the Prison*, trans. Alan Sheridan (New York: Vintage Books, 1979), 195–203.
13 Wright, *An Autobiography* (1932), 90.
14 Wright, *An Autobiography* (1932), 90.
15 Wright, *An Autobiography* (1932), 90.
16 Wright, *An Autobiography* (1943), 91.
17 Wright, *An Autobiography* (1943), 85. The first edition included a curious set of quotes when he writes, "He looked me over with that glance of his that 'went through.'" Wright, *An Autobiography* (1932), 91.
18 Wright, *An Autobiography* (1932), 91; Wright, *An Autobiography* (1943), 91.
19 Wright, *An Autobiography* (1932), 91.
20 Wright, *An Autobiography* (1932), 91.

21 Wright, *An Autobiography* (1932), 91.
22 Wright, *An Autobiography* (1932), 91.
23 Wright, *An Autobiography* (1943), 271. The second edition text was used because of its pleasing syntax. The first edition, with its clumsy coupling of adjectives states, "Ah, that erotic supreme adventure of the mind that was his ornament!" Wright, *An Autobiography* (1932), 269. Wright first used this phrase shortly after Sullivan's death in his homage to his master's work for *Architectural Record*. There he wrote, "Ah, that supreme, erotic, high adventure of the mind that was his ornament!" Frank Lloyd Wright, "Louis Sullivan—His Work," *Frank Lloyd Wright: Essential Texts*, ed. Robert Twombly (New York: W. W. Norton & Company, 2009), 218. Mario Manieri Elia detects a hint of sarcasm in Wright's phrase. This seems unlikely given Wright's comparison to Casanova, Boccaccio, and Rabelais in the following paragraph. See Mario Manieri Elia, *Louis Henry Sullivan* (New York: Princeton Architectural Press, 1996), 60.
24 Wright, *An Autobiography* (1932), 269.
25 Wright had first published this paragraph for a far more limited audience in his homage to Sullivan for the July 1924 issue of *Architectural Record*. Wright, "Louis Sullivan—His Work," 218–19.
26 Gill, *Many Masks*, 79–80; Andrew, *Louis Sullivan and the Polemics of Modern Architecture*, 13, and Gill references an unpublished manuscript by Tim Samuelson.
27 Gill, *Many Masks*, 78.
28 Sullivan, "The Artistic Use of the Imagination," 67.
29 Presented in 1889, it is more than likely that Wright attended the presentation by his boss to a group of young architects. Or maybe Sullivan had even read the presentation to Wright beforehand, as he often did.
30 Sullivan, *Kindergarten Chats*, 29. His conceit of a building as a man shares a similarity to Whitman's conceit of the book as a man: *Lift me close to your face till I whisper, / What you are holding is in reality no book, nor part of a book, / It is a man, flushed and full-blooded—it is I*—So Long! Whitman, *Leaves of Grass*, 242.
31 Sullivan, *Kindergarten Chats*, 30.
32 Whitman, *Leaves of Grass*, 288; Walt Whitman, *Leaves of Grass: The Deathbed Edition* (1892; repr., New York: Quality Paperback Book Club, 1992), 70.
33 Andrew and Gill debate whether the father of the skyscraper construed the building type as ithyphallic. Neither offers anything beyond conjecture. Andrew, *Louis Sullivan and the Polemics of Modern Architecture*, 13. Gill, *Many Masks*, 79 80.
34 Emphasizing the physiological effect of an emotion, Sara Ahmed states, "I will use the idea of 'impression' as it allows me to avoid making analytical distinctions between bodily sensation, emotion and thought as if they could be 'experienced' as distinct realms of human 'experience.'" Ahmed keeps it very close to the *tender* body when she reminds the reader "*We need to remember the 'press' in an impression.*" Teresa Brennan wrote, "By an affect, I mean the physiological shift accompanying a judgment." Ahmed, *The Cultural Politics of Emotion*, 6. Brennan, *The Transmission of Affect*, 5.
35 Bain, *The Emotions and the Will*, 10.

36 William James, *The Principles of Psychology*, Vol. 2 (1890; repr., New York: Dover Publications, 1953), 449. James wrote with threefold emphasis, "My theory, on the contrary, is that *the bodily changes follow directly the perception of the exciting fact, and that our feeling of the same changes as they occur* IS *the emotion.*"
37 With his repeated public extramarital affairs Wright showed again and again his willingness to defy social conventions for what truly mattered to him.
38 Plutarch reminded his reader that while writers failed to name the mothers of ancient Greece's illustrious leaders, "we know even the nurse of Alcibiades, that her country was Lacedæmon, and her name Amycla." Plutarch, *Plutarch's Lives*, 106.
39 There are other similarities between Wright and Alcibiades. Both men were flamboyant, vain, brilliant, and exceedingly clever tricksters who, despite the egregious harm that they inflicted on others, could nonetheless regain their goodwill. But perhaps the other greatest similarity was their shared profligacy with money. Alcibiades is described as a "great taker, [who] would be corrupted with money: and when he had it, he would most licentiously and dishonestly spend it"—a near-perfect description of the immoderate Wright. Plutarch. *The Lives of the Noble Grecians & Romans Compared Together by that Grave Learned Philosopher and Historiographer Plutarke of Chæronia.* Translated from Greek into French by James Amyot, from French into English by Thomas North (London: Nonesuch Press, 1929), 429.
40 Alcibiades was known for his good looks. Plutarch says his "beauty" "bloomed with him in all the ages of his life." According to Plato, even Socrates described it as "immense comeliness of form." Plutarch, *Plutarch's Lives: The Harvard Classics*, 106. Plato, *The Symposium*, trans. R. E. Allen (New Haven: Yale University Press, 1991), 165.
41 Nonetheless, Plutarch referred to Plato as a source.
42 When Wright was over ninety years old, he again selected Alcibiades for singular mention from the forty-eight lives. Wright, "Roots," 20.
43 Sullivan called the École des Beaux-Arts the "fountain head of theory." Sullivan, *The Autobiography of an Idea*, 213.
44 Hendrickson tracked down Wright's university transcript, which indicates that in his first semester he took all of one course in French, for which he never got a grade. The second year he took one course in descriptive geometry and one in mechanical drawing, for which he got "C's." He may have audited a few other courses but the university has no record of it. Hendrickson, *Plagued by Fire*, 46.
45 Wright was clearly surprised to find the Jones along with a copy of Violett le Duc's *Habitations of Man in All Ages* in the library of his Uncle Jones's church, exclaiming, "I got two books you would never expect could be found there." The Jones was probably the 1865 edition because Wright described it as a "reprint but good enough." Wright, *An Autobiography* (1932), 74.
46 Wright stated that he read Ruskin's *Seven Lamps of Architecture, Fors Clavigera, Modern Painters,* and *Stones of Venice,* and Violett le Duc's *Raisonné de l'architecture.* But he does not mention any specific ornamentalists other than Jones. Wright, *An Autobiography* (1932), 31; 52; 74.
47 There were 112 entries for "architectural books" in the auction catalog. Many were multiple-volume entries and sets. I added the total of volumes. At least one was in Italian. Williams, Barker & Severn Co., *Catalogue at Auction*, not paginated.

48 The majority of Sullivan's architectural books were monographs. They evinced a broad array of scholarship, from works by Mrs. Schuyler Van Rensselaer, whom John Wellborn Root dubbed a "mere word-monger," to a five-volume history set by James Ferguson, whom Root placed in "a class of really educated critics." Probably the most influential architecture books he had were Viollet le-Duc's two-volume *Discourses on Architecture* and the folio edition of his *Compositions et Dessine*. Root, *The Meanings of Architecture*, 16.
49 Recall that Sullivan gave a copy of Spencer's *Philosophy* to Wright. It is possible that he had had books by Semper, Riegl, and the others, and gave them away. Many scholars indicate that Sullivan was influenced by Ruskin, but I have yet to find any concrete evidence that he actually read the English critic. What influence he obtained might have come from the Ruskinian idealism that permeated American aesthetic culture prior to the Centennial. Or as both Weingarden and Twombly indicate, he was probably exposed to Ruskin's ideas during his five-month employment with the Philadelphia architectural firm of Furness & Hewitt. Weingarden, *Louis H. Sullivan and a 19th-Century Poetics*, 21; Twombly, *Louis Sullivan: His Life & Work*, 42.
50 The plaster medallions, "Rosace," are the rare exception that are identified by style, and sometimes by manufacturer's address, and sometimes by location found. A. Raguenet, *Matériaux & Documents D/Architecture Classés par Ordre Alphabétique* (Paris: H. Cagnon, 1872). See "Rosace," 1–8.
51 Wright, *An Autobiography* (1932), 361.
52 Owen Jones, *The Grammar of Ornament* (1856, Reprint, London: Studio Editions, 1995), 8.
53 Jones, *The Grammar of Ornament*, see, for instance, the Roman Ornament, plates XXVI and XXVII.
54 In his presentation of Greek ornament, one could assume that the sum of Greek ornament was almost entirely in wallpaper. Jones, *The Grammar of Ornament*, plates XV–XXII.
55 Wright, *An Autobiography* (1932), 74.
56 Frampton, *Studies in Tectonic Culture*, 95–9; Weingarden, *Louis H. Sullivan and a 19th-Century Poetics*, 295.
57 Wright recounts the event in all three editions of his autobiography, Wright, *An Autobiography* (1932), 91; Wright, *An Autobiography* (1943), 91; Frank Lloyd Wright, *An Autobiography*, 3rd edition (New York: Horizon Press, 1977), 113.
58 Kierkegaard, *Either-Or*, 1:231–7. I am indebted to Karsten Harries for his elaboration of the "occasion." See Harries, *Between Nihilism and Faith*, 76–8.
59 Sullivan, *A System of Architectural Ornament*, not paginated.
60 Sullivan, *A System of Architectural Ornament*, Plate 5, not paginated.
61 Schiller, *Naïve and Sentimental Poetry*, 84.
62 Schiller, *Naïve and Sentimental Poetry*, 84.
63 Kant, *The Critique of Judgment*, trans. J. H. Bernard (Amherst, NY: Prometheus Books, 2000), 100.
64 Schiller, *Naïve and Sentimental Poetry*, 84.
65 Wright, *An Autobiography* (1932), 91.
66 Sullivan, *A System of Architectural Ornament*, Plate 5, not paginated. Wright claimed that he had not read Sullivan's writings. Most scholars do not believe this statement. Nonetheless, he claimed that he knew Sullivan's thought and wrote, "he whose thought was, in his own person and presence, an open book to me for many years." Wright, *An Autobiography* (1943), 561.

67 Wright, *An Autobiography* (1932), 104.
68 Wright, *Genius and the Mobocracy*, 101.
69 Wright, *An Autobiography* (1932), 269.
70 Wright claimed it lasted seven years. Wright, "In the Cause of Architecture," 86. Wright, *An Autobiography* (1932), 96.
71 Hitchcock, *In the Nature of Materials*, 7.
72 Mumford saw Sullivan as the link between Richardson's "romantic phase" and Wright's initiation of "modern architecture." Sullivan articulated the ideas that Wright successfully put into formal architectural expression, even "more completely and convincingly" than he managed to do in his own work. Mumford, *The Brown Decades*, 74–5.
73 During the same period Adler and Sullivan designed at least eight more skyscrapers that remained unbuilt, including the Odd Fellows Temple (1891) and The Trust & Savings Bank Building (1893–1895).
74 Wright, *Genius and Mobocracy*, 59. Wright, *Modern Architecture: Being the Kahn Lectures for 1930*, 85.
75 Sullivan, "Style," 46.
76 Mumford, *The Brown Decades*, 74.
77 Sullivan, "The Tall Office Building," 103.
78 Sullivan, "The Tall Office Building," 111. In the essay Sullivan posits the idea and wrote that "form ever follows function." By 1912 he used the more succinct "form follows function." Louis Sullivan, "Lighting the People's Savings Bank, Cedar Rapids, Iowa: An Example of American Twentieth Century Ideas of Architecture and Illumination (1912)," *Louis Sullivan: The Public Papers*, ed. Robert Twombly (Chicago: The University of Chicago Press, 1988), 208.
79 Adler's role in the design of the Auditorium is not to be underestimated. See Menocal, *Architecture as Nature: The Transcendentalist Idea of Louis Sullivan*, xvii. But to the young Wright it wouldn't have mattered.
80 Wright, *Genius and the Mobocracy*, 48–9. Already one of the most celebrated sopranos of the nineteenth century, Patti would not make her Carnegie Hall debut for another five years.
81 Wright, *Genius and the Mobocracy*, 49.
82 Sullivan, *The Autobiography of an Idea*, 316.
83 Wright, *An Autobiography* (1932), 101–2. He deleted this criticism from later editions.
84 Wright, *An Autobiography* (1932), 102.

Chapter 9

1 Sullivan, "Essay on Inspiration," 26.
2 Wright, *Genius and the Mobocracy*, 95. Wright exhibited more than a little ambivalence about Sullivan's status as poet. But when referring to Sullivan the architect, Wright would call him "the lyric poet" and even "the great lyric poet." Wright, *Genius and the Mobocracy*, 59; 109.
3 Sullivan, "Essay on Inspiration," 10.
4 Weingarden defends the poem stating that "what modern readers of Sullivan's theory have described as turgid prose writing can be better appreciated as evidence of Sullivan's emulation of Whitman's technique of parallelism. That

is, his repetition of single words and phrases, and his phonic, syntactical, and grammatical patterns, imitated the 'natural' order of the poet's long, roving prose or verse lines." Conversely, I am inclined to agree with the author, Sullivan himself, who, writing after some thirty-six years of hindsight, described the "Essay" as "a bit sophomoric, and over-exalted, but the thought is sound." Sullivan, *The Autobiography of an Idea*, 303. Weingarden, *Louis H. Sullivan and a 19th-Century Poetics of Naturalized Architecture*, 225.

5 Wright, *Genius and Mobocracy*, 61. Wright used the term "corrupt" to describe the changes he made to Sullivan's work. He then wondered if he should say he was "interpreting" it.
6 Wright, *An Autobiography* (1932), 95.
7 Wright, *An Autobiography* (1932), 268.
8 Wright, *An Autobiography* (1932), 266.
9 Wright, *An Autobiography* (1932), 268.
10 Sullivan, "Ornament in Architecture," 83–4. Wright, *An Autobiography* (1932), 268.
11 Wright, *An Autobiography* (1932), 268.
12 Plato's choice of Eros and the love of the beautiful on the surface seem inconsistent with a rhetorical argument that culminates in the contemplation of wisdom in terms of "true virtue" or the "truth." Might he not have been better served had he begun with encomiums to Athena, the goddess of wisdom? But Plato suggests that wisdom is initiated by "that which we desire and of which we claim to be lovers." It begins with a drive and a feeling, that is, love. It seems so similar to *feeling in idea*, the etymology of sentimentality itself. Even *The Symposium*, in its own way, is a sentimental tale. Plato, *Phaedo, Plato: Complete Works*, edited with an introduction by John M. Cooper (Indianapolis: Hackett Publishing Company, 1997), 58.
13 Plato, *The Symposium*, 154–7.
14 Plato, *The Symposium*, 155.
15 Plato, *The Symposium*, 156.
16 Plato, *The Symposium*, 157.
17 Wright, *An Autobiography* (1932), 268. His capital "B" "Beauty" imitates Plato's capital "B" "Beauty" and the "Beautiful itself," further suggesting Wright's intentional comparison.
18 Wright, *An Autobiography* (1932), 270.
19 Wright described himself as an "unconventional believer in the Good, the True and the Beautiful, as work and life and love." Wright, *An Autobiography* (1932), 192. And in obvious flattery that proved prescient, he bestowed a qualified immortality on his client, Darwin Martin, when he described the Martin house as "a permanent record that will proclaim [Martin] to subsequent generations as a lover of the good! the true! the beautiful!" Quinan, *Frank Lloyd Wright's Martin House*, 126. He indicated "that feeling we call Love. When it takes form we call it Beauty." Frank Lloyd Wright, "To My European Co-Workers," *Frank Lloyd Wright: Collected Writings*, Vol. 1 (1894–1930), ed. Bruce Pfeiffer (New York: Rizzoli International Publications, 1992), 208. And in *The Japanese Print* he wrote, "But the expression we seek and need is that of harmony or of the good; known otherwise as the true, often spoken of as the beautiful, and personified as God." Wright, *The Japanese Print*, 30.
20 Wright, *An Autobiography* (1932), 269.

21 Indeed, Wright even granted immortality to Sullivan. Frank Lloyd Wright, "Louis Henry Sullivan: Beloved Master (1924)," *Frank Lloyd Wright: Essential Texts*, ed. Robert Twombly (New York: W. W. Norton & Company, 2009), 211–12.
22 Harries, *Between Nihilism and Faith*, 88.
23 Wright, *An Autobiography* (1932), 269.
24 Wright, *An Autobiography* (1932), 269. Wright could not overcome early-twentieth-century gender expectations. While he made clear just a few paragraphs later that the wooed god was Eros, in this quote he had Sullivan wooing a goddess.
25 Compare Diotima's Ladder of Love with Sullivan's hierarchy of powers in his *System*. While slightly different characterizations, as to intention the one is the near inverse of the other.
26 Plato, *The Symposium*, 157–8.
27 Plato, *The Symposium*, 161.
28 Plato, *The Symposium*, 160; 168. Plato suggests that Alcibiades nonetheless spoke a certain truth. When asked to rebut him if he fails to speak the truth, Socrates never does. Instead Socrates describes the drunken Alcibiades as "sober."
29 Gill indicates that Wright's relationship with Sullivan was laden with "powerful sexual overtones" but does not believe they were acted upon. Hendrickson excavates his relationships with both Cecil Corwin and Robert (Robie) Lamp (both probably gay) and suggests that Wright was bisexual. (Sullivan was not a primary focus of Hendrickson's study.) As already indicated, many contemporary scholars believe Sullivan was gay. Gill, *Many Masks*, 63. Hendrickson, *Plagued by Fire*, 514.
30 Plato, *The Symposium*, 157.
31 Sullivan, *The Autobiography of an Idea*, 207.
32 Sullivan, *The Autobiography of an Idea*, 163. For other examples, see also *The Autobiography of an Idea*, 16; 17; 41; 46; 91; 163; 224; 231; 274, and Sullivan, *Kindergarten Chats*, 149.
33 Sullivan, *The Autobiography of an Idea*, 224. Even though Sullivan was writing about his education under Monsieur Clopet during his brief tenure at the École des Beaux Arts, he maintained his skepticism of abstraction to convey truth through his final writings. See also Louis Sullivan, "Reflections on the Tokyo Disaster (1924)," *Louis Sullivan: The Public Papers*, ed. Robert Twombly (Chicago: The University of Chicago Press, 1988), 245; Sullivan, *A System of Architectural Ornament*, not paginated; and Sullivan, *Democracy: A Man Search*, 45; 104–3.
34 Nietzsche, *Thus Spoke Zarathustra*, 225–8.
35 Sullivan, *Kindergarten Chats*, 145.
36 Sullivan, *Democracy: A Man Search*, 45.
37 Sullivan, *Democracy: A Man Search*, 382.
38 Sullivan, *Democracy: A Man Search*, 324.
39 Sullivan, *Democracy: A Man Search*, 45.
40 Nietzsche, *Thus Spoke Zarathustra*, 322.
41 Schiller, *Naïve and Sentimental Poetry*, 92. Schiller wrote that "nature is in the *right* in that it speaks truth."
42 Sullivan, *Democracy: A Man Search*, 232. One sentence later he repeated this demand, the second time calling for the removal of "veils of words, ceremonials, traditions, assumptions." See also Sullivan, *Democracy: A Man Search*, 231–3.

43 Sullivan may have come to his aversion to words through his reading of James's "Psychologist's Fallacies." The first is the "Misleading Influence of Speech," where James covers the relationship between words (and speech) and the understanding of phenomena. James, *The Principles of Psychology*, Vol. 1, 194–5. This same set of passages also had considerable influence on Pragmatists like John Dewey. Louis Menand, *The Metaphysical Club* (New York: Farrar, Straus and Giroux, 2001), 328–9.
44 Sullivan, "What Is Architecture?" 191.
45 Sullivan, *The Autobiography of an Idea*, 199–200.
46 Sullivan, *The Autobiography of an Idea*, 199–200.
47 Sullivan, *The Autobiography of an Idea*, 200.
48 T. J. Jackson Lears, *No Place of Grace: Antimodernism and the Transformation of American Culture, 1880–1920* (New York: Pantheon Books, 1981), 167.
49 Lears, *No Place of Grace*, 218.
50 Lears, *No Place of Grace*, 223.
51 Scholars regularly trace one of Sullivan's lineages of influence directly to Emerson. Most base that on a few degrees of separation during his employment in 1873 with Frank Furness. While I have not found anything to indicate that he read the transcendentalist, he did have five volumes of Goethe's *Werke* and two volumes of *Faust* in his library. He also owned two volumes of Grimm's *Life of Goethe* (Boston, 1880). Williams, Barker & Severn Co., *Catalogue at Auction*, not paginated.
52 Lears, *No Place of Grace*, 218.
53 Lears, *No Place of Grace*, 218.
54 Sigmund Freud, *Civilization and Its Discontents*, trans. James Strachey (New York: W. W. Norton & Company, 1962), 11–12. Freud admitted he got the term from Romain Rolland, a friend. Rolland described it as a religious experience.
55 Freud, *Civilization and Its Discontents*, 12.
56 Freud, *Civilization and Its Discontents*, 19.
57 Freud, *Civilization and Its Discontents*, 19.
58 Solomon, *In Defense of Sentimentality*, 8; 11.
59 Weingarden suggests that Sullivan was an "astute student" of contemporary literary theory and practice and that he resorted to poetry as a way of initiating the reader's "spiritual communion with nature." Weingarden, *Louis H. Sullivan and a 19th-Century Poetics of Naturalized Architecture*, 19–20.
60 Sullivan, "What Is Architecture?" 191. This is an important essay to the understanding of Sullivan's worldview that is too easy to dismiss. Unfortunately, like a hot air balloon, as it works its way to a conclusion it inflates into ever more empty aphorisms, platitudes, and circular logic, ascending in a heat of ever more frequent fist-raising capitalization. However, some of his core ideas are summarized in this essay.
61 Sullivan, *The Autobiography of an Idea*, 224.
62 Sullivan, *The Autobiography of an Idea*, 225.
63 Sullivan, "What Is Architecture?" 191.
64 Friedrich Nietzsche, "On Truth and Lie in a Nonmoral Sense," *Philosophy and Truth: Selections from Nietzsche's Notebooks of the Early 1870's*, trans. Daniel Breazeale (New York: Humanity Books, 1979), 81–4.
65 Nietzsche, "On Truth and Lie," 84.

66 Sullivan, "What Is Architecture?" 191–2.
67 Harries, *The Broken Frame*, 59.
68 Harries, *The Broken Frame*, 60.
69 Sherman Paul characterized Sullivan's library as follows: "Science and intellect were the forwarding forces. But, in many, beneath the skepticism was the desire to reconcile science and religion and to ameliorate a brutal naturalism by discovering within it a Christian ethic." Paul, *Louis Sullivan: An Architect in American Thought*, 96.
70 I base this statement on the lists of engineering marvels (structural, electrical, and mechanical to include moving floors, ceilings, and stages) that accompany any description of the building. For a good thorough description, see Twombly, *Louis Sullivan: His Life & Work*, 161–95, or Garczynski, *Auditorium*, 22–38.
71 A. H. Sturtevant calls Wilson's *Cell* one of the most famous textbooks in the history of modern biology. A. H. Sturtevant, *A History of Genetics* (New York: Harper & Row, 1965), 33.
72 Sullivan, "Interlude: The Doctrine of Parallelism," *A System of Architectural Ornament*, not paginated.
73 Wright, *Genius and Mobocracy*, 61.
74 I use the term "fool" with cynical irony. On the last page of *The Ethical Function of Architecture*, Karsten Harries warns that "any architect who today wants to address [architecture's ethical function] has to be aware that he does so without authority, that he is a bit like the fool who says what he thinks needs to be said but can only hope that others will listen." Even if Sullivan managed to articulate an alternative to the modernist conceptions of being, unless someone listened or even cared, he remains that fool. Harries, *The Ethical Function of Architecture*, 367.
75 Nietzsche, *Thus Spoke Zarathustra*, 235.
76 The way the translation is written remains vague. It is an issue of the word "may." Does it mean that the will to love and die *might* overcome a mere image? Or it might not? Or does "may" mean that it is finally liberated to overcome a mere image? Or both? The original German reads "*dass ein Bild nicht nor Bild bleibe*," which suggests a more assertive, "that an image does not remain a mere image." Friedrich Nietzsche, *Also Sprach Zarathustra/Thus Spoke Zarathustra* (German/English Bilingual Text) (Milton Keynes, UK: Jiahu Books, 2013), 166–7.
77 Harries, *The Ethical Function of Architecture*, 225.
78 Harries, *The Ethical Function of Architecture*, 237.
79 Harries, *The Ethical Function of Architecture*, 237; Nietzsche, *Thus Spoke Zarathustra*, 252.
80 Harries, *The Ethical Function of Architecture*, 228–9.
81 Nietzsche, *Thus Spoke Zarathustra*, 235. Recall that at the highest rung of Diotima's ladder, "human life is to be lived: in *contemplating* the Beautiful itself [emphasis added]." Plato, *The Symposium*, 156.
82 According to the auction catalog, Sullivan's copy of Zarathustra was 1896. Most historians suggest that Sullivan had read Whitman in 1886. He had already written to Whitman on February 3, 1887. See Traubel, *With Walt Whitman in Camden (November 1, 1888–January 20, 1889)*, 25–6.
83 Juan A. Herrero Brasas indicates that "leaves" was a term used by printers for the actual leaves or scraps of paper on which Whitman wrote his poems. Herrero Brasas, *Walt Whitman's Mystical Ethics of Comradeship*, 145.

84 Whitman, *Leaves of Grass*, 342–4.
85 Sullivan, "Essay on Inspiration," 18. Both Weingarden and Twombly cite Whitman's "Elemental Drifts" as an important influence on Sullivan's essay. While the correlation of death, love, and beauty is not as explicit as in "Calamus 2," the two poems nonetheless share similar themes. "Elemental Drifts" is haunted with "little corpses," "dead lips," and the "sobbing dirge of Nature." Whitman later revised the title to "As I Ebb'd with the Ocean of Life." Weingarden, *Louis H. Sullivan and a 19th-Century Poetics of Naturalized Architecture*, 224. Twombly, *Louis Sullivan: His Life & Work*, 214.
86 Sullivan, "Essay on Inspiration," 26.
87 Sullivan, "Essay on Inspiration," 15.
88 Sullivan, "Essay on Inspiration," 26–7. Sullivan intends that "serenity" as both that state of utter calm and an essence that he calls "Inscrutable Serenity." Clearly related to that spiritual essence of the "function of all functions," in "The Young Man in Architecture," he also calls it the "Inscrutable Spirit." Sullivan, "Essay on Inspiration," 24. Sullivan "The Young Man in Architecture," 137.
89 Sullivan, *Kindergarten Chats*, 149.
90 Wright, *An Autobiography* (1943), 16.
91 Wright, *An Autobiography* (1932), 1.
92 Wright, *An Autobiography* (1932), 1.
93 Wright, *An Autobiography* (1932), 1.
94 Wright, *An Autobiography* (1932), 2.
95 Wright, *An Autobiography* (1932), 2.
96 Wright, *An Autobiography* (1932), 371.
97 Wright, *An Autobiography* (1932), 371.
98 Wright, *The Japanese Print*, 16–17.
99 In the later editions of his autobiography, Wright cites Heraclitus and his doctrine of change as "perhaps" "the only reality we may see." Wright, *An Autobiography* (1943), 376.
100 Harries, *The Ethical Function of Architecture*, 228. Harries makes the exact same correlation as Wright. Harries illustrates the point. "Take two lines: one a circle, clean and hard, drawn with a compass, the other an expressive squiggle, a swirling line resembling handwriting. The two lines stand in a very different relationship to time: the first comes as close as a visual statement can to the timeless realm of the spirit, while the other has an organic look and seems to embrace time."
101 Harries, *The Ethical Function of Architecture*, 255.
102 Wright, *The Japanese Print*, 15–16.
103 Wright's emotive sensitivity to geometric form could border on the tragic. In a response to criticism from Russell Sturgis he wrote, "I confess to a love for a clean arras; the cube I find comforting, the sphere inspiring. In the opposition of the circle and the square I find motives for architectural themes with all the sentiment of Shakespeare's 'Romeo and Juliet' …." Quinan, Levine, and Alofsin all quote this letter. Quinan, *Frank Lloyd Wright's Larkin Building*, 166. Levine, *The Architecture of Frank Lloyd Wright*, 40. Alofsin, *Frank Lloyd Wright: The Lost Years, 1910–1922*, 154.
104 Wright, *The Japanese Print*, 16; Wright, *Genius and the Mobocracy*, 111, n.
105 Wright, *The Japanese Print*, 18.

106 Mumford offers a good example of the desire to divorce any "spell power" from the logical realization of a building. He criticized Sullivan for suggesting that a skyscraper should be a "proud and soaring thing" instead of simply solving its "functional" requirements. Mumford believed that a building should not be given a "spiritual function to perform." Mumford, *The Brown Decades*, 69–70.
107 Kitarō Nishida, *Sourcebook for Modern Japanese Philosophy: Selected Documents* (Westport, CT: Greenwood Press, 1998), 30.
108 Nishida, *Sourcebook for Modern Japanese Philosophy*, 30–1.
109 Nishida, *Sourcebook for Modern Japanese Philosophy*, 32.
110 Nishida, *Sourcebook for Modern Japanese Philosophy*, 32–3.
111 Nishida, *Sourcebook for Modern Japanese Philosophy*, 34.
112 Wright, *An Autobiography* (1943), 369. Second edition quoted because the phrasing and sentence structure are a little slower, more drawn out, more emphatic. Wright used the same expression earlier in Wendingen with capitalization: "the Eternity that is Now." Wright, "To My European Co-Workers," 162.
113 Wright, *An Autobiography* (1943), 369.
114 Frank Lloyd Wright, *Frank Lloyd Wright: The Natural House* (New York: Bramhall House, 1954), 220.
115 Kakuzo Okakura, *The Book of Tea*, ed. Everett F. Bleiler (1906; repr., New York: Dover Publications, 1964), 19. Wright, *Frank Lloyd Wright: The Natural House*, 220–1. Wright regularly credited Lao Tzŭ (often Laotze) as a source that he "consulted." He recounted the first time he read *The Book of Tea*, and in particular where he read that "the reality of a room, for instance, was to be found in the vacant space enclosed by the roof and walls, not in the roof and walls themselves." Historians often refer to this quote and the influence the book held on Wright. While manifestly present in Wright's work, and in the modernist conception of space that followed, the slight book also offered just as much to his understanding of being. Wright, *An Autobiography* (1943), 561. Wright, *Frank Lloyd Wright: The Natural House*, 220–1.
116 Okakura, *The Book of Tea*, 24.
117 Vincent Scully, "Introduction," *The Nature of Frank Lloyd Wright*, ed. Carol R. Bolon, Robert S. Nelson, and Linda Seidel (Chicago: The University of Chicago Press, 1988), xiv.
118 Scholars from Gill, to Hendrickson, Scully, Secrest, Johnson, Twombly, and Kruty have noted (and debunked) Wright's persistent distortion of the facts. As Gill put it, "He was a virtuoso at bearing false witness, which is to say that he sometimes lied in the name of self-promotion or self-protection and at other times he seems to have lied simply for the pleasure it gave him." Nonetheless, some scholars remain charitable, indeed insightful. Hendrickson claims that Wright's autobiography is "untrue, even as it's gorgeously true (as opposed to factually true) in all the larger ways." Scully states, "So Wright's words cannot invariably be trusted or taken at face value." He reminds the reader that "in art so many incompatible things are usually all true together." What is clear, despite the mendacity of it all, is that Wright sought some higher truth through his work. Yet, as much as he longed for it, he knew the impossibility of the universal and eternal ideal in a finite world. He reveals it in his writing every time he qualifies his strongest assertions with a "maybe," or a question mark, or scare quotes.

Moreover, as the architect who based his work on presumably unchanging "principles," he drove his apprentices crazy with his constant design changes. Tafel indicates that when challenged, Wright had his standard reply: "that was all right yesterday, but it's not right today." Gill, *Many Masks*, 24. Hendrickson, *Plagued by Fire*, 31. Scully, "Introduction," xvi. Tafel, *Apprentice to Genius,* 70; 165.

119 While Wright indicated that later in his career he "turned away from the Greek abstraction," there is no evidence to indicate that he ceased in his desire for "universal principles." Tafel, writing long after Wright's death, implies that the architect never wavered in that belief. Frank Lloyd Wright, "Influences and Inferences," *Frank Lloyd Wright: Writings and Buildings*, ed. Edgar Kaufmann and Ben Raeburn (New York: A Meridian Book, New American Library, 1960), 303. Tafel, *Apprentice to Genius*, 100.

120 Wright, *The Japanese Print*, 67.

121 Wright never abandoned Plato. In *The Symposium,* Plato made essentially the same argument by stating that the ascension of that ladder to the beautiful and truth begins with the drive for immortality that he characterized as love.

122 Wright, *The Japanese Print*, 17–22; 28; 67. Each page makes at least one affirmative reference to either sentiment or sympathy or both.

123 This is a very qualified statement. I am referring specifically to his practice of ornament over the duration of our time period, i.e., until 1924. While his surface ornamentation in all his important works continued on this trajectory and culminated with its complete removal, his practice of ornament structuralized explored alternative expressions of time, including that paradigmatic embrace of time: the spiral of the Guggenheim museum.

124 Wright, *An Autobiography* (1932), 110; Wright, *An Autobiography* (1943), 112. "Father" in quotes again suggests the question of essentiality, gender, imitation, and camp that was covered in Chapter 7. Wright's difficulty with fatherhood is well known. Even he admitted to it: Wright, *An Autobiography* (1932), 111. Just like his "like a man," Wright deleted the quotation marks in the second edition of the autobiography. And "a love for the beautiful," which is also in quotes, implies that he could be referencing another source other than himself. Was he making another reference to the correlation of love and beauty from Plato's *Symposium*? Or is he just quoting himself? And again those quotation marks were deleted in the second edition.

125 Harries, *The Broken Frame*, xi.

126 Harries, *The Broken Frame*, 5.

127 Wright, *Studies and Executed Buildings* (Wasmuth), 14.

128 While this study is about Sullivan and Wright's ornamentation, it should be noted that Wright's commitment to help in articulating a uniquely American architecture continued to evolve in the other elements of his architecture. I do not mean to suggest that categorically, Sullivan "appears to have been the more 'articulate.'" But in his use of ornament purely as such, Sullivan appears to have been more so.

129 Harries raises the serious question of the possibility of a common ethos under liberal democracy and capitalism. Harries, *The Ethical Function of Architecture*, 65. Earlier, Mumford, writing in 1931, criticized Sullivan's work for its "individuality" and argued that "'individuality' cannot be the foundation of a common rule: it is only the irreducible residue that remains after the common rule has been established." Mumford, *The Brown Decades*, 70.

130 Karsten Harries, *The Bavarian Rococo Church: Between Faith and Aestheticism* (New Haven: Yale University Press, 1983), 246.
131 Whitman, "Democratic Vistas," 374. Wright understood this as well. Writing in 1932, he indicated that "a creative architecture for America can only mean an architecture for the individual." Frank Lloyd Wright, "Of Thee I Sing," *Frank Lloyd Wright: Essential Texts*, ed. Robert Twombly (New York: W. W. Norton & Company, 2009), 252.
132 Nickel and Siskind indicate that the term "Sullivanesque" was used as early as 1897. Twombly cites the *American Architect* magazine as using it in 1895. But it is Weingarden who finds the coining of the term by Garczynski in 1890 at the completion of the Auditorium. Nickel and Siskind, *The Complete Architecture of Adler and Sullivan*, 216. Twombly, *Louis Sullivan: His Life & Work*, 33–43. Weingarden, *Louis H. Sullivan and a 19th-Century Poetics of Naturalized Architecture*, 103, fn. 17. Garczynski, *Auditorium*, 71.

Chapter 10

1 Huxtable, *Frank Lloyd Wright*, 89.
2 Huxtable indicates that Wright's primary purpose in their publication was to position himself "as the prophet and prime practitioner of a new American architecture. The publications were to make the case for a 'pure art' that would be 'the expressive vehicle of a pure society'—his buildings would be seen as a pure representation of the progressive American spirit." According to Scully he succeeded in establishing his importance. He characterized Wright's monograph as "one of the three most influential architectural treatises of the twentieth century." Huxtable, *Frank Lloyd Wright: A Life*, 119. Vincent Scully, "Foreword," *Studies and Executed Buildings by Frank Lloyd Wright* (1910: Wasmuth; repr., New York: Rizzoli International Publications, 1990), 5.
3 Huxtable, *Frank Lloyd Wright: A Life*, 89.
4 It would be decades before Wright's work load began to approach the productivity of the time period from 1893 to 1910. While in the 1940s and 1950s the size of his office would exceed this initial time period, it did not produce the frequency of influential works.
5 Twombly, *Louis Sullivan: His Life and Work*, 322.
6 Morrison, *Louis Sullivan: Prophet of Modern Architecture*, 148.
7 Wright, *Genius and Mobocracy*, 3; Wright, *An Autobiography* (1932), 105.
8 In desperation, Sullivan would periodically ask Wright for money, to which Wright often favorably responded. But it could never solve the problem.
9 Neutra, *Life & Shape*, 184.
10 Morrison, *Louis Sullivan: Prophet of Modern Architecture*, 227; Wright, *An Autobiography* (1932), 265; Robert Twombly, *Louis Sullivan: His Life & Work* (Chicago: The University of Chicago Press, 1987), 442; Willard Connely, *Louis Sullivan as He Lived: The Shaping of American Architecture* (New York: Horizon Press, Inc., 1960), 303. Wright indicated that he was with Sullivan the day before he died. Twombly concurs. Twombly and Morrison cite the date of death as April 14, 2016. Connely indicated that the visit occurred April 11.

11 Norris Kelly Smith, *Frank Lloyd Wright*, 108.
12 Secrest indicates that Wright told the press this about his infidelity: "It is infinitely more difficult to live without rules, but that is what the really honest, sincere, thinking man is compelled to do." Secrest, *Frank Lloyd Wright: A Biography*, 212. See also Wright, *An Autobiography* (1932), 202–3; Huxtable, *Frank Lloyd Wright*, 118.
13 Norris Kelly Smith, *Frank Lloyd Wright*, 111.
14 Writing in 1946, his son, John Lloyd Wright wrote, "Something in him died with her, a something lovable and gentle that I knew and loved in my father. As I reflect now I am convinced that the love that united them was deep, sincere and holy in spite of its illegality. " John Lloyd Wright, *My Father Frank Lloyd Wright*, 85. See also Wright, *An Autobiography* (1932), 189–93.
15 Most biographers mention Noel's addiction. Compounding the addiction was her mental instability. Huxtable states, "Today she would be considered schizophrenic." Twombly indicates that Noel left Wright in April, the month of Sullivan's death. Secrest indicates that Noel left Taliesin on May 9, 1924. Huxtable, *Frank Lloyd Wright*, 142. Twombly, *Frank Lloyd Wright: His Life and His Architecture*, 183. Secrest, *Frank Lloyd Wright: A Biography*, 301.
16 It is difficult to imagine the extreme of Wright's experiences. His apprentice, Tafel wrote, "Any lesser man might have given up altogether or gone mad." Tafel, *Apprentice to Genius*, 114.
17 While Wright mentioned the *System* at this time, he did not indicate that it arrived with the autobiography. Wright, *An Autobiography* (1932), 264–5. Twombly, *Louis Sullivan: His Life & Work*, 442.
18 Wright, *An Autobiography* (1932), 264.
19 Wright described his divorced father as alone, never to love again, withdrawing "into the *arid* life of his studies, his books, and his music, where he was oblivious to all else [emphasis added]." Wright, *An Autobiography* (1943), 51.
20 Plato, *The Symposium*, 154.
21 Recall that Wright also made a point of telling the reader that Sullivan, on his deathbed, also had his feet on the floor.
22 Plato, *Phaedo*, 55.
23 Plato, *Phaedo*, 58.
24 Plato, *The Symposium*, 156.
25 Over the course of his entire career, long after the duration of this study, Wright never gave up his practice of ornament. Historians and scholars criticize his later work as having devolved into a kind of exaggerated ornament structuralized that Frampton characterized as "selfconscious exoticism." As if finally liberating his repressed sentimentality, it too often lacks the substance found in so much of his earlier work. Ironically, we may be reminded of Harries's quote, "In the end all that remains is an atmosphere, and it is precisely this atmosphere which Kitsch seeks to elicit." At the extreme, Frampton characterizes the Marin County Courthouse as "ultra-kitsch." Kenneth Frampton, *Modern Architecture: A Critical History* (London: Thames and Hudson, 1985), 189. See also Levine, *The Architecture of Frank Lloyd Wright*, 422, fn. 12, 501–2.
26 Wright, *An Autobiography* (1932), 271.
27 Wright, *An Autobiography* (1943), 268.
28 Wright, *An Autobiography* (1932), 265. All ellipses are Wright's.

BIBLIOGRAPHY

Primary Sources: The writings of Louis H. Sullivan

Sullivan, Louis. "The Artistic Use of the Imagination." *Louis Sullivan: The Public Papers*. Edited by Robert Twombly. Chicago and London: The University of Chicago Press, 1988.

Sullivan, Louis H. *The Autobiography of an Idea*. 1924. Reprint, New York: Dover Publications, 1956.

Sullivan, Louis. "Characteristics of American Architecture." *Louis Sullivan: The Public Papers*. Edited by Robert Twombly. Chicago and London: The University of Chicago Press, 1988.

Sullivan, Louis. "The Chicago Tribune Competition." *Louis Sullivan: The Public Papers*. Edited by Robert Twombly. Chicago and London: The University of Chicago Press, 1988.

Sullivan, Louis. "Concerning the Imperial Hotel." *Louis Sullivan: The Public Papers*. Edited by Robert Twombly. Chicago and London: The University of Chicago Press, 1988.

Sullivan, Louis H. *Democracy: A Man-Search*. Introduction by Elaine Hedges. Detroit: Wayne State University Press, 1961.

Sullivan, Louis. "Development of Construction." *Louis Sullivan: The Public Papers*. Edited by Robert Twombly. Chicago and London: The University of Chicago Press, 1988.

Sullivan, Louis. "Emotional Architecture as Compared to Intellectual: A Study in Subjective and Objective." (1894), *Louis Sullivan: The Public Papers*. Edited by Robert Twombly. Chicago and London: The University of Chicago Press, 1988.

Sullivan, Louis. "Essay on Inspiration." *Louis Sullivan: The Public Papers*. Edited by Robert Twombly. Chicago and London: The University of Chicago Press, 1988.

Sullivan, Louis. "*From* Hooley's New Theater." *Louis Sullivan: The Public Papers*. Edited by Robert Twombly. Chicago and London: The University of Chicago Press, 1988.

Sullivan, Louis H. *Kindergarten Chats and Other Writings*. 1918. Reprint, New York: Dover Publications, 1979.

Sullivan, Louis. "Lighting the People's Savings Bank, Cedar Rapids, Iowa: An Example of American Twentieth Century Ideas of Architecture and Illumination (1912)." *Louis Sullivan: The Public Papers*. Edited by Robert Twombly. Chicago and London: The University of Chicago Press, 1988.

Sullivan, Louis. *Lotos Club Notebook*. New York: Sullivan's personal unpublished notebook found in Avery Architectural and Fine Arts Library, Columbia University.

Sullivan, Louis. "May Not Architecture again Become a Living Art?" *Louis Sullivan: The Public Papers*. Edited by Robert Twombly. Chicago and London: The University of Chicago Press, 1988.
Sullivan, Louis. "Ornament in Architecture." *Louis Sullivan: The Public Papers*. Edited by Robert Twombly. Chicago and London: The University of Chicago Press, 1988.
Sullivan, Louis. "Plastic and Color Decoration of the Auditorium." *Louis Sullivan: The Public Papers*. Edited by Robert Twombly. Chicago and London: The University of Chicago Press, 1988.
Sullivan, Louis. "Reflections on the Tokyo Disaster (1924)." *Louis Sullivan: The Public Papers*. Edited by Robert Twombly. Chicago and London: The University of Chicago Press, 1988.
Sullivan, Louis. "Style." *Louis Sullivan: The Public Papers*. Edited by Robert Twombly. Chicago and London: The University of Chicago Press, 1988.
Sullivan, Louis. "Sub-contracting." *Louis Sullivan: The Public Papers*. Edited by Robert Twombly. Chicago and London: The University of Chicago Press, 1988.
Sullivan, Louis H. *A System of Architectural Ornament According with a Philosophy of Man's Powers*. 1924. Reprint, New York: The Eakins Press, 1967.
Sullivan, Louis. "The Tall Office Building Artistically Considered." *Louis Sullivan: The Public Papers*. Edited by Robert Twombly. Chicago and London: The University of Chicago Press, 1988.
Sullivan, Louis. "What Is Architecture? A Study in the American People of Today," *Louis Sullivan: The Public Papers*. Edited by Robert Twombly. Chicago and London: The University of Chicago Press, 1988.
Sullivan, Louis. "What Is the Just Subordination, in Architectural Design, of Details to Mass?" *Louis Sullivan: The Public Papers*. Edited by Robert Twombly. Chicago and London: The University of Chicago Press, 1988.
Sullivan, Louis. "The Young Man in Architecture." *Louis Sullivan: The Public Papers*. Edited by Robert Twombly. Chicago and London: The University of Chicago Press, 1988.

Primary Sources: The writings of Frank Lloyd Wright

Wright, Frank Lloyd. "The Art and Craft of the Machine," *Frank Lloyd Wright: Writings and Buildings*, Selected by Edgar Kaufmann and Ben Raeburn. New York: A Meridian Book, New American Library, 1974.
Wright, Frank Lloyd. *An Autobiography*. New York: Longmans, Green and Co., 1932.
Wright, Frank Lloyd. *An Autobiography*. New York: Duell, Sloan and Pearce, 1943.
Wright, Frank Lloyd. *An Autobiography*. New York: Horizon Press, 1977.
Wright, Frank Lloyd. "In the Cause of Architecture: The Third Dimension." 1925. *The Work of Frank Lloyd Wright: Wendingen*. Introduction by Mrs. Frank Lloyd Wright. New York: Bramhall House, 1965. [See Wijdeveld].

Wright, Frank Lloyd. "In the Cause of Architecture." *Frank Lloyd Wright: Collected Writings*, Vol. 1 (1894–1930). Edited by Bruce Pfeiffer. New York: Rizzoli International Publications, 1992.

Wright, Frank Lloyd. "The Ethics of Ornament," *The Prairie School Review*, Vol. IV, no. 1 (First Quarter 1967): 16–17.

Wright, Frank Lloyd. *Frank Lloyd Wright: The Natural House*. New York: Bramhall House, 1954.

Wright, Frank Lloyd. *Frank Lloyd Wright: Preliminary Studies, 1889–1916*. Edited by Yukio Futagawa. Text by Bruce Pfeiffer. Tokyo: A. D. A. Edita, 1985.

Wright, Frank Lloyd. *Genius and the Mobocracy*, 2nd Printing. New York: Duell, Sloan and Pearce, 1949.

Wright, Frank Lloyd. "Influences and Inferences." *Frank Lloyd Wright: Writings and Buildings*. Edited by Edgar Kaufmann and Ben Raeburn. New York: A Meridian Book, New American Library, 1960.

Wright, Frank Lloyd. "The Japanese Print: An Interpretation. 1912." *Frank Lloyd Wright, The Japanese Print: An Interpretation*. New York: Horizon Press, 1967.

Wright, Frank Lloyd. "Louis Henry Sullivan: Beloved Master (1924)." *Frank Lloyd Wright: Essential Texts*. Edited by Robert Twombly. New York: W. W. Norton & Company, 2009.

Wright, Frank Lloyd. "Louis Sullivan—His Work. 1924." *Frank Lloyd Wright: Essential Texts*, Edited by Robert Twombly. New York: W. W. Norton & Company, 2009.

Wright, Frank Lloyd. *Modern Architecture: Being the Kahn Lectures for 1930*. 1931. Reprint, Princeton: Princeton University Press, 2008.

Wright, Frank Lloyd. "To My European Co-Workers." *Frank Lloyd Wright: Collected Writings*, Vol. 1 (1894–1930). Edited by Bruce Pfeiffer. New York: Rizzoli International Publications, 1992.

Wright, Frank Lloyd. "New Architecture: Principles." *Frank Lloyd Wright: Writings and Buildings*, Edited by Edgar Kaufmann and Ben Raeburn. New York: A Meridian Book, New American Library, 1960.

Wright, Frank Lloyd. "Prairie Architecture." *Frank Lloyd Wright: Writings and Buildings*. Selected by Edgar Kaufmann and Ben Raeburn. New York: A Meridian Book, New American Library, 1974.

Wright, Frank Lloyd. "Roots." *Frank Lloyd Wright: Writings and Buildings*. Selected by Edgar Kaufmann and Ben Raeburn. New York: A Meridian Book, New American Library, 1974.

Wright, Frank Lloyd. "The Sovereignty of the Individual." *Frank Lloyd Wright: Writings and Buildings*. Selected by Edgar Kaufmann and Ben Raeburn. New York: A Meridian Book, New American Library, 1974.

Wright, Frank Lloyd. *Studies and Executed Buildings by Frank Lloyd Wright*. Reprint of the portfolio edition of 100 lithographs published in 1910 by Verlag Ernst Wasmuth, A. G., Berlin. 1990. Reprint, New York: Rizzoli International Publications, Inc., 1986.

Wright, Frank Lloyd. "Of Thee I Sing." *Frank Lloyd Wright: Essential Texts*. Edited by Robert Twombly. New York: W. W. Norton & Company, 2009.

Wright, Frank Lloyd. *The Work of Frank Lloyd Wright: Wendingen*. Introduction by Olgivanna Lloyd Wright. New York: Bramhall House, 1965. [See Wijdeveld].

General Bibliography:

Ahmed, Sara. *The Cultural Politics of Emotion*. New York: Routledge, 2004.
Allen, Robert C. *Horrible Prettiness: Burlesque and American Culture*. Chapel Hill: University of North Carolina Press, 1991.
Alofsin, Anthony. *Frank Lloyd Wright, The Lost Years, 1910–1922: A Study of Influence*. 1993. Reprint, Chicago: University of Chicago Press, 2009.
Andrew, David S. *Louis Sullivan and the Polemics of Modern Architecture: The Present against the Past*. Urbana and Chicago: University of Chicago Press, 1985.
Atwan, Robert. "Observing a Spear of Summer Grass." *The Kenyon Review*, New Series, Vol. 12, no. 2, Impure Form (Spring 1990) 17–19; 21–5.
Austin, J. L. *How to Do Things with Words: The William James Lectures Delivered at Harvard University in 1955*. Eastford, CT: Martino Fine Books, 2018.
Bain, Alexander. *The Emotions and the Will*. 1875. Reprint, Whitefish, MT: Kessinger Legacy Reprints, n.d.
Balmori, Diana and Joel Sanders. *Groundwork: Between Landscape and Architecture*. New York: The Monacelli Press, 2011.
Barr, Alfred, Jr., Henry-Russell, Jr. Hitchcock, Philip Johnson, and Lewis Mumford. *Modern Architects*. New York: Museum of Modern Art and W. W. Norton & Company, 1932.
Bederman, Gail. *Manliness & Civilization: A Cultural History of Gender and Race in the United States, 1880–1917*. Chicago and London: The University of Chicago Press, 1995.
Beeby, Thomas. "The Grammar of Ornament/Ornament as Grammar." *Via III, Ornament*. Edited by Stephen Kieran. Philadelphia: University of Pennsylvania, Fine Arts, 1977.
Bloomer, Jennifer. "D'Or," *Sexuality and Space*. Edited by Beatriz Colomina. New York: Princeton Architectural Press, 1992.
Bloomer, Kent. *The Nature of Ornament: Rhythm and Metamorphosis in Architecture*. New York: W. W. Norton & Company, 2000.
Brennan, Teresa. *The Transmission of Affect*. Ithaca, NY: Cornell University Press, 2004.
Brooks, H. Allen. "Frank Lloyd Wright and the Destruction of the Box." *Journal of the Society of Architectural Historians*, Vol. 38, no. 1 (March 1979). http://olli.illinois.edu/downloads/courses/Spring%202016/Architecture%20of%20Frank%20Lloyd%20Wright/Destruction_of_the_Box_FLW.pdf [accessed April 6, 2016].
Brooks, H. Allen. *The Prairie School: Frank Lloyd Wright and His Midwest Contemporaries*. Toronto: University of Toronto Press, 1972.
Butler, Judith. *Bodies That Matter: On the Discursive Limits of "Sex."* New York: Routledge, 1993.
Butler, Judith. "Imitation and Gender Insubordination." *The Lesbian and Gay Studies Reader*. Edited by Henry Abelove et al. New York and London: Routledge, 1993.
Cadwell, Michael. *Strange Details*. Cambridge, MA; London: MIT Press, 2007.
Carpenter, Edward. *Days with Walt Whitman: With Some Notes on His Life and Work*. 1906. Reprint, London: George Allen & Unwin Ltd, 1921.

Chauncey, George. *Gay New York: Gender, Urban Culture and the Makings of the Gay Male World, 1890–1940*. New York: Basic Books, 1994.

Connely, Willard. *Louis Sullivan as He Lived: The Shaping of American Architecture*. New York: Horizon Press, 1960.

Davis II, Charles L. "Louis Sullivan and the Physiognomic Translation of American Character." *Journal of the Society of Architectural Historians*, Vol. 76, no. 1 (March 2017). https://jsah.ucpress.edu/content/76/1/63.full.pdf+html [accessed September 11, 2019].

De Kock, Charles Paul. *Edmond and His Cousin*. Translated by Edith Mary Norris. Boston: The Frederick J. Quinby Company, 1904.

de Wit, Wim, ed. *Louis Sullivan: The Function of Ornament*. New York: W. W. Norton & Company, 1986.

Dow, Arthur W. *Composition: A Series of Exercises in Art Structure for the Use of Students and Teachers*, 13th edition. N.D. Reprint, Berkeley: University of California Press, 1997.

Dow, Arthur W. *Composition: A Series of Exercises Selected from a New System of Art Education*, 4th edition. New York: The Baker and Taylor Company, 1902.

Drennan, William R. *Death in a Prairie House: Frank Lloyd Wright and the Taliesin Murders*. Madison, WI: Terrace Books, University of Wisconsin Press, 2007.

Dresser, Christopher. *The Language of Ornament: Style in the Decorative Arts*. Reprint of *Studies in Design*, 1876. New York: Portland House, 1988.

Drinka, George Frederick, M. D. *The Birth of Neurosis: Myth, Malady, and the Victorians*. New York: Simon and Schuster, 1984.

Elia, Mario Manieri. *Louis Henry Sullivan*. New York: Princeton Architectural Press, 1996.

Emerson, Ralph Waldo. *Representative Men: Seven Lectures*, "Swedenborg; or, the Mystic." Cambridge, MA: The Riverside Press, 1884.

Flaubert, Gustave. *A Sentimental Education: The Story of a Young Man*. Translated with and introduction by Douglas Parmée. Oxford: Oxford University Press, 2000.

Foucault, Michel. *Discipline & Punish: The Birth of the Prison*. Translated by Alan Sheridan. New York: Vintage Books, 1979.

Foucault, Michel. *The History of Sexuality, Volume I: An Introduction*. Translated by Robert Hurley. New York: Vintage Books, 1990.

Frampton, Kenneth. *Modern Architecture: A Critical History*. London: Thames and Hudson, 1985.

Frampton, Kenneth. *Studies in Tectonic Culture: The Poetics of Construction in Nineteenth and Twentieth Century Architecture*. Cambridge MA and London: MIT Press, 1995.

Frank, Marie. *Denman Ross and American Design Theory*. Hanover: University Press of New England, 2011.

Freud, Sigmund. *Civilization and Its Discontents*. Translated by James Strachey. New York: W. W. Norton & Company, Inc., 1962.

Freud, Sigmund. *New Introductory Lectures on Psycho-Analysis*. Translated and edited by James Strachey. New York: W. W. Norton & Company, 1965.

Freud, Sigmund and Josef Breuer. *Studies on Hysteria*. Translated by James Strachey in collaboration with Anna Freud. New York: Basic Books, Inc., 1957.

Friedland, Roger and Harold Zellman. *The Fellowship: The Untold Story of Frank Lloyd Wright and the Taliesin Fellowship*. New York: Harper Perennial, 2007.
Garczynski, Edward. *Auditorium*. New York: Exhibit Publishing Co., 1890.
Gay, Peter. *Why the Romantics Matter*. New Haven and London: Yale University Press, 2015.
Geddes, Patrick and J. Arthur Thomson. *The Evolution of Sex*. London: Walter Scott, 1889. Reprint, Ann Arbor, University Microfilms International, 1983.
Gill, Brendan. *Many Masks: A Life of Frank Lloyd Wright*. New York: G. P. Putnam's Sons, 1987.
Gray, Asa. *Gray's School and Field Book of Botany*. New York and Chicago: Ivison Blakeman and Company, 1878.
Greenberg, Clement. "Avant-Garde and Kitsch." *Art and Culture: Critical Essays*. Boston: Beacon Press, 1969.
HABS, Historic American Buildings Survey. "Auditorium Building." HABS No. ILL-1007.
Haeckel, Ernst. *The Riddle of the Universe at the Close of the Nineteenth Century*. Translated by Joseph McCabe. New York: Harper & Brothers Publishers, 1901.
Hall, G. Stanley. *Adolescence: Its Psychology and Its Relations to Physiology, Anthropology, Sociology, Sex, Crime, Religion and Education*, Vol. 1. New York: D. Appleton and Company, 1904.
Harries, Karsten. *The Bavarian Rococo Church: Between Faith and Aestheticism*. New Haven: Yale University Press, 1983.
Harries, Karsten. *Between Nihilism and Faith: A Commentary on Either/Or*. Berlin and New York: Walter de Gruyter GmbH & Co. KG, 2010.
Harries, Karsten. *The Broken Frame: Three Lectures*. Washington, DC: The Catholic University of America Press, 1989.
Harries, Karsten. *The Ethical Function of Architecture*. Cambridge, MA: MIT Press, 1997.
Harries, Karsten. *The Meaning of Modern Art: A Philosophical Interpretation*. Evanston, IL: Northwestern University Press, 1968.
Hayden, Dolores. *The Grand Domestic Revolution: A History of Feminist Designs for American Homes, Neighborhoods and Cities*. Cambridge, MA: MIT Press, 1982.
Hayden, Dolores. *Redesigning the American Dream: The Future of Housing, Work and Family Life*. New York: W. W. Norton & Company, 2002.
Heinz, Thomas A. *Frank Lloyd Wright's Stained Glass & Lightscreens*. Salt Lake City: Gibbs Smith, Publisher, 2000.
Hendrickson, Paul. *Plagued by Fire: The Dreams and Furies of Frank Lloyd Wright*. New York: Alfred A. Knopf, 2019.
Herrero Brasas, Juan A. *Walt Whitman's Mystical Ethics of Comradeship: Homosexuality and the Marginality of Friendship at the Crossroads of Modernity*. Albany: State University of New York Press, 2010.
Hess, Alan. *Frank Lloyd Wright: The Houses*. New York: Rizzoli International Publications, 2005.
Hitchcock, Jr. Henry-Russell. *Modern Architecture: Romanticism and Reintegration*. New York: Payson & Clarke, Ltd., 1929.
Hitchcock, Jr. Henry-Russell. *In the Nature of Materials, 1887–1941, The Buildings of Frank Lloyd Wright*. New York: Duell, Sloan and Pearce, 1942.

Hofstadter, Richard. *Social Darwinism in American Thought*. Revised edition, 3rd printing. New York: George Braziller, Inc., 1969.

Huxtable, Ada Louise. *Frank Lloyd Wright: A Life*. 2004. Reprint, New York: Penguin Books, 2008.

James, Cary. *The Imperial Hotel: Frank Lloyd Wright and the Architecture of Unity*. Rutland, Vermont: Charles E. Tuttle Company, 1968.

James, William. *The Principles of Psychology*, Vols. 1 and 2. 1890. Reprint, New York: Dover Publications, 1950.

Johnson, Donald Leslie. *On Frank Lloyd Wright's Concrete Adobe: Irving Gill, Rudolph Schindler and the American Southwest*. Surrey, England: Ashgate Publishing Limited, 2013.

Johnson, Philip. "Is Sullivan the Father of Functionalism?" *Art News*, Vol. 55, no. 8 (December 1956): 45–6; 56–7.

Jones, Owen. *The Grammar of Ornament*. 1856. Reprint, London: Studio Editions, 1995.

Kant, Immanuel. *The Critique of Judgment*. Translated by J. H. Bernard. Amherst, NY: Prometheus Books, 2000.

Kantrowitz, Arnie. "Edward Carpenter." *Walt Whitman: An Encyclopedia*. http://www.whitmanarchive.org/criticism/current/encyclopedia/index.html [accessed February 6, 2014].

Kaufman, Mervyn D. *Father of Skyscrapers: A Biography of Louis Sullivan*. Boston: Little, Brown and Company, 1969.

Kaufmann, Walter. *Nietzsche: Philosopher, Psychologist, Antichrist*. 3rd edition. Princeton: Princeton University Press, 1968.

Kierkegaard, Søren. *Either/Or*, Vol. 1. Translated by David F. Swenson and Lillian Marvin Swenson with introduction by Howard Johnson. Garden City, NY: Anchor Books, 1959.

Kruty, Paul. *Frank Lloyd and Midway Gardens*. Urbana and Chicago: University of Illinois Press, 1998.

Lavater, Johann Caspar. *Essays on Physiognomy*. London: C. Whittingham for H. D. Symonds, 1804.

Lears, T. J. Jackson. *No Place of Grace: Antimodernism and the Transformation of American Culture, 1880–1920*. New York: Pantheon Books, 1981.

Lears, T. J. Jackson. *Rebirth of a Nation: The Making of North America, 1877–1920*. New York: HarperCollins Publishers, 2009.

Leland, Charles Godfrey. *The Alternate Sex or the Female Intellect in Man, and the Masculine in Woman*. London: William Rider & Son, Ltd., 1904.

Leonard, Thomas C. *Illiberal Reformers: Race, Eugenics & American Economics in the Progressive Era*. Princeton: Princeton University Press, 2016.

Levine, Neil. *The Architecture of Frank Lloyd Wright*. Princeton, NJ: Princeton University Press, 1996.

Loos, Adolf. "Ornament and Crime." *Programs and Manifestoes of 20th-Century Architecture*. Edited by Ulrich Conrads. Translated by Michael Bullock. Cambridge, MA: MIT Press, 1989.

Lorch, Emil. "Some Considerations upon the Study of Architectural Design." *The Inland Architect and News Record*, Vol. 37, no. 5 (June 1901).

Maher, George W. "A Plea for an Indigenous Art." *Architectural Record*, Vol. 21 (June 1907): 433.

Mallgrave, Harry Francis and Elaftherios Ikonomu, introduction and translation. *Empathy, Form, and Space: Problems in German Aesthetics 1873–1893*. Santa Monica, CA: The Getty Center for the History of art and the Humanities, 1994.
Massey, Jonathan. *Crystal and Arabesque: Claude Bragdon, Ornament, and Modern Architecture*. Pittsburgh: University of Pittsburgh Press, 2009.
Meech-Pekarik, Julia. "Frank Lloyd Wright's Other Passion." *The Nature of Frank Lloyd Wright*. Edited by Carol R. Bolon, Robert S. Nelson, and Linda Seidel. Chicago: The University of Chicago Press, 1988.
Menand, Louis. *The Metaphysical Club*. New York: Farrar, Straus and Giroux, 2001.
Menocal, Narciso. *Architecture as Nature: The Transcendentalist Idea of Louis Sullivan*. Madison: The University of Wisconsin Press, 1981.
Miller, Edwin Haviland, ed. *Walt Whitman's: "Song of Myself:" A Mosaic of Interpretations*. Iowa City: University of Iowa Press, 1989. http://whitmanarchive.org/criticism/current/pdf/anc.01063.pdf [accessed December 24, 2012].
Morrison, Hugh. *Louis Sullivan: Prophet of Modern Architecture*. New York: W. W. Norton & Company, 1998.
Mumford, Lewis. *The Brown Decades: A Study of the Arts in America, 1865–1895*. 1931. Reprint, New York: Dover Publications, 1971.
Neutra, Richard. *Life & Shape*. 1962. Reprint, Los Angeles: Atara Press, 2009.
Nickel, Richard and Aaron Siskind, *The Complete Architecture of Adler & Sullivan*. Chicago: The Richard Nickel Committee, 2010.
Nietzsche, Friedrich. *Also Sprach Zarathustra/Thus Spoke Zarathustra*. (German/English Bilingual Text). Milton Keynes, UK: Jiahu Books, 2103.
Nietzsche, Friedrich. "'Thus Spoke Zarathustra', and 'On Truth and Lie.'" *The Portable Nietzsche*. Edited and translated with an introduction by Walter Kaufmann. New York: Penguin Books, 1976.
Nietzsche, Friedrich. "On Truth and Lie in a Nonmoral Sense." *Philosophy and Truth: Selections from Nietzsche's Notebooks of the Early 1870's*. Edited and translated with an introduction by Daniel Breazeale. New York: Humanity Books, 1979.
Nishida, Kitarō. *Sourcebook for Modern Japanese Philosophy: Selected Documents*. Translated and edited by David A. Dilworth et al. Westport, CT: Greenwood Press, 1998.
Nordau, Max. *Degeneration*. Translated from the Second Edition of the German Work. New York: D. Appleton and Company, 1895.
Nute, Kevin. *Frank Lloyd Wright and Japan: The Role of Traditional Japanese Art and Architecture in the Work of Frank Lloyd Wright*. New York: Van Nostrand Reinhold, 1993.
Okakura, Kakuzo. *The Book of Tea*. Edited by Everett F. Bleiler. 1906. Reprint, New York: Dover Publications, 1964.
Paul, Sherman, *Louis Sullivan: An Architect in American Thought*. Englewood Cliffs, NJ: Prentice-Hall, 1962.
Picon, Antoine. "Ornament and Its Users: From the Vitruvian Tradition to the Digital Age." *Histories of Ornament: From Global to Local*. Edited by Gülru Necipoğlu and Alina Payne. Princeton and Oxford: Princeton University Press, 2016.

Plato. *Phaedo, Plato Complete Works*. Edited with introduction by John M. Cooper. Indianapolis and Cambridge: Hackett Publishing Company, 1997.

Plato. *Philebus, Plato Complete Works*. Edited with introduction by John M. Cooper. Indianapolis and Cambridge: Hackett Publishing Company, 1997.

Plato. *The Symposium*. Translated with Commentary by R. E. Allen. New Haven and London: Yale University Press, 1991.

Plutarch. *The Lives of the Noble Grecians & Romans Compared Together by that Grave Learned Philosopher and Historiographer Plutarke of Chæronia*. Translated from Greek into French by James Amyot, from French into English by Thomas North. London: Nonesuch Press, 1929.

Plutarch. *Plutarch's Lives of Themistocles, Pericles, Aristides, Alcibiades and Coriolanus, Demosthenes and Cicero, Cæsar and Antony*. The Harvard Classics. Edited by Charles W. Eliot, LL.D. Translation called Dryden's Corrected and revised by Arthur Hugh Clough. New York: P. F. Collier & Son Company, 1909.

Pond, Irving K. *The Meaning of Architecture: An Essay in Constructive Criticism*. Boston: Marshall Jones Company, 1918.

Potvin, John. *Bachelors of a Different Sort: Queer Aesthetics, Material Culture and the Modern Interior in Britain*. Manchester: Manchester University Press, 2014.

Quinan, Jack. *Frank Lloyd Wright's Larkin Building: Myth and Fact*. Cambridge, Mass: MIT Press, 1987.

Quinan, Jack. *Frank Lloyd Wright's Martin House: Architecture as Portraiture*. New York: Princeton Architectural Press, 2004.

Raguenet, A. *Matériaux & Documents D'Architecture Classés par Ordre Aphabétique*. Paris: H. Cagnon, 1872.

Rohan, Timothy. M. "Rendering the Surface: Paul Rudolph's Art and Architecture Building at Yale." *Grey Room*, Vol. 1 (Fall 2000): 84–107.

Root, John. *The Meanings of Architecture: Buildings and Writings of John Wellborn Root*. Collected by Donald Hoffmann. New York: Horizon Press, 1967.

Ross, Denman W. *A Theory of Pure Design: Harmony, Balance, Rhythm*. New York: Peter Smith, 1933.

Ruskin, John. *The Seven Lamps of Architecture*. New York: The Noonday Press, 1974.

Rydell, Robert W. *All the World's a Fair: Visions of Empire at American International Expositions, 1876–1916*. Chicago: University of Chicago Press, 1984.

Schiller, Friedrich von. *Naïve and Sentimental Poetry and on the Sublime: Two Essays*. Translated with an introduction by Julius A. Elias. New York: Frederick Ungar Publishing Co., 1966.

Schmidgall, Gary. "Herrero Brasas, Juan A. Walt Whitman's Mystical Ethics of Comradeship: Homosexuality and the Marginality of Friendship at the Crossroads of Modernity [review]." *Walt Whitman Quarterly Review*, Vol. 28, no. 1 (2010).

Schopenhauer, Arthur. *The Essays of Arthur Schopenhauer*. Translated by T. Bailey Saunders. New York: A. L. Burt Company, n. d.

Schopenhauer, Arthur. *The Essays of Arthur Schopenhauer*. Translated by T. Bailey Saunders. New York: Willey Book Company, n. d.

Schopenhauer, Arthur. "On Physiognomy." *Essays*. Translated by T. Bailey Saunders. New York: Willey Book Company, n. d.

Schopenhauer, Arthur. *The World as Will and Representation*, Vols. 1 and 2. Translated by E. F. J. Payne. New York: Dover Publications, 1969.

Schramm, Geoffrey Saunders. "Whitman's Lifelong Endeavor: *Leaves of Grass* at 150." *The Walt Whitman Archive.* http://www.whitmanarchive.org/about/articles/anc.00007.html [accessed October 20, 2013].

Schuyler, Montgomery. *American Architecture and Other Writings*, Edited by William H. Jordy and Ralph Coe. 1961. Reprint, New York: Atheneum, 1964.

Scully, Jr., Vincent. *Architecture: The Natural and the Manmade.* New York: St. Martin's Press, 1991.

Scully, Jr., Vincent. "Foreword." *Studies and Executed Buildings by Frank Lloyd Wright.* 1910: Wasmuth; Reprint, New York: Rizzoli International Publications, 1990.

Scully, Jr., Vincent. *Frank Lloyd Wright.* New York: George Braziller, Inc., 1960.

Scully, Jr., Vincent. "Introduction." *The Nature of Frank Lloyd Wright.* Edited by Carol R. Bolon, Robert S. Nelson, and Linda Seidel. Chicago: The University of Chicago Press, 1988.

Scully, Jr., Vincent. "Louis Sullivan's Architectural Ornament." *Perspecta 5: The Yale Architectural Journal.* Edited by Edwin Close, II. New Haven: School of Art and Architecture, Yale University, 1959.

Scully, Jr., Vincent. *The Shingle Style and the Stick Style: Architectural Theory and Design from Downing to the Origins of Wright.* 1955. Reprint, New Haven: Yale University Press, 1971.

Secrest, Meryle. *Frank Lloyd Wright: A Biography.* Chicago: The University of Chicago Press, 1998.

Shand-Tucci, Douglass. *The Crimson Letter: Harvard, Homosexuality, and the Shaping of American Culture.* New York: St. Martin's Press, 2003.

Sinclair, Upton. *The Jungle.* New York: Penguin Books, 2006.

Siry, Joseph M. *Unity Temple: Frank Lloyd Wright and Architecture for Liberal Religion.* Cambridge: Cambridge University Press, 1996.

Smith, Kathryn. *Frank Lloyd Wright, Hollyhock House and Olive Hill: Buildings and Projects for Aline Barnsdall.* New York: Rizzoli International Publications, Inc., 1992.

Smith, Norris Kelly. *Frank Lloyd Wright: A Study in Architectural Content.* Englewood Cliffs, NJ: Prentice-Hall, 1966.

Solomon, Jeff. "How Whitman Seduced Us with a Photograph." *The Gay and Lesbian Review*, Vol. 17, no. 4 (July–August 2010): 43-4.

Solomon, Robert C. *In Defense of Sentimentality.* Oxford: Oxford University Press, 2004.

Sontag, Susan. "Notes on 'Camp.'" *Against Interpretation and Other Essays.* New York: Picador; Farrar, Straus and Giroux, 1966.

Spencer, Herbert. *The Data of Ethics.* New York: A. L. Burt Company, n.d.

Spencer, Herbert. *First Principles of a New System of Philosophy.* New York: D. Appleton and Company, 1864.

Spuybroek, Lars. *The Sympathy of Things: Ruskin and the Ecology of Design.* Rotterdam: Lars Spuybroek and V2_Publishing, 2011.

Streitmatter, Rodger. *Outlaw Marriages: The Hidden Histories of Fifteen Extraordinary Same-Sex Couples.* Boston: Beacon Press, 2012.

Sturtevant, A. H. *A History of Genetics.* New York: Harper & Row, 1965.

Symonds, John Addington. *The Life of Michelangelo Buonarroti*, Vols. 1 and 2. London: John C. Nimmo, 1893.

Tafel, Edgar. *Apprentice to Genius: Years with Frank Lloyd Wright*. New York: McGraw-Hill Book Company, 1979.
Tebben, Joseph R. *The Old Home: Louis Sullivan's Newark Bank*. Granville, OH: The McDonald & Woodward Publishing Company, 2014.
Trachtenberg, Marvin and Isabelle Hyman. *Architecture: From Prehistory to Post-Modernism/the Western Tradition*. New York: Harry N. Abrams, Inc., 1986.
Traubel, Horace. *With Walt Whitman in Camden (March 28–July 14, 1888)*. 1905. Reprint, New York: Rowman and Littlefield, Inc., 1961.
Traubel, Horace. *With Walt Whitman in Camden (November 1, 1888–January 20, 1889)*. 1914. Reprint, New York: Rowman and Littlefield, Inc., 1961.
Twombly, Robert C. *Frank Lloyd Wright: An Interpretive Biography*. New York: Harper & Row, Publishers, 1973.
Twombly, Robert C. *Frank Lloyd Wright: His Life and His Architecture*. New York: John Wiley & Sons, 1979.
Twombly, Robert C. *Louis Sullivan: His Life and Work*. Chicago: University of Chicago Press, 1986.
Twombly, Robert and Narciso Menocal. *Louis Sullivan: The Poetry of Architecture*. New York and London: W. W. Norton & Company, 2000.
Van Zanten, David. "Schooling the Prairie School: Wright's Early Style as a Communicable System." *The Nature of Frank Lloyd Wright*. Edited by Carol R. Bolon, Robert S. Nelson, and Linda Seidel. Chicago: The University of Chicago Press, 1988.
Warner, Michael, ed. *The Portable Walt Whitman*. New York: Penguin Books, 2003.
Weingarden, Lauren S. *Louis H. Sullivan: The Banks*. Cambridge, MA: MIT Press, 1987.
Weingarden, Lauren S. *Louis H. Sullivan and a 19th-Century Poetics of Naturalized Architecture*. Burlington, VT and Surrey, England: Ashgate publishing Limited, 2009.
Weingarden, Lauren S. "Louis Sullivan's *System of Architectural Ornament*." *Louis H. Sullivan: A System of Architectural Ornament*. New York: Rizzoli, 1990.
Weininger, Otto. *Sex and Character*. New York: G. P. Putnam's Sons, n.d.
Whitman, Walt. "Democratic Vistas." *Walt Whitman: Prose Works 1892, Volume II, Collect and Other Prose*. Edited by Floyd Stovall. New York: New York University Press, 1964.
Whitman, Walt. *Leaves of Grass*. Philadelphia: Rees Welsh & Co., 1882 [Sullivan's personal copy found in the Library of Congress].
Whitman, Walt. *Leaves of Grass, 1860: The 150th Anniversary Facsimile Edition*. Iowa City: University of Iowa Press, 2009.
Whitman, Walt. *Leaves of Grass: The Deathbed Edition*. 1892. Reprint, New York: Quality Paperback Book Club, 1992.
Whitman, Walt. *The Uncollected Poetry and Prose of Walt Whitman*, 2 vols. Edited by Emory Holloway. Garden City, NY, and Toronto: Doubleday Page and Company, 1921.
Wijdeveld, H. Th., ed. *The Life Work of Frank Lloyd Wright with Contributions by Frank Lloyd Wright, An Introduction by H. Th. Wijdeveld, and Many Articles by Famous European Architects and American Writers*. Santpoort, Holland: C. A. Mees [Original Wendingen Edition], 1925.

Williams, Barker and Severn Co. *Catalogue at Auction: Household Effects, Library, Oriental Rugs, Paintings, Etc. of Mr. Louis Sullivan.* Chicago: Ryerson & Burnham Archives, Art Institute of Chicago, Accession # 1931.1, 1909.

Willis, A. E. *Encyclopædia of Human Nature and Physiognomy.* Chicago: Loomis and Company, Publishers, 1889.

Wilson, Edmund B., Ph. D. *The Cell in Development and Inheritance.* New York: The Macmillan Company, 1911.

Wolff, Arnold. *The Cologne Cathedral.* 2nd edition. Translated by Margret Maranuk-Rohmeder. *Köln* [Cologne]: Verlag Kölner Dom, 1999.

Wright, John Lloyd. *My Father, Frank Lloyd Wright.* 1946. Reprint, New York: Dover Publications, 1992.

INDEX

Note: Locators with letter 'n' refer to notes.

abstract concept/truth 3, 174, 176, 178–80, 186
abstraction 39, 43, 73, 92–100, 105, 110, 112, 129, 133, 134, 136, 148, 164, 180, 186, 190–1, 234 n.111, 235 n.7, 248 n.33, 253 n.119
Addams, Jane 17, 19, 54, 215 n.33
Adler, Dankmar 12, 23, 39, 89, 154, 167, 179, 198, 246 n.73, 246 n.79
"aesthetic approach." *See* Harries; love, and aesthetic approach
affect xxiii, 177, 184, 204 n.8
Alcibiades 84, 88, 160–1, 169, 174–5, 202
Alofsin, Anthony 97, 133, 231 n.71
Alternate Sex, The (Leland) 57–8, 65, 66–7
Andrew, David S. 41, 52, 53, 216 n.63, 218 n.91
Anthony, Susan B. 19
"art for art's sake" 25, 26
"Artistic Use of the Imagination, The" (Sullivan) 47, 168
Art Nouveau 94
Auditorium Building (Adler and Sullivan) 31–4, 39, 41, 71, 73, 153–4, 167, 169, 171, 179, 180, 195, 246 n.79
Ausgeführte Bauten und Entwürfe von Frank Lloyd Wright (Wasmuth) 197. *See also* Wasmuth
Autobiography, An (Wright) xxiii, 15, 18, 44, 83–9, 110, 112, 144, 145, 159, 167, 184–5
Autobiography of an Idea, The (Sullivan) xxiii, 43–4, 47, 62–4, 199, 200

Bain, Alexander 45, 159, 215 n.37
Barnsdall, Aline 136
Baumgarten, Alexander Gottlieb 147, 190, 210 n.109
beauty, notion of 31, 66, 97, 172–5, 181–2, 190–1. *See also* love, and beauty; Wright, Frank Lloyd, on beauty
   Nietzsche notion of 52–3, 181–2
   Platonic notion of 99, 172–6, 181, 184–6, 190–1, 201
   Whitman notion of 182
Bederman, Gail 17–19, 45, 64, 86
Beeby, Thomas H. 112–15, 120–1, 236 n.27, 236 n.38
being, notion of xxiii, 26, 46, 47, 70, 77, 165–7, 172, 177, 178, 181–4, 186, 187, 188, 189–90
   Japanese notion of non-being 187–8
   Platonic notion of 100, 146, 172–5, 181, 186, 187–9, 201, 202
Birth of Venus (Cabanel; painting) 145, 147
bisexual 65, 67, 68
Blondel, Jacques-François 54
Bloomer, Kent 21, 22–3, 25, 133, 141
Book of Tea, The (Okakura) 188, 252 n.115
Bragdon, Claude 167, 212 n.42
Brancusi, Constantin 136
Brasas, Herrero 220 n.14
'Breaking Home Ties' (Hovenden; painting) 95, 191
Bride Stripped Bare by Her Bachelors, Even (The Large Glass) (Duchamp) 136
Broken Frame, The (Harries) 190
Bryan, William Jennings 19

Burnham, Daniel 154, 169
Butler, Judith 146

Cabanel, Alexandre 145, 147, 241 n.55
"Cardboard House, The" (Wright) 111
Carnegie Hall 32, 33–4, 39, 73
Carpenter, Edward 69, 213 n.11
Cell in Development and Heredity, The (Wilson) 56, 179, 219 n.99
Chauncey, George 68, 69, 223 n.62
Cheney, Edwin H. 85, 228 n.35
Cheney, Mamah Borthwick 85, 127, 134, 136, 199, 228 n.35
Chicago Architectural Sketch Club 157-8
Chicago Auditorium theater. *See* Auditorium
Chicago Stock Exchange (Sullivan) 167, 168
civilization, conception of 5, 17–18, 20, 24, 46, 47, 169, 176, 177, 181. *See also* nature, *vs.* culture/civilization
Civilization and Its Discontents (Freud) 177–8
Classical Revival 13, 208 n.50
Cologne Cathedral 11
Columbian Exposition, 1893 17, 19, 95
conventionalization 92–4, 99–100, 133, 136, 143, 231 n.71, 234 n.111
Coonley Residence (Wright) 91, 121, 122, 197
Corwin, Cecil 1, 154, 248 n.29
Cours d'architecture (Blondel) 54
Cubism 96, 232 n.90, 235 n.7
curvilinear/sinuous design 89, 90, 94, 109, 185–6, 190, 191

Dana House (Wright) 90, 99, 123, 124
Darwin, Charles 31, 66, 222 n.46
Davis II, Charles L. 54
Days with Walt Whitman (Carpenter) 69, 213 n.11
decoration 20–3, 25–6, 32, 34, 37, 39, 48, 73, 90–2, 105, 129, 133, 141, 162, 194
Degeneration (Nordau) 54, 223 n.61

de Kock, Charles Paul 15, 165, 178
Democracy (Sullivan) 58, 176, 215 n.39
Democratic Vistas (Whitman) 75
doomsday, notion of 129, 132, 134, 136, 237 n.9
Dow, Arthur Wesley 97–100
Doyle, Peter 69
dualism 176, 177, 183
Duchamp, Marcel 136

Eakins, Thomas 95
École des Beaux-Arts 44, 54, 70, 161, 244 n.43
Edelmann, John 52
Either/Or (Kierkegaard) 9, 11
Elmslie, George Grant 195
Emerson, Ralph Waldo 71, 89, 177, 209 n.89, 231 n.65, 249 n.51
emotion/body correlation 158–9, 160, 180
Emotions and the Will, The (Bain) 159
emotions, tender. *See* tender emotions
empathy 46
Empedocles 58
Encyclopædia of Human Nature and Physiognomy (Willis) 54
Endless Column (Brancusi; sculpture) 136
Ennis House (Wright) 138, 139, 141–2, 240 n.47
Eros (Plato) 172, 173, 174
"Essay on Inspiration" (Sullivan) 169, 171, 182
Essays (Schopenhauer) 52, 217 n.67
Essays on Physiognomy (Lavater) 54
"ethical function". *See* Harries
ethos 24–5, 56, 75–6, 134, 143, 177, 180, 181, 194, 195, 253 n.129. *See also* love, and ethos
Evolution of Sex (Geddes and Thompson) 65

Fallingwater (Wright) 143
femininity 67, 68, 180, 228 n.25
Fenollosa, Ernest 97, 100
"First Love, The" (Kierkegaard) 9, 14
First Love, The (Scribe) 9–10, 15, 207 n.35

Flaubert, Gustave, 31
foliation 76, 89–93, 115, 120
Foucault, Michel 68, 154, 204 n.9
Frampton, Kenneth 138
Frank Lloyd Wright: Ausgeführte Bauten (Wasmuth) 197. *See also* Wasmuth
Frank Lloyd Wright and Midway Gardens (Kruty) 88–9
Freeman House (Wright) 138, 140, 141
Freud, Sigmund xxiii, 177, 178
  oceanic feeling (*see* oceanic feeling)
  repression xxiii
Froebel "Gifts" 94, 106, 125, 232 n.88
"From Pent-up Aching Rivers" (Whitman) 158
functionalism 73–4

Gage building 71, 226 n.87
Geddes, Patrick 65, 66, 221 n.34, 222 n.35
gender, construction of 17–18, 65–7, 68, 71, 77, 145, 146, 159
  in architecture 71
geometry/geometric design 49–50, 58–9, 71, 76–7, 89, 92, 94, 96, 99–100, 105–6, 109, 113–14, 125, 133–4, 136, 138, 147–8, 171–2, 180, 185–91, 202, 234 n.111, 235 n.21, 251 n.103
Getty Tomb 34–5, 41
Gill, Brendan 2–3, 6, 157, 204 n.2, 227 n.4, 228 n.25, 228 n.33, 248 n.29, 252 n.118
Goethe, Johann Wolfgang von 66, 177
good, the 2, 11, 173, 175, 193
Gothic architecture 6–9, 11–12, 15, 24–5, 85, 146, 155, 166, 207 n.44
Grammar of Ornament (Jones, Owen) 155, 161, 163, 164
Gray, Asa 56–8, 179, 193, 219 n.96
Gray's School and Field Book of Botany (Gray) 56, 179
Griffin, Marion Mahony 122–3, 240 n.41
Griffin, Walter 122–3, 240 n.41
Guaranty Building 36–9, 71, 212 n.38

Haeckel, Ernst 57–9, 193, 219 n.106
Hall, Stanley 18, 42
Harries, Karsten 14, 24, 25, 26, 76, 141, 179, 194
  "aesthetic approach" 24–6, 73, 75, 190, 191, 192, 195
  embrace of time 76
  "ethical function" 24, 25, 75, 194
  kitsch 14–16, 174
  "perennial Platonism" 182, 186
  "terror of time" 182, 186, 192, 201, 202
Harrison, William Henry 169
Heidegger, Martin 24, 239 n.32
Heinz, Thomas 99
Heller House (Wright) 89
Hendrickson, Paul 84, 209 n.86, 228 n.24, 237 n.1, 244 n.44, 248 n.29
"High Building Question, The" (Sullivan) 168
Hitchcock, Henry-Russell, Jr. 129, 167, 230 n.62, 237 n.11
Hollyhock House (Wright) 127, 136–7, 138, 192, 206 n.27, 236 n.29
Home Building Association Bank 73, 74
Homer 200
Homer, Winslow 95
homosexuality 18, 65, 68–70, 77, 224–5 n.73, 224 n.66, 224 n.69
Hovenden, Thomas 95
Hubbard, Elbert 87, 88, 229 n.54, 230 n.56
Hull House 17, 19, 54
Husser House (Wright) 89
Huxtable, Ada Louise 197, 228 n.33, 254 n.2

Il Redentore 8–9, 13
Imperial Hotel (Wright) 85, 127–38, 188, 192, 197, 239 n.34
In Defense of Sentimentality (Solomon) 15
Independent Presbyterian Church of Savannah, GA xxii, 20, 21
"Inorganic and the Organic, The" 42, 48–50, 183
instinct xxii, 42, 45–6, 52, 67, 83, 110–11, 181

integral ornament, Wright's concept xxi, 26, 110–11, 125, 144, 147, 149, 191–4, 203, 235 n.11
  "imagination giving natural pattern to structure itself"/"ornament structuralized" 111–13, 118, 120, 121, 125, 126, 128, 129, 132, 134, 136, 138, 144, 191, 192, 236 n.27, 237 n.11, 253 n.123, 255 n.25
  "surface qualified by human imagination"/"surface ornament" 111, 112, 126, 132, 138, 140, 143, 144, 191

Jacobs House (Wright) 143
James, Cary 129
James, William 159
"Japanese Print: An Interpretation, The" (Wright) 92–3, 100, 186–7, 189
Japan/Japanese architecture/prints 85, 91–3, 97–8, 100, 128–36, 143, 146, 186–9, 202, 205–6 n.13, 228 nn.36–7, 231 n.69, 234 n.112, 238 n.19, 239 n.25, 239 n.32
Jerusalem Church, Rincon, GA 20, 22
Johnson, S. C. and Son, Administration Building and Research Tower (Wright) 143
Jones, Owen 113, 155–6, 161–5, 184, 231 n.71
Jones, Rev. Jenkin Lloyd 19, 161, 162
Jones, Richard Lloyd 19, 209 n.86
Jungle, The (Sinclair) 17

Kant, Immanuel 166, 176, 183, 190, 191
Kierkegaard, Søren 9–11, 14, 146–7
  "occasion" 165
Kindergarten Chats (Sullivan) 45–6, 54, 75, 176, 198, 215 n.32
King of Kings (Brancusi; sculpture) 136
Kiss (Lovers), The (Klimt; painting) 105
kitsch 14–16, 20, 85, 96, 100, 145–7, 163, 165, 173, 174, 178, 191, 208 n.64, 241 n.54, 255 n.25

Klimt, Gustav 105
"knit-block" 240 n.41
Kruty, Paul 88–9, 103, 230 nn.60–1, 234 n.6, 235 n.7, 235 n.9

Ladies' Home Journal 197
Lange, Carl 159
Larkin Building (Wright) 92–4, 197
Lavater, Johann Caspar 54
"Laws of Sexual Attraction" (Weininger) 65
Lears, T. J. Jackson 177
Leaves of Grass (Whitman) 61–3, 64, 87–8, 171, 182–3, 219 n.3, 220 n.5, 221 n.17, 225 n.74, 226 n.97, 230 n.56
Le Corbusier 68, 112, 210 n.96
Leland, Charles Godfrey 57–8, 65–8, 71, 222 n.46
Levine, Neil 128–9, 133, 136–8
Liberty magazine 95
Lives (Plutarch) 84, 160, 244 n.38
Lombroso, Cesare 54
Longfellow, Henry Wadsworth 81
Loos, Adolf 68
Lorch, Emil 97, 98, 99, 233 n.94, 233 n.101
Louis H. Sullivan and a 19th-Century Poetics of Naturalized Architecture (Weingarden) 47
Louisiana Purchase Exposition 91
love
  and aesthetic approach 25, 190–2
  and beauty 172–5, 181, 182, 183, 189–91, 201–3
  and ethos 194–5
  and knowledge 189, 201–3
  and ornament 193–4
  and sentimentality 2, 3, 4, 8, 9–11, 13–14, 20, 25, 47, 201–3
  between Sullivan and Wright xx, 156, 159–61, 167–9, 175, 184, 200
Lowell, James Russell 81

Mahony, Marion. *See* Griffin, Marion Mahony
manliness/masculinity discourse 17–18, 45, 64–5, 71, 144–8, 180
Marshall Field's Warehouse 54, 158

Martin, Darwin D. House (Wright) 197, 231 n.66, 247 n.19
Matériaux & Documents D'Architecture Classés par Ordre Alphabétique (Raguenet) 161–3
Meaning of Architecture, The (Pond) 54, 55
Meaning of Modern Art, The (Harries) 14
Meech-Pekarik, Julia 95, 234 n.112
Menocal, Narciso 71
Michelangelo 68, 69, 70
Midway Gardens (Wright) 84–5, 88–9, 92–101, 103–12, 125–6, 127, 144, 147–9, 186, 197, 203
  demolished in 1929 148–9
  and Hollyhock House, comparison with 137
  and Imperial Hotel, comparison with 128–34
  and "textile block" houses, comparison with 138, 140, 142
  and Wainwright Building, comparison with Sullivan's 108–10
Millard House (Wright) 138, 139–40, 141, 237 n.5
Milwaukee County Courthouse 12, 13, 15
Monadnock Building 32, 37
Mumford, Louis 169

naïve, *see* Schiller, Friedrich
Naïve and Sentimental Poetry (Schiller) 4
Nature 4, 5, 75, 77, 146, 171, 176, 189
  vs. culture/civilization 5, 6, 29, 45–7
  as subject/object 5, 135
nature-pattern 137
Navajo sandpaintings 136
Neoclassical Revival 12–13
Neutra, Richard 198
"new masculinity" 20, 45, 86, 157
New Materialism 166, 216 n.51
Nietzsche, Friedrich Wilhelm 52–3, 59, 176, 178–9, 181–3, 194, 201, 213 n.11, 216 n.63
Nile Club (Mahony and Griffin) 122, 123

Nishida, Kitarō 187
Noel, Miriam 199, 255 n.15
nonobjective art 98–9, 136
Nordau, Max 54, 223 n.61
"Notes on 'Camp'" (Sontag) 145, 241 n.54

object. *See* subject/object
"oceanic feeling" 176–7, 181
  and gender 177
"of-the-thing-not-on-it" 30, 31, 34, 36, 39, 48, 73, 94, 111, 138, 142, 180, 191, 192
Okakura, Kakuzo 188
organic/inorganic architecture/ornamentation 6, 42, 48–51, 57–9, 71, 74, 76–7, 85, 100, 110, 125, 135, 138, 164, 192, 238 n.20, 241 n.60
ornament. *See also* love, and ornament
  and decoration 21–3, 25, 73, 141
  definitions xxi, 20–3, 25–6, 111
  etymology 20–1, 25
  "ornament purely as such"/pure ornament 192–4
  problem of xxi, 23–4, 25, 30, 110, 163, 164 (*see also* Sullivan, solve problem, and Wright, solve problem)
  and sentimentality xxii, 20, 126, 155, 163, 193–4, 203
  and sympathy 48, 59
"Ornament in Architecture" (Sullivan) 41, 48, 53, 168
ornament structuralized. *See* "integral ornament"
Orth, Michael 63, 220 n.16

Palladio, Andrea 8
pattern, concept of 110–13, 115, 121, 125, 132, 137–8, 140, 148, 164, 241 n.61
Peoples Savings and Loan 72, 73, 226 n.88
physiognomy 54–6, 172
"Plastic and Color Decoration of the Auditorium" (Sullivan) 32
plastic ornamentation 31–7, 48, 71, 73, 75, 94, 112, 174, 180

Plato 9, 77, 98–100, 106, 137, 138, 146, 160–1, 172–5, 176, 178, 181–2, 184, 186–91, 200–2, 233 n.97, 238 n.19, 244 n.41, 247 n.12, 248 n.28, 253 n.121
Plutarch 84, 88, 160, 230 n.58, 244 n.38, 244 n.40
Pond, Irving K. 31, 54, 210 n.103, 210 n.114, 212 n.42
Portrait of Adele Bloch-Bauer I (Klimt) 105
power, concept 44, 53, 67. *See also* Sullivan, and power
Prairie-style houses 17, 90, 110, 113, 128, 129, 132, 138, 143, 239 n.26
Primitivism 45–6, 75, 97, 99–100, 133–4
Principles of Psychology, The (James, William) 159
Purcell, William Gray 195
"pure design" 97–8, 99, 232 n.88, 233 n.93
"pure form" 39, 54, 96, 99–101, 106, 109, 110, 121, 125–6, 129, 132–8, 143, 147, 186, 191
"pure invention" 98–9

Quinan, Jack 93–4

Raguenet, A. 155–6, 161–5, 178, 184
realism 89–96, 100, 108, 148, 164, 180, 186, 191, 232 n.84, 235 n.7
Reims, Cathedral of Notre Dame 7, 8–9, 11
Remington, Frederic 18, 95, 215 n.33, 221 n.26
Renaissance architecture 7, 8, 9, 12–13, 77, 101, 207 n.44
repression. *See* Freud
Richardson, H. H. 54, 158, 167, 231 n.71, 246 n.72
Riddle of the Universe (Haeckel) 57
Robie House (Wright) 197
Rogers, John 95, 96
Rogers, Will 87
Rogers Group, The 95, 191
Rohe, Mies van der 112
Roosevelt, Teddy 18

Root, John Wellborn 12, 23, 32, 39, 154, 210 n.103, 210 n.114, 231 n.71, 245 n.48
Ross, Denman 97–9, 233 n.94, 233 n.97
Ruskin, John 25, 82, 89–90, 112, 162, 216–17 n.64, 231 n.71, 245 n.49

S. C. Johnson and Son Administration Building (Wright) 143
Saint-Gaudens, Augustus 95
Schiller, Friedrich 4–13, 24, 26, 166, 176, 202, 241 n.59
 "naïve" 4–6, 10, 83, 135, 146, 162, 177, 184, 200
 sentimental/sentimentality 4–13, 30, 47, 135, 162, 166, 202
Schiller Building (Sullivan) 41, 167
Schmidgall, Gary 220 n.14
Schopenhauer, Arthur 11, 12, 52–6, 59, 181, 191, 216 n.63, 217 nn.66–7
Scribe, Augustin Eugène 9–10, 14, 15, 207 n.35
Scully, Vincent 46, 133, 188, 240 n.47, 252 n.118, 254 n.2
Secessionists 91, 94, 105, 210 n.103, 231 n.71
seed germ 52, 53, 56–9, 183, 217 n.64
sentiment, definitions 3–4, 205 n.12
Sentimental Education, A (Flaubert) 31
sentimentality
 in architecture 11–15, 147, 154, 193
 and civilization 5–6, 17, 30
 definitions xxi, 3–4, 15, 20, 158–9
 etymology 3
 and gender 18, 19, 20, 159
 Kierkegaard's 9–10, 11, 147
 and kitsch 14, 15, 95–6
 and love (*see* love, and sentimentality)
 and narcissism 10, 20, 177–8
 and ornament xxii, 159, 163, 193, 203
 repression of xxi, 20
 for Schiller 4–6, 9–10, 12–13
 for Schopenhauer 11
 semantic shift xxi, 9–11, 20
 for Solomon 15–16, 18–19, 20
 for Sullivan xxi–xxiii, 15, 16, 20, 42, 47, 77, 148, 166, 183

for Wright xxi–xxiii, 2–4, 6–14, 20, 84, 85–7, 99–101, 110, 126, 135–6, 147, 148–9, 166, 169, 189, 190, 205–6 n.13
Sex and Character (Weininger) 65
Shakespeare 66
Shand-Tucci, Douglass 68, 223 n.62
Silsbee, Joseph Lyman 12, 154, 155, 231 n.71
Sinclair, Upton 17
skyscraper xx, 17, 35, 167–9, 243 n.33, 246 n.73, 252 n.106
Smith, Norris Kelly 198
Social Darwinism 17, 19, 42
Socrates 160–1, 169, 172–5, 184, 186, 197, 200–2, 233 n.97, 244 n.40, 248 n.28
Solomon, Robert 15–16, 18, 20, 46, 47, 148, 178, 209 n.92
Solomon R. Guggenheim Museum (Wright) 143
"Song of Myself" (Whitman) 61, 62, 63, 64, 220 n.16
Sontag, Susan 145, 241 n.54, 241 n.59
Spencer, Herbert 19, 31, 42, 45, 209 n.89, 213 n.8, 213 n.11, 215 n.37, 245 n.49
Sprecher, Adolph 83, 144, 240 n.52
Storer House (Wright) 138
style 8, 9, 34, 37, 39, 90, 206 n.32, 207 n.46
    problem of 12, 23–4, 162
    and ornament 23–4
    and sentimentality 12–14, 24
"Style" (Sullivan) 169
subject/object 5, 46, 47, 59, 77, 135, 148, 165, 177, 183–4, 201
Sullivan, Louis H.
    and Adler partnership 153–4, 167, 198
    autobiography xiii, 43–4, 62–4, 199
    in Chicago 16–17
    decline and death of xx–xxi, 197–203
    early life/education/career 29–30, 43–4, 61, 161
    and erotic expression 63, 64, 70, 156–8, 167, 180
    function, conception of 56–7, 73, 74, 75, 169, 183, 219 n.96
    and gender expression 44, 45, 64–7, 71, 180
    influenced by Whitman 46–7, 61–3, 64, 69–70, 75, 158, 182
    library books 15, 54, 57, 65, 68–9, 159, 161, 162, 179, 215 n.33
    "master craftsman" 42, 43, 53, 70, 213 n.11, 225 n.77
    and nature 29, 30, 31, 75, 76, 77, 87
    "of-the-thing-not-on-it" (*see* "of-the-thing-not-on-it")
    ornament aesthetics/ornamentation xxi, 16, 30–9, 41–59, 71–7, 109, 110, 111–26, 161–3, 180–4, 193–5
    ornament, solve problem of xxi, 37, 39, 73, 75–7, 174, 180, 181
    ornamentation, Wright's account 30–2, 34, 112, 153–69, 171–5
    plastic and color decorations 31–5, 48, 73, 75, 112
    and poetry 178–80, 181, 184
    and power 30, 42, 43, 44, 45, 46, 48, 52, 53, 59, 64, 67, 213 n.4
    sentimentality (*see* sentimentality)
    sexuality 68–9
    "spiritual results" 32, 73–4, 226 n.90
    and sympathy 44, 45, 46–7, 48, 50, 59, 61, 64, 66–7, 69, 70, 75, 77–8, 181–3
    truth, notion of 175–81, 183, 184
    and words 176–8, 184 (*see also* oceanic feeling)
    and Wright xx, 153–69, 171–95
    and Wright's style, comparison 113–25, 143
Swedenborg, Emanuel 71
"Swedenborg: Or the Mystic," (Emerson) 71
Symonds, John Addington 68, 69, 70
sympathy 20, 44–8, 50, 59, 61, 64, 66, 67, 69, 70, 75, 77, 159, 182–3, 201–3, 253 n.122
    defined 46, 47

love and 189–90
Symposium, The (Plato) 160, 172–4, 181, 186, 189–90, 201
System of Architectural Ornament[*System*], *A* (Sullivan) 41–3, 45–53, 56–9, 67, 75–6, 113, 115–17, 165, 179, 181, 183, 199, 200

"Tale of the Midway Gardens, The" (Wright) 89, 94
Taliesin I, destruction of xx, 127, 129, 134
Taliesin II (Wright) 127, 143
Tallmadge, Thomas 73
"Tall Office Building Artistically Considered" (Sullivan) 169
tender emotions/feelings 3, 10, 15–17, 19, 20, 66, 77, 86, 145–6, 148, 159, 183, 193–4, 202–3
"textile block" houses (Wright) 127, 138–43, 197, 240 n.41, 240 n.46
Theory of Pure Design (Ross) 97–8
"There Was a Child Went Forth" (Whitman) 46, 70
Thompson, J. Arthur 65, 66, 221 n.34, 222 n.35
Thus Spoke Zarathustra (Nietzsche) 52–3, 176, 181–3
time, conceptions of 76, 181–3, 185–9
  Japanese conception of 187–8
  Platonic conception of 100, 172, 173, 181–2, 201
Tobin, Catherine (Kitty) Lee 1, 2, 159, 199, 205 nn.9–10
Transportation Building (Sullivan) 19, 35, 208 n.52
Traubel, Horace 69, 224 nn.65–6, 229 n.47
truth, conception of 2–6, 11, 94, 99, 146, 156, 159–60, 173, 175–86, 188–9, 191, 193, 201–2, 247 n.12
Tuthill, William Burnet 33, 212 n.32
Twombly, Robert 169, 171

ukiyo-e (Japanese prints) 85, 93
Union Trust Building (Sullivan) 167

Unity Temple (Wright) 91–3, 99, 113–21, 125, 138, 197, 234 n.111, 240 n.46

Van Nostrand Science Series 179
Victoria Hotel (Adler and Sullivan) 89
Vitruvian Figure 77

Wagner, Richard 68, 154, 169, 223 n.61, 225 n.77
Wainwright Building (Sullivan) 34–7, 108–9, 115, 167, 168, 193
Washington, Booker T. 19
Wasmuth, Verlag Ernst, A. G., Berlin 97, 110, 111, 143, 192, 197. See also *Ausgeführte Bauten und Entwürfe von Frank Lloyd Wright* and *Frank Lloyd Wright: Ausgeführte Bauten*
Weingarden, Lauren 41, 42, 47, 50, 51, 69, 73, 213 n.2, 213 n.11, 216 n.64
Weininger, Otto 65, 66, 68, 71
Western Association of Architects 12, 39, 171
"What is Architecture?: Study in the American People Today" (Sullivan) 67, 179
"What is the Just Subordination of Details to Masses?" (Sullivan) 73
Whitman, Walt 19, 46–7, 61–4, 68–71, 75, 87–8, 158, 171, 182–3, 194, 201, 213 n.11, 219 n.115, 220 nn.4–5
Whittier, John Greenleaf 81
Wilde, Oscar 68, 223 n.60
will, concept xxii, 52–3, 59, 181
Willis, A. E. 54–6
Wilson, Edmund B. 56–8, 179, 193, 219 n.99, 250 n.71
Winslow House (Wright) 89, 90
With Walt Whitman in Camden (Traubel) 69
"woman in man" 66–7
Works of Charles Paul de Kock, The 15
World as Will and Representation, The (Schopenhauer) 52, 217 n.67
World's Fair, 1904 91

Wright, Frank Lloyd
　appreciation of Asian (Japanese) art/architecture (*see* Japan/Japanese architecture/prints)
　autobiography xxiii, 15, 18, 44, 83–7, 110, 111–12, 144–5, 159, 167, 184–5, 190
　and beauty 184–5, 238 n.19
　"damn," paradigm of 2, 82, 85–9, 94, 100–1, 136, 146, 148, 229 n.46
　early architectural style and design 88–101
　and erotic expression 156–61, 166, 167, 172–5, 192, 202
　fashion and sartorial flair 87–8
　and gender expression 18, 44, 45, 81–4, 86–8, 144–8, 157, 159, 160, 174, 190, 191–2
　vs. his mother's beliefs 1–2, 10–11, 81–2
　and his wife (*see* Tobin, Catherine (Kitty) Lee)
　and integral ornament (*see* integral ornament)
　and Mamah Borthwick Cheney (*see* Cheney, Mamah Borthwick)
　move to Chicago 16–17, 84
　natural *vs.* sentimental 2, 4, 6–8, 85, 89, 90, 111, 135, 147
　Nature/truth, conceptions of 1–2, 6, 10, 11, 82, 90, 97, 135, 146
　"of-the-thing-not-on-it" (*see* "of-the-thing-not-on-it")
　ornament, solve problem of xxi, 34, 91, 110, 143–4, 147–8, 163–4, 192
　ornamentation xxi, 23, 89–94, 99–101, 105–44, 191–5
　principles, first, basic, universal 96–100, 133–5, 141, 148, 163–4, 172–5, 188–9, 191, 238 n.19, 252 n.118
　pure form 96, 99–101, 106, 109, 110, 121, 125–6, 129, 132–8, 143, 191
　reality, conceptions of 93, 100, 137, 138
　romance, conception of 134, 135, 136–8
　sentimental art and architecture 11–14, 85, 88–9, 95, 101, 126, 135–6, 147, 154–5, 173
　sentimentality (*see* sentimentality, for Wright)
　start-up firm 197
　structure, conceptions of 85, 100, 125, 138
　and Sullivan (apprenticeship under/accounts of) xx, 16–19, 30–1, 44–5, 84, 86, 89–90, 154–7, 159–69, 197–203
　Sullivan as sentimental 169, 171, 172
　Sullivan's work 30–1, 34–5, 169, 171–5
　Taliesin tragedy 127–8, 134
　and the tender emotions 86, 145–8, 174, 189–90
　time, notion of 186–9, 202
　trip to Europe/Japan 85, 94, 97, 100, 128, 136
　truth, notion of 2–6, 11, 99, 146, 159, 173–5, 184–9, 191, 202
Wright, John Lloyd 86, 127, 148